• 42784

D1197357

The
Levinas Reader

1989

Emmanuel Levinas

EDITED BY SEÁN HAND

BLACKWELL
Oxford UK & Cambridge USA

Withdrawn / Retire
University of
Sudbury

Copyright © Introduction and editorial apparatus, Seán Hand 1989 Copyright ©'The Phenomenological Theory of Being', 'There Is', 'Time and the Other', 'Martin Buber and the Theory of Knowledge', 'Ethics as First Philosophy', 'Substitution', 'Reality and Its Shadow', 'The Transcendence of Words', 'The Servant and her Master', 'The Other in Proust', 'God and Philosophy', 'Revelation in the Jewish Tradition', 'The Pact', 'Ideology and Idealism', 'Judaism', 'Judaism and the Present', 'The State of Israel and the Religion of Israel', 'Means of Identification', 'The State of Caesar and the State of David', 'Politics After', 'Assimilation and New Culture', 'Ethics and Politics', Emmanuel Levinas, 1930, 1946, 1947, 1963, 1984, 1968, 1948, 1949, 1966, 1947, 1975, 1977, 1982, 1973, 1971, 1960, 1951, 1963, 1971, 1979, 1980, 1982

First published 1989
Reprinted 1992

Blackwell Publishers
108 Cowley Road, Oxford OX4 1JF, UK

Three Cambridge Center,
Cambridge, MA 02142, USA

All rights reserved. Except for the quotation of short passages for the purposes of criticism and review, no part of this publication may be reproduced, stored in a retrieval system, or transmitted, in any form or by any means, electronic, mechanical, photocopying, recording or otherwise, without the prior permission of the publisher.

Except in the United States of America, this book is sold subject to the condition that it shall not, by way of trade or otherwise, be lent, re-sold, hired out or otherwise circulated without the publisher's prior consent in any form of binding or cover other than that in which it is published and without a similar condition including this condition being imposed on the subsequent purchaser.

British Library Cataloguing in Publication Data

A CIP catalogue record for this book is available from the British Library

Library of Congress Cataloging in Publication Data

Levinas, Emmanuel.
[Selections. English. 1989]
The Levinas reader/edited by Seán Hand.
p.   cm.
Bibliography: p.
Includes index.
ISBN 0–631–16446–4. — ISBN 0–631–16447–2 (pbk.)
1. Ontology.   2. Ethics.   3. Aesthetics.   4. Religion.
5. Political science.   I. Hand, Seán.   II. Title.
B2430.L482E6   1989   89–14865
194—dc20   CIP

Typeset in 10 on 12 pt Plantin
by Graphicraft Typesetters, Ltd
Printed in Great Britain
by Athenaeum Press Ltd, Newcastle upon Tyne.

Contents

Contents

Preface

Emmanuel Levinas is one of the most profound, exacting and original philosophers of twentieth-century Europe. His post-rational ethics stands as the ultimate and exemplary challenge to the solitude of Being, a rigorous and moving testimony of one's infinite obligation to the other person. Levinas's teaching reveals ethics to be the first philosophy: his call to responsibility henceforth obliges thought to refer not to the *true* but to the *good*. In assuming this colossal responsibility, Levinas has changed the course of contemporary philosophy.

The Levinas Reader is the most comprehensive introduction to Levinas's work yet published in English. The essays chosen encompass every aspect of his thought: the early phenomenological studies written under the guidance and inspiration of Husserl and Heidegger; the fully developed ethical critique of such totalizing philosophies; the pioneering essays on the moral dimension to aesthetics; the rich and subtle readings of the Talmud which are an exemplary model of an ethical, transcendental philosophy at work; the admirable meditations on current political issues. Given the extraordinary range of these texts, their specialized vocabulary and assumed knowledge, each essay has been prefaced by a brief introduction presenting the basic issues and the necessary background, and suggesting ways to study the text further. The general introduction to the edition presents a clear résumé of the circumstances surrounding Levinas's thought and each stage of its development, in the hope that the beginner as well as the specialist will be able to benefit from Levinas's inspiring teaching. A full bibliography has also been provided.

The Levinas Reader has both used the best of several extant English-language versions of his work, and commissioned translations especially for this volume. Given the very nature of Levinas's thought, involving an infinite responsibility for the other and an equally infinite interpretability of those texts which are the bedrock of our culture, the attempt to homogenize these translations to an excessive degree would directly contravene the very spirit of his philosophy. The notion of a true translation is precisely the impossible goal of Levinas's ethical enterprise. Editorial intervention has therefore been undertaken primarily to help the reader: minor stylistic changes have been made, and a glossary explaining the main Judaic references has been provided at the end of the volume. Certain conventions concerning the translation of the term 'other' have been observed: *autrui*, *autre*, and *Autre* have been rendered as 'Other', 'other' and 'Other (*l'Autre*)' respectively. In general, quotations from the Bible have been taken from the Collins Revised Standard Version, and quotations from the Talmud come from *The Babylonian Talmud*, under the editorship of Isidore Epstein (London: Soncino Press), 1948.

I should like to thank my editor at Basil Blackwell, Stephan Chambers, my desk editor, Andrew McNeillie, and my copy editor, Alex McIntosh, for the commitment and complete professionalism which all of them brought to the production of this volume. The Bodleian Library, the Taylor Institution recondite material. Sarah Richmond produced superb translations of difficult works with impressive efficiency. Michael Holland brought his expert knowledge of Blanchot to bear on his translation. Roland Lack, Jonathan Romney and Michael Temple worked hard to produce their new translations. Daniel Frank of the Oxford Centre for Postgraduate Hebrew Studies generously helped me to read specific passages of the Talmud. Above all, I should like to thank Emmanuel Levinas for his kind support, and for the continuously inspiring nature of his work, based on responsibility for the other. Any errors which remain in this work must be my own responsibility.

Seán Hand

Acknowledgements

The editor and publishers would like to thank the following for permission to include the material collected in this edition: for 'The Phenomenological Theory of Being', Northwestern University Press; for 'There is', 'Substitution', 'Reality and its Shadow' and 'God and Philosophy', Martinus Nijhoff Publishers (division of Kluwer academic publishers); for 'Time and the Other', Duquesne University Press; for 'Martin Buber and the Theory of Knowledge', Open Court Publishing Company; for 'Ethics as First Philosophy', Editions de l'Université de Bruxelles; for 'The Transcendence of Words', 'The Servant and her Master' and 'The other in Proust', Editions Fata Morgana; for 'Revelation in the Jewish Tradition', 'The Pact', 'The State of Caesar and the State of David', 'Politics After!' and 'Assimilation and New Culture', Editions de Minuit; for 'Prayer Without Demand', Presses Universitaires de France; for 'Ideology and Idealism', Ohio State University Press; for 'Judaism', 'Judaism and the Present', 'The State of Israel and the Religion of Israel' and 'Means of Identification', Johns Hopkins University Press; for 'Ethics and Politics', the editor, *Les nouveaux cahiers*.

Introduction

'We are all responsible for everyone else – but I am more responsible than all the others.' This remark, spoken by Alyosha Karamazov in *The Brothers Karamazov*, is one Levinas is fond of quoting. It is a neat indication of the nature of a thought that, in the words of Jacques Derrida, 'can make us tremble'.[1] Its challenge is an excessive one: a mode of being and saying where I am endlessly obligated to the Other, a multiplicity in being which refuses totalization and takes form instead as fraternity and discourse, an ethical relation which forever precedes and exceeds the egoism and tyranny of ontology.

It is not surprising that the remark is taken from Dostoyevsky. Emmanuel Levinas was born in Lithuania in 1906 of Jewish parents. His earliest memories include the news of the death of Tolstoy, and the tricentennial celebrations of the house of Romanov. The First World War, which uprooted the family, and the 1917 revolution, merge in his memories with his father's bookshop in Kovno. A particular confluence of the old and the new was therefore much in evidence. Judaism had been developed to a high spiritual point in Lithuania, and in the eighteenth century had produced arguably the last Talmudist of genius, the Gaon of Vilna. At the same time, Levinas's parents belonged to a generation that saw their future in the Russian language and culture. Levinas's earliest reading therefore involved not only the Hebrew Bible, but the great Russians: Pushkin, Gogol, Dostoyevsky and Tolstoy. It was the preoccupations of these Russian writers that led Levinas in 1923 to Strasbourg (the closest French city to Lithuania) in order to study philosophy under such teachers as Charles Blondel and Maurice Pradines. At this time the writings of Bergson were making a strong impact among the students, and Levinas has always insisted on the importance of Bergson's theory of duration. He quickly made friends with Maurice Blanchot, who introduced him to the work of Proust and Valéry. In 1928–9, Levinas then attended a series of lectures given in Freiburg by Husserl on phenomenological psychology and the constitution of intersubjectivity. It was at this time that he began to write his dissertation on Husserl's theory of intuition. He also discovered Heidegger's *Being and Time*, and attended the famous 1929 encounter between Heidegger and Cassirer at Davos, which for Levinas marked 'the end of a certain humanism'. In the thirties, he took French nationality, married and worked in the administrative section of the Alliance Israélite Universelle. At the outbreak of war, Levinas was mobilized as an interpreter of Russian and German. He was quickly made a prisoner of war, reading Hegel, Proust and Rousseau in between periods of forced labour. Levinas's book, *Existence and Existents*, with its description of anonymous existence, and the states of insomnia, sleep, horror, vertigo, appetite, fatigue and indolence, was begun in captivity. After the war he returned to Paris to become the director of the *Ecole Normale Israélite Orientale* and at the *Collège philosophique*, founded by Jean Wahl, he gave a series of papers which were to become *Time and the Other*. Since 1957 he has contributed to the annual Talmud Colloquium of French Jewish intellectuals. His 1961 doctoral thesis earned him an appointment at the University of Poitiers. This was followed by a move to Paris-Nanterre in 1967 and to the Sorbonne in 1973.

These biographical details delineate the major influences on the work of Levinas, a work which progressively analyses the alterity of existence in *Existence and Existents*; subjectivity, time and eros in *Time and the Other*; ethics as first philosophy in *Totality and Infinity*; the importance of language in *Otherwise than Being or Beyond Essence*; and the question of God in *De Dieu qui vient à l'idée*.

The most important of these influences is undoubtedly phenomenology. Husserlian phenomenology involves the methodical analysis of lived experience from which can be derived the necessary and universal truths of all experience. Human experience is no longer seen as pure *cogito*, but as always tending towards something in the real world. Rather than proceed by abstract deduction, or dialectic, the phenomenological method enables consciousness to become reflexive, to recognize the intentionality that allows an object to emerge as meaningful. The lack of presuppositions in such a method reveals the relation between logical judgement and perceptual experience. Truth and meaning are shown to be *generated*.

Heidegger builds on Husserl's phenomenology while rejecting some of its central features. The notion of phenomenology is retained in *Being and Time* though the idea that one can isolate and so examine the purely conscious status of objects is rejected. The growing importance of the ego in Husserl, which leads him in *Cartesian Meditations* to redefine phenomenology as an 'egology' is rejected, though the notion of a transcendental constitution is still held. Heidegger shifts attention from the existence of beings to our very understanding of Being. Existential moods are now seen as the ontological ways in which we come to understand our being-in-the-world. *Dasein* is thus first of all an intrinsic part of the world, though it becomes ontological through its primary and unique concern with its own identity. It is through this concern that it relates to other *Daseins* and objects. The time necessary to such self-awareness is obviously most crucially perceived in the advent of one's own death. The fact of dying for and by ourselves is what gives the self authenticity, making it a 'being-toward-death'.

Chapters 1 and 2 below offer a clear illustration of Levinas's indebtedness to the phenomenology of this period. The critical position he takes up with regard to it is summarized in one of the interviews with Philippe Nemo published in *Ethics and Infinity*:

> The work that I did then on 'the theory of intuition' in Husserl was . . . influenced by *Sein und Zeit*, to the extent that I sought to present Husserl as having perceived the ontological problem of being, the question of the *status* rather than the *quiddity* of beings. Phenomenological analysis, I said, in searching for the constitution of the real for consciousness, does not undertake so much to search for transcendental conditions in the idealist sense of the term that it does not wonder about the signification of the being of 'beings' in the diverse regions of knowledge.
>
> In *Sein und Zeit*'s analyses of anxiety, care and being-toward-death, we witness a sovereign exercise of phenomenology . . . For Heidegger one does not 'reach' nothingness through a series of theoretical steps, but, in anxiety, from a direct and irreducible access. Existence itself, as through the effect of an intentionality, is animated by a meaning, by the primordial ontological meaning of nothingness. It does not derive from what one can know *about* the destiny of man, or *about* his causes, or *about* his ends; existence in its very event of existence signifies, in anxiety, nothingness, as if the verb to exist had a direct complement.
>
> *Sein und Zeit* has remained the very model of ontology. The Heideggerian notions of finitude, being-there, being-toward-death, etc., remain fundamental. Even if one frees oneself from the systematic rigours of this thought, one remains marked by the very style of *Sein und Zeit*'s analyses, by the 'cardinal points' to which the 'existential analytic' refers.[2]

It is clear from the Heideggerian dramatization given to Husserl in the above quotation that the latter was guilty in Levinas's eyes of tainting his intuitionism with an objectifying 'intellectualism'. Levinas felt that as Husserl conceived of philosophy as a universally valid science, like geometry, this meant that philosophy occupies the same place in the metaphysical destiny of man as the exercise of the theoretical sciences. His conclusion, in *The Theory of Intuition*, was that in such a conception 'philosophy seems as independent of the historical situation of man as any theory that tries to consider everything *sub specie aeternitatis*'.[3]

So in practice, Husserl's system does not admit meanings that are irreducible to representation. But for Levinas, these non-representational intentionalities are precisely the ethical encounter with another human being. It is this contestation of the ontological by the ethical that ultimately leads Levinas to disagree also with Heidegger. Even as the latter heralds the end of the metaphysics of presence, he continues to think of being as a coming-into-presence. Philosophy is still an egology in the way in which Heidegger subordinates the relation with the Other to the relation with Being. But whereas Heidegger locates signification in existence as a project, Levinas locates it in responsibility for the Other. The communication which must be established in order to enter into relation with the being of the Other means that this relation is not ontology, but rather religion, a place where knowledge cannot take precedence over sociality. This is seen above all in Levinas's view of time and death. The temporality of Heideggerian *Dasein*, which reaches absolute autenticity in an ecstatic being-toward-death, reveals less a sense of alterity than the area in which I come into what is absolutely and precisely mine, *mineness* or *Jemeinigkeit*, as §9 of *Being and Time* makes plain:

> Dasein is mine to be in one way or another. Dasein has always made some sort of decision as to the way in which it is in each case mine (*je meines*). That entity which in its Being has this very Being as an issue, comports itself towards its Being as its own ownmost possibility. In each case Dasein *is* its possibility, and it 'has' this possibility, but not just as a property (*eigenschaftlich*), as something present-at-hand would. And because Dasein is in each case essentially its own possibility, it *can*, in its very Being, 'choose' itself and win itself; it can also lose itself and never lose itself; or only 'seem' to do so. But only in so far as it is essentially something which can be *authentic* – that is, something of its own – can it have lost itself and not yet won itself. As modes of Being, *authenticity* and *inauthenticity* (these expressions have been chosen terminologically in a strict sense) are both grounded in the fact that any Dasein whatsoever is characterized by mineness (*dass Dasein überhaupt durch Jemeinigkeit bestimmt ist*).[4]

Levinas does not view death, however, in this way. Rather than see it as the ultimate test of virility and authenticity, as the proof of mineness, his ethical reaction is to view it as the other's death, in which we recognize the limits of the possible in suffering (see chapter 3 below). Levinas quotes Pascal's *Pensées* as an epigraph to *Otherwise than Being or Beyond Essence*: '"That is my place in the sun". That is how the usurpation of the whole world began.' The statement amounts to a rejection of the violence at the heart of ontology as first philosophy in the face of one's responsibility for the Other's death, an inescapable answerability which is that which makes me an individual 'I'. This 'I' questions its right to be, but only given its unquestionable and primary obligation to the other. Ethical philosophy must remain the first philosophy (see chapter 5 below).

Totality and Infinity is the book which most explicitly criticizes the totalizing vision of previous philosophical systems in the West. In it Levinas rejects the synthesizing of phenomena in favour of a thought that is open to the face of the other. The term 'face' here denotes the way in which the presentation of the other to me exceeds all idea of the other in me. The proximity of this face-to-face relation cannot be subsumed into a totality; rather, it concretely produces a relation to the commandment and judgement of infinity. The face thus signifies the philosophical priority of the existent over Being. My presence before the face is therefore an epiphany. It creates an asymmetrical indebtedness on my part towards the Other's moral summons which is based not on a prior knowledge or *Jemeinigkeit*, but on the primacy of the other's right to exist, and on the edict: 'You shall not kill'. This commandment undermines the *conatus essendi* that bases itself on an appeal to nature. Ethics arises from the presence of infinity within the human situation, which from the beginning summons and puts me into question in a manner that recalls Descartes's remark in his third Meditation that 'in some way I have in me the notion of the infinite earlier than the finite.' Consequently, to be oneself is to be for the other. Levinas has summarized this fundamental point in an article entitled 'Beyond Intentionality':

> The sense of the human is not to be measured by presence, not even by self-presence. The meaning of proximity exceeds the limits of ontology, of the human essence, and of the world. It signifies by way of transcendence and the relationship-to-God-in-me (*l'à-Dieu-en-moi*) which is the putting of myself into question. The face signifies in the fact of summoning, of *summoning me* – in its nudity or its destitution, in everything that is precarious in questioning, in all the hazards of mortality – to the unresolved alternative between Being and Nothingness, a questioning which, *ipso facto, summons me*.
>
> The Infinite in its absolute difference witholds itself from presence in me; the Infinite does not come to meet me in a contemporaneousness like that in which noesis and noema meet simultaneously together, nor in the way in which the interlocutors responding to one another may meet. The Infinite is not indifferent to me. It is in calling me to other men that transcendence concerns me. In this unique intrigue of transcendence, the non-absence of the Infinite is neither presence, nor re-presentation. Instead, the idea of the Infinite is to be found in my responsibility for the Other.[5]

This 'first philosophy', which bears testimony to the revelation of the Infinite, has important consequences for the nature of philosophical speech.

Philosophical saying is no longer devoted to knowledge and the process of thematization culminating in self-presence. Speech is put in question since it is the locus of a face-to-face relation in which the Infinite reveals itself in its absolute difference. The primacy of the other's edict means that language is not simply enacted within a consciousness, as Levinas believes it ultimately remains in both Husserl and Heidegger, where it is still bound to the process of comprehension. For Levinas, it is language which conditions rational thought, and the primordial face to face of language constitutes reason itself. Reason lives in language, since the first signification is the infinity of the intelligence which expresses itself in the face. For Levinas, society and signification precede the impersonal structures of knowledge and reason. This makes Levinas particularly open to artistic expression (see chapters 7 to 10) and to the entire nature of philosophical discourse (see chapter 11).

This attention to language, and the meontological subjectivity which it carries is most strongly experienced in *Otherwise than Being or Beyond Essence*. Levinas's earlier descriptions of eros now become the basic language of the responsibility for the other, as 'having-the-other-in-one's skin' (see p. 104 below). In the way in which this vocabulary contests 'intellectualism', it bears witness to an ethical relationship with alterity. For Levinas sees the act of saying, and the exposure it entails, as the mark, and the very possibility, of ethical sincerity. Whereas ontology ultimately must reduce saying to the totalizing closure of the said, saying is a state of openness to the other. It is for that reason that Levinas has to speak of a state that is otherwise than Being, or being's other, since the ontological terms of philosophy in Husserl and Heidegger dissimulate and subordinate the primordial subjectivity structured as responsibility in which one finds oneself as soon as one enters language, prior to any assumption of that role. Saying is 'the commitment of an approach, the one for the other, the very signifyingness of signification'[6] prior to being a communication in which a truth is manifested. Saying therefore breaks through the noema involved in intentionality, stripping me in extreme passivity of every identical quiddity. Subjectivity is the dis-interested vulnerability of saying.

This offering of oneself is not a role that is assumed, but is a goodness that occurs despite oneself. The Biblical 'Here I am!' (I Samuel, 3: 4) which is offered as a responsibility for the other prior to commitment does not involve the reduction of subjectivity to consciousness. Instead it is *subjectum*, subjectivity as substitution and expiation for the other. The philosophical language of the book, and the book's philosophical view of language, enact a discourse in terms of 'otherwise than being' that frees subjectivity from the ontic or ontological programme.

The responsibility for the other represented by 'Here I am!' is therefore a sacred history rather than an epistemological one. The 'Here I am!' is the place through which the Infinite enters without delivering itself up to vision. In the Jewish Revelation, the freedom of Being becomes the 'difficult freedom' of the ethical 'Here I am!', an open greeting based on a deferring to a towards-God, an *à-Dieu*. Levinas is not afraid to use the term God to designate this ethical exigency: invisible, infinite, non-thematizable and irreducible to intentionality. But God is not an absolute rule; rather, He 'comes to the idea' as the absolute alterity revealed in the sacredness of the face-to-face relation. It is in this sense, as a revelation depending on an absolute ethical Law, which is never experienced as a stigma or enslavement, that the meontological subjectivity unfolded in Levinas's philosophy could be called Judaic, obedience to the Most High by way of the ethical relationship with the Other. The individual is not just *Dasein*; he is also the site of transcendence, responding to the unfulfillable obligation of the Revelation. Sacred history, fidelity to the commandments of the Torah, points beyond ontology in affirming how *being-for-itself* is conditional on the unconditioned responsibility of *being-for-the-other*. Torah is anterior to being (see chapters 12 to 14 below).

This solicitation of phenomenology by sacred history is part of an anarchic signifying practice. This means Levinas can quote Psalm 82 to shake the foundations of ontology with the primordial necessity of justice, or read the inhabitants of Canaan as a comment on the Heideggerian order.[7] But, equally, it means that the question of institutional justice and the politics of the modern state are at the heart of first philosophy as they are at the heart of the Talmud. *Otherwise than Being or Beyond Essence* is therefore dedicated for quite fundamental reasons 'to the memory of those who were closest among the six million assassinated by the National Socialists, and of the millions on millions of all confessions and all nations, victims of the same hatred of the other man, the same anti-semitism.' Political self-affirmation means from the outset a responsibility for all. Levinas therefore views the state of Israel as the possibility of going beyond *realpolitik* and the dangers inherent in idealism towards the embodiment of a truly prophetic morality. The tension between identity and assimilation in a modern state whose monotheistic politics are those of a chosen and persecuted people is to be transcended ultimately by the original responsibility beyond any universalism, an ethically necessary politics that will mark the end of such concepts as assimilation and identity, together with the possibility of totalitarianism which they to some degree indicate and preserve (see chapters 15 to 18).

This moral combat, based on peace for the other, is one more indication of the radical challenge to thought posed by the philosophy of Levinas. In the age of Auschwitz, Levinas shows that to be or not to be is not the ultimate question: it is but a commentary on the better than being, the infinite demand of the ethical relation.

NOTES

1 Jacques Derrida, 'Violence and Metaphysics' in *Writing and Difference*, trans. Alan Bass (London and Henley: Routledge and Kegan Paul, 1978), p. 82.
2 *Ethics and Infinity*, trans. Richard A. Cohen (Pittsburgh: Duquesne University Press, 1985), pp. 39–41.
3 *The Theory of Intuition*, trans. André Orianne (Evanston: Northwestern University Press, 1973), p. 155.
4 Martin Heidegger, *Being and Time* (Oxford: Basil Blackwell, 1962), p. 68.
5 'Beyond Intentionality' in *Philosophy in France Today*, edited by Alan Montefiore (Cambridge: Cambridge University Press, 1983), pp. 112–13.
6 *Otherwise than Being or Beyond Essence*, trans. Alphonso Lingis (The Hague: Martinus Nijhoff, 1981), p. 5.
7 *Quatre lectures talmudiques* (Paris: Editions Minuit, 1968) p. 129.

PART I

From Existence to Ethics

1

The Phenomenological Theory of Being

'The Phenomenological Theory of Being: the Absolute Existence of Consciousness' is taken from Levinas's first book, *La théorie de l'intuition dans la phénoménologie de Husserl* (Paris: Alcan), published in 1930. The book was subsequently reprinted by Vrin in 1963 and 1970 before being published in English in 1973 as *The Theory of Intuition in Husserl's Phenomenology*, translated by André Orianne (Evanston: Northwestern University Press).

While agreeing to the inclusion of this chapter in *The Levinas Reader*, Levinas asked me to stress that such work is 'ancient history' for him today. It is true that it was produced almost sixty years ago while Levinas was still emerging from the shadow of his teachers, Husserl and Heidegger, and that in some ways it is still an apprentice piece. But it is of much more than merely historical interest: the book remains one of the best commentaries ever produced on Husserl's *Ideen I*, despite being written at a time when Husserl's philosophy was virtually unknown in France. In the late 1920s French philosophy was still dominated by the pre-war intuitionism of Bergson and the equally conservative rationalism of Brunschvicq, increasingly out of touch with the younger generation of philosophers who were being influenced by such writers as Proust and Valéry.

The need to distinguish Husserl's idealism from that of contemporary French idealists, therefore, together with the Heideggerian slant that Levinas himself brought to bear on his analysis of Husserl's 'intellectualism', condition the way in which Levinas concentrates on the absoluteness of consciousness. He examines how Husserl moves beyond Descartes's absolute *knowledge* of the existence of consciousness towards the absoluteness of consciousness itself, one that exists prior to reflection. Consciousness is a primary domain which thereafter enables us to speak of and understand such terms as subject and object. It is the dehistoricized nature of this phenomenological reduction which Levinas will eventually come to criticize. Though locating being in concrete life, Husserl gives himself 'the freedom of theory'. Even in this early examination of how Husserlian phenomenology overcomes naturalistic ontology, therefore, we can see the beginnings of the 'difficult freedom' of Levinas's mature ethics.

For further discussion of this early work, one may usefully consult: R. Sokolowski, *The Formation of Husserl's Concept of Constitution* (The Hague: Martinus Nijhoff, 1964), which makes use of Levinas's interpretations; a review of *La théorie de l'intuition* by J. Héring published in the *Revue Philosophique de la France et de l'Etranger*, CXIII (1932), nos 5–6, 474–81; and André Orianne's introduction to the English edition, which also stresses the translation policies adopted.

S.H.

If *to be* means to exist the way nature does, then everything which is given as refractory to the categories and to the mode of existence of nature will, as such, have no objectivity and will be, a priori and unavoidably, reduced to something natural. The characteristics of such objects will be reduced to purely subjective phenomena which, with their multifarious structure, are the products of natural causality. Let us illustrate this with an example. The beauty which is manifested in an aesthetic experience presents itself as belonging to the realm of objectivity. The beauty of a work of art is not simply a 'subjective feeling' occasioned by such and such properties of the work which, in itself, is beyond beauty or ugliness. *Aesthetic objects themselves are beautiful* – at least this is the intrinsic meaning of an aesthetic experience. But this object, value, or beauty, with its *sui generis* mode of existence, is incompatible with the categories applied to it by naturalism.[1] If it is granted that these categories are the only norms of reality, then naturalism, which attempts to reduce whatever is real in an aesthetic experience to such categories, could possibly preserve the meaning of such an experience, but this experience would still be considered as being intrinsically a psychological phenomenon in nature. As long as the naturalistic ontology is accepted, existence, including the existence of nature, is not determined by the meaning of life. Rather, life itself must, in order to exist, be conceived on the model of nature. That is, life must be integrated in causal chains and granted reality only inasmuch as it belongs to them. The intrinsic meaning of this experience would be only a property, a phenomenon among others. Faithful to its principle, naturalism reduces the meaning of acts of consciousness, no matter how original or irreducible,[2] to nature, which alone really exists. Naturalistic descriptions have a descriptive value, but they cannot be used to derive any assertion concerning the existence of values. Beauty, in our example, is real only *qua* psychological phenomenon within the causal course of nature. A descriptive psychology cannot by itself go beyond naturalism.

Therefore, in order to go conclusively beyond naturalism and all its consequences,[3] it is not enough to appeal to descriptions which emphasize the particular character, irreducible to the naturalistic categories, of certain objects. It is necessary to dig deeper, down to the very meaning of the notion of being, and to show that the origin of all being, including that of nature, is determined by the intrinsic meaning of conscious life and not the other way around. It is only then that the descriptions which deal with the intrinsic meaning of consciousness, descriptions which must be provided by intuition, will have more than a merely psychological value. On this depends the philosophical standing of intuition. It is not without reason that Husserl saw the main failing of the first edition of the *Logische Unter-suchungen* in the fact that, in the introduction to Volume II, he had characterized phenomenology as descriptive psychology.[4]

We must therefore determine which theory of being may, negatively, detach itself from the naturalistic ideal of existence and may, positively, rely solely on the internal meaning of life.

In an earlier section of *The Theory of Intuition* we tried to show how the world of physical science, whose absolute rights are proclaimed by the physicist, refers essentially to a series of subjective phenomena. We also emphasized that this relation to subjectivity must not be understood as a relation between container and contained, and that it would be premature to see here a new form of Berkeleian idealism. Nevertheless, some relation to subjectivity is inherent in the very meaning of these subjective phenomena. The different sides of a table that are successively discovered from different points of view in some way presuppose a consciousness capable of orienting itself. We will postpone the study of this relation,[5] but all our analyses lead us to say, with Husserl, that 'the world of transcendent *res* necessarily depends on (*ist ange-wiesen an*) consciousness.'[6]

Someone may object that material things extend beyond the realm of our present perception. It belongs to their very essence to be more than what is intimated or revealed in a continuum of subjective aspects at the moment of perception. They are also there when we do not perceive them: they exist in themselves. Is it then possible to find a necessary connection between the mode of existing of material objects and a continuous series of 'subjective phenomena'?

Husserl recognizes that the independence from instantaneous perception exhibited by material things is not merely an illusion. But he thinks that he is able to account for this within the framework of a theory which puts external things in a necessary relation to consciousness.

The concept of consciousness includes more than the central sphere of awakened and active consciousness. Husserl is far from ignoring that – as has been perceived by Bergson and James – each moment of consciousness is surrounded by a halo, by fringes, or, in Husserl's terms, by *horizons*, which are, so to speak, in the margin of the central phenomenon:[7] 'Each perception is an *ex-ception* (*jedes Erfassen ist ein Herausfassen*).'[8] Cogitation makes the *cogitatum* its own by extracting it from a background which constantly accompanies it and which may become itself the object of an *Herausfassung*.[9] In the latter case, what was originally kept in sight falls into

the background without totally disappearing from the field of consciousness. In a new *cogito*, 'the preceding *cogito* ceases to shine, falls in the
darkness, but is still kept alive, although in a different manner.'[10] It may
remain, in certain cases, as the mere possibility of our going back to it, a
possibility implicitly contained in each present moment.

The opposition between central and marginal consciousness is not proper
to perception alone, and its manifestation in the guise of *Herausfassung* by
one's attention is but a particular case of it. It can be found in all the acts
of consciousness: acts of memory, imagination, pleasure, will, etc.[11] In the
background of conscious life there is a multitude of cogitations. This
background is not a vagueness beyond the reaches of analysis, a sort of fog
within consciousness; it is a field already differentiated. One can distinguish
in it various types of acts: acts of belief (the dawning of a genuine belief, a
belief that precedes knowledge etc.),[12] of pleasure or displeasure, of desire,
etc. Something like tentative acts are present before the acts themselves:
tentative judgements, pleasure, desire, etc.[13] There are even decisions of
this type which are present 'before our accomplishment of a genuine *cogito*,
before our ego becomes active by judging, being pleased, desiring or
willing.'[14]

Without going into the details of this structure, we can oppose actual
consciousness to the sphere of possibilities which are contained implicitly in
the actual life of consciousness and form a not-yet-actualized or *potential*
consciousness.[15]

With the help of the notion of actual and potential consciousness, we can
understand the independence shown by the material world with respect to
subjectivity. *It is an independence only with respect to actual consciousness.* The
object which we do not have actually in sight does not disappear from
consciousness. It is given potentially as the object of a possible actual
consciousness. 'Horizons', as Husserl calls them, in the form of marginal
phenomena or in the more indeterminate form of implicit possibilities of
consciousness, accompany that which is given clearly and explicitly. We
may let our sight wander around these horizons, illuminating certain aspects
of them and letting others fall into darkness. *The property of the world of
things of being 'in itself' means nothing else than this possibility of going back to
the same thing and reidentifying it.*[16] This conception is of even greater
philosophical interest because the potential sphere does not belong to
consciousness contingently but as a necessary part of its structure, and so
does the possibility for the various moments of the potential sphere to
become actual and to be, in turn, surrounded by potentialities. 'The flux of
consciousness cannot be made of pure actuality.'[17] It is necessary 'that a
continuous and progressive chain of cogitations be always surrounded by a
sphere of inactuality which is always ready to become actual.'[18]

In summary, the existence of an unperceived material thing can only be its capability of being perceived. This capability is not an empty possibility in the sense that everything that is not contradictory is possible; rather, it is a possibility[19] which belongs to the very essence of consciousness. The existence of the totality of physical reality which forms the background of what is actually perceived represents the positive possibility of the appearance of subjective phenomena of a certain type, an appearance which can be anticipated to a certain extent through the meaning of that which is actually perceived.

> To say that it [the material object] is there, means that starting from the present perceptions, with their effectively apprehended background, some sequence of possible perceptions . . . lead to those sets of perceptions in which the object could appear and be perceived.[20]

So far we have spoken of the existence of the physical objects relative to consciousness. Now we want to make clearer another character of their existence. Not only is their existence relative to a multiplicity of aspects in which they are intimated but, moreover, these aspects never exhaust things: by right, their number is infinite. The aspects which we see at any given moment always indicate further aspects, and so on. Things are never known in their totality; an essential character of our perception of them is that of being inadequate.[21]

A material thing refers to a double relativity. On the one hand, a thing is relative to consciousness – to say that it exists is to say that it meets consciousness.[22] On the other hand, since the sequence of subjective phenomena is never completed, existence remains relative to the degree of completion of the sequence of 'phenomena', and further experience may, in principle, falsify and reduce to a hallucination what had seemed to be acquired by a preceding perception.[23]

This characterization of the existence of material things is meant by Husserl to be only temporary, so its definitive elaboration is one of the main problems of phenomenology.[24] Yet it allows us to understand how, as Husserl says, 'the existence of *transcendent objects*[25] is purely phenomenal',[26] how 'the existence of a thing is never necessarily required by its mode of being given but is always in a certain way contingent',[27] and also how 'all that is given of a thing in person could also not exist.'[28] Finally, it allows us to understand Husserl's assertion concerning 'the dubitable character of transcendent perception'.[29]

It is obvious that this thesis does not assert that there is something doubtful about the perception of the world and that it is not opposed to the naive and natural attitude of the man who lives in the existing world. *It is not a sceptical thesis.* It does not deny the value of external perception[30] by asserting its illusory character, its inadequation to genuine being. Such a sceptical thesis would not express a specifically philosophical attitude. While taken a stand opposite to that of the naive attitude, it would still leave us on the same level as that of naive life, since then philosophy would merely deny everything which is asserted in the natural attitude. We would be discussing the existence or the non-existence of the world, but we would still presuppose an unclarified concept of existence. We would fail to question this concept or we would rely implicitly on a pretheoretical non-critical concept of existence.

The novelty of the analyses which we have just described is precisely that, instead of making assertions about the certain or uncertain existence of things, they are asserting theses concerning the *very mode of existence of external things*, and this puts the problem on a new level. We could formulate the result of our analyses in the following way: the existence of material things contains in itself a nothingness, a possibility of not-being. This does not mean that things do not exist but that their mode of existing contains precisely the possible negation of itself.[31] This negation is not merely a characteristic of knowledge, as if we were only saying that knowledge of the physical world can never posit with certainty the existence of the world. Instead, one must take this possible negation as a constitutive element of the very existence of things.[32]

To avoid any misunderstanding, we must add that the contingency of material things that we assert here should not be taken to mean that existence is not included in the essence of material things, as it is in the essence of God, according to the famous ontological argument. The negation or contingency, which is inherent in existence, expresses no more than the duality of how external things reveal themselves and exist. This duality consists in the facts that a being is intimated, but it is intimated in an infinite sequence of subjective phenomena; that the existence of things is assimilated to the concordance of those phenomena, but this concordance is not necessary; hence, the claim of things to exist is relative to those phenomena which, at any moment, may become discordant. *Contingency, here, is not a relation between the essence and the existence of an object but a determination of the existence itself.* The purely phenomenal character of the existence of external things which Kant determines by opposition to the 'things in themselves' appears here as an internal determination of this existence.

Furthermore, if *contingency* had to be understood here by opposition to the necessity of the ontological argument, then the necessity of the existence of consciousness, which we shall study presently and which is opposed to the contingency of the physical world in Husserl's philosophy, would have to be understood in the sense of the ontological argument. But Husserl denies this explicitly.[33]

Nothing is granted to the sceptics. On the contrary, the origin and the true reasons for the mistakes of a scepticism are explained. In the relative character of the existence of material things we find the foundation of scepticism. Scepticism created a chasm by hypostatizing as *being in itself* the claim of the subjective phenomena, to existence, while calling *knowledge* these same subjective phenomena, in the flux of their becoming. Noticing that the intimated thing is, in principle, inadequate to the phenomena which constitute it, scepticism seems to find the right to assert that we do not know being and that we are constantly misled by our senses. But scepticism is precisely so called because it does not recognize the value of being to what we know and is guided by an idea of being which expresses the existence of things in only one way, the way in which things claim to transcend the phenomena which constitute them. The great interest of Husserl's conception then seems to be his starting point (the phenomenological starting point *par excellence*): to have tried to locate the existence of external things, not in their opposition to what they are for consciousness, but in the aspect under which they are present in concrete conscious life. What exists for us, what we consider as existing is not a reality hidden behind phenomena that appear as images or signs of this reality.[34] The world of phenomena itself makes up the being of our concrete life. It is a world of phenomena that have no clearly defined limits and are not mathematically precise; they are full of 'almost' and 'so to speak', obeying the vague laws that are expressed by the word 'normality'.[35]

We can perceive how, with such an attitude, one can go beyond any philosophy which thinks it must start from the theory of knowledge, as a study of our faculty of knowing, in order to see whether and how a subject can reach being. Any theory of knowledge presupposes, indeed, the existence of an object and of a subject that must come in contact with each other. Knowledge is then defined as this contact, and this always leaves the problem of determining whether knowledge does not falsify the being which it presents to the subject. But this problem is exposed as fictitious once we understand that the origin of the very idea of 'an object' is to be found in the concrete life of a subject; that a subject is not a substance in need of a bridge, namely, knowledge, in order to reach an object, but that the secret of its subjectivity is its being present in front of objects. The modes of appearing of things are not, therefore, characters which are superimposed on existing things by the process of consciousness; they make up the very existence of things.

Until now, however, we have proceeded negatively. We have shown that existence does not necessarily mean existence in the manner of things and that the existence of things in some way refers back to the existence of consciousness. What meaning does the being of consciousness have? How can it be positively determined? We must clarify these matters in order to reach the very heart of Husserl's ontology.

The fundamental intuition of Husserlian philosophy consists of attributing absolute existence to concrete conscious life and transforming the very notion of conscious life. This conscious life, which has an absolute existence, cannot be the same as what is meant by consciousness in Berkeleian idealism, a sort of closed world which has in fact the same type of existence as that of things. Conscious life must be described as life in the presence of transcendent beings. It must be understood that when we speak of the absolute existence of consciousness, when we assert that the external world is solely constituted by consciousness, we do not fall back into Berkeleianism; rather, we are going back to a more original phenomenon of existence that alone makes possible the subject and object of traditional philosophy. Those two terms are only abstractions based on the concrete phenomenon which is expressed by the Husserlian concept of consciousness.

We shall first describe the absolute character of the existence of consciousness and then show[36] how this existence consists in being intentional. It will then follow that consciousness is the origin of all being and that the latter is determined by the intrinsic meaning of the former. Thus we shall be in a position to understand how the study of conscious life, when understood in a certain way, may have a philosophical value.[37]

To determine the essence of consciousness, Husserl starts from the totality of those phenomena which are included in the Cartesian *cogito*.

> We are taking as a starting point 'consciousness' in the pregnant sense of the term, in the sense which first comes to mind and which can be most easily expressed as the Cartesian *cogito*, as 'I think'. As we know, Descartes understood the *cogito* in a wide sense, in such a way as to include any state such as: 'I perceive, I remember, I imagine, I judge, I desire, I want' and, similarly, all analogous ego states (*Icherlebnisse*) in their innumerable successive formations.[38]

Those states of life, those *Erlebnisse*, do not form a region of reality which is simply beside the world of nature.[39] It is only in terms of 'empty categories'[40] that we may use the word 'being' with respect to both the world of things and the world of consciousness. The *Erlebnisse* have a different mode of existence. We insist on this from the beginning. 'Consciousness has in itself its proper being . . . It constitutes *a region of being original in principle.*'[41] Elsewhere, Husserl says, even more explicitly,

'There emerges an essential and fundamental difference between *being qua consciousness* and *being qua thing*.'[42] 'In this way is intimated a difference in principle between the *modes of existence* of consciousness and of reality, the most important difference that there is.'[43]

If we concentrate on the manner in which consciousness is revealed to reflective insight, we shall notice that, in the perception of consciousness or reflection (*immanent* perception, in Husserl's terminology), there is no duality between what is revealed and what is only intimated, as in external, transcendent perception.[44] 'Ein Erlebnis schattet sich nicht ab.'[45] 'For any being in this region it is nonsense to speak of appearance (*erscheinen*) or of representation by *Abschattungen*.'[46]

> Psychical being, being as 'phenomenon', is in principle not a unity that could be experienced in several separate perceptions as individually identical, not even in perceptions of the same subject. In the psychical sphere there is, in other words, no distinction between appearance and being, and if nature is a being that appears in appearances, still appearances themselves (which the psychologist certainly looks upon as psychical) do not constitute a being which itself appears by means of appearances lying behind it.[47]

The flux of consciousness is always given in immanent perception as something absolute, something which is what it is, and not as an object which is anticipated on the basis of a sequence of phenomena which may further contradict or destroy one another and consequently disappoint our expectations. Unlike the perception of external things, immanent perception is adequate.

> The perception of an *Erlebnis* is a direct vision (*schlichtes Erschauen*) of something which is given (or could be given) . . . in perception as something absolute and not as that which is identical in many *Abschattungen* . . . A feeling does not appear through *Abschattungen*. Whenever I consider it I have . . . something absolute which has no sides that could be presented once in one way, once in another.[48]

That they may always turn out to be nothing is a characteristic of the existence of material things and is alien to a being which is revealed directly rather than in a sequence of *Abschattungen*. 'In this absolute sphere . . . there is no room for discordance[49] or mere appearance, or for the possibility of being something else.[50] It is a sphere of absolute position.'[51] The analysis of immanent perception leads us to the absolute position of consciousness, to the impossibility of denying its existence.

When reflective perception is directed toward my *Erlebnis*, what is perceived

is an absolute *self* (*absolutes Selbst*), the existence of which cannot, in principle, be denied; that is, it is in principle impossible to suppose that it does not
exist. To say of an *Erlebnis* given in such a way that it does not exist would be
nonsense.[52]

We seem to be in the presence of the Cartesian *cogito*; there is no doubt
about the relationship between the two ideas, and Husserl realizes it.

We shall return to the connections that can be found between Husserl's
attitude and that of the Cartesian *cogito*, but let us say now that by stretching the connection too far, one could distort the most original thought of
the German philosopher. Indeed, for Husserl, the absoluteness of consciousness means more than the indubitability of internal perception.
This absoluteness does not concern only the truths pertaining to consciousness and their certainty but also the very existence of consciousness itself.
To posit as absolute the existence of consciousness means more than the fact
that it is absurd to doubt it.

It is important to show that Husserl has done more than render comprehensible the absolute evidence of the *cogito* by appealing to the fact that
internal perception is adequate. For Husserl, it is the absoluteness of
consciousness itself which makes possible an adequate perception. The
absolute evidence of the *cogito* is founded on the mode of being of consciousness. 'Only for the ego, and for the flux of experience in its relation to
itself, do we find this exceptional situation; only here there is, and there
must be, something like immanent perception.'[53]

It is not only as object of reflection that consciousness, being given
adequately, necessarily exists; the meaning of its existence consists precisely
in not existing as an object of reflection only. Conscious life exists even
when it is not an object of reflection. 'What is perceived in it [in reflection]
is precisely characterized as not having existence and duration in perception
only, but as having been already there before becoming object of perception.'[54] Here, the existence of consciousness reveals its independence with
respect to internal perception, as opposed to external objects, whose very
existence refers us back to consciousness.[55] It is no longer a reflection on
consciousness that constitutes its existence; the former is made possible by
the latter.

Furthermore, we have wondered whether the assertion that consciousness has an absolute existence remains, for Husserl, a mere thesis that he
does not attempt to clarify. Indeed, we cannot say that the clarification of
the meaning of this absoluteness has ever been attempted explicitly by
Husserl. This is certainly one of the most serious gaps in his theory. He will
study the notion of existence proper to the various regions of being; but, in
the case of consciousness, back to which all regions refer, he will assert only

its absolute existence.[56] And yet it seems to us that there is at least the beginning of an analysis which goes in that direction. Husserl characterizes the existence of consciousness and its independence from reflection by saying that consciousness 'is ready to be perceived (*Wahrnehmungsbereit*).'[57] But for external objects, according to their mode of existing, to be ready to be perceived always means to be already in some way an object of consciousness – if only implicitly, as a part of the horizon of an actual perception.[58] Consciousness, on the other hand, is ready to be perceived in a quite different manner. For consciousness, to be perceivable does not mean to be already an object of consciousness but, more precisely, to exist in this special manner which is opposed to the mode of presence of objects to subjects. Consciousness is ready to be perceived 'through the simple modality of its existence . . . for the ego to which it belongs.'[59] This possibility of being perceived, a possibility which is inherent in the very existence of consciousness, derives, according to another text, from the fact that 'all *Erlebnisse* are conscious.'[60] *Erlebnisse* are conscious. They know themselves in some manner, but this consciousness is not analogous to the perception of external objects or even to the immanent perception of reflection. Indeed, we also learn, and we can only make a note of it, that the existence of those experiences is equivalent to their being 'constituted in the immanent consciousness of time'.[61] 'The consciousness . . . of time functions as perceptive consciousness.'[62] But Husserl adds:

> This universal (*allumfassende*) consciousness of time is obviously not a continuous perception, in the pregnant sense of the term. . . . In other words, it is obviously not a continuous internal reflection for which *Erlebnisse* would be objects, *posited* in the specific meaning of the term and apprehended as existing.[63]

The specific mode of existence of consciousness – its absoluteness and its independence from reflection – consists in its existing for itself, prior to being taken in any way as an object by reflection. Consciousness exists in such a way that it is constantly present to itself.

> All real *Erlebnisse*, *qua* existing and present, or, as we could also say, *qua* temporal unity constituted in the phenomenological consciousness of time, carry in some sense, in themselves, their character of being *in a way analogous to perceived objects*.[64]

But that the 'existence of *Erlebnisse*'[65] is in principle conscious does not mean that conscious life exists and then becomes conscious of itself. 'It is certainly an absurdity to speak of a content of which we are "unconscious", one of which we are conscious only later.'[66] Consciousness constitutes the very being of *Erlebnisse*. From this we understand the great importance of the phenomenological investigations on the constitution of immanent time.

To summarize: consciousness presents itself as a sphere of absolute existence. This absolute existence not only expresses the indubitable character of the *cogito* but also, *qua* positive determination of the very being of consciousness, founds the possibility of an indubitable *cogito*.

It is in this, we believe, that Husserl's conception of the *cogito* differs from Descartes's. For Descartes, indeed, the distinction between thought and space is, above all, a distinction between two types of knowledge, one absolutely certain, the other doubtful. There may be many reasons in favour of the truths that I can formulate, but they are never incontrovertible because, by its very nature, our sensibility is subject to error. The analysis of sensibility by Descartes exposes as relative and fallible what we assert on the basis of our senses. This analysis, however, is not presented as an analysis of the being of sensible things, but as an analysis of knowledge, that is, of the channels that put a subject in contact with being.

From among those doubtful truths there is, for Descartes, one that is privileged, namely, the *cogito*; but it is only one privileged piece of knowledge among others, a sort of axiom from which all the others should be deduced. 'The soul is easier to know than the body.' Because of the force of its certainty, knowledge of the soul is superior to knowledge of the body. One can then understand that, after the *cogito*, Descartes intends to deduce from the existence of consciousness that of God and of the external world. Descartes does not go back to the source of the evidence of the *cogito*; he does not search for its root in the being of consciousness which renders this evidence possible. For him, the meaning of existence is not a problem. He is probably led by the idea that to exist means always and everywhere the same thing, and he then simply wants to show that the external world exists just as he has shown that consciousness exists. For Husserl, the necessary existence of consciousness does not follow from the *cogito*; rather, this necessary existence is none other than an existence that allows a *cogito*. The *cogito* is not merely a means to attain a first certainty so as to deduce the existence of the world outside the *cogito*. What is interesting is the mode of existence of the *cogito*, the type of original existence that characterizes it. Hence Descartes is still on the grounds of dogmatic philosophy, if we call 'dogmatic' a philosophy that begins with an unclarified idea of existence borrowed from the existence of hypostatized external things and then applies this type of existence to all the regions of being. For such a philosophy, the question is not to know what it is to be, but to know whether such and such an object exists. Against such a theory, scepticism has an easy task when it reduces the totality of being to appearance: if we admit that to exist is to exist in the manner of things, then we are forced to admit that such an existence is always problematic. Of course, the novelty of Cartesian philosophy consists in wanting to go beyond scepticism by abandoning the idea of existence conceived on the model of external things. If what appears does not exist, we are at least certain that the act of appearing exists. But Descartes did not follow his discovery to the end. Once he had reached, in consciousness, a domain of absolute existence, he did not see that the term 'existence' is used there with a quite different meaning from the one it has when applied to the world of spatial things. He interpreted the former on the model of the latter. The soul, for Descartes, is a substance which has an existence parallel to that of extended substances and is distinguished from them solely by the certainty we have of its existence. The specific character of the *cogito* is not understood by Descartes as the internal character of the substantiality of consciousness.

This is where Husserl has made progress. The evidence of the *cogito* is grounded on the mode of existence of consciousness in the same way that appearing characterizes the very being of external things. The difference between those two modes of knowing is not limited to their degree of certainty: it is a difference in nature. An abyss separates the adequation of internal perception and the non-adequation of external perception. Husserl's step forward beyond Descartes consists in not separating the knowledge of an object – or, more generally, the mode of appearing of an object in our life – from its being; it consists of seeing the mode of its being known as the expression and the characteristic of its mode of being. This is why, in Husserl's philosophy, there is for the first time a possibility of passing from and through the theory of knowledge to the theory of being. The latter will consist of directly studying the essence of beings that are revealed to consciousness, and of studying the modes of existence in the different regions of objects. Let us say, incidentally, that with the idea of a different existence for external things and for consciousness, there arises the very possibility of different modes of existence.

We have tried to characterize the absolute existence of consciousness by indicating the conscious character of *Erlebnisse*, the character by virtue of which they are always present to themselves. This absolute existence should not be understood as it would be in an 'ontological argument'.

Husserl explicitly states that, for him, the existence of consciousness is simply factual. 'Clearly, the necessity of the existence of each actual *Erlebnis* is not a pure essential necessity, i.e., a pure eidetic[67] particularization of an eidetic law. It is a factual necessity.'[68] The *Seinsnotwendigkeit* of consciousness must mean something quite different from an existence that follows necessarily from an essence. It concerns not the fact that consciousness exists but the mode of its existence. It does not mean that consciousness necessarily exists but that inasmuch as it exists its existence does not contain the possibility of its not-being which is the characteristic of spatial exist-ence. *To exist*, in the case of consciousness, does not mean *to be perceived* in a series of subjective phenomena, but *to be* continuously present to itself, which is what the term 'consciousness' expresses.

Now we can understand how Husserl could meet the objection raised by Hering in *Phénoménologie et philosophie religieuse*. Hering's objection con-cerns the impossibility of passing from the indubitability of the *cogito* to the assertion of its necessary existence. 'Indeed,' says Hering,

> in this case the fact in question derives its indubitability not from the idea of the *cogito* (as is the case for the ideal existence of an essence or in the case of the actual existence of God for the ontologists) but from the particularly favourable situation of the observer. So Paul could perfectly well imagine a world in which the consciousness of Pierre would not exist.[69]

Hering is perfectly right in saying that the existence of the *cogito* does not have the same meaning as 'the existence of God for the ontologists', since, as we have tried to show, Husserl himself admits this. However, if the necessity of consciousness is, according to our interpretation, a charac-teristic of the mode and not of the fact of its existence, one can no longer appeal to its privileged situation which allows it to reflect upon itself, in order to dispute the necessary character of the existence of consciousness. The possibility of such a *privileged situation* is precisely what characterizes the existence of consciousness. In the being of consciousness is founded the very possibility of reflection. 'Only for the ego and for the flux of experience in its relation to itself, do we find this exceptional situation; only here there is, and there must be, something like immanent perception.'[70]

The analyses of the existence which is proper to external things and to consciousness have not shown, as a superficial reading of Husserl's works could lead one to believe, that only consciousness exists and that the external world does not. Both exist, but according to two different modes.

However, we must now emphasize a certain primacy of consciousness which is crucial for the whole of Husserl's philosophy and which, above all, is vital for understanding the function and the place of intuition in his system. Consciousness exists absolutely; this is guaranteed by every mo-ment of its existence.[71] But to say that consciousness, in the concrete totality of its course, carries with it the guarantee of its being amounts to saying that existence should not be looked for somewhere behind it, but that, with all the wealth of its details and meanderings, it is itself being, and that it is here that the notion of existence must be sought. Husserl's assertion in § 49 of *Ideen* that consciousness '*nulla re indiget ad existendum*' does not, we believe, mean anything else. It is in this primacy of conscious life that naturalism is definitively superseded. Its last objection against that for which the intrinsic meaning of our conscious life bears witness could consist, as we have shown, in presenting all that life means as a purely subjective phenomenon incapable of saying anything about *being*. We have tried to establish that the norm of being used by naturalism does not apply to all beings, and that consciousness exists in a different way. Furthermore, our analyses have shown that the existence of consciousness is absolute and that consciousness carries in itself the guarantee of its being, while the being of naturalism returns back to consciousness, which it presupposes as its source. Only consciousness can make intelligible to us the meaning of the being of the world which is a certain mode of meeting consciousness or of appearing to it.[72] The world of nature, from which naturalism derives its notion of existence, only exists itself in the measure in which it enters the life of consciousness.[73] But, precisely, because concrete life contains in different manners different regions of objects, *to be* does not mean the same thing for each of those regions. Their proper mode of being met by, or constituted for, consciousness must become the object of philosophy, and, as we shall see, it must, according to Husserl, constitute philosophy's central problem.[74]

However, by presenting the idea of a sphere which is the origin of all beings and prompts us to transform the very concept of being, seeing it no longer as the idea of substance but as that of subjectivity, do we not fall back into a form of Berkeleian idealism where to be contained in consciousness is the total measure of reality?

It is clear enough from our previous considerations that we are not dealing here with an idealism for which the assertion of the purely phenomenal existence of the external world means a devaluation of it. The external world exists, it is what it is, and to see it as being only a phenomenon is to clarify the sense of its existence; it is to show, after having looked at the life in which it is given, what its mode of occurring in life is.[75]

There is another matter which separates Husserlian idealism from that of someone like Berkeley. For Husserl, it is not a matter of reducing the world of spatial objects to contents of consciousness,[76] and in fact of attributing to these contents the mode of existence of the material objects which have been drowned in them. On the contrary, the point is to show – and we have indefatigably emphasized it – that the sphere to which all existence refers back has a specific manner of existing. This specific existence lets us surmise that we are not in the presence here of a subject opposed to an object, of a being which is antithetical to objects and, for that reason, is precisely on the same level as them. For Husserl, consciousness is a primary domain which alone renders possible and comprehensible an 'object' and a 'subject', terms that are already derivative.

It is in this last point that the main difference between Husserl and

Berkeleian idealism lies. Consciousness for Husserl and consciousness for British empiricism (highly tainted with naturalism) have nothing in common but the name. So far we have characterized the existence of the absolute sphere of life as *consciousness*, i.e., as existing by being, prior to any reflection, present to itself. But we still must establish a characteristic of the other structural elements of consciousness, which are as important as the first.

NOTES

1 Edmund Husserl, 'Ideen zu einer reinen Phänomenologie und phänomenologischen Philosophie', in *Jahrbuch für Philosophie und phänomenologische Forschung*, I (Halle, 1913), § 152. Henceforth abbreviated as *Ideen*.
2 Ibid., § 19.
3 Concerning the motives which led Husserl to criticize and go beyond naturalism, see ibid., §18.
4 Husserl, 'Bericht über deutsche Schriften zur Logik in den Jahren 1895–99', *Archiv für systematische Philosophie*, X (1903), 397–400; *Logical Investigations*, trans. J. N. Findlay (New York: Humanities, 1970); *Ideen*, §49.
5 See *Theory of Intuition*, ch. 3.
6 *Ideen*, § 49.
7 We shall see later how, despite the 'continuity' of the various moments of consciousness and despite those fringes which make impossible any exact delimitation of psychic life, Husserl has not condemned the intellect. See *Theory of Intuition*, ch. 6.
8 *Ideen*, §35.
9 Ibid., § 113.
10 Ibid., §115.
11 Ibid., § 35.
12 Ibid., § 115.
13 Ibid., § 84.
14 Ibid., § 115.
15 Ibid., § 35.
16 Ibid., § 45; § 47.
17 Ibid., § 35.
18 Ibid.
19 Concerning the distinction of various types of possibility, see ibid, § 140.
20 Ibid., § 45. Aron Gurwitsch, 'La Philosophie phénoménologique en Allemagne,' *Revue de métaphysique et de morale*, XXXV, (1928), no. 4 illuminates very well the role of *potentiality* in Husserlian idealism.
21 See *Ideen*, § 3; § 44; § 138; and *passim*.
22 Ibid., § 50.
23 Ibid., § 46; § 138.
24 Ibid., § 55; § 96.

25 The term *transcendent* means, for Husserl, everything which is not a constitutive part of the flux of consciousness (ibid., § 38). Hence, it means mainly material objects.

26 Ibid., § 44.

27 Ibid., § 46.

28 Ibid.

29 Ibid.

30 See ibid., § 32; and especially § 55.

31 Ibid., § 46; § 49; § 138.

32 Ibid., § 44. The mode of perception of a thing depends on the thing's 'specific meaning'.

33 Ibid., § 46.

34 Ibid., § 43.

35 This notion of normality is introduced in ibid., § 44.

36 See *The Theory of Intuition*, ch. 3.

37 See ibid., ch. 7.

38 *Ideen*, § 34. See also § 28. The concept of consciousness here does not yet include the potential sphere. This is why Husserl speaks of consciousness 'in the pregnant sense of the term'.

39 Ibid., § 39; § 49.

40 Ibid., § 49; § 76.

41 Ibid., § 33, (my italics).

42 Ibid., § 42.

43 Ibid., (my italics); see also § 35.

44 For this terminology, see ibid., § 38.

45 Ibid., § 42; § 44.

46 Ibid., and § 49.

47 'Philosophie als strenge Wissenschaft' in *Logos*, I (1910), (trans. Quentin Lauer, in *Edmund Husserl: Phenomenology and the Crisis of Philosophy* (New York: Harper and Row, 1965), p. 312.

48 *Ideen*, § 44.

49 *Discordance* may take place between successive phenomena which constitute the appearance of a material thing: the sequence of phenomena which intimate a 'man' may be contradicted by the rest of the experience, which shows that it was a tree taken to be a man. This possibility – that the perceived object is, in truth, *something else* (that, in our example, the man is actually a tree) – is essentially inherent in the way external things appear.

50 See preceding note.

51 *Ideen*, § 46.

52 Ibid.

53 Ibid. See also, in § 45, an expression such as 'zur Seinsart der Erlebnisses gehört es', etc. Similarly, § 79: 'Jede Seinsart ... hat wesensmässig ihre Gegebenheitsweisen'. See also ibid., § 111.

54 Ibid., § 45.

55 Ibid., § 38. Concerning the notions of 'dependent' and 'independent', see *The Theory of Intuition*, pp. 109ff.

56 See *The Theory of Intuition*, especially ch. 7.
57 *Ideen*, § 45.
58 See above.
59 *Ideen*, § 45.
60 Ibid.
61 Ibid., § 113.
62 Ibid.
63 Ibid.
64 Ibid.; see also § 114; § 118.
65 Ibid., § 45.
66 'Husserls Vorlesungen zur Phänomenologie des inneren Zeitbewusstsein', ed. Martin Heidegger, in *Jahrbuch für Philosophie und phänomenologische Forschung*, X, Halle, 1928. Translated by James S. Churchill as *The Phenomenology of Internal Time-Consciousness* (Bloomington: Indiana University Press, 1947), p. 472.
67 Concerning this term, see *The Theory of Intuition*, p. 104.
68 *Ideen*, § 46.
69 Jean Hering, *Phénoménologie et philosophie religieuse* (Paris: Alcan, 1925), p. 85.
70 *Ideen*, § 46.
71 Ibid.
72 Ibid., § 76.
73 Ibid., § 47.
74 See *The Theory of Intuition*, ch. 7 and Conclusion.
75 *Ideen*, § 55.
76 Ibid., § 98.

Translated by André Orianne

2

There is: Existence without Existents

Originally published in 1946 in *Deucalion (Cahiers de Philosophie)*, I, 141–54, 'There is' was subsequently incorporated into the Introduction and chapter 3, section 2 of *De l'existence à l'existant* (Paris: Fontaine; reissued in the same year by Vrin), translated as *Existence and Existents* by Alphonso Lingis (The Hague: Martinus Nijhoff, 1978). It is consequently one of the first and most abiding examples of Levinas's original thought. Considered by Blanchot to be one of his most fascinating propositions, it is one that recurs in *Time and the Other, Totality and Infinity* and *Difficult Freedom*.

'There is' is anonymous and impersonal being in general, like 'it is raining' or 'it is hot'. It exists prior even to nothingness, the rumbling within silence that one hears when putting a shell to one's ear, the horrifying silence confronting the vigilant insomniac who is and is not an 'I'. It marks the end of objectivizing consciousness, since it is not an object of perception or thought, and cannot be grasped or intentionally constituted. As such, one cannot avoid the experience of the 'there is', since one is steeped in it. It is this unavoidability that Levinas is suggesting when, towards the end of the extract, he speaks of 'the impossibility of death'.

What is important about the notion of *there is* is not just its effect on philosophical language (Levinas's references are to Shakespeare rather than to Plato or Hegel, and the poetic nature of a piece dealing with insomnia, sleep and horror can be read as a similar, and entirely logical, challenge) but also that such language permits a contestation of the Sartrean *en-soi*, and the Heideggerian *es gibt*. The presence of absence and the horror of being described by *there is* are the opposite of the inner peace of *en-soi*; instead, they reveal a without self, the absence of all self, a *sans-soi*. More crucially, the impersonality on which Levinas insists contradicts the generosity of the German version of 'there is', the *es gibt*, from the verg *geben*, to give (see *Being and Time*, p. 255). Prior to the essence of Being, therefore, which in Heidegger is to give and confer its truth, Levinas sees an eternal vigilance which we cannot avoid by falling asleep, and which therefore characterizes existence as bathed in infinity. Whereas Heidegger shows the temporalizing movement of our existence bringing meaning and worth to the world as a kind of generous project, Levinas's phenomenological inquiry is here already introducing the alterity and infinity that will structure his later ethics.

For further information on *Existence and Existents*, one can consult two reviews of the work: Richard A. Cohen in *Man and World*, 12 (1979), 521–6; and C.R. Vasey in *The Thomist*, 44 (1980), no. 3, 466–73.

S.H.

Let us imagine all beings, things and persons, reverting to nothingness. One cannot put this return to nothingness outside of all events. But what of this nothingness itself? Something would happen, if only night and the silence of nothingness. The indeterminateness of this 'something is happening' is not the indeterminateness of a subject and does not refer to a substantive. Like the third person pronoun in the impersonal form of a verb, it designates not the uncertainly known author of the action, but the characteristic of this action itself which somehow has no author. This impersonal, anonymous, yet inextinguishable 'consummation' of being, which murmurs in the depths of nothingness itself we shall designate by the term *there is*. The *there is*, inasmuch as it resists a personal form, is 'being in general'.

We have not derived this notion from exterior things or the inner world – from any 'being' whatever. For *there is* transcends inwardness as well as exteriority; it does not even make it possible to distinguish these. The anonymous current of being invades, submerges every subject, person or thing. The subject–object distinction by which we approach existents is not the starting point for a meditation which broaches being in general.

We could say that the night is the very experience of the *there is*, if the term experience were not inapplicable to a situation which involves the total exclusion of light.

When the forms of things are dissolved in the night, the darkness of the night, which is neither an object nor the quality of an object, invades like a presence. In the night, where we are riven to it, we are not dealing with anything. But this nothing is not that of pure nothingness. There is no longer *this* or *that*; there is not 'something'. But this universal absence is in its turn a presence, an absolutely unavoidable presence. It is not the dialectical counterpart of absence, and we do not grasp it through a thought. It is immediately there. There is no discourse. Nothing responds to us, but this silence; the voice of this silence is understood and frightens like the silence of those infinite spaces Pascal speaks of. *There is*, in general, without it mattering what there is, without our being able to fix a substantive to this term. *There is* is an impersonal form, like in it rains, or it is warm. Its anonymity is essential. The mind does not find itself faced with an apprehended exterior. The exterior – if one insists on this term – remains uncorrelated with an interior. It is no longer given. It is no longer a world. What we call the I is itself submerged by the night, invaded, depersonalized, stifled by it. The disappearance of all things and of the I leaves what cannot disappear, the sheer fact of being in which *one* participates, whether one wants to or not, without having taken the initiative, anonymously. Being remains, like a field of forces, like a heavy atmosphere belonging to no one, universal, returning in the midst of the negation which put it aside, and in all the powers to which that negation may be multiplied.

There is a nocturnal space, but it is no longer empty space, the transparency which both separates us from things and gives us access to them, by which they are given. Darkness fills it like a content; it is full, but full of the nothingness of everything. Can one speak of its continuity? It is surely uninterrupted. But the points of nocturnal space do not refer to each other as in illuminated space; there is no perspective, they are not situated. There is a swarming of points.

Yet this analysis does not simply illustrate Professor Mosch Turpin's thesis, in the *Tales of Hoffman*, that night is the absence of day. The absence of perspective is not something purely negative. It becomes an insecurity. Not because things covered by darkness elude our foresight and that it becomes impossible to measure their approach in advance. For the insecurity does not come from the things of the day world which the night conceals; it is due just to the fact that nothing approaches, nothing comes, nothing threatens; this silence, this tranquility, this void of sensations constitutes a mute, absolutely indeterminate menace. The indeterminateness constitutes its acuteness. There is no determined being, anything can count for anything else. In this ambiguity the menace of pure and simple presence of the *there is*, takes form. Before this obscure invasion it is impossible to take shelter in oneself, to withdraw into one's shell. One is exposed. The whole is open upon us. Instead of serving as our means of access to being, nocturnal space delivers us over to being.

The things of the day world then do not in the night become the source of the 'horror of darkness' because our look cannot catch them in their 'unforeseeable plots'; on the contrary, they get their fantastic character from this horror. Darkness does not only modify their contours for vision; it reduces them to undetermined, anonymous being, which sweats in them.

One can also speak of different forms of night that occur right in the daytime. Illuminated objects can appear to us as though in twilight shapes. Like the unreal, invented city we find after an exhausting trip, things and beings strike us as though they no longer composed a world, and were swimming in the chaos of their existence. Such is also the case with the 'fantastic', 'hallucinatory' reality in poets like Rimbaud, even when they

name the most familiar things and the most accustomed beings. The misunderstood art of certain realistic and naturalistic novelists, their prefaces
and professions of faith to the contrary, produces the same effect: beings
and things that collapse into their 'materiality', are terrifyingly present in
their destiny, weight and shape. Certain passages of Huysmans or Zola, the
calm and smiling horror of de Maupassant's tales do not only give, as is
sometimes thought, a representation 'faithful to' or exceeding reality, but
penetrate behind the form which light reveals into that materiality which,
far from corresponding to the philosophical materialism of the authors,
constitutes the dark background of existence. It makes things appear to us
in a night, like the monotonous presence that bears down on us in insomnia.

The rustling of the *there is* . . . is horror. We have noted the way it
insinuates itself in the night, as an undetermined menace of space itself
disengaged from its function as receptable for objects, as a means of access
to beings. Let us look further into it.

To be conscious is to be torn away from the *there is*, since the existence of
a consciousness constitutes a subjectivity, a subject of existence, that is, to
some extent a master of being, already a name in the anonymity of the
night. Horror is somehow a movement which will strip consciousness of its
very 'subjectivity'. Not in lulling it into unconsciousness, but in throwing it
into an *impersonal vigilance*, a *participation*, in the sense that Levy-Bruhl
gives to the term.

What is new in the idea of participation which Levy-Bruhl introduced to
describe an existence where horror is the dominant emotion, is in the
destruction of categories which had hitherto been used to describe the
feelings evoked by 'the sacred'. In Durkheim if the sacred breaks with
profane being by the feelings it arouses, these feelings remain those of a
subject facing an object. The identity of each of these terms does not seem
compromised. The sensible qualities of the sacred are incommensurable
with the emotional power it emits and with the very nature of this emotion,
but their function as bearers of 'collective representations' accounts for this
disproportion and inadequateness. The situation is quite different in Lévy-
Bruhl. Mystical participation is completely different from the Platonic
participation in a genus; in it the identity of the terms is lost. They are
divested of what constituted their very substantivity. The participation of
one term in another does not consist in sharing an attribute; one term *is the
other*. The *private* existence of each term, mastered by a subject that is, loses
this private character and returns to an undifferentiated background; the
existence of one submerges the other, and is thus no longer an existence of
the one. We recognize here the *there is*. The impersonality of the sacred in

primitive religions, which for Durkheim is the 'still' impersonal God from which will issue one day the God of advanced religions, on the contrary describes a world where nothing prepares for the apparition of a God. Rather than to a God, the notion of the *there is* leads us to the absence of God, the absence of any being. Primitive men live before all Revelation, before the light comes.

Horror is nowise an anxiety about death. According to Lévy-Bruhl, primitive peoples show only indifference to death, which they take as a natural fact. In horror a subject is stripped of his subjectivity, of his power to have private existence. The subject is depersonalized. 'Nausea', as a feeling for existence, is not yet a depersonalization; but horror turns the subjectivity of the subject, his particularity qua *entity*, inside out. It is a participation in the *there is*, in the *there is* which returns in the heart of every negation, in the *there is* that has 'no exits'. It is, if we may say so, the impossibility of death, the universality of existence even in its annihilation.

To kill, like to die, is to seek an escape from being, to go where freedom and negation operate. Horror is the event of being which returns in the heart of this negation, as though nothing had happened. 'And that,' says Macbeth, 'is more strange than the crime itself.' In the nothingness which a crime creates a being is condensed to the point of suffication, and draws consciousness out of its 'retreat'. A corpse is horrible; it already bears in itself its own phantom, it presages its return. The haunting spectre, the phantom, constitutes the very element of horror.

The night gives a spectral allure to the objects that occupy it still. It is the 'hour of crime', 'hour of vice', which also bear the mark of a supernatural reality. Evil-doers are disturbing to themselves like phantoms. This return of presence in negation, this impossibility of escaping from an anonymous and uncorruptible existence constitutes the final depths of Shakespearean tragedy. The fatality of the tragedy of antiquity becomes the fatality of irremissible being.

Spectres, ghosts, sorceresses are not only a tribute Shakespeare pays to his time, or vestiges of the original material he composed with; they allow him to move constantly toward this limit between being and nothingness where being insinuates itself even in nothingness, like bubbles of the earth ('the Earth hath bubbles'). Hamlet recoils before the 'not to be' because he has a foreboding of the return of being ('to dye, to sleepe, perchance to Dreame'). In Macbeth, the apparition of Banquo's ghost is also a decisive experience of the 'no exit' from existence, its phantom return through the fissures through which one has driven it. 'The times have been, that when the Brains were out, the man would dye, and there an end; But now they rise again . . . and push us from our stools. This is more strange than such a murther is.' 'And it is over with' is impossible. The horror does not come from the danger. 'What man dare, I dare . . . Approach thou like the rugged Russian Bear . . . Take any shape but that, and my firm Nerves shall never tremble . . . Hence horrible Shadow, unreal mockery hence . . . ' It is the shadow of being that horrifies Macbeth; the profile of being takes form in nothingness.

The horror of the night, as an experience of the *there is*, does not then reveal to us a danger of death, nor even a danger of pain. That is what is essential in this analysis. The pure nothingness revealed by anxiety in Heidegger's analysis does not consitute the *there is*. There is horror of being and not anxiety over nothingness, fear of being and not fear for being; there is being prey to, delivered over to something that is not a 'something'. When night is dissipated with the first rays of the sun, the horror of the night is no longer defineable. The 'something' appears to be 'nothing'.

Horror carries out the condemnation to perpetual reality, to existence with 'no exits'.

The sky, the whole world's full of my forefathers.
Where may I hide? Flee to infernal night.
How? There my father holds the urn of doom . . .

Phaedra discovers the impossibility of death, the eternal responsibility of her being, in a full universe in which her existence is bound by an unbreakable commitment, an existence no longer in any way private.

We are opposing, then, the horror of the night, 'the silence and horror of the shades', to Heideggerian anxiety, the fear of being to the fear of nothingness. While anxiety, in Heidegger, brings about 'being toward death', grasped and somehow understood, the horror of the night 'with no exits' which 'does not answer' is an irremissible existence. 'Tomorrow, alas! one will still have to live' – a tomorrow contained in the infinity of today. There is horror of immortality, perpetuity of the drama of existence, necessity of forever taking on his burden.[1]

When, in the last chapter of *Creative Evolution*, Bergson shows that the concept of nothingness is equivalent to the idea of being crossed out, he seems to catch sight of a situation analogous to that which led us to the notion of the *there is*.

According to Bergson, negation has a positive meaning as a movement of the mind which rejects one being in order to think of another being; but, when applied to the totality of being, it no longer makes sense. To deny the totality of being is for consciousness to plunge into a kind of darkness, where it would at least remain as an operation, as the consciousness of that darkness. Total negation then would be impossible, and the concept of nothingness illusory. But Bergson's critique of nothingness only aims at the necessity of a being, a 'something' which exists. It always approaches Being as 'a being', and ends up with a residual entity. The darkness into which consciousness plunges, which has put out every glimmering of light in being, is also understood as content. The fact that it is a content obtained through the negation of all content remains unconsidered. But this is just what is new in this situation. Darkness, as the presence of absence, is not a purely present content. There is not a 'something' that remains. There is the atmosphere of presence, which can, to be sure, appear later as a content, but originally is the impersonal, non-substantive event of the night and the *there is*. It is like a density of the void, like a murmur of silence. There is nothing, but there is being, like a field of forces. Darkness is the very play of existence which would play itself out even if there were nothing. It is to express just this paradoxical existence that we have introduced the term 'there is'. We want to call attention to this being a density, an atmosphere, a field, which is not to be identified with an object that would have this density, or that would be taken up in the breath of existence or situated within a field of forces. We want to call attention to the existential density of the void itself, devoid of all being, empty even of void, whatever be the power of negation applied to itself. Negation does not end up with being as a structure and organization of objects; that which affirms and imposes itself in the extreme situation we have imagined, and which we approach in the night and in the tragic, is being as an impersonal field, a field without proprietor or master, where negation, annihilation and nothingness are events like affirmation, creation and subsistence, but impersonal events. A presence of absence, the *there is* is beyond contradiction; it embraces and dominates its contradictory. In this sense being has no outlets.

In modern philosophy the idea of death and of anxiety in face of death was opposed to the Bergsonian critique of nothingness. To 'realize' the concept of nothingness is not to see nothingness, but to die. As death, and an attitude taken with respect to death, the negation of being is not merely an impassive thought. But nothingness is here still conceived independently of the *there is*, without recognizing the universality of the *there is*; the dialectical character of the presence of absence is not taken note of. One starts with being, which is a content limited by nothingness. Nothingness is still envisaged as the end and limit of being, as an ocean which beats up against it on all sides. But we must ask if 'nothingness,' unthinkable as a limit or negation of being, is not possible as interval and interruption; we must ask whether consciousness, with its aptitude for sleep, for suspension, for *epochè*, is not the locus of this nothingness-interval.

NOTE

1 Maurice Blanchot's *Thomas L'Obscur* (Paris: Gallimard, 1941), opens with the description of the *there is* . . . (see in particular ch. II, pp. 13–16). The presence of absence, the night, the dissolution of the subject in the night, the horror of being, the return of being to the heart of every negative movement, the reality of irreality are there admirably expressed.

Translated by Alphonso Lingis

3

Time and the Other

The following extract from *Time and the Other* originally comprised the final two lectures of a series of four, which were delivered in 1946–7 at the *Ecole philosophique* founded by Jean Wahl. The series was subsequently published in *Le Choix – Le Monde – L'Existence*, a collection edited by Jean Wahl (Grenoble-Paris: Arthaud, 1947), pp. 125–96, together with contributions from Jeanne Hersch, Alphonse de Waelhens and Jean Wahl. With a new preface, it was reissued as a separate book in 1979 (Montpellier: Fata Morgana) and translated into English, with two additional essays, by Richard A. Cohen in 1987 (Pittsburgh, Pennsylvania: Duquesne University Press). Cohen also provides an excellent introduction and copious footnotes.

Time and the Other marks a further stage in the way Levinas uses phenomenological structure to move beyond the noetic-noematic correlation. Its general aim is to show that time is not the achievement of an isolated subject, but the very relationship which that subject has with the Other. Beginning with the concept of 'there is' as 'the irremissibility of pure existing', Levinas goes on to see consciousness as therefore being the ability to withdraw from such an anonymous vigilance. This in turn leads to a discussion of solitude and materiality, which is the existent identical to itself and occupied with itself. Part II then introduces this subject into the world. Everyday life, by creating an interval between ego and self, *saves* the subject by overcoming this unbearable weight of existence. The salvation provided by 'being-in-the-world' leads Levinas to view the relationship between subject and world not in terms of the use of tools, as in Heidegger, but in terms of nourishment and enjoyment, which are prior to theory and practice. This conception of earthly enjoyment, whose forgetfulness of self is the first morality, marks a decisive break with *Dasein*, and is returned to in later works such as *Totality and Infinity* (pp. 127–39, 143–51) and *Otherwise than Being* (pp. 72–4).

The different sense of temporality created by this 'luminosity of enjoyment' leads Parts III and IV, which are reproduced here, to confront the crucial issue of the Heideggerian being-toward-death. Rather than see death as the subject's ultimate test of authenticity and virility, Levinas views it as something absolutely unknowable that comes at subjectivity from beyond its possibilities. The mystery of death, which is the limit of the subject's virility and always in the future, replaces the project of *Dasein* with a recognition of the relationship with the other. As this assumption of the other involves mystery rather than achievement, Levinas characterizes this face to face as Eros.

The use of concepts such as the feminine and fecundity in the phenomenology of voluptuousness led Simone de Beauvoir to accuse Levinas of sexism (for references to this and subsequent reactions, see note 27). It is true that Levinas on occasions appears to offer a male-oriented discourse, and no attempt has been made in this book to disguise such a trend when it occurs. But it must also be recognized that Levinas emphasizes the formal and cultural nature of the difference between the sexes; and that the priority of the Other forms the very basis of his philosophy. This last point, however, has in turn led Jacques Derrida to reply that Levinas 'pushes the respect for dissymmetry so far that it seems to us impossible, essentially impossible, that [his work] could have been written by a woman. Its philosophical subject is man (*vir*)' (see *Writing and Difference* (London: Routledge and Kegan Paul, 1978), p. 321). For further material by Levinas on this subject, see 'Judaism and the feminine element' (translated by Edith Wyschogrod), *Judaism*, 18 (1969), 30–8; while a remarkable feminist reading of Levinas's phenomenology of Eros is offered by Luce Irigaray's essay 'The Fecundity of the Caress' in *Face to Face with Levinas*, edited by Richard A. Cohen (Albany: State University of New York Press, 1986), pp. 231–56.

S.H.

III

I have dealt with the subject alone, alone due to the very fact that it is an existent. The solitude of the subject results from its relationship with the existing over which it is master. This mastery over existing is the power of beginning, of starting out from itself, starting out from itself neither to act nor to think, but to be.

I then showed that liberation with regard to the existent's anonymous existing becomes an enchainment to self, the very enchainment of identification. Concretely, the relationship of identification is the encumbrance of the ego by the self, the care that the ego takes of itself, or materiality. The subject – an abstraction from every relationship with a future or with a past – is thrust upon itself, and is so in the very freedom of its present. Its solitude is not initially the fact that it is without succour, but its being thrown into feeding upon itself, its being mixed in itself. This is materiality. So in the very instant of the transcendence of need, placing the subject in front of nourishments, in front of the world as nourishment, this transcendence offers the subject a liberation from itself. The world offers the subject participation in existing in the form of enjoyment, and consequently permits it to exist at a distance from itself. The subject is absorbed in the object it absorbs, and nevertheless keeps a distance with regard to that object. All enjoyment is also sensation – that is, knowledge and light. It is not just the disappearance of the self, but self-forgetfulness, as a first abnegation.

Work

But this instantaneous transcendence through space does not manage to escape solitude. The light that permits encountering something other than the self, makes it encountered as if this thing came from the ego. The light, brightness, is intelligibility itself; making everything come from me, it reduces every experience to an element of reminiscence. Reason is alone. And in this sense knowledge never encounters anything truly other in the world. This is the profound truth of idealism. It betokens a radical difference between spatial exteriority and the exteriority of instants in relation to one another.

In the concreteness of need, the space that keeps us away from ourselves is always to be conquered. One must cross it and take hold of an object – that is, one must work with one's hands. In this sense, 'the one who works not, eats not' is an analytic proposition. Tools and the manufacture of tools pursue the chimerical ideal of the suppression of distances. In the perspective that opens upon the tool, beginning with the modern tool – the machine – one is much more struck by its function which consists in suppressing work, than by its instrumental function, which Heidegger exclusively considered.

In work – meaning, in effort, in its pain and sorrow – the subject finds the weight of the existence which involves its existent freedom itself. Pain and sorrow are the phenomena to which the solitude of the existent is finally reduced.

Suffering and Death[1]

In pain, sorrow, and suffering, we once again find, in a state of purity, the finality that constitutes the tragedy of solitude. The ecstasis of enjoyment does not succeed in surmounting this finality. Two points must be emphasized: I am going to pursue the analysis of solitude in the pain of need and work, not in the anxiety of nothingness; and I am going to lay stress on the pain lightly called physical, for in it engagement in existence is without any equivocation. While in moral pain one can preserve an attitude of dignity and compunction, and consequently already be free; physical suffering in all its degrees entails the impossibility of detaching oneself from the instant of existence. It is the very irremissibility of being. The content of suffering merges with the impossibility of detaching oneself from suffering. And this is not to define suffering by suffering, but to insist on the *sui generis* implication that constitutes its essence. In suffering there is an absence of all refuge. It is the fact of being directly exposed to being. It is made up of the impossibility of fleeing or retreating. The whole acuity of suffering lies in this impossibility of retreat. It is the fact of being backed up against life and being. In this sense suffering is the impossibility of nothingness.

But in suffering there is, at the same time as the call to an impossible nothingness, the proximity of death. There is not only the feeling and the knowledge that suffering can end in death. Pain of itself includes it like a paroxysm, as if there were something about to be produced even more rending than suffering, as if despite the entire absence of a dimension of withdrawal that constitutes suffering, it still had some free space for an event, as if it must still get uneasy about something, as if we were on the verge of an event beyond what is revealed to the end in suffering. The structure of pain, which consists in its very attachment to pain, is prolonged further, but up to an unknown that is impossible to translate into terms of light – that is, that is refractory to the intimacy of the self with the ego to which all our experiences return. The unknown of death, which is not given straight off as nothingness but is correlative to an experience of the impossibility of nothingness, signifies not that death is a region from which no one has returned and consequently remains unknown as a matter of fact; the unknown of death signifies that the very relationship with death cannot take place in the light, that the subject is in relationship with what does not come from itself. We could say it is in relationship with mystery.

This way death has of announcing itself in suffering, outside all light, is an experience of the passivity of the subject, which until then had been active and remained active even when it was overwhelmed by its own nature, but reserved its possibility of assuming its factual state. To say 'an experience of passivity' is only a way of speaking, for experience always already signifies knowledge, light, and initiative, as well as the return of the object to the subject. Death as mystery contrasts strongly with experience thus understood. In knowledge all passivity is activity through the intermediary of light. The object that I encounter is understood and, on the whole, constructed by me, even though death announces an event over which the subject is not master, an event in relation to which the subject is no longer a subject.

I at once take note of what this analysis of death in suffering presents that is unusual, in relation to the celebrated Heideggerian analyses of *being toward death*. Being toward death, in Heidegger's autentic existence, is a supreme lucidity and hence a supreme virility. It is *Dasein*'s assumption of the uttermost possibility of existence, which precisely makes possible all other possibilities,[2] and consequently makes possible the very feat of grasping a possibility – that is, it makes possible activity and freedom. Death in Heidegger is an event of freedom, whereas for me the subject seems to reach the limit of the possible in suffering. It finds itself enchained, overwhelmed, and in some way passive. Death is in this sense the limit of idealism.

I even wonder how the principal trait of our relationship with death could have escaped philosophers' attention. It is not with the nothingness of death, of which we precisely know nothing, that the analysis must begin, but with the situation where something absolutely unknowable appears. Absolutely unknowable means foreign to all light, rendering every assumption of possibility impossible, but where we ourselves are seized.

Death and the Future[3]

This is why death is never a present. This is a truism. The ancient adage designed to dissipate the fear of death – 'If you are, it is not; if it is, you are not'[4] – without doubt misunderstands the entire paradox of death, for it effaces our relationship with death, which is a unique relationship with the future. But at least the adage insists on the eternal futurity of death. The fact that it deserts every present is not due to our evasion[5] of death and to an unpardonable diversion at the supreme hour, but to the fact that death is *ungraspable*, that it marks the end of the subject's virility and heroism. The now is the fact that I am master, master of the possible, master of grasping the possible. Death is never now. When death is here, I am no longer here, not just because I am nothingness, but because I am unable to grasp. My mastery, my virility, my heroism as a subject can be neither virility nor heroism in relation to death. There is in the suffering at the heart of which we have grasped this nearness of death – and still at the level of the phenomenon – this reversal of the subject's activity into passivity. This is not just in the instant of suffering where, backed against being, I still grasp it and am still the subject of suffering, but in the crying and sobbing toward which suffering is invertèd. Where suffering attains its purity, where there is no longer anything between us and it, the supreme responsibility of this extreme assumption turns into supreme irresponsibility, into infancy. Sobbing is this, and precisely through this it announces death. To die is to return to this state of irresponsibility, to be the infantile shaking of sobbing.

Allow me to return once again to Shakespeare, in whom I have over-indulged in the course of these lectures. But it sometimes seems to me that the whole of philosophy is only a meditation of Shakespeare. Does not the hero of tragedy assume death? I will allow myself a very brief analysis of Macbeth's end. Macbeth learns that Birnam Wood marches on the castle of

Dunsinane, and is the sign of defeat: death approaches. When this sign comes true, Macbeth says: 'Blow wind! come, wrack!' But right afterward: 'Ring the alarm-bell! [etc . . .] At least we'll die with harness on our back.' Prior to death there will be battle. The second sign of defeat has not yet come about. Had not the witches predicted that a man of woman born could do nothing against Macbeth? But here is Macduff, who was not of woman born. Death is coming now. 'Accursed by that tongue that tells,' cries Macbeth to Macduff who learns of his power over him, 'for it hath cow'd my better part of man! . . . I'll not fight with thee.'

This is the passivity when there is no longer hope. This is what I have called the 'end of virility'. But immediately hope is reborn, and here are Macbeth's last words:

> Though Birnam Wood be come to Dunsinane, and thou oppos'd, being of no woman born, yet I will try the last.

Prior to death there is always a last chance; this is what heroes seize, not death. The hero is the one who always glimpses a last chance, the one who obstinately finds chances. Death is thus never assumed, it comes. Suicide is a contradictory concept. The eternal immanence of death is part of its essence. In the present, where the subject's mastery is affirmed, there is hope. Hope is not added to death by a sort of *salto mortale*,[6] by a sort of inconsequence; it is in the very margin that is given, at the moment of death, to the subject who is going to die. *Spiro/spero*.[7] *Hamlet* is precisely a lengthy testimony to this impossibility of assuming death. Nothingness is impossible. It is nothingness that would have left humankind the possibility of assuming death and snatching a supreme mastery from out of the servitude of existence. 'To be or not to be'[8] is a sudden awareness of this impossibility of annihilating oneself.

The Event and the Other (*L'Autre*)

What can we infer from this analysis of death? Death becomes the limit of the subject's virility, the virility made possible by the hypostasis at the heart of anonymous being, and manifest in the phenomenon of the present, in the light. It is not just that there exist ventures impossible for the subject, that its powers are in some way finite; death does not announce a reality against which nothing can be done, against which our power is insufficient – realities exceeding our strength already arise in the world of light. What is important about the approach of death is that at a certain moment we are no longer *able to be able* (*nous ne 'pouvons plus pouvoir'*).[9] It is exactly thus that the subject loses its very mastery as a subject.

This end of mastery indicates that we have assumed existing in such a way that an *event* can happen to us that we no longer assume, not even in the way we assume events – because we are always immersed in the empirical world – through vision. An event happens to us without our having absolutely anything 'a priori', without our being able to have the least project, as one says today. Death is the impossibility of having a project. This approach of death indicates that we are in relation with something that is absolutely other, something bearing alterity not as a provisional determination we can assimilate through enjoyment, but as something whose very existence is made of alterity. My solitude is thus not confirmed by death but broken by it.

Right away this means that existence is pluralist. Here the plural is not a multiplicity of existents; it appears in existing itself. A plurality insinuates itself into the very existing of the existent, which until this point was jealously assumed by the subject alone and manifest through suffering. In death the existing of the existent is alienated. To be sure, the other (*l'Autre*) that is announced does not possess this existing as the subject possesses it; its hold over my existing is mysterious. It is not unknown but unknowable, refractory to all light. But this precisely indicates that the other is in no way another myself, participating with me in a common existence.[10] The relationship with the other is not an idyllic and harmonious relationship of communion, or a sympathy[11] through which we put ourselves in the other's place; we recognize the other as resembling us, but exterior to us; the relationship with the other is a relationship with a Mystery. The other's entire being is constituted by its exteriority, or rather its alterity, for exteriority is a property of space and leads the subject back to itself through light.

Consequently only a being whose solitude has reached a crispation through suffering, and in relation with death, takes its place on a ground where the relationship with the other becomes possible. The relationship with the other will never be the feat of grasping a possibility. One would have to characterize it in terms that contrast strongly with the relationships that describe light. I think the erotic relationship furnishes us with a prototype of it. Eros, strong as death,[12] will furnish us with the basis of an analysis of this relationship with mystery – provided it is set forth in terms entirely different from those of the Platonism that is a world of light.

But it is possible to infer from this situation of death, where the subject no longer has any possibility of grasping, another characteristic of existence with the other. The future is what is in no way grasped. The exteriority of the future is totally different from spatial exteriority precisely through the fact that the future is absolutely surprising. Anticipation of the future and projection of the future, sanctioned as essential to time by all theories from

Bergson[13] to Sartre, are but the present of the future and not the authentic future; the future is what is not grasped, what befalls us and lays hold of us. The other is the future. The very relationship with the other is the relationship with the future. It seems to me impossible to speak of time in a subject alone, or to speak of a purely personal duration.

Other and the Other[14]

I have just shown the possibility of an event in death. And I have contrasted this possibility, where the subject is no longer master of the event, with the possibility of the object, which the subject always masters and with which it is, in short, always alone. I have characterized this event as mystery, precisely because it could not be anticipated – that is, grasped; it could not enter into a present or it could enter into it as what does not enter it. But the death thus announced as other, as the alienation of my existence, is it still *my* death? If it opens a way out of solitude, does it not simply come to crush this solitude, to crush subjectivity itself? In death there is indeed an abyss between the event and the subject to whom it will happen. How can the event that cannot be grasped still happen to me? What can the other's relationship with a being, an existent, be? How can the existent exist as mortal and none the less persevere in its 'personality', preserve its conquest over the anonymous 'there is', its subject's mastery, the conquest of its subjectivity? How can a being enter into relation with the other without allowing its very self to be crushed by the other?

This question must be posed first, because it is the very problem of the preservation of the ego in transcendence. If the escape from solitude is meant to be something other than the absorption of the ego in the term toward which it is projected, and if, on the other hand, the subject cannot assume death, as it assumes an object, how can this reconciliation between the ego and death come about? How, too, can the ego assume death without meanwhile assuming it as a possibility? If in the face of death one is no longer able to be able, how can one still remain a self before the event it announces?

The same problem is implied in a description faithful to the very phenomenon of death. The pathos of suffering does not consist solely in the impossibility of fleeing existing, of being backed up against it, but also in the terror of leaving this relationship of light whose transcendence death announces. Like Hamlet we prefer this known existence to unknown existence. It is as though the adventure into which the existent has entered by hypostasis were its sole recourse, its sole refuge against what is intolerable in that adventure. In death there is Lucretius' temptation of nothingness, and Pascal's desire for eternity.[15] These are not two distinct attitudes: we want both to die and to be.

The problem does not consist in rescuing an eternity from the jaws of death, but in allowing it to be welcomed, keeping for the ego – in the midst of an existence where an event happens to it – the freedom acquired by hypostasis. Such is the situation one can call the attempt to vanquish death, where at one time the event happens and yet the subject, without welcoming it, as one welcomes a thing or object, faces up to the event.

I have just described a dialectical situation. I am now going to show a concrete situation where this dialectic is accomplished. It is impossible for me to explain this method at length here; I have resorted to it again and again. One sees in any event that it is not phenomenological to the end.

The relationship with the Other, the face-to-face with the Other, the encounter with a face that at once gives and conceals the Other, is the situation in which an event happens to a subject who does not assume it, who is utterly unable in its regard, but where none the less in a certain way it is in front of the subject. The other 'assumed' is the Other.

Time and the Other[16]

I hope to be able to show that the relationship with the Other is as entirely different from what the existentialists propose as it is from what the Marxists propose. For the moment I would like to at least indicate how time itself refers to this situation of the face-to-face with the Other.

The future that death gives, the future of the event, is not yet time. In order for this future, which is nobody's and which a human being cannot assume, to become an element of time, it must also enter into relationship with the present. What is the tie between two instants that have between them the whole interval, the whole abyss, that separates the present and death, this margin at once both insignificant and infinite, where there is always room enough for hope? It is certainly not a relationship of pure contiguity, which would transform time into space, but neither is it the élan of dynamism and duration, since for the present this power to be beyond itself and to encroach upon the future seems to me precisely excluded by the very mystery of death.

Relationship with the future, the presence of the future in the present, seems all the same accomplished in the face-to-face with the Other. The situation of the face-to-face would be the very accomplishment of time; the encroachment of the present on the future is not the feat of the subject alone, but the intersubjective relationship. The condition of time lies in the relationship between humans, or in history.

IV

Part III began with suffering as the event whereby the existent manages to accomplish all its solitude – that is, all the intensity of its tie with itself, all the finality of its identity – and at the same time it is that whereby the subject finds itself in relationship with the event that it does not assume, which is absolutely other, and in regard to which it is a pure passivity and no longer able to be able. This future of death determines the future for us, the future insofar as it is not present. It determines what in the future contrasts strongly with all anticipation, projection, and élan. Starting from such a notion of the future to understand time, one never again meets with time as a 'moving image of eternity'.[17]

When one deprives the present of all anticipation, the future loses all co-naturalness with it. The future is not buried in the bowels of a pre-existent eternity, where we would come to lay hold of it. It is absolutely other and new. And it is thus that one can understand the very reality of time, the absolute impossibility of finding in the present the equivalent of the future, the lack of any hold upon the future.

To be sure, the Bergsonian conception of freedom through duration tends toward the same end. But it preserves for the present a power over the future: duration is creation. To criticize this deathless philosophy it is not enough to situate it within the whole drift of modern philosophy, which makes creation the principal attribute of the creature. It is a matter of showing that creation itself presupposes an opening onto a mystery. The subject's identity by itself is incapable of yielding this. To uphold this thesis I have insisted upon the anonymous and irremissible existing that constitutes an entire universe, and upon the hypostasis that ends in the mastery of an existent over existing, but which by the same token is shut up within the finality of the identity that its spatial transcendence does not undo. It is not a matter of contesting the fact of anticipation, to which the Bergsonian descriptions of duration have accustomed us. It is a matter of showing their ontological conditions, which are the feat rather than the work[18] of a subject in relation with mystery, which is, so to say, the very dimension that is opened to a subject shut up in itself. This is precisely the reason why the work of time is profound. It is not simply a renewal through creation, which remains attached to the present, giving the creature but the sadness of Pygmalion. More than the renewal of our moods and qualities, time is essentially a new birth.

Power and Relationship with the Other

The strangeness of the future of death does not leave the subject any initiative. There is an abyss between the present and death, between the ego and the alterity of mystery. It is not the fact that death cuts existence short, that it is end and nothingness, but the fact that the ego is absolutely without initiative in the face of it. Vanquishing death is not a problem of eternal life. Vanquishing death is to maintain, with the alterity of the event, a relationship that must still be personal.

What, then, is this personal relationship other than the subject's power over the world, meanwhile protecting its personality? How can the subject be given a definition that somehow lies in its passivity? Is there another mastery in the human other than the virility of grasping the possible, the *power to be able* ('*pouvoir de pouvoir*')? If we find it, it is in it, in this relation that very place of time will consist. I already said in Part III that this relation is the relationship with the Other.

But a solution does not consist in repeating the terms of the problem. It is a matter of specifying what this relationship with the Other can be. Someone has objected to me that in my relationship with the Other it is not only the Other's future that I encounter, that the other as existent already has a past for me and, consequently, does not have a privilege over the future. This objection will allow me to approach the main part of my exposition here. I do not define the other by the future, but the future by the other, for the very future of death consists in its total alterity. But my main response will consist in saying that the relationship with the other, taken at the level of our civilization, is a complication of our original relationship; it is in no way a contingent complication, but one itself founded upon the inner dialectic of the relationship with the Other. I cannot develop this here.[19] I will simply say that this dialectic appears when one pushes further all the implications of hypostasis that have thus far been treated very schematically, and in particular when one shows, next to the transcendence toward the world, the transcendence of expression that founds the contemporaneousness of civilization and the mutuality of every relationship. But this transcendence of expression itself presupposes the future of alterity, to which I limit myself here.

If the relationship with the other involves more than relationships with mystery, it is because one has accosted the other in everyday life where the solitude and fundamental alterity of the other are already veiled by decency. One is for the other what the other is for oneself; there is no exceptional place for the subject. The other is known through sympathy, as another (my)self, as the alter ego.[20] In Blanchot's novel *Aminadab*, this situation is pushed to the absurd. Between the persons circulating in the strange house where the action takes place, where there is no work to pursue, where they only abide – that is, exist – this social relationship becomes total reciprocity. These beings are not interchangeable but reciprocal, or rather they are interchangeable because they are reciprocal. And then the relationship with the other becomes impossible.

But already, in the very heart of the relationship with the other that characterizes our social life, alterity appears as a nonreciprocal relationship – that is, as contrasting strongly with contemporaneousness. The Other as Other is not only an alter ego: the Other is what I myself am not.[21] The Other is this, not because of the Other's character, or physiognomy, or psychology, but because of the Other's very alterity. The Other is, for example, the weak, the poor, 'the widow and the orphan',[22] whereas I am the rich or the powerful. It can be said that intersubjective space is not symmetrical.[23] The exteriority of the other is not simply due to the space that separates what remains identical through the concept, nor is it due to any difference the concept would manifest through spatial exteriority. The relationship with alterity is neither spatial nor conceptual. Durkheim has misunderstood the specificity of the other when he asks in what Other rather than myself is the object of a virtuous action.[24] Does not the essential difference between charity and justice come from the preference of charity for the other, even when, from the point of view of justice, no preference is any longer possible?[25]

Eros[26]

In civilized life there are traces of this relationship with the other that one must investigate in its original form. Does a situation exist where the alterity of the other appears in its purity? Does a situation exist where the other would not have alterity only as the reverse side of its identity, would not comply only with the Platonic law of participation where every term contains a sameness and through this sameness contains the Other? Is there not a situation where alterity would be borne by a being in a positive sense, as essence? What is the alterity that does not purely and simply enter into the opposition of two species of the same genus? I think the absolutely contrary contrary (*le contraire absolument contraire*), whose contrariety is in no way affected by the relationship that can be established between it and its correlative, the contrariety that permits its terms to remain absolutely other, is the *feminine*.[27]

Sex is not some specific difference. It is situated beside the logical division into genera and species. This division certainly never manages to reunite an empirical content. But it is not in this sense that it does not permit one to account for the difference between the sexes. The difference between the sexes is a formal structure, but one that carves up reality in another sense and conditions the very possibility of reality as multiple, against the unity of being proclaimed by Parmenides.

Neither is the difference between the sexes a contradiction. The contradiction of being and nothingness leads from one to the other, leaving no room for distance. Nothingness converts into being, which has led us to the notion of the 'there is'. The negation of being occurs at the level of the anonymous existing of being in general.

Neither is the difference between the sexes the duality of two complementary terms, for two complementary terms presuppose a preexisting whole. To say that sexual duality presupposes a whole is to posit love beforehand as fusion.[28] The pathos of love, however, consists in an insurmountable duality of beings. It is a relationship with what always slips away. The relationship does not *ipso facto* neutralize alterity but preserves it. The pathos of voluptuousness lies in the fact of being two. The other as other is not here an object that becomes ours or becomes us; to the contrary, it withdraws into its mystery. Neither does this mystery of the feminine – the feminine: essentially other – refer to any romantic notions of the mysterious, unknown, or misunderstood woman. Let it be understood that if, in order to uphold the thesis of the exceptional position of the feminine in the economy of being, I willingly refer to the great themes of Goethe or Dante, to Beatrice and the *ewig Weibliches*, to the cult of the *Woman* in chivalry and in modern society (which is certainly not explained solely by the necessity of lending a strong arm to the weaker sex) – if, more precisely, I think of the admirably bold pages of Léon Bloy in his *Letters to his Fiancée*,[29] I do not want to ignore the legitimate claims of the feminism that presupposes all the acquired attainments of civilization. I simply want to say that this mystery must not be understood in the ethereal sense of a certain literature; that in the most brutal materiality, in the most shameless or the most prasaic appearance of the feminine, neither her mystery nor her modesty is abolished. Profanation is not a negation of mystery, but one of the possible relationships with it.

What matters to me in this notion of the feminine is not merely the unknowable, but a mode of being that consists in slipping away from the light. The feminine in existence is an event different from that of spatial transcendence or of expression that go toward light. It is a flight before light. Hiding is the way of existing of the feminine, and this fact of hiding is precisely modesty. So this feminine alterity does not consist in the object's simple exteriority. Neither is it made up of an opposition of wills. The Other is not a being we encounter that menaces us or wants to lay hold of us. The feat of being refractory to our power is not a power greater than ours. Alterity makes for all its power. Its mystery constitutes its alterity. A fundamental comment: I do not initially posit the Other as freedom, a characteristic in which the failure of communication is inscribed in advance.

For with a freedom there can be no other relationship than that of submission or enslavement. In both cases, one of the two freedoms is annihilated. The relationship between master and slave can be grasped at the level of struggle, but then it becomes reciprocal. Hegel has shown precisely how the master becomes slave of the slave and the slave becomes master of the master.[30]

In positing the Other's alterity as mystery, itself defined by modesty, I do not posit it as a freedom identical to and at grips with mine; I do not posit another existent in front of me, I posit alterity. Just as with death, I am not concerned with an existent, but with the event of alterity, with alienation. The other is not initially characterized as freedom, from which alterity would then be deduced; the other bears alterity as an essence. And this is why I have sought this alterity in the absolutely original relationship of eros, a relationship that is impossible to translate into powers and must not be so translated, if one does not want to distort the meaning of the situation.

I am thus describing a category that falls neither into the being-nothingness opposition, nor into the notion of the existent. It is an event in existing different from the hypostasis by which an existent arises. The existent is accomplished in the 'subjective' and in 'consciousness'; alterity is accomplished in the feminine. This term is on the same level as, but in meaning opposed to, consciousness. The feminine is not accomplished as a *being* (*étant*) in a transcendence toward light, but in modesty.

The movement here is thus inverse. The transcendence of the feminine consists in withdrawing elsewhere, which is a movement opposed to the movement of consciousness. But this does not make it unconscious or subconscious, and I see no other possibility than to call it mystery.

Even when by positing the Other as freedom, by thinking of the Other in terms of light, I am obliged to admit the failure of communication, I have merely admitted the failure of the movement that tends to grasp or to possess a freedom. It is only by showing in what way eros differs from possession and power that I can acknowledge a communication in eros. It is neither a struggle, nor a fusion, nor a knowledge. One must recognize its exceptional place among relationships. It is a relationship with alterity, with mystery – that is to say, with the future, with what (in a world where there is everything) is never there, with what cannot be there when everything is there – not with a being that is not there, but with the very dimension of alterity. There where all possibles are impossible, where one can no longer be able, the subject is still a subject through eros. Love is not a possibility, is not due to our initiative, is without reason; it invades and wounds us, and nevertheless the *I* survives in it.

A phenomenology of voluptuousness, which I am only going to touch upon here – voluptuousness is not a pleasure like others, because it is not solitary like eating or drinking – seems to confirm my views on the exceptional role and place of the feminine, and on the absence of any fusion in the erotic.

The caress is a mode of the subject's being, where the subject who is in contact with another goes beyond this contact. Contact as sensation is part of the world of light. But what is caressed is not touched, properly speaking. It is not the softness or warmth of the hand given in contact that the caress seeks. The seeking of the caress constitutes its essence by the fact that the caress does not know what it seeks. This 'not knowing', this fundamental disorder, is the essential. It is like a game with something slipping away, a game absolutely without project or plan, not with what can become ours or us, but with something other, always other, always inaccessible, and always still to come (*à venir*). The caress is the anticipation of this pure future (*avenir*)[31] without content. It is made up of this increase of hunger, of ever richer promises, opening new perspectives onto the ungraspable. It feeds on countless hungers.

This intentionality of the voluptuous - the sole intentionality of the future itself, and not an expectation of some future fact – has always been misunderstood by philosophical analysis. Freud himself says little more about the libido than that it searches for pleasure, taking pleasure as a simple content, starting with which one begins an analysis but which itself one does not analyze. Freud does not search for the significance of this pleasure in the general economy of being. My thesis, which consists in affirming voluptuousness as the very event of the future, the future purified of all content, the very mystery of the future, seeks to account for its exceptional place.

Can this relationship with the other through Eros be characterized as a failure? Once again, the answer is yes, if one adopts the terminology of current descriptions, if one wants to characterize the erotic by 'grasping', 'possessing', or 'knowing'. But there is nothing of all this, or the failure of all this, in eros. If one could possess, grasp, and know the other, it would not be other. Possessing, knowing, and grasping are synonyms of power.

Furthermore, the relationship with the other is generally sought out as a fusion. I have precisely wanted to contest the idea that the relationship with the other is fusion. The relationship with the Other is the absence of the other; not absence pure and simple, not the absence of pure nothingness, but absence in a horizon of the future, an absence that is time. This is the horizon where a personal life can be constituted in the heart of the transcendent event, what I called above the 'victory over death'. I must say a few words about it in concluding.

Université	University
de	of
Sudbury	Sudbury

Fecundity[32]

I am going to return to the consideration that led me from the alterity of death to the alterity of the feminine. Before a pure event, a pure future, which is death, where the ego can in no way be able – that is, can no longer be an ego – I seek a situation where none the less it is possible for it to remain an ego, and I have called this situation 'victory over death'. Once again, this situation cannot be qualified as power. How, in the alterity of a you, can I remain I, without being absorbed or losing myself in that you? How can the ego that I am remain myself in a you, without being none the less the ego that I am in my present – that is to say, an ego that inevitably returns to itself? How can the ego become other to itself? This can happen only in one way: through paternity.

Paternity is the relationship with a stranger who, entirely while being Other, is myself, the relationship of the ego with a myself who is none the less a stranger to me. The son, in effect, is not simply my work, like a poem or an artifact, neither is he my property. Neither the categories of power nor those of having can indicate the relationship with the child. Neither the notion of cause nor the notion of ownership permit one to grasp the fact of fecundity. I do not *have* my child; I *am* in some way my child. But the words 'I am' here have a significance different from an Eleatic or Platonic significance. There is a multiplicity and a transcendence in this verb 'to exist', a transcendence that is lacking in even the boldest existentialist analyses. Then again, the son is not any event whatsoever that happens to me – for example, my sadness, my ordeal, or my suffering. The son is an ego, a person. Lastly, the alterity of the son is not that of an alter ego. Paternity is not a sympathy through which I can put myself in the son's place. It is through my being, not through sympathy, that I am my son. The return of the ego to itself that begins with hypostasis is thus not without remission, thanks to the perspective of the future opened by eros. Instead of obtaining this remission through the impossible dissolution of hypostasis, one accomplishes it through the son. It is thus not according to the category of cause, but according to the category of the father that freedom comes about and time is accomplished.

Bergson's notion of *élan vital*, which merges artistic creation and generation in the same movement – what I call 'fecundity' – does not take account of death, but above all it tends toward an impersonal pantheism, in the sense that it does not sufficiently note the crispation and isolation of subjectivity, which is the ineluctable moment of my dialectic. Paternity is not simply the renewal of the father in the son and the father's merger with him, it is also the father's exteriority in relation to the son, a pluralist existing. The fecundity of the ego must be appreciated at its correct ontological value, which until now has never been done. The fact that it is a biological – and psychological – category in no way neutralizes the paradox of its significance.

I began with the notions of death and the feminine, and have ended with that of the son. I have not proceeded in a phenomenological way. The continuity of development is that of a dialectic starting with the identity of hypostasis, the enchainment of the ego to the self, moving toward the maintenance of this identity, toward the maintenance of the existent, but in a liberation of the ego with regard to self. The concrete situations that have been analyzed represent the accomplishment of this dialectic. Many intermediaries have been skipped. The unity of these situations – death, sexuality, paternity – until now appeared only in relation to the notion of power that they exclude.

This was my main goal. I have been bent on emphasizing that alterity is not purely and simply the existence of another freedom next to mine. I have a power over such a freedom where it is absolutely foreign to me, without relation to me. The coexistence of several freedoms is a multiplicity that leaves the unity of each intact, or else this multiplicity unites into a general will. Sexuality, paternity, and death introduce a duality into existence, a duality that concerns the very existing of each subject. Existing itself becomes double. The Eleatic notion of being is overcome. Time constitutes not the fallen form of being, but its very event. The Eleatic notion of being dominates Plato's philosophy, where multiplicity was subordinated to the one, and where the role of the feminine was thought within the categories of passivity and activity, and was reduced to matter. Plato did not grasp the feminine in its specifically erotic notion. In his philosophy of love he left to the feminine no other role than that of furnishing an example of the Idea, which alone can be the object of love. The whole particularity of the relationship of one to another goes unnoticed. Plato constructs a Republic that must imitate the world of Ideas; he makes a philosophy of a world of light, a world without time. Beginning with Plato, the social ideal will be sought for in an ideal of fusion. It will be thought that, in its relationship with the other, the subject tends to be identified with the other, by being swallowed up in a collective representation,[33] a common ideal. It is the collectivity that says 'we', that, turned toward the intelligible sun, toward the truth, feels the other at its side and not in front of itself. This collectivity necessarily establishes itself around a third term, which serves as an intermediary. *Miteinandersein*, too, remains the collectivity of the 'with', and is revealed in its authentic form around the truth. It is a collectivity around something common. Just as in all the philosophies of communion, sociality in Heidegger is found in the subject alone; and it is in terms of solitude that the analysis of *Dasein* in its authentic form is pursued.

Against this collectivity of the side-by-side, I have tried to oppose the 'I-you' collectivity,[34] taking this not in Buber's sense, where reciprocity remains the tie between two separated freedoms, and the ineluctable character of isolated subjectivity is underestimated.[35] I have tried to find the temporal transcendence of the present toward the mystery of the future. This is not a participation in a third term, whether this term be a person, a truth, a work, or a profession. It is a collectivity that is not a communion. It is the face-to-face without intermediary, and is furnished for us in the eros where, in the other's proximity, distance is integrally maintained, and whose pathos is made of both this proximity and this duality.

What one presents as the failure of communication in love precisely constitutes the positivity of the relationship; this absence of the other is precisely its presence as other.

Set against the cosmos that is Plato's world, is the world of the spirit (*l'esprit*) where the implications of eros are not reduced to the logic of genus, and where the ego takes the place of the same and the *Other* takes the place of the other.

NOTES

All notes are by the translator, unless otherwise indicated.

1 The themes of this section are taken up and developed in the section entitled 'Time and the Will: Patience', in *Totality and Infinity*, pp. 236–40.

2 Levinas: Death in Heidegger is not, as Jean Wahl says 'the impossibility of possibility', but 'the possibility of impossibility'. (See Heidegger, *Being and Time*, pp. 294, 307.) This apparently Byzantine distinction has a fundamental importance. (See *Totality and Infinity*, p. 235.)

3 The themes of this section are later taken up and developed in *Totality and Infinity*, in the section entitled 'The Will and Death' (pp. 232–6), which directly precedes – rather than follows – the section of *Totality and Infinity* indicated in note 1 above, thus reversing the order of development found in *Time and the Other*.

4 Epicurus, Letter to Menoeceus.

5 The earliest published text containing what is perhaps the nascent kernel of Levinas's thought – hidden within the husks of Heideggerian ontology – is entitled 'De l'évasion' ('On Evasion') (*Recherches philosophiques*, 5 (1935–6), 373–92); republished as a book (Montpellier: Fata Morgana, 1982) introduced and annotated by J. Rolland. Its main theme is the escape of the self from its enchainment with itself. It is noteworthy, furthermore, in that it contains, nearly three years before the publication of Sartre's famous novel *Nausea*, several pages describing 'the very experience of pure being' in terms of the experience of nausea!

6 A somersault (literally: 'deadly-jump'). This expression reappears in *Totality and Infinity*, p. 246.

7 ['If] I breathe, I hope'.
8 In English in original. Jankélévitch also protests against this seemingly all-inclusive disjunction; see the section entitled 'Etre ou n'être pas?' ('To be or not to be?') in his *Philosophie première* (Paris: Presses Universitaires de France, 1954), pp. 36–8.

Almost thirty-five years after *Time and the Other*, Levinas again recalls Hamlet's famous question in 'Bad Conscience and the Inexorable', where he writes: 'To be or not to be – this is probably not the question par excellence' (in *Face to Face with Levinas*, ed. Richard A. Cohen (Albany: State University of New York Press, 1986), p. 40).

9 The verb *pouvoir* means 'to be able' or 'can'; the noun means 'power', 'force', 'means'. Levinas's idea seem to be that in the face of the mystery of death, the subject not only loses its various powers, it loses its very ability to have powers, its 'I can' – that is to say, its very self-constitution as an existent.

In his translation of Levinas's *Totality and Infinity*, Alphonso Lingis also notes this peculiar doubling of the verb *pouvoir* (pp. 39, 198, 236).

10 Although Levinas is explicitly discussing the encounter with the alterity of death, this sentence and the ones following it conjure up the encounter with the alterity of the other person. What is common to death and social life is an encounter with radical alterity.

This important shift from solitude to social life, evinced by death, does not result, therefore, from an intellectual confusion or a fallaciously employed ambiguity. As will soon become clear (see especially the penultimate paragraph of the next section below), and as Levinas says unequivocally in *Totality and Infinity*, the encounter with the alterity of death is like nothing so much as the encounter with the alterity of the other person, 'as though the approach of death remained one of the modalities of the relationship with the Other' (p. 234).

It is alterity, then, not shared attributes, that is the key to social life.

In the above critical sentence, Levinas doubtless has in mind the alternative version of social life expressed in particular by Heidegger's notion of *mitsein* (previously mentioned) and Husserl's notion of 'associative pairing', found in the fifth meditation of Edmund Husserl's *Cartesian Meditations* (trans. D. Cairns (The Hague: Martinus Nijhoff, 1970), pp. 89–151), a text that Levinas, along with Gabrielle Pfeiffer, translated into French for publication in 1931. (It is relevant, then, to note that Pfeiffer translated the first three meditations and Levinas translated the longer and final two meditations as well as Husserl's brief conclusion.)

11 See Max Scheler, *The Nature of Sympathy*, trans. P. Heath (New Haven: Yale University Press, 1954); first German edition published in 1913, the second in 1923.

12 'L'Eros, *fort comme la mort . . .* ' This expression is found in the Song of Songs, 8: 6. Franz Rosenzweig begins Part 2, Book 2, of *The Star of Redemption* with it; Lev Shestov refers to it in his book, *Athens and Jerusalem*, trans. B. Martin (New York: Simon and Schuster, 1968), p. 144.

13 It is perhaps curious that Levinas includes Bergson here (as he does, similarly, in *Existence and Existents*, p. 94). Levinas often acknowledges his indebtedness to

Bergson, who was, after all, *the* dominant French thinker at the beginning of the twentieth century, and led the way in rethinking time and its insertion of newness into being.

It was Bergson who argued, against previous notions of time (and proleptically against Heidegger's notion of time), that we must 'succeed in conceiving the radically new and unforeseeable', which means rejecting the idea of '"possibles" outlined beforehand . . . as if the will was limited to "bringing about" one of them' (Henri Bergson, *The Creative Mind*, trans. M. Andison (New York: Philosophical Library, 1945), pp. 18–19).

In the opening comments and the third section of part IV of *Time and the Other*, Levinas will give his reasons for criticizing Bergson in this regard.

14 *Autre et autrui.*

15 See Lucretius, *The Way Things Are*, book 3; Blaise Pascal, *Pensées*, passim.

16 *Temps et autrui.*

17 Plato, *Timaeus*, 37; also see p. 129 below.

18 *le fait plutôt que l'oeuvre.*

19 For these developments, see the section entitled 'Intentions' in *Existence and Existents*, pp. 37–45; and the section entitled 'The Truth of the Will' in *Totality and Infinity*, pp. 240–7.

20 It is at the level of the 'decency' of 'everyday life' then, that Levinas finds a place for the sympathy and pairing that he has rejected as ultimately constitutive of the inter-subjective relationship (see notes 50 and 51, above).

21 For Levinas this formulation does not necessarily lead to the conclusion of the German Idealists – namely, that alterity is only encountered through *negation*. Philosophers can perhaps hardly be reminded too often of this difference. For Levinas the alterity encountered through negativity is merely a relative, not an absolute, alterity. To grasp alterity *outside* even negativity, and thus in a truly positive 'sense', is perhaps the essence of Levinas's entire effort. See, in particular, the section entitled 'Transcendence is Not Negativity' in *Totality and Infinity*, pp. 40–2; and the Preface to *Time and the Other*, p. 32.

22 The Hebrew Bible contains many references to the orphan and the widow jointly: Exodus 22: 21; Deuteronomy 10: 18, 24: 17, 24: 19, 24: 20, 24: 21, 26: 12, 27: 19; Isaiah 1: 17, 9: 16, 10: 2; Jeremiah 7: 6, 22: 3, Ezekiel 22: 7; Zechariah 7: 10; Malachi 3: 5; Psalms 68: 6, 109: 9, 146: 9; Lamentations 5: 3. Relevant to Levinas's emphasis on the alterity of the other, in all these instances (except Isaiah, and at 69: 6 in Psalms where the 'solitary' is mentioned; and, one should add, in James 1: 27, where the orphan and the widow are mentioned together), the *stranger* is always also mentioned in conjunction with the orphan and the widow.

23 See the section entitled 'Asymmetry of the Interpersonal' in *Totality and Infinity*, pp. 215–16, also p. 251 and passim.

24 According to Durkheim, 'morality is the product of the collective' and not the result of the face-to-face encounter. See 'The Determination of Moral Facts' and 'Replies to Objections' in Emile Durkheim, *Sociology and Philosophy*, trans. D. Pocock (New York: MacMillan, 1974), pp. 35–79.

25 Although, inasmuch as our culture is predominantly Christian, one might see

here an allusion only to the alleged opposition between 'Christian mercy' and 'Jewish justice', in addition to being an internal Christian opposition (often enough, it is true, expressed in terms of a Christian vision of Judaism), the allusion here is certainly also to an ancient and properly internal Jewish opposition – namely, that between God's *chesed*, kindness, and God's *gevurah*, justice. To be sure, this opposition is equally a secular, moral opposition.

26 For a fuller development of the analysis of eros and fecundity (the topic of the next section), see section 4, 'Beyond the Face', of *Totality and Infinity*, pp. 254–85. Also see 'Phenomenology of the Face and Carnal Intimacy' by Alphonso Lingis in his book, *Libido: The French Existential Theories* (Bloomington: Indiana University Press, 1985), pp. 58–73; and 'The Fecundity of the Caress' by Luce Irigaray in *Face to Face with Levinas*, ed. Richard A. Cohen (Albany: State University of New York Press, 1986), pp. 231–56.

27 This sentence and some of those that follow were cited by Simone de Beauvoir in 1949 in *The Second Sex*, trans. H. Parshley (New York: Bantam Book, 1970), p. xvi, n. 3, to condemn Levinas for sexism.

De Beauvoir takes Levinas to task for allegedly assigning a secondary derivative status to women: subject (he) as absolute, woman as other. The issue is important but certainly not as simple as de Beauvoir, in this instance, makes it out to be, because for Levinas the other has a priority over the subject. For a more sympathetic treatment of Levinas's thought on this issue, see Catherine Chalier, *Figures du féminin* (Paris: La nuit surveillée, 1982).

For Levinas's most recent thoughts on this issue, with regard to *Time and the Other*, see 'Love and Filiation' in Levinas, *Ethics and Infinity*, trans. Richard A. Cohen (Pittsburgh: Duquesne University Press, 1985), pp. 65–72.

28 This is Aristophanes' position in Plato's *Symposium*.

29 *Lettres à sa Fiancée* (Paris: Stock, 1922); English translation (New York: Sheed and Ward, 1937). Léon Bloy (1846–1917) was a prolific French Catholic writer with a strong Jansenist bent.

30 Surely, in addition to Hegel, Levinas has Sartre's philosophy of freedom in mind. *Being and Nothingness* was published only five years earlier than *Time and the Other* (although Levinas, a German captive for the duraton of World War Two, had not read it in 1946, by his own admission (see Jean Wahl, *A Short History of Existentialism*, trans. F. Williams and S. Maron (New York: Philosophical Library, 1949), p. 51).

For some recent critical remarks by Levinas on the early Sartre, see Richard Kearney's 'Dialogue with Emmanuel Levinas', in *Face to Face with Levinas*, ed. Richard A Cohen (Albany: State University of New York Press, 1986), pp. 16–17.

31 *Venir* is a verb meaning 'to come' or – especially in the construction *à venir* – 'about to come'; *avenir* is a noun meaning 'future'. These latter two terms sound exactly the same in French. Levinas is emphasizing the essential connection between their meanings: the future is what is always about to come – that is, what is always about to come into the present but has not yet done so and never will (lest it be present rather than future).

32 See note 26, above.

33 The term 'collective representation' was used by the *l'année sociologique* group of anthropologists, including Durkheim, Mauss, and Lévy-Bruhl. See, again, Lucian Lévy-Bruhl, *How Natives Think* (Princeton University Press, 1985), trans. L. Clare; especially the Introduction and part 1, ch. 1, 'Collective Representation in Primitives' Perceptions and the Mystical Character of Such', pp. 13–76.

34 Of course Sartre also rejects the collectivity of the side-by-side in the name of the 'I-you' (Sartre, *Being and Nothingness*, part 3, ch. 1). But, as we have seen, for Levinas, Sartre's criticism is inadequate because the 'I-you' it proposes remains an antagonistic relationship of two freedoms, a failure of communication.

35 For a deeper understanding of Levinas's reading of Buber, see (among other articles) the following chapter, 'Martin Buber and the Theory of Knowledge'; and the subsequent correspondence between Levinas and Buber in 'Dialogue avec Martin Buber', in Levinas, *Noms Propres* (Montpellier: Fata Morgana, 1976), pp. 51–5.

Translated by Richard A. Cohen

4

Martin Buber and the Theory of Knowledge

Written in 1958, 'Martin Buber and the Theory of Knowledge' is unusual in having been published originally in German in 1963 ('Martin Buber und die Erkenntnis-theorie' in *Martin Buber, Philosophen des 20. Jahrhunderts*, edited by Paul Arthur Schilpp and Maurice Friedman (Stuttgart: Kohlhammer), pp. 119–34), and then translated into English in 1967 (in *The Philosophy of Martin Buber*, edited by P. A. Schilpp and M. Friedman (La Salle, Illinois: Open Court Publishing Company; London: Cambridge University Press), pp. 133–50), before finally appearing in French only in 1976 in the book of essays entitled *Noms propres* (Montpellier: Fata Morgana), pp. 29–50.

Martin Buber (1878–1965) was a Jewish philosopher and theologian whose main thought is contained in the 1923 book *I and Thou*. In it he makes a radical distinction between two basic relations: the I-Thou and the I-It. The former is a relation of reciprocity and mutuality between two subjects; the latter is the relation between subject and passive object, and unlike the former can be viewed in some independent manner. Every Thou will at times become an It; every I-It has the potential to become I–Thou. Buber's notion of God is that of the eternal Thou. This is the only I–Thou relation that can be sustained indefinitely, for God is wholly other.

Levinas begins his argument where our extract from *Time and the Other* in chapter 3 leaves off. He agrees with Buber that the self is not a substance but a relation, existing only as an 'I' addressing itself to a 'Thou'. This 'I–Thou' has priority over the 'I-It' relation, since the former is a necessary condition for the intentionality of the latter. Indeed, the I–Thou relation is the first relation, or *a priori* of relation: 'the movement which relates the Thou is not like one that sets any theme of discourse'.

But having assimilated Buber's thoughts to the problem of knowledge in contemporary philosophical thought, Levinas then goes on to criticize Buber's concept of intersubjectivity in terms of its reciprocity, its formality and its exclusiveness. The I–Thou relation in Buber is one in which a response is obtained from a friendly partner in a reciprocal dialogue. This ideal cannot account for the ethical import of the I–Thou relation, in which I am already obligated to the other in an asymmetrical manner. Buber's position is not ethical in the sense that it is a purely formal encounter that levels down the epiphany of the Other, and exists instead in a kind of ether, devoid of any concrete structure that might account for enjoyment, or sickness, or hunger. Consequently, such a relation is exclusive of the universe and can give rise to no sense of the justice necessary in order to go beyond the pure spiritualism of a narcissistic 'I–Thou'. Indeed, no true dialogue is possible for Levinas without such a *fürsorge*. For Levinas, therefore, Buber's 'I–Thou' relation can ultimately offer no place to the relation between the emergence of the I's independence, and the sense of *social* communion. As Buber fails to show the act of separateness involved in the process of subjectivation, the rupture of the individual within the whole, it is Levinas's belief that Buber fails to account for philosophy itself.

For a complete guide to the complex and changing relations between Levinas and Buber, see Robert Bernasconi's essay '"Failure of Communication" as a Surplus: Dialogue and Lack of Dialogue between Buber and Levinas' in *The Provocation of Levinas: Rethinking the Other*, edited by Robert Bernasconi and David Wood (London and New York: Routledge, 1988), pp. 100–35.

S.H.

The Problem of Truth

The theory of knowledge is a theory of truth.[1] Like the Parmenides of Plato it poses the question: how can the absolute being manifest itself in truth? For to be known, it must manifest itself in the world where error is possible. How can a being, subject to error, touch the absolute being without impairing its absolute character? It is reasonable to suggest that the efforts of ancient Greek philosophy were largely devoted to this question of how to mediate between appearance and reality. For in a universe conceived as a single whole, the gap between the two had to be bridged; and it was assumed that the mind need only reflect on itself to discover the One from which it derived.

The problem of the subject–object relation which arises in modern discussions on theory of knowledge, is an extension of this preoccupation of antiquity with the problem of truth. But it is no longer assumed that the agent of knowledge occupies a distinctive position in the hierarchy of beings which constitute the universe. The individual existent who aspires to the truth is radically separated from being as such. But if the implications of this separation were made clear, we would have to ascribe the metaphysical source of his being to the individual himself. For the latter is posited on the basis of an inferiority which is not directed to anything *other*, i.e., the individual is fixed in a dimension where it has only itself as term. The individual is subsequently identified with the subject of knowledge or consciousness. Hence understanding is construed not as one of the many activities of mind or as the superior function of mind, but as its very nature, i.e., that which constitutes its existence as parted, as breaking out from himself. Thus for awareness or for the consciousness which accompanies our acts, nothing, in fact, is external. Every movement of mind, including that which relates it to an external reality such as the acts of affirming, negating, willing, and even acts such as sensation which indicate a dependence on an external reality, is construed as a *pensée* in the Cartesian sense of the term. The consciousness where finally the existence of those movements is acted – the knowledge included in it – is in the origin of all that comes from the exteriority. If one identifies the subject with consciousness, therefore, any event which occurs, including shock or injury which disrupts the continuity of consciousness, has its source in a subject of awareness which exists in and by itself, i.e.: is separated. Philosophy, to employ Husserl's term, is an egology. But if the phenomenology of Husserl which has contributed to the repudiation of the idealist notion of the subject, is an egology, i.e., rediscovers the universe within the subject which constitutes it, it is still an egology which has always interpreted the self in terms of a consciousness which conceptualizes reality.

Theory of knowledge, then, in the contemporary sense of the expression, acquires a peculiar significance for it leads us to *original being*. The subject has that function precisely because it is a subject of knowledge. Thus theory of knowledge is prior to all other types of philosophical inquiry not only as a propaedeutic of knowledge but also as a theory of the absolute. Understanding which is the very life and essence of being, implies a relationship to the object. The object is constituted by the subject as opposed to subject. But that opposition remains in the power of subject.

Both ontology and the theory of the subject–object relation have in common a notion of the truth as an expressible content, regardless of the particular structure of being revealed by that content. Hence the truth is expressible in words but the original function of truth on which such expression depends, is to signify an inner meaning, of a solitary mind, which appeals to no interlocutor. The monumental solidity of being hinges on this possibility of expressing the truth and of conceiving it as an achieved result although being has in fact been interpreted from the time of the Parmenides and Sophist of Plato, as a relation, or since Descartes, as thought, while the object in turn has been interpreted as the intelligible though irrepresentable object of the physico-mathematical sciences. One of the most interesting facets of Buber's thought consists in his attempt to show that the truth is not a content and that words cannot summarize it in any way; that it is more subjective, in a sense, than any other type of subjectivity; yet, as distinct from all purely idealist conceptions of the truth, it provides the only means of access to what is more objective than any other type of objectivity, i.e., to that which the subject can never possess since it is totally *other*. It is this aspect of Buber's philosophy which is closely related to certain main tendencies in contemporary philosophical thought.

From the Object to Being

For contemporary thought, the history of the theory of knowledge is synonymous with the history of the vanishing of the subject–object problem. The subject, closed upon himself, once the metaphysical source of both the self and the world, is held to be an abstraction. The consistency of the self is resolved into intentional relations as for Husserl, or into the being-in-the-world or *Miteinandersein* of Heidegger, or else it is identified with a continuous process of renovation, typified by Bergson's duration. The concrete reality is man already entering into relations with the world and already projected beyond the present moment of his existence. Such relations are incapable of being characterized as representation, for the theoretical representation would only tend to confirm the autonomy of the thinking subject. But to combat successfully this view of an autonomous subject, analysis must discover underlying the objective representation, the wholly different relations: man is *in* a situation before he takes his place, but this is not to say that this adherence to being is reducible to a certain status in a hierarchically organized universe or to the performance of a specific function as part of a physical mechanism without any recourse to any truth. What must be insisted on is that a relation with the object is not identical with a relation to being, and objective knowledge, therefore, does not trace the original itinerary of truth. Objective knowledge is already bathed in a light which illuminates its way, and a light is required to see the light, for the philosopher as for the psalmist. It is in this sense, then, that we must reject the propaedeutic and ontological privileges possessed by a theory of knowledge solely concerned with the way in which a subject may be said to know an object.

Our critique leads us, therefore, to a knowledge of being and to a theory about this knowledge. But the knowledge of being does not resemble an object-relation with the difference that it is concerned with an object of a greater density and impenetrability, so to speak, an object more vast than the object of scientific knowledge. The original meaning of truth as a communication with being consists in not being truth about anything. It consists in not being a discourse about being. Being is not a theme of discourse. But in the original communication we have with being, the possibility of such discourse is revealed, and the context within which objective propositions may be meaningful is delimited. For Heidegger, revelation of the truth diffuses that light which is necessary to see the light, and one must first react to the light before one can speak *of* it. For Bergson, truth is synonymous with choice, invention, creation, and is not a mere reflection of being.[2] And Bergsonian intuition does not merely imply a union with being which extends beyond any purely external perception of being: Unity with being *is* invention and creation, i.e., truth is the essential act of being itself.

Thus knowledge for contemporary philosophy is directed beyond the object towards being but it does not seek being in the same way as it does the object. Our problem is to provide a positive description of this new orientation, of the search for a theory of more ultimate knowledge. The philosophy of Buber should be envisaged in this perspective.

Experience and Meeting

Consistent with contemporary views, the self, for Buber, is not a substance but a relation. It can only exist as an 'I' addressing itself to a 'Thou', or grasping an 'It'. But it is not to be construed as the same relation with two different terms. The relation itself, as for phenomenology, is related to each of these two terms in a different way.

The sphere of the It coincides with everything which the I comes into contact with in its objective and practical experience. Experience and practice are here associated (45) without consideration being given to the *non-objective* structure of practice which, it is now perceived, already anticipates the commitment of the self to being. For Buber, as for Bergson, the sphere of utilization implies the most superficial type of relation and is identifiable with the objective cognition of things. In effect, the sphere of the It is posited as the correlate of all our mental acts whether willed or felt, in so far as they are directed to an object. 'I perceive something. I have a sensation of something. I conceptualize something for myself. I think of something … All this and anything similar to it, constitutes the sphere of the *It*' (16). The It is described, in this connection, in the same terms as those used by Husserl to denote the intentional object. Thus in the measure that the I–Thou relation is distinguished from the I–It relation, the former designates what is not intentional but what for Buber is rather the condition of all intentional relations. Prior to Heidegger's, yet compatible with Bergson's views, Buber, then, pursues his inquiry into ontological structures anterior to those which characterize the objectifying intellect.

Human beings when we speak of them in the third person, 'he', 'she', 'they', as well as my own private psychological states, belong to the sphere of the It. The I experiences these; but only explores their surface without committing its whole being (15–16), and its experiences do not extend beyond itself (17). The It is neutral. The neuter gender suggests, moreover, that in the It, individuals do not enter into the type of unifying relation in which their otherness is distinctive, where they are, so to speak, other than the others. The individual is rather regarded as that which one may dispose of, what is significant only with respect to the actions of its physical being. Thus the actual purpose of all knowing, i.e., the effort to grasp what is independent of it, what is completely other, is not fulfilled in this case. Being is cast in the role, as the need may be, of an anonymous article of exchange, a funded past, or else is experienced in the actual moment of enjoyment, and cannot be properly interpreted as a real presence (25).

The I–Thou relation consists in confronting a being external to oneself, i.e., one which is radically other, and in recognizing it as such. This recognition of otherness, however, is not to be confused with the *idea* of otherness. To have an idea of something is appropriate to the I–It relation. What is important is not thinking *about* the other, even *as* an other, but of directly confronting it and of saying Thou to it. Hence a real access to the otherness of the other does not consist in a perception but in thou-saying, and this is at once an immediate contact and an appeal which does not posit an object (30), but of which the object-relation is, in fact, a distortion. This does not mean that the Thou is some unknown sort of object but rather that the movement which relates the Thou is not like one that sets any theme of discourse. The being who is invoked in this relation is ineffable because the I speaks *to* him rather than *of* him and because in the latter case all contact is broken off with the Thou. To speak *to* him is to let him realize his own otherness. The I–Thou relation, therefore, escapes the gravitational field of the I–It in which the externalized object remains imprisoned.

The I–Thou relation is one in which the self is no longer a subject who always remains alone and is for this reason Relation *par excellence*, for it extends beyond the boundaries of the self (404–9) (although it is questionable what these boundaries mean for Buber, for he never described positively the isolation and the limitation of the I). The relation is the very essence of the I: whenever the I truly affirms itself, its affirmation is inconceivable without the presence of the Thou (23, 40, passim). The Thou, as index of the dimension in which the I seeks (and therefore in a measure already finds) another being, the Thou as the indeterminate horizon of the encounter, is a priori or innate (39). The I is the term of a relation which cannot be expressed in terms of thought, for the latter only acts to dissolve the relation. Furthermore, I, in the relation, rediscovers 'its original community with the totality of being' (443–5). The allegiance of the primitive mind to the law of participation, according to Buber, testifies to the original nature of the relation and the primacy of the I–Thou to the I–It (30–3).

The distinction between the experience of an object and a meeting in which one being confronts another – a difference which concerns the nature of the relation itself and not merely of its terms, and which implies consequences whose scope Feuerbach, the first to formulate the I–Thou relation, could not foresee; a concern to base human experience on the meeting – these are the fundamental contributions of Buber to theory of knowledge. It is of spiritual significance that this relation to being underlying all of our objective knowledge does not involve an impersonal, neutral unity – the *Sein des Seiendes* of Heidegger – but a *Seiendes* which is the being of the other, and hence implies a social communion considered as the primary act of being.

Finally, we may observe the phenomenological character of Buber's descriptions: they are all based on the concrete reality of perception and do not require any appeal to abstract principle for their justification; the non-theoretical modes of existence are themselves ascriptive of meaning and the ontological structures with which they are associated are not separable from these.

The Ontology of the Interval, or the 'Between'

The Relation cannot be identified with a 'subjective' event because the I does not represent the Thou but meets it. The meeting, moreover, is to be distinguished from the silent dialogue the mind has with itself (204–5); the I–Thou meeting does not take place in the subject but in the realm of being. (26–7) However, we must avoid an interpretation of the meeting as something objectively apprehended by the I, for the ontological realm is not a block universe but an occurrence. The interval between the I and Thou, the *Zwischen*, is the locus where being is being realized (27).

The interval between the I and Thou cannot be conceived as a kind of stellar space existing independently of the two terms which it separates. For the dimension itself of the interval opens uniquely to the I and to the Thou which enter into each meeting (458), and the utmost transcendence is bound to the utmost particularity of the terms. Buber has made an effort to do more than merely define a kind of being which may be distinguished from the being of nature or of things, as, for instance, the process of becoming is distinguished from the Eleatic being. The interval between the I and Thou is inseparable from the adventure in which the individual himself participates, yet is more objective than any other type of objectivity, precisely because of that personal adventure. The *Zwischen* is reconstituted in each fresh meeting and is therefore always novel in the same sense as are the moments of Bergsonian duration.

If the notion of 'betweenness' functions as the fundamental category of being, however, man is the locus where the act of being is being acted (455). Man must not be construed as a subject constituting reality but

rather as the articulation itself of the meeting. The personality is for Buber
not merely a being among other beings, but is a category, in Kant's sense of
the term, and it is Nietzsche who has compelled our acceptance of this
(387). Man does not meet, he is the meeting. He is something that *distances*
itself and in this distancing the anonymous existence of the world of things
affirms itself by the various uses we make of it, and in that distancing we
can also enter into relations with this alien world.[3] By this double movement, Man is situated at the centre of being and philosophy is identifiable
with anthropology. But he is not at the centre in so far as he is a thinking
subject, but with respect to his whole being, since only a total commitment
can be the realization of his fundamental situation. That situation underlies
his thought and already implies a transcendence. 'Only when we try to
understand the human person in his whole situation, in the possibilities of
his relation to all that is not himself, do we understand man.' 'Man can
become whole not by virtue of a relation to himself but only by virtue of a
relation to another self.'[4]

Man, construed as the possibility of both distancing and relatedness, is
not a subject confronting the natural world nor is he a part of the latter. To
affirm that the I–Thou relation is not psychological but ontological, does
not mean that it is a natural relation. The interval in which the act of being
is being acted and which the individual at once creates and bridges, compels
us to abandon the notion of a being-content, an already actualized being, or
a being as theme of discourse. It is the abandoning of this notion which is
the principal feature of present-day ontology.

Communication and Inclusion

What is the structure of this encounter which is both a knowing relation
and an ontological event?

The I–Thou relation is a relation of true knowledge because it preserves
the integrity of the otherness of the Thou instead of relegating the Thou to
the anonymity of the It. It should be observed that the act whereby the I
withdraws and thus distances itself from the Thou or 'lets it be', in Heidegger's terms, is the same act which renders a union with it possible. In effect,
there is no union worthy of the name except in the presence of this sort of
otherness: union, *Verbundenheit*, is a manifestation of otherness (44). The
presence of the Thou, of the other, *ipso facto* implies a 'word' which is
addressed directly to me and which requires a response. 'Whoever refuses
to reply, no longer perceives the "word"' (196). It is impossible to remain a
spectator of the Thou, for the very existence of the Thou depends on the
'word' it addresses to me. And, it must be added, only a being who is
responsible for another being can enter into dialogue with it. Responsibility,

in the etymological sense of the term, not the mere exchange of words, is what is meant by *dialogue*, and it is only in the former case that there is meeting. The futility of remaining a spectator is not due to our tragic participation in a situation which is not of our choice, to our dereliction, but to the necessity of responding to the 'word'. There is a transcendent reality to which I am somehow committed which 'tells me something' (143–4), nor is this phrase a metaphor, for it expresses the very essence of language.

Truth, therefore, is not grasped by a dispassionate subject who is a spectator of reality, but by a commitment in which the other remains in his otherness. Although the Absolute could not be attained for the philosophers of antiquity except by means of contemplative detachment, and *the impossibility of the latter is precisely what led to the separation of being and truth in the Parmenides of Plato*, commitment, for Buber, is what gains access to otherness. For only what is other can elicit an act of responsibility (197). Buber attempts to maintain the radical otherness of the Thou in the Thou relation: the I does not construe the Thou as object, nor ecstatically identify itself with the Thou, for the terms remain independent despite the relation into which they enter. Thus the problem of truth raised by the Parmenides is resolved in terms of a social or intersubjective relation.

Commitment is a strictly personal relation. Truth does not consist in a reflection on that commitment, but is the commitment itself. The category of man, moreover, is each one of us (349) and not man in general which is typical of the I–It relation. We may recognize this as one of the prominent themes of the philosophy of existence, viz, the singularity of existence as forming the basis of knowledge, without, however, implying relativism (328).

Unlike Bergson and certain themes of the philosophy of existence, however, it is not held here that, as opposed to the representation of being, knowledge by commitment coincides with being. In order to know pain, 'the mind must cast itself into the depths of a felt pain' (436), instead of contemplating it as a spectacle; this is equally the case with 'all the events of the soul, which resemble mystery rather than spectacle, and whose meaning remains hidden to whoever refuses to enter into the dance.' But even for pain which has a privileged status and presupposes a coincidence with being, Buber requires a relation of a different kind which is dialogical in nature, a communication with the 'pain in the world' (438).

The relations implied by responsibility, by the dialogue or the original relation with the being is reciprocal. The ultimate nature of dialogue is revealed in what Buber calls *Umfassung*, or inclusion, and which is one of the most original notions of his philosophy. In the I–Thou relation, the reciprocity is directly experienced and not merely known about: the I in its relation with the Thou is further related to itself by means of the Thou, i.e., it is related to the Thou as to someone who in turn relates itself to the I, as though it had come into delicate contact with himself through the skin of the Thou. It thus returns to itself by means of the Thou. This relation should be distinguished from the psychological phenomenon of *Einfühlung* where the subject puts itself completely in the other's place, thus forgetting itself. In the case of *Einfühlung*, then, the I forgets itself, and does not feel itself as a Thou of the Thou, whereas in the *Umfassung* the I sharply maintains its active reality (280).

Truth

Verbundenheit characterizes the reciprocity of the I–Thou relation and of the dialogue where I commit myself to the Thou just because it is absolutely other. The essence of the 'word' does not initially consist in its objective meaning or descriptive possibilities, but in the response that it elicits. The assertion is not true because the thought that it expresses corresponds to the thing or because it is revelatory of being. It is true only when it derives from the I–Thou relation identical with the ontological process itself. The assertion is true when it realizes the reciprocity of the relation by eliciting a response and singling out an individual who alone is capable of responding. This conception of the truth has nothing in common with the static notion of truth as an expressible content. But it is not to be assumed that a Heraclitian or Bergsonian becoming, also inexpressible because the word is necessarily a changeless entity and cannot apply to what is always changing, is the sole reality that may be opposed to immutable being. For Buber describes a sphere of being which cannot be told because it is a living dialogue between individuals who are not related as objective contents to one another: *one individual has nothing to say about the other*. The sensitivity of the I–Thou relation lies in its completely formal nature. To apprehend the other as a content is tantamount to relating oneself to him as an object and is to enter into an I–It relation instead.

The notion of truth (with respect to which Buber's language is insufficiently didactic) is determined by the I–Thou relation construed as the fundamental relation to being. We must distinguish Truth possessed, Truth as an impersonal result, called also objective Truth (283) from the Truth as a 'way of being', a manner of truly being which denotes God. But truth also signifies a 'concrete attitude towards being', '*Realverhältnis zum Seienden*' (198–9) and the living test which verifies it (*Bewährung*). 'To know signifies for the creature to fulfill a relation with being, for everyone in his own particular way, sincerely (*wahrhaft*) and with complete responsibility, accepting it on faith in all its various manifestations and therefore open to its real possibilities, integrating these experiences according to its own nature. It is only in this way that the living truth emerges and can be preserved' (283).

Citing Kierkegaard, Buber asserts that the particular is a verification when it 'expresses what has been said (*das Gesagte*) by the personal existent': thus truth does not consist in a correspondence with being, but is the correlate of a life authentically lived. Buber however, finds that a correction is necessary here: 'I should have said', he writes, 'that the particular verifies by expressing what has not been said (*das Nicht-Gesagte*) by the individual being' (201). Thus Buber wishes to remove from his conception of the truth any association with an assertion or objective content. The truth is wholly an attitude *towards*, an inquiry *into*, a struggle *for*, the truth (213), i.e., the authenticity of a particular existence rather than an agreement between appearance and reality: 'Eine menschliche Wahrheit, die Wahrheit menschlicher, Existenz' (297). The expression, 'living truth', so frequently employed by Buber designates an existence which can be understood only in terms of its authenticity and non-authenticity, rather than an existence directed by any 'true idea'.

However, within that sphere of responsibility which relates the I to the Thou, there is an 'inquiry into the truth' which gives authenticity to the personality of the I, liberating it from the strictures imposed by an anonymous collectivity and from the activities of the unconscious whose instrument it would otherwise be (251ff.). The I–Thou relation becomes a personal commitment through its inquiry into the truth, which is not determined by the authenticity but determines it. From this point of view, the truth again seems to assume an intellectualistic physiognomy, and the I–Thou relation, without which the I can have no being, presents once again the spectre of a discarded subjectivity of philosophical idealism.

The Formal Nature of the Meeting

The I–Thou relation is nothing but a realization of the meeting. The Thou has no qualities which the I aspires to have or know. The privileged examples of this relation are selected in 'Dialogue' from beings who do not *know* one another in this sense of the term (134). 'Between the I and the Thou there is no conceptual structure, no prediction, fantasy, purpose, desire or anticipation. All intermediaries are obstacles. It is only when these vanish that the meeting occurs' (23–4). A content would imply mediation, and therefore would compromise the integrity and simplicity of the act. Buber denotes by the use of the term *Geschehen* (133) ('happening') this transparent act of transcendence which is incapable of being described. Each encounter must be considered as a unique event, a momentary present which cannot be connected to other temporal instants in order to form a history or biography; each is a spark (234) like Bergson's moment of intuition or the 'almost nothing' of his disciple Jankélévitch, where the relation of awareness to its content becomes progressively more attenuated and finally touches on the limit where consciousness no longer has a content but is a needle point penetrating being. The relation is a fulguration of moments without continuity, not a coherent connection of parts nor a final possession (118; 232; 456–7). Perhaps this conception of being springs from Buber's religious liberalism, from his religiosity as opposed to his religion, and is a reaction against the rigid, ossified forms of a spiritual dogmatism, placing contact above content and the pure and unqualified presence of God above all dogmas and rules. The question remains however, whether transcendence without any dogmatic content can receive a content from the dimension of height which Buber does not take into consideration. As we shall see, the *ethical* aspects of the I–Thou relation, so frequently evoked in Buber's descriptions are not determinant, and the I–Thou relation is also possible with respect to things.

Although Buber accords a privileged status to the purely intersubjective aspects of the I–Thou relation, the reciprocity of which may be expressed in language, the meeting is also construed as a relation with God as well as with things. For we can behave towards God too, as if we were called (18), and the tree, too, instead of being of use to me or dissolving into a series of phenomenal appearances, can confront me in person, speak to me and elicit a response. For Husserl, the presentational immediacy of the thing is merely one mode of its representation; for Buber, the former alters its representational character and commits me; the thing in this case is not given, for I am in a measure obligated by it, and the commitment is even reciprocal (20–8; 44, passim). The thing which is merely given and which I can dominate belongs to the sphere of the It. But the specific way in which the artist, for example, confronts the thing in creating a work of art, may be construed as a response to an appeal, and therefore, as a meeting.

In one of his later works, *Der Mensch und Sein Gebild*, Buber indicates that the empirical world, offered up for our use, and for the satisfaction of our needs, the world, in short, of the It, is itself conditioned by the encounter and therefore by the intersubjective I–Thou relation as well as the I–Thou relation which relates us to God and to Nature. Thus even perception which lies at the source of all human behavior (*Der Mensch und sein Gebild*), is not a purely subjective reality. Perception is the response of man to a meeting with the unknown object *x* of science what, inaccessible to representation, awaits Man (Ibid.). Man's response is a formative vision (*Schau*), a 'formative fidelity dedicated to what is unknown and which collaborates with the latter; the fidelity is not devoted to the phenomenon but to the inaccessible being with whom we are in communication' (Ibid.). Buber makes use of Gestalt psychology, in this connection, but he does not revert to the conception of things as constituted out of sensations: for what is realized is done in the *Zwischen*, and the latter belongs to being, i.e., what is neither subject nor object. Buber has continued to affirm this dating from the *Ich und Du* (102): 'The formation of the world and its vanishing are neither internal nor external to me; they have no being at all for they forever recreate themselves (*Geschehen*) and this creation depends on my own life.' In *Der Mensch und sein Gebild*, Buber includes the meeting as a part of nature so that perception is exercised to the same purpose as other vital acts. 'Man does not belong to the natural order solely by virtue of his (other) vital activities or in so far as he is responsible for his acts, but also as a perceiving being. My perceptions are acts in the natural order in which both the self and the object participate, without derogation from the spiritual nature of subjective existence' (*Der Mensch und sein Gebild*). 'Nature aspires to a state of totality, that is, to what is perceived' (Ibid).

What these assertions are designed to show is that Nature is neither subjective appearance nor objective existence, for both are abstractions. The true notion of being is that of the meeting between beings who are abstractions when considered in themselves. If perception is the original act of being, then we may say that the empirical world is more 'objective' than objectivity. Perception is the primordial act of being: the being is an act. However, it is typical of Buber's theory of knowledge that both the relation to things and the relation to man have something in common. Thus responsibility which we noted is at the basis of language, never assumes a strictly ethical import, for the response that the self makes to the unknown object x of perception, is construed by Buber, as an imperfect form of the I–Thou relation (*Der Mensch und sein Gebild*). The intersubjective relation, on the other hand, with its ethical overtones based on the mediation or imitation of God (and a theology somewhat too well-informed on the nature of God) (214–15; 221), is only a special case of the encounter. Buber, of course, admits that the perceptual meeting is transcended by four other kinds of meeting: Knowledge, love, art and belief. But none of these can be logically inferred from the purely formal structure of the I–Thou relation. Thus the meeting preserves its formal nature apart. Does this imply a vacillation in Buber's thought? Dating from the publication of *Ich und Du*, Buber admitted that things too can enter into the I–Thou relation, yet it frequently seems that the relation between humans – as soon as the Thou has a human face – has a privileged status and even conditions all other relations: 'everything else lives in its light' (20). Furthermore: 'one can have confidence, confidence in the world because this man exists' (281). Consequently the light of the Thou – just as the intelligible sun in Plato, the idea of the Good, and the phosphorescence of the *Sein des Seienden* later on in Heidegger – would be the primal truth which is the source of all other truths.

Some Objections

How are we to preserve the specificity of the intersubjective I–Thou relation without ascribing a strictly ethical import to responsibility, and conversely, how ascribe an ethical meaning to the relation and still maintain the reciprocity on which Buber insists? Does not the ethical begin only at the point where the I becomes conscious of the Thou as beyond itself?

We shall direct our criticism mainly to the reciprocity of the I–Thou relation. Ethical themes frequently occur in the writings of Buber, but with respect to the I–Thou relation, a more formal structure involving distance and relatedness is underlying the I–It relation. But it is questionable whether the relation with the otherness of the Other which appears as a dialogue of question and answer can be described without emphasizing paradoxically a difference of level between the I and the Thou. The originality of the relation lies in the fact that it is not known from the outside but only by the I which realizes the relation. The position of the I, therefore, is not interchangeable with that of the Thou. But how can we characterize this ipseity? For if the self becomes an I in saying Thou, as Buber asserts, my position as a self depends on that of my correlate and the relation is no longer any different from other relations: it is tantamount to a spectator speaking of the I and Thou in the third person. The formal meeting is a symmetrical relation and may therefore be read indifferently from either side. But in the case of ethical relations, where the Other is at the same time higher than I and yet poorer than I, the I is distinguished from the Thou not by the presence of specific attributes, but by the dimension of height, thus implying a break with Buber's formalism. The primacy of the other, like his nakedness, does not qualify what is a purely formal relation to the other, *posterior* to the act of relating, but directly qualifies otherness itself. Otherness is thus qualified, but not by any attribute.

Thus the relation is more than an empty contact which may always be renewed and of which spiritual friendship is the apogee (285). The reiteration of these '*spirituel*' themes (compensated for by a fruitful analysis of the connection between the I–Thou relation and the crowd which is opposed to the views of Kierkegaard and Heidegger, and a correction of earlier texts which relegated the third person plural, 'they' to the sphere of the It), and the '*spirituel*' language employed by Buber, are limitations in a work which is otherwise rich in insight. Like the simplified materialism of bodily contact, however, the pure spiritualism of friendship does not correspond to the facts. Buber strongly protests against Heidegger's notion of *Fürsorge*, or care for the other, which for Heidegger, permits access to the other (401–2). Of course, we need not turn to Heidegger for insight into the love for humanity or for social justice. However, *Fürsorge*, inasmuch as it is a response to the essential misery of the other, *does* give access to the otherness of the other. It accounts for the dimension of height and of human distress to a greater degree than *Umfassung*, and it may be conjectured that clothing those who are naked and nourishing those who go hungry is a more authentic way of finding access to the other than the rarefied ether of a spiritual friendship. Is dialogue possible without *Fürsorge*? If we criticize Buber for extending the I–Thou relation to things, then, it is not because he is an animist with respect to our relations with the physical world, but because he is too much the artist in his relations with man.

The transition from the subject-object relation to that of the I–Thou implies the passage of consciousness to a new sphere of existence, viz., the interval, betweenness or *Zwischen*; and this is a passage from thought to *Umfassung*. Buber forcefully affirms in this connection the radical difference between the silent dialogue of the mind with itself and the real dialogue it has with the other (204–5; 418). But is it not, after all, in consciousness that *Zwischen* and *Umfassung* are revealed? Buber himself admits that 'all dialogue derives its authenticity from consciousness of *Umfassung*' (281); it is *only* in consciousness that we can know the latter. A theory of ontological knowledge based on the nature of the 'space' existing in the sphere of betweenness should indicate how the Relation by itself, apart from its term, differs from consciousness. It should also be shown how that 'space' 'deforms', transforms and inverts the act of immediate awareness as it does the act of knowledge itself, once we admit that the I–It relation does in fact corrode the I–Thou (45).

Finally, we may turn to a problem of more general concern, not restricted therefore to Buber's particular philosophy. It is one which confronts any epistemology which bases truth on a non-theoretical activity or on existence. And it places in question the existence of epistemology itself for it concerns 'the truth about the truth', i.e., it asks about the nature of the knowledge epistemology itself claims to have when it communicates the truth. It is here that the theoretical nature of philosophy becomes evident. But perhaps this is due only to the practical exigencies of teaching, and merely corresponds to the return of the philosopher to the Cave where he is compelled to employ the language of enchained slaves?[5] If this is the case, then to philosophize is to live in a certain manner and, according to Buber, to practice to a greater extent than the others, in one's capacity of artist, friend or believer, the dialogue with the real. Is not philosophy then, an attitude distinct from all others – is not *philo sophari* essentially different from *vivere*? If this is so, then perhaps theory of knowledge is not based on any dialogical step that we need take. The truth is rather obtainable in a wholly different kind of dialogue which does not manifest its concern for Relation so much as it does a desire to assure to the I its independence, even if this independence is only possible in a union (*Verbunden*). Philosophy, then, is definable in terms of a rupture of the individual with the whole, and it is for this reason that it is abstract or critical in nature and implies a full possession of oneself. We need not insist at this point on Buber's indifference to the approximations of scientific knowledge which are hastily classified with our visual observations of reality, without his offering any explanation for the scope of our physico-mathematical knowledge. Although Buber has penetratingly described the Relation and the act of distancing, he has not taken separation seriously enough. Man is not merely identifiable with the category of distance and meeting, he is a being *sui generis*, and it is impossible for him to ignore or forget his avatar of subjectivity. He realizes his own separateness in a process of subjectification which is not explicable in terms of a recoil from the Thou. Buber does not explain that act, distinct from both distancing and relating, in which the I realizes itself without recourse to the other.

NOTES

1 Textual references are to the *Dialogisches Leben. Gesammelte philosophische und pädagogische Schriften* (Zurich: Gregor Müller Verlag, 1947), containing the collected philosophical works of Buber published up to 1947. The numbers in parentheses appearing in the text of this chapter refer to the appropriate page of the *Dialogisches*; reference to the relevant work is omitted.

2 Maurice Friedman's article, 'Martin Buber's Theory of Knowledge', *Review of Metaphysics* (Dec., 1954) gives a penetrating analysis of the essential features of Buber's epistemology without, however, showing the narrow connection of the latter with current philosophical tendencies. Although the I–Thou relation may not be specifically stressed, the subject-object relation together with its supporting ontology has everywhere been abandoned. Further, we may remark that Bergson was not the theoretician of the It, as the author suggests. See the excellent bibliography which exhibits the extent of Buber's influence or suggests the theme of the I–thou relation independently of that influence.

3 Cf. 'Distance and Relation', *Hibbert Journal*, 49 (1951), 105–13; *Psychiatry*, 20 (1957), 97–104.

4 'What is Man?', in *Between Man and Man*, trans. R. G. Smith (London: Collins, 1961), pp. 168–81.

5 As Bergson undoubtedly assumed when he began his essay in 1888 with the words: 'We must express ourselves in words...'

5

Ethics as First Philosophy

Published for the first time in *Justifications de l'éthique* (Bruxelles: Editions de l'Université de Bruxelles), 1984, pp. 41–51, and specially translated for this volume, 'Ethics as First Philosophy' is a clear and powerful summary of Levinas's methodical and yet radical move away from Husserl's transcendental idealism and Heidegger's hermeneutics towards the ethical question of the meaning of being, presented in the face-to-face relation. Beginning with the phenomenological legacy which reveals knowledge as built on an intentionality in contact with concrete reality, Levinas quickly brings us to the point where we must recognize the closed and circular nature of this self-conscious awareness. Intentionality reduces wisdom to a notion of increasing self-consciousness, in which anything that is non-identical is absorbed by the identical. In this way, self-consciousness affirms itself as absolute being. But for Levinas the non-intentional subsists in duration itself, which cannot be controlled by will. This non-intentionality is an *unhappy consciousness* that exists without attributes or aims. As a result of the passivity of this *mauvaise conscience*, one affirms one's being by having to respond to one's *right* to be. This response means that responsibility for the Other preexists any self-consciousness, so that from the beginning of any face to face, the question of being involves the right to be. This is what Levinas means when he mentions the face of the Other: I do not grasp the other in order to dominate; I respond, instead, to the face's epiphany. As such, what is produced in a concrete form is the idea of infinity rather than totality. The relation is metaphysical, and precedes any ontological programme. Prior to a state-of-mind in which one finds oneself, therefore, the infinite vigilance we display with regard to the other, suspending all notion of totality, is that which founds and *justifies* being as the very being of being.

For a larger development of the various stages involved in this complex and challenging philosophy, see *Totality and Infinity*, especially section I.A.4: 'Metaphysics Precedes Ontology', and above all section III.B: 'Ethics and the Face'. Levinas answers questions on the phenomenology of the face in a recent interview published in *The Provocation of Levinas, Rethinking the Other*, edited by Robert Bernasconi and David Wood (London and New York: Routledge, 1988), pp. 168–80.

S.H.

I

The correlation between *knowledge*, understood as disinterested contemplation, and *being*, is, according to our philosophical tradition, the very site of intelligibility, the occurrence of meaning (*sens*). The comprehension of being – the semantics of this verb – would thus be the very possibility of or the occasion for wisdom and the wise and, as such, is *first philosophy*. The intellectual, and even spiritual life, of the West, through the priority it gives to knowledge identified with Spirit, demonstrates its fidelity to the first philosophy of Aristotle, whether one interprets the latter according to the ontology of book Γ of the *Metaphysics* or according to the theology or onto-theology of book Λ where the ultimate explanation of intelligibility in terms of the primary causality of God is a reference to a God defined by being *qua* being.

The correlation between knowledge and being, or the thematics of contemplation, indicates both a difference and a difference that is *overcome* in the *true*. Here the known is understood and so *appropriated* by knowledge, and as it were *freed* of its otherness. In the realm of truth, being, as the *other* of thought becomes the characteristic *property* of thought as knowledge. The ideal of rationality or of sense (*sens*) begins already to appear as the immanence of the real to reason; just as, in being, a privilege is granted to the *present*, which is presence to thought, of which the future and the past are modalities or modifications: re-presentations.

But in knowledge there also appears the notion of an intellectual activity or of a reasoning will – a way of doing something which consists precisely of thinking through knowing, of seizing something and making it one's own, of reducing to presence and representing the difference of being, an activity which *appropriates* and *grasps* the otherness of the known. A certain grasp: as an entity, being becomes the characteristic property of thought, as it is grasped by it and becomes known. Knowledge as perception, concept, comprehension, refers back to an act of grasping. The metaphor should be taken literally: even before any technical application of knowledge, it expresses the principle rather than the result of the future technological and industrial order of which every civilisation bears at least the seed. The immanence of the known to the act of knowing is already the embodiment of seizure. This is not something applied like a form of magic to the 'impotent spirituality' of thinking, nor is it the guarantee of certain psycho-physiological conditions, but rather belongs to that unit of knowledge in which *Auffassen* (*understanding*) is also, and always has been, a *Fassen* (*gripping*). The mode of thought known as knowledge involves man's concrete existence in the world he inhabits, in which he moves and works and possesses. The most abstract lessons of science – as Husserl showed in his *The Crisis of European Sciences and Transcendental Phenomenology* – have their beginnings in the 'world of life' and refer to things within hand's reach. It is to this hand that the idea of a 'given world' concretely refers. Things contain the promise of satisfaction – their concreteness puts them on a scale fit for a knowing form of thought. Thought as knowledge is already the labour of thought. A thought that assesses what is equal and adequate, and can give satis-faction. The rationality of beings stems from their presence and adequation. The operations of knowledge reestablish rationality behind the diachrony of *becoming* in which presence occurs or is foreseen. Knowledge is re-presentation, a return to presence, and nothing may remain *other* to it.

Thought is an activity, where something is appropriated by a knowledge that is independent, of course, of any finality exterior to it, an activity which is disinterested and self-sufficient and whose self-sufficiency, sovereignty, *bonne conscience*[1] and happy solitude are asserted by Aristotle. 'The wise man can practise contemplation by himself' says Book Ten of the *Nicomachean Ethics*.[2] This is a regal and as it were unconditioned activity, a sovereignty which is possible only as solitude, an unconditioned activity, even if limited for man by biological needs and by death. But it is a notion that allows a second one to be sustained, the notion of the pure *theoretic*, of its freedom, of the equivalence between wisdom and freedom, of that partial coincidence of the human domain with the divine life of which Aristotle speaks at the end of the seventh section of Book Ten of the *Ethics*. Here already the strange and contradictory concept of a *finite freedom* begins to take shape.

Throughout the whole history of Western philosophy, *contemplation* or *knowledge* and the *freedom of knowledge* are inspiration for the mind (*l'esprit*). Knowing is the psyche or pneumatic force of thought, even in the act of *feeling* or *willing*. It is to be found in the concept of *consciousness* at the dawn of the modern age with the interpretation of the concept of *cogito* given by Descartes in his Second Meditation. Husserl, returning to a medieval tradition, then, describes it as intentionality, which is understood as 'consciousness of something', and so is inseparable from its 'intentional object'. This structure has a noetic-noematic composition in which representation or objectivization is the incontestable model. The whole of human lived experience, in the period up to and above all including the present, has been expressed in terms of experience, that is, has been converted into accepted doctrine, teachings, sciences. Relationships with neighbours, with social groups, with God equally represent collective and religious *experiences*.

Modernity will subsequently be distinguished by the attempt to develop from the identification and appropriation of being *by* knowledge toward the identification of being *and* knowledge. The passage from the *cogito* to the *sum* leads to that point where the free activity of knowledge, an activity alien to any external goal, will also find itself on the side of what is known. This free activity of knowledge will also come to constitute the mystery of being *qua* being, whatever is known by knowledge (*le connu du savoir*). The *Wisdom of first philosophy* is reduced to self-consciousness. Identical and non-identical are identified. The labour of thought wins out over the otherness of things and men. Since Hegel, any goal considered alien to the disinterested acquisition of knowledge has been subordinated to the freedom of knowledge as a science (*savoir*); and within this freedom, *being* itself is from that point understood as *the active affirming of that same being*, as *the strength and strain of being*. Modern man persists in his being as a sovereign who is merely concerned to maintain the *powers of his sovereignty*. Everything that is possible is permitted. In this way the experience of Nature and Society would gradually get the better of any exteriority. A miracle of modern Western freedom unhindered by any memory or remorse, and opening onto a 'glittering future' where everything can be rectified. Only by death is this freedom thwarted. The obstacle of death is insurmountable, inexorable and fundamentally incomprehensible. The recognition of finitude will of course characterize a new test for ontology. But finitude and death will not have called into question the *bonne conscience* with which the freedom of knowledge operates. They will simply have put a check on its powers.

II

In this essay we wish to ask whether thought understood as knowledge, since the ontology of the first philosophy, has exhausted the possible modes of meaning for thought, and whether, beyond knowledge and its hold on being, a more urgent form does not emerge, that of wisdom. We propose to begin with the notion of intentionality, as it figures in Husserlian phenomenology, which is one of the culminating points in Western philosophy. The equivalence of thought and knowledge in relation to being is here formulated by Husserl in the most direct manner. Whilst successfully isolating the idea of an originary, non-theoretical intentionality from the active emotional life of consciousness, he continues to base his theory on *representation*, the objectivizing act, adopting Brentano's thesis at this point, in spite of all the precautions he takes in his new formulation of this thesis. Now, within consciousness – which is consciousness of something – knowledge is, by the same token, a relation to an *other* of consciousness and almost the aim or the will of that other which is an *object*.

Husserl, inviting us to question the intentionality of consciousness, wants us also to ask 'worauf sie eigentlich hinauswill' (*What are you getting at?*), an intention or wish which, incidentally, would justify calling the units of consciousness acts. At the same time, knowledge, within the intuition of truth, is described as a 'filling out' that gratifies a longing for the being as object, given and received in the original, *present* in a representation. It is a hold on being which equals a constitution of that being. This Transcendental Reduction suspends all independence in the world other than that of consciousness itself, and causes the world to be rediscovered as *noema*. As a result, it leads – or ought to lead – to full self-consciousness affirming itself as absolute being, and confirming itself as an *I* that, through all possible 'differences', is identified as master of its own nature as well as of the universe and able to illuminate the darkest recesses of resistance to its powers. As Merleau-Ponty in particular has shown, the I that constitutes the world comes up against a sphere in which it is by its very flesh implicated; it is implicated in what it otherwise would have constituted and so is implicated in the world. But it is present in the world as it is present in its own body, an intimate incarnation which no longer purely and simply displays the exteriority of an object.[3]

But this reduced consciousness – which, in reflecting upon itself, rediscovers and masters its own acts of perception and science as objects in the world, thereby affirming itself as self-consciousness and absolute being – also remains a non-intentional consciousness of itself, as though it were a surplus somehow devoid of any wilful aim. A non-intentional consciousness operating, if one may put it like this, unknowingly as knowledge, as a non-objectivizing knowledge. As such it accompanies all the intentional processes of consciousness and of the *ego* (*moi*) which, in that consciousness, 'acts' and 'wills' and has 'intentions'. Consciousness of consciousness, indirect, implicit and aimless, without any initiative that might refer back to an ego; passive like time passing and ageing me without my intervening (*sans moi*). A 'non-intentional' consciousness to be distinguished from philosophical reflection, or the internal perception to which, indeed, non-intentional consciousness might easily offer itself as an internal object and for which it might substitute itself by making explicit the implicit messages it bears. The intentional consciousness of reflection, in taking as its object the transcendental ego, along with its mental acts and states, may also thematize and grasp supposedly implicit modes of non-intentional lived experience. It is invited to do this by philosophy in its fundamental project which consists in enlightening the inevitable transcendental naivety of a consciousness forgetful of its horizon, of its implicit content and even of the time it lives through.

Consequently one is forced, no doubt too quickly, to consider in philoso-

phy all this immediate consciousness merely as a still confused representation to be duly brought to 'light'. The obscure context of whatever is
thematized is converted by reflection, or intentional consciousness, into
clear and distinct data, like those which present the perceived world or a
transcendental reduced consciousness.

One may ask, however, whether, beneath the gaze of reflected consciousness taken as self-consciousness, the non-intentional, experienced as the
counterpoint to the intentional, does not conserve and free its true meaning.
The critique of introspection as traditionally practised has always been
suspicious of a modification that a supposedly spontaneous consciousness
might undergo beneath the scrutinizing, thematizing, objectivizing and
indiscreet gaze of reflection, and has seen this as a violation or distortion of
some sort of secret. This is a critique which is always refuted only to be
reborn.

The question is what exactly happens, then, in this non-reflective
consciousness considered merely to be pre-reflective and the implicit partner of an intentional consciousness which, in reflection, intentionally aims
for the thinking self (*soi*), as if the thinking ego (*moi*) appeared in the world
and belonged to it? What might this supposed confusion or implication
really mean? One cannot simply refer to the formal notion of potentiality.
Might there not be grounds for distinguishing between the envelopment of
the particular in the conceptual, the implicit understanding of the pre-
supposition in a notion, the potentiality of what is considered possible
within the horizon, on the one hand, and, on the other hand, the intimacy
of the non-intentional within what is known as pre-reflective consciousness
and which is duration itself?

III

Does the 'knowledge' of pre-reflective self-consciousness really know? As a
confused, implicit consciousness preceding all intentions – or as duration
freed of all intentions – it is less an act than a pure passivity. This is not
only due to its being-without-having-chosen-to-be or its fall into a confused
world of possibilities already realised even before any choice might be
made, as in Heidegger's *Geworfenheit*. It is a 'consciousness' that signifies
not so much a knowledge of oneself as something that effaces presence or
makes it discreet. Phenomenological analysis, of course, describes such a
pure duration of time within reflection, as being intentionally structured by
a play of retentions and protentions which, in the very duration of time, at
least remain non-explicit and suppose, in that they represent a flow, another
sort of time. This duration remains free from the sway of the will, absolutely outside all activity of the ego, and exactly like the ageing process which is

probably the perfect model of passive synthesis, a lapse of time no act of remembrance, reconstructing the past, could possibly reverse. Does not the temporality of implicit time, like the implication of the implicit, here signify otherwise than as knowledge taken on the run, otherwise than a way of representing presence or the non-presence of the future and the past? Duration as pure duration, non-intervention as being without insistence, as being that dare not speak its name, being that dare not be; the agency of the instant without the insistence of the ego, which is already a lapse in time, which is 'over before it's begun'! This implication of the non-intentional is a form of *mauvaise conscience*: it has no intentions, or aims, and cannot avail itself of the protective mask of a character contemplating in the mirror of the world a reassured and self-positing portrait. It has no name, no situation, no status. It has a presence afraid of presence, afraid of the insistence of the identical ego, stripped of all qualities. In its non-intentionality, not yet at the stage of willing, and prior to any fault, in its non-intentional identification, identity recoils before its affirmation. It dreads the insistence in the return to self that is a necessary part of identification. This is either *mauvaise conscience* or timidity; it is not guilty, but accused; and responsible for its very presence. It has not yet been invested with any attributes or justified in any way. This creates the reserve of the stranger or 'sojourner on earth', as it says in the Psalms, the countryless or 'homeless' person who dare not enter in. Perhaps the interiority of the mental is originally an insufficient courage to assert oneself in one's being or in body or flesh. One comes not into the world but into question. By way of reference to this, or in 'memory' of this, the ego (*moi*) which is already declaring and affirming itself (*s'affirme*) — or making itself firm (*s'affermit*) – itself in being, still remains ambiguous or enigmatic enough to recognise itself as hateful, to use Pascal's term, in this very manifestation of its emphatic identity of its ipseity, in the 'saying I'. The superb priority of $A = A$, the principle of intelligibility and meaning,[4] this sovereignty, or freedom within the human ego, is also, as it were, the moment when humility occurs. This questions the affirmation and strengthening of being found in the famous and facilely rhetorical quest for the meaning of life, which suggests that the absolute ego, already endowed with meaning by its vital, psychic and social forces, or its transcendental sovereignty, then returned to its *mauvaise conscience*.

Pre-reflective, non-intentional consciousness would never be able to return to a moral realization of this passivity, as if, in that form of consciousness, one could already see a subject postulating itself in the 'indeclinable nominative', assured of its right to be and 'dominating' the timidity of the non-intentional like a spiritual infancy that is outgrown, or an attack of weakness that becomes an impassive psyche. The non-intentional is from the start passivity, and the accusative in some way its 'first case'. (Actually, this passivity, which does not correlate to any activity, is not so much something that describes the *mauvaise conscience* of the non-intentional [as] something that is described by it). This *mauvaise conscience* is not the finitude of existence signalled by anguish. My death, which is always going to be premature, does perhaps put a check on being which, *qua* being, perseveres in being, but in anguish this scandal fails to shake the *bonne conscience* of being, or the morality founded upon the inalienable right of the *conatus* which is also the right and the *bonne conscience* of freedom. However, it is in the passivity of the non-intentional, in the way it is spontaneous and precedes the formulation of any metaphysical ideas on the subject, that the very justice of the position within being is questioned, a position which asserts itself with intentional thought, knowledge and a grasp of the here and now. What one sees in this questioning is being as *mauvaise conscience*; to be open to question, but also to questioning, to have to respond. Language is born in responsibility. One has to speak, to say *I*, to be in the first person, precisely to be me (*moi*). But, from that point, in affirming this *me* being, one has to respond to one's right to be. It is necessary to think through to this point Pascal's phrase, 'the I (*moi*) is hateful'.

IV

One has to respond to one's right to be, not by referring to some abstract and anonymous law, or judicial entity, but because of one's fear for the Other. My being-in-the-world or my 'place in the sun',[5] my being at home,[6] have these not also been the usurpation of spaces belonging to the other man whom I have already oppressed or starved, or driven out into a third world; are they not acts of repulsing, excluding, exiling, stripping, killing? Pascal's 'my place in the sun' marks the beginning of the image of the usurpation of the whole earth. A fear for all the violence and murder my existing might generate, in spite of its conscious and intentional innocence. A fear which reaches back past my 'self-consciousness' in spite of whatever moves are made towards a *bonne conscience* by a pure perseverance in being. It is the fear of occupying someone else's place with the *Da* of my *Dasein*; it is the inability to occupy a place, a profound utopia.

In my philosophical essays, I have spoken a lot about the face of the Other as being the original site of the sensible. May I now briefly take up again the description, as I now see it, of the irruption of the face into the phenomenal order of appearances?

The proximity of the other is the face's meaning, and it means from the very start in a way that goes beyond those plastic forms which forever try to cover the face like a mask of their presence to perception. But always the face shows through these forms. Prior to any particular expression and beneath all particular expressions, which cover over and protect with an immediately adopted face or countenance, there is the nakedness and destitution of the expression as such, that is to say extreme exposure, defencelessness, vulnerability itself. This extreme exposure – prior to any human aim – is like a shot 'at point blank range'. Whatever has been invested is extradited, but it is a hunt that occurs prior to anything being actually tracked down and beaten out into the open. From the beginning there is a face to face steadfast in its exposure to invisible death, to a mysterious forsakenness. Beyond the visibility of whatever is unveiled, and prior to any knowledge about death, mortality lies in the Other.

Does not expression resemble more closely this extreme exposure than it does some supposed recourse to a code? True *self*-expression stresses the nakedness and defencelessness that encourages and directs the violence of the first crime: the goal of a murderous uprightness is especially well-suited to exposing or expressing the face. The first murderer probably does not realize the result of the blow he is about to deliver, but his violent design helps him to find the line with which death may give an air of unimpeachable rectitude to the face of the neighbour; the line is traced like the trajectory of the blow that is dealt and the arrow that kills.

But, in its expression, in its mortality, the face before me summons me, calls for me, begs for me, as if the invisible death that must be faced by the Other, pure otherness, separated, in some way, from any whole, were my business. It is as if that invisible death, ignored by the Other, whom already it concerns by the nakedness of its face, were already 'regarding' me prior to confronting me, and becoming the death that stares me in the face. The other man's death calls me into question, as if, by my possible future indifference, I had become the accomplice of the death to which the other, who cannot see it, is exposed; and as if, even before vowing myself to him, I had to answer for this death of the other, and to accompany the Other in his mortal solitude. The Other becomes my neighbour precisely through the way the face summons me, calls for me, begs for me, and in so doing recalls my responsibility, and calls me into question.

Responsibility for the Other, for the naked face of the first individual to come along. A responsibility that goes beyond what I may or may not have done to the Other or whatever acts I may or may not have committed, as if I were devoted to the other man before being devoted to myself. Or more exactly, as if I had to answer for the other's death even before *being*. A guiltless responsibility, whereby I am none the less open to an accusation of which no alibi, spatial or temporal, could clear me. It is as if the other established a relationship or a relationship were established whose whole intensity consists in not presupposing the idea of community. A responsibility stemming from a time before my freedom – before my (*moi*) beginning, before any present. A fraternity existing in extreme separation. *Before*, but in what past? Not in the time preceding the present, in which I might have contracted any commitments. Responsibility for my neighbour dates from before my freedom in an immemorial past, an unrepresentable past that was never present and is more ancient than consciousness of . . . . A responsibility for my neighbour, for the other man, for the stranger or sojourner, to which nothing in the rigorously ontological order binds me – nothing in the order of the thing, of the something, of number or causality.

It is the responsibility of a hostage which can be carried to the point of being substituted for the other person and demands an infinite subjection of subjectivity. Unless this anarchic responsibility, which summons me from nowhere into a present time, is perhaps the measure or the manner or the system of an immemorial freedom that is even older than being, or decisions, or deeds.

V

This summons to responsibility destroys the formulas of generality by which my knowledge (*savoir*) or acquaintance (*connaissance*) of the other man re-presents him to me as my fellow man. In the face of the other man I am inescapably responsible and consequently the unique and chosen one. By this freedom, humanity in me (*moi*) – that is, humanity as me – signifies, in spite of its ontological contingence of finitude and mortality, the anteriority and uniqueness of the non-*interchangeable*.

This is the anteriority and chosen nature of an excellence that cannot be reduced to the features distinguishing or constituting individual beings in the order of their world or people, in the role they play on history's social stage, as characters, that is, in the mirror of reflection or in self-consciousness.

Fear for the Other, fear for the other man's death, is *my* fear, but is in no way an *individual's* taking fright. It thus stands out against the admirable phenomenological analysis of *Befindlichkeit*[7] found in *Sein und Zeit*: a reflective structure expressed by a pronominal verb, in which emotion is always emotion for something moving you, but also emotion for oneself. Emotion therefore consists in being moved – being scared by something, overjoyed by something, saddened by something, but also in feeling joy or sadness for oneself. All affectivity therefore has repercussions for my being-for-death. There is a double intentionality in the *by* and the *for* and so there is a turning back on oneself and a return to anguish for oneself, for one's finitude: in the fear inspired *by* the wolf, an anguish *for* my death. Fear for the other man's death does not turn back into anguish for my death. It extends beyond the ontology of the Heideggerian *Dasein* and the *bonne conscience* of being in the sight of that being itself. There is ethical awareness and vigilance in this emotional unease. Certainly, Heidegger's being-for-death marks, for the being (*étant*), the end of his being-in-the-sight-of-that-being as well as the scandal provoked by that ending, but in that ending no scruple of being (*être*) is awakened.

This is the hidden human face behind perseverance in being! Hidden behind the affirmation of being persisting analytically – or animally – in its being, and in which the ideal vigour of identity identifying and affirming and strengthening itself in the life of human individuals and in their struggle for vital existence, whether conscious or unconscious or rational, the miracle of the ego vindicated in the eyes of the neighbour – or the miracle of the ego (*moi*) which has got rid of self (*soi*) and instead fears for the Other – is thus like the suspension, or epochè, of the eternal and irreversible return of the identical to itself and of the intangible nature of its logical and ontological privilege. What is suspended is its ideal priority, which wipes out all otherness by murder or by all-encompassing and totalizing thought; or war and politics which pass themselves off as the relation of the Same to the Other (*l'Autre*). It is in the laying down by the ego of its sovereignty (in its 'hateful' modality), that we find ethics and also probably the very spirituality of the soul, but most certainly the question of the meaning of being, that is, its appeal for justification. This first philosophy shows through the ambiguity of the identical, an identical which declares itself to be *I* at the height of its unconditional and even logically indiscernable identity, an autonomy above all criteria, but which precisely at the height of this unconditional identity confesses that it is hateful.

The ego is the very crisis of the being of a being (*de l'être de l'étant*) in the human domain. A crisis of being, not because the sense of this verb might still need to be understood in its semantic secret and might call on the powers of ontology, but because I begin to ask myself if my being is justified, if the *Da* of my *Dasein* is not already the usurpation of somebody else's place.

This question has no need of a theoretical reply in the form of new information. Rather it appeals to responsibility, which is not a practical stopgap measure designed to console knowledge in its failure to match being. This responsibility does not deny knowledge the ability to comprehend and grasp; instead, it is the excellence of ethical proximity in its sociality, in its love without concupiscence. The human is the return to the interiority of non-intentional consciousness, to *mauvaise conscience*, to its capacity to fear injustice more than death, to prefer to suffer than to commit injustice, and to prefer that which justifies being over that which assures it.

VI

To be or not to be – is that the question? Is it the first and final question? Does being human consist in forcing oneself to be and does the under-standing of the meaning of being – the semantics of the verb to be – represent the first philosophy required by a consciousness which from the first would be knowledge and representation conserving its assurance in being-for-death, asserting itself as the lucidity of a thought thinking itself right through, even unto death and which, even in its finitude – already or still an unquestioned *mauvaise conscience* as regards its right to be – is either anguished or heroic in the precariousness of its finitude? Or does the first question arise rather in the *mauvaise conscience*, an instability which is different from that threatened by my death and my suffering? It poses the question of my right to be which is already my responsibility for the death of the Other, interrupting the carefree spontaneity of my naive persever-ance. The right to be and the legitimacy of this right are not finally referred to the abstraction of the universal rules of the Law – but in the last resort are referred, like that law itself and justice – or for the other of my non-indifference, to death, to which the face of the Other – beyond my ending – in its very rectitude is exposed. Whether he regards me or not, he 'regards' me. In this question being and life are awakened to the human dimension. This is the question of the meaning of being: not the ontology of the understanding of that extraordinary verb, but the ethics of its justice. The question *par excellence* or the question of philosophy. Not 'Why being rather than nothing?', but how being justifies itself.

NOTES

1 We have decided to leave the phrases *bonne conscience* and *mauvaise conscience* in the original French. This is because, in addition to suggesting a good and a bad conscience (which is how they are translated in *Time and the Other*, p. 110, for example) or a clear and a guilty conscience, they also carry the connotation of consciousness and *unhappy consciousness*. For Hegel, unhappy consciousness (*das unglückliches Bewusstsein*) is an inwardly disrupted one, with a dual and essentially contradictory nature. It is therefore 'the gazing of one self-consciousness into another, and itself *is* both' (*Phenomenology of Spirit*, p. 126). It is the coexistence of master and slave, eternal and mortal, 'the Unchangeable' and the 'changeable'. Critics are divided, however, over whether or not this duality is a sincerely felt representation of Christianity.
2 Aristotle, *The Nicomachean Ethics* (Harmondsworth: Penguin, 1955, 1981).
3 A reference to Merleau-Ponty's 'body intentionality'. See the *Phenomenology of Perception*, part 1, pp. 67–199. In addition, see *Totality and Infinity*, p. 181.
4 Hegel characterizes the Absolute as A=A in the Preface to the *Phenomenology of*

Spirit, p. 9. The equation is in turn a reference to Leibniz, who calls A=A 'the law of identity', arguing ultimately that no distinctions are real, and that identity with itself is the only ultimate equivalence.

5 A reference to Pascal's *Pensées* (Brunzschvicq 295/Lafume 112).

6 Levinas is alluding here to Heidegger's sense of *bei sich*, the real and originary sense in which the existent comes to exist 'for itself'. The meaning of '*bei*' is close to that of 'at' in 'at home' or '*chez*' in '*chez moi*'. Cf. *Being and Time*, p. 80, H.54: 'The expression "*bin*" is connected with "*bei*", and so "*ich bin*" (I am) mean in its turn "I reside" or "dwell alongside" the world, as that which is familiar to me in such and such a way. "Being" (*Sein*), as the infinitive of "*ich bin*" (that is to say, when it is understood as an *existentiale*), signifies "to reside alongside . . . ", "to be familiar with . . . ". "*Being-in*" *is thus the formal existential expression for the Being of Dasein, which has Being-in-the-world as its essential state.*'

7 *Befindlichkeit* has always been translated into English as 'state-of-mind', an expression also used for '*befinden*' and '*befindlich*'. More literally, it means 'the state in which one may be found', which is the sense it carries here in Levinas. As such, Heidegger's translators make it clear that 'the "of-mind" belongs to English idiom, has no literal counterpart in the structure of the German word, and fails to bring out the important connotation of finding oneself' (*Being and Time*, footnote to H.134, p. 172).

Translated by Seán Hand and Michael Temple

6

Substitution

First published in October 1968 in the *Revue Philosophique de Louvain*, 66, no. 91, 487–508, and subsequently incorporated into *Autrement qu'être ou au-delà de l'essence*, 1974 (translated into English in 1981 by Alphonso Lingis under the title *Otherwise than Being or Beyond Essence*), 'Substitution' forms the central chapter of what is undoubtedly Levinas's most challenging and ambitious work. In *Otherwise than Being* responsibility is a pre-original or an-archic fact: it exists prior to any act through which one might *assume* responsibility for a role or action, and extends beyond my death in its implications. This infinitely growing answerability moves us beyond even the positions outlined in *Totality and Infinity*. Whereas the latter was still structured by the phenomenological terms of self and other (wherein the realms of enjoyment and dwelling are followed by the relationships with things, the ethical dimension to which the face gives rise, and the voluptuosity which in turn can go beyond ethics), *Otherwise than Being* begins with this last element. The intellectual structure of intentionality is preceded by direct sensuous contact. It is not a being-toward-death that conditions the form of the book, but the veracity of saying and unsaying whose exposure is described in directly corporeal terms, as an act denuding itself of its skin, a stripping beyond nudity. Instead of ontological philosophy, Levinas offers a powerful and radical discourse in terms of 'otherwise than being' based on a relationship not with death but with alterity. The *original* form of openness is therefore my exposure to alterity in the face of the other. I literally put myself in the place of another. Moreover, this substitution is not an abnegation of responsibility, but a passivity that bears the burden of everything for which the other is responsible. I become a subject in the physical sense of being hostage to the other. The unconditionality of this responsibility means that we are always already beyond essence.

Two helpful guides to *Otherwise than Being* can be consulted: the introduction to the English edition of the work by Alphonso Lingis; and the review by Adriaan Peperzak, 'Beyond being', *Research in Phenomenology*, 8 (1978), 239–61. Jacques Derrida has also produced a deep and involved reading of Levinas in part inspired by *Otherwise than Being* in 'En ce moment même dans cet ouvrage me voici', in *Textes pour Emmanuel Levinas*, edited by François Laruelle (Paris: Jean-Michel Place, 1980), pp. 21–60.

S.H.

Ich bin du, wenn
ich ich bin

Paul Celan

Principle and Anarchy

In the relationship with beings, which we call consciousness, we identify beings across the dispersion of silhouettes in which they appear; in self-consciousness we identify ourselves across the multiplicity of temporal phases. It is as though subjective life in the form of consciousness consisted in being itself losing itself and finding itself again so as to *possess itself* by showing itself, proposing itself as a theme, exposing itself in truth. This identification is not the *counterpart* of any image; it is a claim of the mind, proclamation, saying, kerygma. But it is not at all arbitrary, and consequently depends on a mysterious operation of schematism, in language, which can make an ideality correspond to the dispersion of aspects and images, silhouettes or phases. To become conscious of a being is then always for that being to be grasped across an ideality and on the basis of a said. Even an empirical, individual being is broached across the ideality of logos. Subjectivity *qua* consciousness can thus be interpreted as the articulation of an ontological event, as one of the mysterious ways in which its 'act of being' is deployed. Being a theme, being intelligible or open, possessing oneself, the moment of *having in being* – all that is articulated in the movement of essence, losing itself and finding itself out of an ideal principle, an ἀρχή, in its thematic exposition, being thus carries on its affair of being. The detour of ideality leads to coinciding with oneself, that is, to certainty, which remains the guide and guarantee of the whole spiritual adventure of being. But this is why this adventure is no adventure. It is never dangerous; it is self-possession, sovereignity, ἀρχή. Anything unknown that can occur to it is in advance disclosed, open, manifest, is cast in the mould of the known, and cannot be a complete surprise.

For the philosophical tradition of the West, all spirituality lies in consciousness, thematic exposition of being, knowing.

In starting with sensibility interpreted not as a knowing but as proximity, in seeking in language contact and sensibility, behind the circulation of information it becomes, we have endeavoured to describe subjectivity as irreducible to consciousness and thematization. Proximity appears as the relationship with the other, who cannot be resolved into 'images' or be exposed in a theme. It is the relationship with what is not disproportionate to the ἀρχή in thematization, but incommensurable with it, with what does not derive its identity from the kerygmatic logos, and blocks all schematism.

Not able to stay in a theme, not able to appear, this invisibility which becomes contact and obsession is due not to the nonsignifyingness of what is approached, but to a way of signifying quite different from that which connects exposition to sight. Here, beyond visibility there is exposed no signification that would still be thematized in its sign. It is the very transcending characteristic of this beyond that is signification. Signification is the contradictory trope of the-one-for-the-other. The-one-for-the-other is not a lack of intuition, but the surplus of responsibility. My responsibility for the other is the *for* of the relationship, the very signifyingness of signification, which signifies in saying before showing itself in the said. The-one-for-the-other is the very signifyingness of signification! It is not that the 'beyond' would be 'further' than everything that appears, or 'present in absence', or 'shown by a symbol'; that would still be to be subject to a principle, to be given in consciousness. Here what is essential is a refusal to allow oneself to be tamed or domesticated by a theme. The movement going 'beyond' loses its own signifyingness and becomes an immanence as soon as logos interpellates, invests, presents and exposes it, whereas its adjacency in proximity is an absolute exteriority. Incommensurable with the present, unassemblable in it, it is always 'already in the past' behind which the present delays, over and beyond the 'now' which this exteriority disturbs or obsesses. This way of passing, disturbing the present without allowing itself to be invested by the ἀρχή of consciousness, striating with its furrows the clarity of the ostensible, is what we have called a trace.[1] Proximity is thus *anarchically* a relationship with a singularity without the mediation of any principle, any ideality. What concretely corresponds to this description is my relationship with my neighbour, a signifyingness which is different from the much-discussed 'meaning-endowment', since signification is this very relationship with the other, the-one-for-the-other. This incommensurability with consciousness, which becomes a trace of the *who knows where*, is not the inoffensive relationship of knowing in which everything is equalized, nor the indifference of spatial contiguity; it is an assignation of me by another, a responsibility with regard to men we do not even know. The relationship of proximity cannot be reduced to any modality of distance or geometrical contiguity, nor to the simple 'representation' of a neighbour; it is already an assignation, an extremely urgent assignation – an obligation, anachronously prior to any commitment. This anteriority is 'older' than the a priori. This formula expresses a way of being affected which can in no way be invested by spontaneity: the subject is affected without the source of the affection becoming a theme of representation. We have called this relationship irreducible to consciousness obsession. The relationship with exteriority is 'prior' to the act that would effect it. For this relationship is not an act, not a thematizing, not a position in the Fichtean sense. Not everything that is in consciousness would be posited by consciousness – contrary to the proposition that seemed to Fichte to be fundamental.

Obsession is irreducible to consciousness, even if it overwhelms it. In consciousness it is betrayed, but thematized by a said in which it is manifested. Obsession traverses consciousness countercurrentwise, is inscribed in consciousness as something foreign, a disequilibrium, a delirium. It undoes thematization, and escapes any *principle*, origin, will, or ἀρχή, which are put forth in every ray of consciousness. This movement is, in the original sense of the term, an-archical. Thus obsession can nowise be taken as a hypertrophy of consciousness.

But anarchy is not disorder as opposed to order, as the eclipse of themes is not, as is said, a return to a diffuse 'field of consciousness' prior to attention. Disorder is but another order, and what is diffuse is thematizable.[2] Anarchy troubles being over and beyond these alternatives. It brings to a halt the ontological play which, precisely *qua* play, is consciousness, where being is lost and found again, and thus illuminated. In the form of an ego, anachronously *delayed* behind its present moment, and unable to recuperate this delay – that is, in the form of an ego unable to conceive what is 'touching' it,[3] the ascendancy of the other is exercised upon the same to the point of interrupting it, leaving it speechless. Anarchy is persecution. Obsession is a persecution where the persecution does not make up the content of a consciousness gone mad; it designates the form in which the ego is affected, a form which is a defecting from consciousness. This inversion of consciousness is no doubt a passivity – but it is a passivity beneath all passivity. It cannot be defined in terms of intentionality, where undergoing is always also an assuming, that is, an experience always anticipated and consented to, already an origin and ἀρχή. To be sure, the intentionality of consciousness does not designate voluntary intention only. Yet it retains the initiating and incohative pattern of voluntary intention. The given enters into a thought which recognizes in it or invests it with its own project, and thus exercises mastery over it. What affects a consciousness presents itself at a distance from the first, manifests itself a priori from the first, is represented, does not knock without announcing itself, leaves, across the interval of space and time, the leisure necessary for a welcome. What is realized in and by intentional consciousness offers itself to protention and diverges from itself in retention, so as to be, across the divergency, identified and possessed. This play in being is consciousness itself: presence to self through a distance, which is both loss of self and recovery in truth. The *for itself* in consciousness is thus the very power which a being exercises upon itself, its will, its sovereignty. A being is equal to itself and is in possession of itself in this form; domination is in consciousness as such. Hegel thought that the *I* is but consciousness mastering itself in self-equality, in what he calls 'the freedom of this infinite equality'.

The obsession we have seen in proximity conflicts with this figure of a being possessing itself in an equality, this being ἀρχή. How can the passivity of obsession find a place in consciousness, which is wholly, or is in the end, freedom? For in consciousness everything is intentionally assumed. Consciousness is wholly equality (equality of self with self, but also equality in that for consciousness responsibility is always strictly measured by freedom, and is thus always limited). How in consciousness can there be an undergoing or a passion whose active source does not, in any way, occur in consciousness? This exteriority has to be empasized. It is not objective or spatial, recuperable in immanence and thus falling under the orders of – and in the order of – consciousness; it is obsessional, non-thematizable and, in the sense we have just defined, anarchic.

It is in a *responsibility that is justified by no prior commitment*, in the responsibility for another – in an ethical situation – that the me-ontological and metalogical structure of this anarchy takes form, undoing the logos in which the apology by which consciousness always regains its self-control, and commands, is inserted. This passion is absolute in that it takes hold without any a priori. The consciousness is affected, then, before forming an image of what is coming to it, affected in spite of itself. In these traits we recognize a persecution; being called into question prior to questioning, responsibility over and beyond the logos of response. It is as though persecution by another were at the bottom of solidarity with another. How can such a passion[4] take place and have its time in consciousness?

Recurrence

But consciousness, knowing of oneself by oneself, is not all there is to the notion of subjectivity. It already rests on a 'subjective condition', an identity that one calls ego or I. It is true that, when asking about the meaning of this identity, we have the habit either of denouncing in it a reified substance, or of finding in it once again the for-itself of consciousness. In the traditional teaching of idealism, subject and consciousness are equivalent concepts. The *who* or the *me* are not even suspected. This one is a nonrelation, but absolutely a term. Yet this term of an irreversible assignation is perhaps dissimulated, under the outdated notion of the soul. It is a term not reducible to a relation, but yet is in recurrence. The ego is in itself like a sound that would resound in its own echo, the node of a wave which is not once again consciousness.[5] The term in recurrence will be sought here beyond or on the hither side of consciousness and its play, beyond or on the hither side of being which it thematizes, outside of being, and thus in itself as in exile. It will be found under the effect of an expulsion, whose positive meaning has to be explicated. Under the effect of such an expulsion outside of being, it is in itself. There is expulsion in that it assigns me before I show myself, before I set myself up. I am assigned without recourse, without fatherland, already sent back to myself, but without being able to stay there, compelled before commencing. Nothing here resembles self-consciousness. It has meaning only as an upsurge in me of a responsibility prior to commitment, that is, a responsibility for the other. There I am one and irreplaceable, one inasmuch as irreplaceable in responsibility. This is the underside of a fabric woven where there is consciousness and which takes place in being.

Nothing here resembles self-consciousness. The reduction of subjectivity to consciousness dominates philosophical thought, which since Hegel has been trying to overcome the duality of being and thought, by identifying, under different figures, substance and subject. This also amounts to undoing the substantivity of substance, but in relationship with self-consciousness. The successive and progressive disclosure of being to itself would be produced in philosophy. Knowing, the dis-covering, would not be added on to the being of entities, to essence.[6] Being's essence carries on like a vigilance exercised without respite on this very vigilance, like a self-possession. Philosophy which states essence as an ontology, concludes this essence, this lucidity of lucidity, by this logos. Consciousness fulfills the being of entities. For Sartre as for Hegel, the oneself is posited on the basis of the for-itself. The identity of the I would thus be reducible to the turning back of essence upon itself. The I, or the oneself that would seem to be its subject or condition, the oneself taking on the figure of an entity among entities, would in truth be reducible to an abstraction taken from the concrete process of self-consciousness, or from the exposition of being in history or in the stretching out of time, in which, across breaks and recoveries, being shows itself to itself. Time, essence, essence as time, would be the absolute itself in the return to self. The multiplicity of unique subjects, entities immediately, empirically, encountered, would proceed from this universal self-consciousness of the Mind: bits of dust collected by its movement or drops of sweat glistening on its forehead because of the labour of the negative it will have accomplished. They would be forgettable moments of which what counts is only their identities due to their positions in the system, which are reabsorbed into the whole of the system.

The reflection on oneself proper to consciousness, the ego perceiving the self, is not like the antecendent recurrence of the oneself, the oneness without any duality of oneself, from the first backed up against itself, up against a wall, or twisted over itself in its skin, too tight in its skin, in itself already outside of itself. Its restlessness also does not convey dispersion into phases, exterior to one another, in a flux of immanent time in the Husserlian sense, retaining the past and biting on the future. The oneself is not the ideal pole of an identification across the multiciplicity of psychic silhouettes kerygmatically proclaimed to be the same by virtue of a mysterious schematism of discourse.[7] The oneself does not bear its identity as entities, identical in that they are said without being unsaid, and thus are thematized and appear to consciousness. The uncancellable recurrence of the oneself in the subject is prior to any distinction between moments which could present themselves to a synthesizing activity of identification and assemblage to recall or expectation. The recurrence of the oneself is not relaxed and lighted up again, illuminating itself thereby like consciousness which lights up by interrupting itself and finding itself again in the temporal play of retentions and protentions. The oneself does not enter into that play of exposings and dissimulations which we call a phenomenon (or phenomenology, for the appearing of a phenomenon is already a discourse). The oneself takes refuge or is exiled in its own fullness, to the point of explosion or fission, in view of its own reconstitution in the form of an identity identified in the said. Verbs, possessive adjectives and the syntactic figures one would like to use to disarticulate the singular torsion or contraction of the oneself bear already the mark of the oneself, of this torsion, this contraction, this fission. That is perhaps also the meaning of Leibniz' mysterious formula, 'the ego is innate to itself.' The self involved in maintaining oneself, losing oneself or finding oneself again is not a result, but the very matrix of the relations or events that these pronominal verbs express. The evocation of maternity in this metaphor suggests to us the proper sense of the oneself. The oneself cannot form itself; it is already formed with absolute passivity. In this sense it is the victim of a persecution that paralyzes any assumption that could awaken in it, so that it would posit itself *for* itself. This passivity is that of an attachment that has already been made, as something irreversibly past, prior to all memory and all recall. It was made in an irrecuperable time which the present, represented in recall, does not equal, in a time of birth or creation, of which nature or creation retains a trace, unconvertible into a memory. Recurrence is more past than any rememberable past, any past convertible into a present. The oneself is a creature, but an orphan by birth or an atheist no doubt ignorant of its Creator, for if it knew it it would again be taking up its commencement. The recurrence of the oneself refers to the hither side of the present in which every identity identified in the said is constituted. It is already constituted when the act of constitution first originates. But in order that there be produced in the drawing out of essence, coming out like a colourless thread from the distaff of the Parques, a break in the same, the nostalgia for return, the hunt for the same and the recoveries, and the clarity in which consciousness plays, in order that this divergency from self and this recapture be produced, the retention and protention by which every present is a representation – behind all the articulations of these movements there must be the recurrence of the oneself. The disclosure of being to itself lurks there. Otherwise essence, exonerated by itself, constituted in immanent time, will posit only indiscernible points,[8] which would, to be sure, be together, but which would neither block nor fulfill any fate. Nothing would make itself. The breakup of 'eternal rest' by time, in which being becomes consciousness and self-consciousness by equalling itself after the breakup, presuppose the oneself. To present the knot of ipseity in the straight thread of essence according to the model of the intentionality of the for-itself, or as the openness of reflection upon oneself, is to posit a new ipseity behind the ipseity one would like to reduce.

The oneself has not issued from its own initiative, as it claims in the plays and figures of consciousness on the way to the unity of an Idea. In that idea, coinciding with itself, free inasmuch as it is a totality which leaves nothing outside, and thus, fully reasonable, the oneself posits itself as an always convertible term in a relation, a self-consciousness. But the oneself is hypostasized in another way. It is bound in a knot that cannot be undone in a responsibility for others. This is an anarchic plot, for it is neither the underside of a freedom, a free commitment undertaken in a present or a past that could be remembered, nor slave's alienation, despite the gestation of the other in the same, which this responsibility for the other signifies. In the exposure to wounds and outrages, in the feeling proper to responsibility, the oneself is provoked as irreplaceable, as devoted to the others, without being able to resign, and thus as incarnated in order to offer itself, to suffer and to give. It is thus one and unique, in passivity from the start, having nothing at its disposal that would enable it to not yield to the provocation. It is one, reduced to itself and as it were contracted, expelled into itself outside of being. The exile or refuge in itself is without conditions or support, far from the abundant covers and excuses which the essence exhibited in the said offers. In responsibility as one assigned or elected from the outside, assigned as irreplaceable, the subject is accused in its skin, too tight for its skin. Cutting across every relation, it is an individual unlike an entity that can be designated as τόδε τι. Unless, that is, the said derives from the uniqueness of the oneself assigned in responsibility the ideal unity necessary for identification of the diverse, by which, in the amphibology of being and entities, an entity signifies. The hypostasis is exposed as oneself in the accusative form, before appearing in the said proper to knowing as the bearer of a name. The metaphor of a sound that would be audible only in its echo meant to approach this way of presenting one's passivity as an underside without a right side.

Prior to the return to itself proper to consciousness, this hypostasis, when it shows itself, does so under the borrowed mask of being. The event in which this unity or uniqueness of the hypostasis is brought out is not the grasping of self in consciousness. It is an assignation to answer without evasions, which assigns the self to be a self. Prior to the play of being, before the present, older than the time of consciousness that is accessible in memory, in its 'deep yore, never remote enough', the oneself is exposed as a hypostasis, of which the being it is as an entity is but a mask. It bears its name as a borrowed name, a pseudonym, a pro-noun. In itself, the oneself is the one or the unique separated from being.

The oneself proper to consciousness is then not again a consciousness, but a term in hypostasis. It is by this hypostasis that the person, as an identity unjustifiable by itself and in this sense empirical or contingent, emerges substantively. In its stance it is resistant to the erosion of time and history, that is, struck by a death always violent and premature. An identity prior to the for-itself, it is not the reduced or germinal model of the relationship of oneself with oneself that cognition is. Neither a vision of oneself by oneself, nor a manifestation of oneself to oneself, the oneself does not coincide with the identifying of truth, is not statable in terms of consciousness, discourse and intentionality. The unjustifiable identity of ipseity is expressed in terms such as ego, I, oneself, and, this work aims to show throughout, starting with the soul, sensibility, vulnerability, materni-ty and materiality, which describe responsibility for others. The 'fulcrum' in which this turning of being back upon itself which we call knowing or mind is produced thus designates the singularity par excellence. It can indeed appear in an indirect language, under a proper name, as an entity, and thus put itself on the edge of the generality characteristic of all said, and there refer to essence. But it is first a non-quiddity, no one, clothed with purely borrowed being, which masks its nameless singularity by con-ferring on it a role. The locus of support for the mind is a personal pronoun. If the return to self proper to cognition, the original truth of being, consciousness, can be realized, it is because a recurrence of ipseity has already been produced. This is an inversion in the process of essence, a withdrawing from the game that being plays in consciousness. It is a withdrawal-in-oneself which is an exile in oneself, without a foundation in anything else, a non-condition. This withdrawal excludes all spontaneity, and is thus always already effected, already past. Ipseity is not an abstract point, the centre of a rotation, identifiable on the basis of the trajectory traced by this movement of consciousness, but a point already identified from the outside, not having to identify itself in the present nor to state its identity, already older than the time of consciousness.

The identity already realized, the 'fact' or the 'already done' that the oneself contributes to consciousness and knowing, does not refer mythically to a duration prior to duration, to a fabric that would still be loose enough so as to permit the flexion upon oneself of the for-itself. The for-itself is a torsion irreducible to the beating of self-consciousness, the relaxing and recovering proper to the same. The oneself comes from a past that could not be remembered, not because it is situated very far behind, but because the oneself, incommensurable with consciousness which is always equal to itself, is not 'made' for the present. The oneself, an inequality with itself, a deficit in being, a passivity or patience and, in its passivity not offering itself to memory, not affecting retrospective contemplation, is in this sense undeclinable, with an undeclinability which is not that of a pure actuality. It is the identity of the singular, modified only in the erosion of ageing, in the permanence of a loss of self. It is unsayable, and thus unjustifiable. These negative qualifications of the subjectivity of the oneself do not consecrate some ineffable mystery, but confirm the presynthetic, pre-logical and in a certain sense atomic, that is, in-dividual, unity of the self, which prevents it from splitting, separating itself from itself so as to contemplate or express itself, and thus show itself, if only under a comic mask, to name itself otherwise than by a pro-noun. This prevention is the positivity of the one. It is in a certain sense atomic, for it is without any rest in itself, 'more and more one', to the point of breakup, fission, openness. That this unity be a torsion and a restlessness, irreducible to the function that the oneself exercises in the ontology accomplished by consciousness, which, by the oneself, operates its turning back over itself, presents a problem. It is as though the atomic unity of the subject were exposed outside by breathing, by divesting its ultimate substance even to the mucous membrane of the lungs, continually splitting up.

The oneself does not rest in peace under its identity, and yet its restlessness is not a dialectical scission, nor a process equalizing difference. Its unity is not just added on to some content of ipseity, like the indefinite article which substantifies even verbs, 'nominalizing' and thematizing them. Here the unity precedes every article and every process; it is somehow itself the content. Recurrence is but an 'outdoing' of unity. As a unity in its form and in its content, the oneself is a singularity, prior to the distinction between the particular and the universal. It is, if one likes, a relationship, but one where there is no disjunction between the terms held in relationship, a relationship that is not reducible to an intentional openness upon oneself, does not purely and simply repeat consciousness in which being is gathered up, as the sea gathers up the waves that wash the shore. The ego is not in itself like matter which, perfectly espoused by its form, is what it is; it is in itself like one is in one's skin, that is, already tight, ill at ease in one's own skin. It is as though the identity of matter resting in

itself concealed a dimension in which a retreat to the hither side of immediate coincidence were possible, concealed a materiality more material
than all matter – a materiality such that irritability, susceptibility or
exposedness to wounds and outrage characterizes its passivity, more
passive still than the passivity of effects. Maternity in the complete being
'for the other' which characterizes it, which is the very signifyingness
of signification, is the ultimate sense of this vulnerability. This hither
side of identity is not reducible to the for-itself, where, beyond its immediate identity, being recognizes itself in its difference. We have to formulate
what the irremissibility and, in the etymological sense of the term, the
anguish of this in-itself of the oneself are. This anguish is not the existential
'being-for-death', but the constriction of an 'entry inwards', or the 'hither
side' of all extension. It is not a flight into the void, but a movement into
fullness, the anguish of contraction and breakup.[9] This describes the relation in which a subject is immolated without fleeing itself, without entering
into ecstasy, without taking a distance from itself, in which it is pursued
into itself, to the hither side of rest in itself, of its coincidence with itself.
This recurrence, which one can, to be sure, call negativity (but a negativity
antecedent to discourse, the unexceptionable homeland of dialectical negativity), this recurrence by contraction, is the self.

It is the negativity characteristic of the *in itself* without the openness of
nothingness, penetrating into the plenum – *in itself* in the sense of *an sich*
and *in sich*. It lies behind the distinction between rest and movement,
between the being at home with oneself (*chez soi*) and wandering, between
equality and difference. This negativity reminds us of the formulas of the
Parmenides concerning the moment in which the One 'being in
motion . . . [it] comes to a stand, or being at rest, (. . .) changes to being in
motion,' and in which it 'must not be at any time' (156cc). 'This strange
sort of nature' which 'is situated between motion and rest' (156d)[10] is not a
cross-section of time at a point that preserves dynamically, in potency, the
contradiction between the present and the future or the past. Nor is it an
extra-temporal ideality which dominates temporal dispersion, for both
points and idealities in their own way presuppose the ontological adventure.
This 'strange sort of nature' is something on the hither side, without any
reference to thematization, without even references to references rising in it,
like 'itch', witout any dialectical germination, quite sterile and pure, completely cut off from adventure and reminiscence. No grounds (*non-lieu*),
meanwhile or contra-tempo time (or bad times (*malheur*)), it is on the hither
side of being and of the nothingness which is thematizable like being.

The expression 'in one's skin' is not a metaphor for the in-itself; it refers
to a recurrence in the dead time or the *meanwhile* which separates inspiration and expiration, the diastole and systole of the heart beating dully

against the walls of one's skin. The body is not only an image or figure here; it is the distinctive in-oneself of the contraction of ipseity and its breakup.[11] This contraction is not an impossibility to forget oneself, to detach oneself from oneself, in the concern for oneself. It is a recurrence to oneself out of an irrecusable exigency of the other, a duty overflowing my being, a duty becoming a debt and an extreme passivity prior to the tranquillity, still quite relative, in the inertia and materiality of things at rest. It is a restlessness and patience that support prior to action and passion. Here what is due goes beyond having, but makes giving possible. This recurrence is incarnation. In it the body which makes giving possible makes one *other* without alienating. For this other is the heart, and the goodness, of the same, the inspiration or the very psyche in the soul.

The recurrence of ipseity, the incarnation, far from thickening and tumefying the soul, oppresses it and contracts it and exposes it naked to the other to the point of making the subject expose its very exposedness, which might cloak it, to the point of making it an uncovering of self in saying. The concept of the incarnate subject is not a biological concept. The schema that corporeality outlines submits the biological itself to a higher structure; it is dispossession, but not nothingness, for it is a negativity caught up in the impossibility of evading, without any field of initiative. It is, improbably enough, a retreat into the fullness of the punctual, into the inextendedness of the one. Responsibility prior to any free commitment, the oneself outside of all the tropes of essence, would be responsibility for the freedom of the others. The irremissible guilt with regard to the neighbour is like a Nessus tunic my skin would be.

The Self

Returning now to the theme of the first part of this exposition, we have to ask if this folding back upon oneself proper to ipseity (which does not even have the virtue of being an act of folding itself, but makes the act of consciousness turning back upon itself possible), this passive folding back, does not coincide with the anarchic passivity of an obsession. Is not obsession a relationship with the outside which is prior to the act that would open up this exterior? The total passivity of obsession is more passive still than the passivity of things, for in their 'prime matter' things sustain the kerygmatic logos that brings out their outlines in matter. In falling under this saying that ordains, matter takes on meaning, and shows itself to be this or that – a thing. This fall – or, this case – a pure surrender to the logos, without regard for the propositions that will make of the thing a narrative to which the logos belongs, is the essence of the accusative. The logos that informs prime matter in calling it to order is an accusation, or a category. But obsession is anarchical; it accuses me beneath the level of prime matter. For as a category takes hold of matter, it takes as its model still what resistance, impenetrability, or potency remains in that matter, that 'being in potency'. Prime matter, presented as a being in potency, is still potency, which the form takes into account. It is not by chance that Plato teaches us that matter is eternal, and that for Aristotle matter is a *cause*; such is the truth for the order of *things*. Western philosophy, which perhaps is reification itself, remains faithful to the order of things and does not know the absolute passivity, beneath the level of activity and passivity, which is contributed by the idea of creation.[12] Philosophers have always wished to think of creation in ontological terms, that is, in function of a preexisting and indestructible matter.

In obsession the accusation effected by categories turns into an absolute accusative in which the ego proper to free consciousness is caught up. It is an accusation without foundation, to be sure, prior to any movement of the will, an obsessional and persecuting accusation. It strips the ego of its pride and the dominating imperialism characteristic of it. The subject is in the accusative, without recourse in being, expelled from being, outside of being, like the one in the first hypotheses of *Parmenides*, without a foundation, reduced to itself, and thus without condition. In its own skin. Not at rest under a form, but tight in its skin, encumbered and as it were stuffed with itself, suffocating under itself, insufficiently open, forced to detach itself from itself, to breathe more deeply, all the way, forced to dispossess itself to the point of losing itself. Does this loss have as its term the void, the zero point and the peace of cemeteries, as though the subjectivity of a subject meant nothing? Or do the being encumbered with oneself and the suffering of constriction in one's skin, better than metaphors, follow the exact trope of an alteration of essence, which inverts, or would invert, into a recurrence in which the expulsion of self outside of itself is its substitution for the other? Is not that what the self emptying itself of itself would really mean? This recurrence would be the ultimate secret of the incarnation of the subject; prior to all reflection, prior to every positing, an indebtedness before any loan, not assumed, anarchical, subjectivity of a bottomless passivity, made out of assignation, like the echo of a sound that would precede the resonance of this sound. The active source of this passivity is not thematizable. It is the passivity of a trauma, but one that prevents its own representation, a deafening trauma, cutting the thread of consciousness which should have welcomed it in its present, the passivity of being persecuted. This passivity deserves the epithet of complete or absolute only if the persecuted one is liable to answer for the persecutor. The face of the neighbour in its persecuting hatred can by this very malice obsess as something pitiful. This equivocation or enigma only the persecuted one who does not evade it, but is without any references, any recourse or help (that is its uniqueness or its identity as unique!) is able to endure. To undergo from the other is an absolute patience only if by this from-the-other is already for-the-other. This transfer, other than interested, 'otherwise than essence', is subjectivity itself. 'To give his cheek to the smiter and to be filled with insults',[13] to demand suffering in the suffering undergone (without producing the act that would be the exposing of the other cheek) is not to draw from suffering some kind of magical redemptive virtue. In the trauma of persecution it is to pass from the outrage undergone to the responsibility for the persecutor, and, in this sense from suffering to expiation for the other. Persecution is not something added to the subject-ivity of the subject and his vulnerability; it is the very movement of recur-rence. The subjectivity as *the other in the same*, as an inspiration, is the put-ting into question of all affirmation for-oneself, all egoism born again in this very recurrence. (This putting into question is not a preventing!) The subje-ctivity of a subject is responsibility of being-in-question[14] in the form of the total exposure to offence in the cheek offered to the smiter. This responsib-ility is prior to dialogue, to the exchange of questions and answers, to the thematization of the said, which is superposed on my being put into ques-tion by the other in proximity, and in the saying proper to responsibility is produced as a digression.

The recurrence of persecution in the oneself is thus irreducible to inten-tionality in which, even in its neutrality as a contemplative movement, the will is affirmed. In it the fabric of the same, self-possession in a present, is never broken. When affected the ego is in the end affected only by itself, freely. Subjectivity taken as intentionality is founded on auto-affection as an auto-revelation, source of an impersonal discourse. The recurrence of the self in responsibility for others, a persecuting obsession, goes against inten-tionality, such that responsibility for others could never mean altruistic will, instinct of 'natural benevolence', or love. It is in the passivity of obsession, or incarnated passivity, that an identity individuates itself as unique, with-out recourse to any system of references, in the impossibility of evading the assignation of the other without blame. The re-presentation of self grasps it already in its trace. The absolution of the one is neither an evasion,[15] nor an abstraction; it is a concreteness more concrete than the simply coherent in a totality. For under accusation by everyone, the responsibility for everyone goes to the point of substitution. A subject is a hostage.

Obsessed with responsibilities which did not arise in decisions taken by a subject 'contemplating freely', consequently accused in its innocence, subjectivity in itself is being thrown back on oneself. This means concrete-ly: accused of what the others do or suffer, or responsible for what they do or suffer. The uniqueness of the self is the very fact of bearing the fault of another. In responsibility for another subjectivity is only this unlimited passivity of an accusative which does not issue out of a declension it would have undergone starting with the nominative. This accusation can be reduced to the passivity of the self only as a persecution, but a persecution that turns into an expiation. Without persecution the ego raises its head and covers over the self. Everything is from the start in the accusative. Such is the exceptional condition or unconditionality of the self, the signification of the pronoun *self* for which our Latin grammars themselves know no nominative form.

The more I return to myself, the more I divest myself, under the traumatic effect of persecution, of my freedom as a constituted, wilful, imperialist subject, the more I discover myself to be responsible; the more just I am, the more guilty I am. I am 'in myself' through the others. The psyche is the other in the same, without alienating the same.[16] Backed up against itself, in itself because without any recourse in anything, in itself like in its skin, the self in its skin both is exposed to the exterior (which does not happen to things) and obsessed by the others in this naked exposure. Does not the self take on itself, through its very impossibility to evade its own identity, toward which, when persecuted, it withdraws? Does not a beginning rise in this passivity? The undeclinability of the ego is the irremissibility of the accusation, from which it can no longer take a distance, which it cannot evade. This impossibility of taking any distance and of slipping away from the Good is a firmness more firm and more profound than that of the will, which is still a tergiversation.

The inability to decline indicates the anachronism of a debt preceding the loan, of an expenditure overflowing one's resources, as in effort. It would be an exigency with regard to oneself where what is possible is not measured by a reflection on oneself, as in the for-itself. In this exigency with regard to oneself the self answering to the exigency does not show itself in the form of a direct object complement – which would be to suppose an equality between self and self. This exigency with regard to oneself without regard for what is possible, that is, beyond all equity, is produced in the form of an accusation preceding the fault, borne against oneself despite one's innocence. For the order of contemplation it is something simply demented. This extreme accusation excludes the declinability of the self, which would have consisted in measuring the possibles in oneself, so as to accuse oneself of this or that, of something committed even if in the form of original sin. The accusation that weighs on the self as a self is an exigency without consideration for oneself. The infinite passion of responsibility, in its return upon itself goes further than its identity,[17] to the hither side or beyond being and the possible, and puts the being in itself in deficit, making it susceptible of being treated as a negative quantity.

But how does the passivity of the self become a 'hold on oneself'? If that is not just a play on words, does it not presuppose an activity behind the absolutely anarchical passivity of obsession, a clandestine and dissimulated freedom? Then what is the object of the exposition developed to this point? We have answered this question in advance with the notion of substitution.

Substitution

In this exposition of the in itself of the persecuted subjectivity, have we been faithful enough to the anarchy of passivity? In speaking of the recurrence of the ego to the self, have we been sufficiently free from the postulates of ontological thought, where the eternal presence to oneself subtends even its absences in the form of a quest, where eternal being, whose possibles are also powers, always takes up what it undergoes, and whatever be its submission, always arises anew as the principle of what happens to it? It is perhaps here, in this reference to a depth of anarchical passivity, that the thought that names creation differs from ontological thought. It is not here a question of justifying the theological context of ontological thought, for the word creation designates a signification older than the context woven about this name. In this context, this said, is already effaced the absolute diachrony of creation, refractory to assembling into a present and a representation. But in creation, what is called to being answers to a call that could not have reached it since, brought out of nothingness, it obeyed before hearing the order. Thus in the concept of creation *ex nihilo*, if it is not a pure nonsense, there is the concept of a passivity that does not revert into an assumption. The self as a creature is conceived in a passivity more passive still than the passivity of matter, that is, prior to the virtual coinciding of a term with itself. The oneself has to be conceived outside of all substantial coinciding of self with self. Contrary to Western thought which unites subjectivity and substantiality, here coinciding is not the norm that already commands all non-coinciding, in the quest it provokes. Then the recurrence to oneself cannot stop at oneself, but goes to the hither side of oneself; *in* the recurrence to oneself there is a going to the hither side of oneself. A does not, as in identity, return to A, but retreats to the hither side of its point of departure. Is not the signification of responsibility for another, which cannot be assumed by any freedom, stated in this trope? Far from being recognized in the freedom of consciousness, which loses itself and finds itself again, which, as a freedom, relaxes the order of being so as to reintegrate it in a free responsibility, the responsibility for the other, the responsibility in obsession, suggests an absolute passivity of a self that has never been able to diverge from itself, to then enter into its limits, and identify itself by recognizing itself in its past. Its recurrence is the contracting of an ego, going to the hither side of identity, gnawing away at this very identity – identity gnawing away at itself – in a remorse. Responsibility for another is not an accident that happens to a subject, but precedes essence in it, has not awaited freedom, in which a commitment to another would have been made. I have not done anything and I have always been under accusation – persecuted. The ipseity, in the passivity without arche characteristic of identity, is a hostage. The word *I* means *here I am*, answering for everything and for everyone. Responsibility for the others has not been a return to oneself, but an exasperated contracting, which the limits of identity cannot retain. Recurrence becomes identity in breaking up the limits of identity, breaking up the *principle* of being in me, the intolerable rest in itself characteristic of definition. The self is on the hither side of rest; it is the impossibility to come back from all things and concern oneself only with oneself. It is to hold on to oneself while gnawing away at oneself. Responsibility in obsession is a responsibility of the ego for what the ego has not wished, that is, for the others. This anarchy in the recurrence to oneself is beyond the normal play of action and passion in which the identity of a being is maintained, in which it *is*. It is on the hither side of the limits of identity. This passivity undergone in proximity by the force of an alterity in me is the passivity of a recurrence to oneself which is not the alienation of an identity betrayed. What can it be but a substitution of me for the others? It is, however, not an alienation, because the other in the same is my substitution for the other through responsibility, for which I am summoned as someone irreplaceable. I exist through the other and for the other, but without this being alienation: I am inspired. This inspiration is the psyche. The psyche can signify this alterity in the same without alienation in the form of incarnation, as being-in-one's-skin, having-the-other-in-one's-skin.

In this substitution, in which identity is inverted, this passivity more passive still than the passivity conjoined with action, beyond the inert passivity of the designated, the self is absolved of itself. Is this freedom? It is a different freedom from that of an initiative. Through substitution for others, the oneself escapes relations. At the limit of passivity, the oneself escapes passivity or the inevitable limitation that the terms within relation undergo. In the incomparable relationship of responsibility, the other no longer limits the same, it is supported by what it limits. Here the overdetermination of the ontological categories is visible, which transforms them into ethical terms. In this most passive passivity, the self liberates itself ethically from every other and from itself. Its responsibility for the other, the proximity of the neighbour, does not signify a submission to the non-ego; it means an openness in which being's essence is surpassed in inspiration. It is an openness of which respiration is a modality or a foretaste, or, more exactly, of which it retains the aftertaste. Outside of any mysticism, in this respiration, the possibility of every sacrifice for the other, activity and passivity coincide.

For the venerable tradition to which Hegel refers, the ego is an equality with itself, and consequently the return of being to itself is a concrete universality, being having separated itself from itself in the universality of the concept and death. But viewed out of the obsession of passivity, of itself anarchical, there is brought out, behind the equality of consciousness, an inequality. This inequality does not signify an inadequation of the apparent being with the profound or sublime being, nor a return to an original innocence (such as the inequality of the ego itself in Nabert, who is perhaps faithful to the tradition in which non-coincidence is only privation). It signifies an inequality in the oneself due to substitution, an effort to escape concepts without any future but attempted anew the next day. It signifies a uniqueness, under assignation, of responsibility, and because of this assignation not finding any rest in itself. The self without a concept, unequal in identity, signifies itself in the first person, setting forth the plane of saying, pro-ducing itself in saying as an ego or as me, that is, utterly different from any other ego, that is, having a meaning despite death. Contrary to the ontology of death this self opens an order in which death can be not recognized. An identity in diastasis, where coinciding is wanting. I am a self in the identifying recurrence in which I find myself cast back to the hither side of my point of departure! This self is out of phase with itself, forgetful of itself, forgetful in biting in upon itself, in the reference to itself which is the gnawing away at oneself to remorse. These are not events that happen to an empirical ego, that is, to an ego already posited and fully identified, as a trial *that* would lead it to being more conscious of itself, and make it more apt to put itself in the place of others. What we are here calling oneself, or the other in the same, where inspiration arouses respiration, the very pneuma of the psyche, precedes this empirical order, which is a part of being, of the universe, of the State, and is already conditioned in a system. Here we are trying to express the unconditionality of a subject, which does not have the status of a principle. This unconditionality confers meaning on being itself, and welcomes its gravity. It is as resting on a self, supporting the whole of being, that being is assembled into a unity of the universe and essence is assembled into an event. The self is a *sub-jectum*; it is under the weight of the universe, responsible for everything. The unity of the universe is not what my gaze embraces in its unity of apperception, but what is incumbent on me from all sides, regards me in the two senses of the term, accuses me, is my affair. In this sense, the idea that I am sought out in the intersidereal spaces is not science-fiction fiction, but expresses my passivity as a self.

The self is what inverts the upright imperturbable work, without exemptions, in which being's essence unfolds. To be in-oneself, backed up against oneself, to the extent of substituting oneself for all that pushes one into this null-place, is for the I to be in itself, lying in itself beyond essence. The reclusion of the ego in itself, on the hither side of its identity, in the other, the expiation supporting the weight of the non-ego, is neither a triumph nor a failure. Failing already presupposes a freedom and the imperialism of a political or ecclesiastical ego, that is, a history of constituted and free egos. The self as an expiation is prior to activity and passivity.

In opposition to the vision of thinkers such as Eugen Fink or Jeanne Delhomme, who require, among the conditions of the world, a freedom without responsibility, a freedom of play, we discern in obsession a responsibility that rests on no free commitment, a responsibility whose entry into being could be effected only without any choice. To be without a choice can seem to be violence only to an abusive or hasty and imprudent reflection, for it precedes the freedom non-freedom couple, but thereby sets up a vocation that goes beyond the limited and egoist fate of him who is only for-himself, and washes his hands of the faults and misfortunes that do not begin in his own freedom or in his present. It is the setting up of a being that is not for itself, but is for all, is both being and disinterestedness. The for itself signifies self-consciousness; the for all, responsibility for the others, support of the universe. Responsibility for the other, this way of answering without a prior commitment, is human fraternity itself, and it is prior to freedom. The face of the other in proximity, which is more than representation, is an unrepresentable trace, the way of the infinite. It is not because among beings there exists an ego, a being pursuing ends, that being takes on signification and becomes a universe. It is because in an approach, there is inscribed or written the trace of infinity, the trace of a departure, but trace of what is inordinate, does not enter into the present, and inverts the *arche* into anarchy, that there is forsakenness of the other, obsession by him, responsibility and a self.[18] The non-interchangeable par excellence, the I, the unique one, substitutes itself for others. Nothing is a game. Thus being is transcended.

The ego is not just a being endowed with certain qualities called moral which it would bear as a substance bears attributes, or which it would take on as accidents in its becoming. Its exceptional uniqueness in the passivity or the passion of the self is the incessant event of subjection to everything, of substitution. It is a being divesting itself, emptying itself of its being, turning itself inside out, and if it can be put thus, the fact of 'otherwise than being'. This subjection is neither nothingness, nor a product of a transcendental imagination. In this analysis we do not mean to reduce an entity that would be the ego to the act of substituting itself that would be the being of this entity. Substitution is not an act; it is a passivity inconvertible into an act, the hither side of the act-passivity alternative, the exception that cannot be fitted into the grammatical categories of noun or verb, save in the said that thematizes them. This recurrence can be stated only as an in-itself, as the underside of being or as otherwise than being.[19] To be oneself, otherwise than being, to be dis-interested, is to bear the wretchedness and bankruptcy of the other, and even the responsibility that the other can have for me. To be oneself, the state of being a hostage, is always to have one degree of responsibility more, the responsibility for the responsibility of the other.[10]

Why does the other concern me? What is Hecuba to me? Am I my brother's keeper? These questions have meaning only if one has already supposed that the ego is concerned only with itself, is only a concern for itself. In this hypothesis it indeed remains incomprehensible that the absolute outside-of-me, the other, would concern me. But in the 'prehistory' of the ego posited for itself speaks a responsibility. The self is through and through a hostage, older than the ego, prior to principles. What is at stake for the self, in its being, is not to be. Beyond egoism and altruism it is the religiosity of the self.

It is through the condition of being hostage that there can be in the world pity, compassion, pardon and proximity – even the little there is, even the simple 'After you, sir'. The unconditionality of being hostage is not the limit case of solidarity, but the condition for all solidarity. Every accusation and persecution, as all interpersonal praise, recompense, and punishment, presupposes the subjectivity of the ego, substitution, the possibility of putting oneself in the place of the other, which refers to the transference from the 'by the other' into a 'for the other', and in persecution from the outrage inflicted by the other to the expiation for his fault by me. But the absolute accusation, prior to freedom, constitutes freedom which, allied to the Good, situates beyond and outside of all essence.

All the transfers of feeling, with which the theorists of original war and egoism explain the birth of generosity (it is, however, not certain that war was at the beginning, before the altars), would not succeed in being fixed in the ego if it were not with its whole being, or rather with its whole disinterestedness, subjected not, like matter, to a category, but to the unlimited accusative of persecution. The self, a hostage, is already substituted for the others. 'I am an other', but this is not the alienation Rimbaud refers to. I am outside of any place, in myself, on the hither side of the autonomy of auto-affection and identity resting on itself. Impassively undergoing the weight of the other, thereby called to uniqueness, subjectivity no longer belongs to the order where the alternative of activity and passivity retains its meaning. We have to speak here of expiation as uniting identity and alterity. The ego is not an entity 'capable' of expiating for the others: it is this original expiation. This expiation is voluntary, for it is prior to the will's initiative (prior to the origin). It is as though the unity and uniqueness of the ego were already the hold on itself of the gravity of the other. In this sense the self is goodness, or under the exigency for an abandon of all having, of all *one's own* and all *for oneself*, to the point of substitution. Goodness is, we have said, the sole attribute which does not introduce multiplicity into the One that a subject is, for it is distinct from the One. If it showed itself to the one, it would no longer be a goodness in it. Goodness invests me in my obedience to the hidden Good.

The individuation or superindividuation of the ego consists in being in itself, in its skin, without sharing the *conatus essendi* of all beings which are beings in themselves. It consists in my being faced with everything that is only because I am by regard for all that is. It is an expiating for being. The self is the very fact of being exposed under the accusation that cannot be assumed, where the ego supports the others, unlike the certainty of the ego that rejoins itself in freedom.

Communication

It is with subjectivity understood as self, with the exciting and dispossession, the contraction, in which the ego does not appear, but immolates itself, that the relationship with the other can be communication and transcendence, and not always another way of seeking certainty, or the coinciding with oneself. Paradoxically enough, thinkers claim to derive communication out of self-coinciding.[21] They do not take seriously the radical reversal, from cognition to solidarity, that communication represents with respect to inward dialogue, to cognition of oneself, taken as the trope of spirituality. They seek for communication a full coverage insurance, and do not ask if inward dialogue is not beholden to the solidarity that sustains communication. In expiation, the responsibility for the others, the relationship with the non-ego, precedes any relationship of the ego with itself. The relationship with the other precedes the auto-affection of certainty, to which one always tries to reduce communication.

But communication would be impossible if it should have to begin in the ego, a free subject, to whom every other would be only a limitation that invites war, domination, precaution and information. To communicate is indeed to open oneself, but the openness is not complete if it is on the watch for recognition. It is complete not in opening to the spectacle of or the recognition of the other, but in becoming a responsibility for him. The overemphasis of openness is responsibility for the other to the point of substitution, where the for-the-other proper to disclosure, to monstration to the other, turns into the for-the-other proper to responsibility. This is the thesis of the present work. The openness of communication is not a simple change of place, so as to situate a truth outside instead of keeping it in oneself. What is surprising is the idea or the folly of situating it outside. Would communication be something added on? Or is not the ego a substitution in its solidarity as something identical, a solidarity that begins by bearing witness of itself to the other? Is it not then first of all a communicating of communication, a sign of the giving of signs, and not a transmission of something in an openness? It is to singularly displace the question to ask if what shows itself in this openness is as it shows itself, if its appearing is not an appearance. The problem of communication reduced to the problem of the truth of this communication for him that receives it amounts to the problem of certainty of the coinciding of self with self, as though coinciding were the ultimate secret of communication, and as though truth were only disclosure. The idea that truth can signify a witness given of the infinite[22] is not even suggested. In this preeminence of certainty, the identity of a substance is taken on for the ego, is said to be a monad, and is henceforth incapable of communication, save by a miracle. One is then led to look for a theory, from Cassirer to Binswanger, according to which a prior dialogue sustains the ego which states it, rather than the ego holding forth a conversation.

Those who wish to found on dialogue and on an original *we* the upsurge of egos, refer to an original communication behind the *de facto* communication (but without giving this original communication any sense other than the empirical sense of a dialogue or a *manifestation* of one to the other – which is to presuppose that *we* that is to be founded), and reduce the problem of communication to the problem of its certainty. In opposition to that, we suppose that there is in the transcendence involved in language a relationship that is not an empirical speech, but responsibility. This relationship is also a resignation (prior to any decision, in passivity) at the risk of misunderstanding (like in love, where, unless one does not love with love, one has to resign oneself to not being loved), at the risk of lack of and refusal of communication. The ego that thematizes is also founded in this responsibility and substitution. Regarding communication and transcendence one can indeed only speak of their uncertainty. Communication is an adventure of a subjectivity, different from that which is dominated by the concern to recover itself, different from that of coinciding in consciousness; it will involve uncertainty. It is by virtue of its eidos possible only in sacrifice, which is the approach of him for whom one is responsible. Communication with the other can be transcendent only as a dangerous life, a fine risk to be run. These words take on their strong sense when, instead of only designating the lack of certainty, they express the gratuity of sacrifice. In a fine risk to be run, the word 'fine' has not been thought about enough. It is as antithetical to certainty, and indeed to consciousness, that these terms take on their positive meaning, and are not the expression of a makeshift.

It is only in this way that the absolutely exterior other is near to the point of obsession. Here there is proximity and not truth about proximity, not certainty about the presence of the other, but responsibility for him without deliberation, and without the compulsion of truths in which commitments arise, without certainty. This responsibility commits me, and does so before any truth and any certainty, making the question of trust and norms an *idle* question, for in its uprightness a consciousness is not only naivety and opinion.[23]

The ethical language we have resorted to does not arise out of a special moral experience, independent of the description hitherto elaborated. The ethical situation of responsibility is not comprehensible on the basis of ethics. It does indeed arise from what Alphonse de Waelhens called non-philosophical experiences, which are ethically independent. The constraint that does not presuppose the will, nor even the core of being from which the will arises (or which it breaks up), and that we have described starting with persecution, has its place between the necessity of 'what cannot be otherwise' (Aristotle, *Metaphysics*, E), of what today we call eidetic necessity, and the constraint imposed on a will by the situation in which it finds itself, or by other wills and desires, or by the wills and desires of others. The tropes of ethical language are found to be adequate for certain structures of the description: for the sense of the approach in its contrast with knowing, the face in its contrast with a phenomenon.

Phenomenology can follow out the reverting of thematization into anarchy in the description of the approach. Then ethical language succeeds in expressing the paradox in which phenomenology finds itself abruptly thrown. For ethics, beyond politics, is found at the level of this reverting. Starting with the approach, the description finds the neighbour bearing the trace of a withdrawal that orders it as a face. This trace is significant for behaviour; and one would be wrong to forget its anarchic insinuation by confusing it with an indication, with the monstration of the signified in the signifier. For that is the itinerary by which theological and edifying thought too quickly deduces the truths of faith. Then obsession is subordinated to a principle that is stated in a theme, which annuls the very anarchy of its movement.[24] The trace in which a face is ordered is not reducible to a sign: a sign and its relationship with the signified are synchronic in a theme. The approach is not the thematization of any relationship, but is this very relationship, which resists thematization as anarchic. To thematize this relation is already to lose it, to leave the absolute passivity of the self. The passivity prior to the passivity-activity alternative, more passive than any inertia, is described by the ethical terms accusation, persecution, and responsibility for the others. The persecuted one is expelled from his place and has only himself to himself, has nothing in the world on which to rest his head. He is pulled out of every game and every war. Beyond auto-affection, which is still an activity, even if it is strictly contemporaneous with its passivity, the self is denuded in persecution, from which an accusation is inseparable, in the absolute passivity of being a creature, of substitution. In divesting the ego of its imperialism, the hetero-affection establishes a new undeclinability: the self, subjected to an absolute accusative, as though this accusation which it does not even have to assume came from it. The self involved in the *gnawing away at oneself* in responsibility, which is also incarnation, is not an objectification of the self by the ego. The self, the persecuted one, is accused beyond his fault before freedom, and thus in an unavowable innocence. One must not conceive it to be in the state of original sin; it is, on the contrary, the original goodness of creation. The persecuted one cannot defend himself by language, for the persecution is a disqualification of the apology. Persecution is the precise moment in which the subject is reached or touched with the mediation of the logos.[25]

'Finite Freedom'

The views that have been expounded can then not be reproached for the imprudence of affirming that the first word of the 'mind', that which makes all the others possible, and even the words 'negativity' and 'consciousness', would be the naive unconditioned 'Yes' of submission, negating truth, and all the highest values! The unconditionality of this *yes* is not that of an infantile spontaneity. It is the very exposure to critique, the exposure prior to consent, more ancient than any naive spontaneity. We have been accustomed to reason in the name of the freedom of the ego – as though I had witnessed the creation of the world, and as though I could only have been in charge of a world that would have issued out of my free will. These are presumptions of philosophers, presumptions of idealists! Or evasions of irresponsible ones. That is what Scripture reproaches Job for. He would have known how to explain his miseries if they could have devolved from his faults! But he never wished evil! His false friends think like he does: in a meaningful world one cannot be held to answer when one has not done anything. Job then must have forgotten his faults! But the subjectivity of a subject come late into a world which has not issued from his projects does not consist in projecting, or in treating this world as one's project. The 'lateness' is not insignificant. The limits it imposes on the freedom of subjectivity are not reducible to pure privation. To be responsible over and beyond one's freedom is certainly not to remain a pure result of the world.

To support the universe is a crushing charge, but a divine discomfort. It is better than the merits and faults and sanctions proportionate to the freedom of one's choices. If ethical terms arise in our discourse, before the terms freedom and non-freedom, it is because before the bipolarity of good and evil presented to choice, the subject finds himself committed to the Good in the very passivity of supporting. The distinction between free and non-free would not be the ultimate distinction between humanity and inhumanity, nor the ultimate mark of sense and nonsense. To understand intelligibility does not consist in going back to the beginning. There was a time irreducible to presence, an absolute unrepresentable past. Has not the Good chosen the subject with an election recognizable in the responsibility of being hostage, to which the subject is destined, which he cannot evade without denying himself, and by virtue of which he is unique? A philosopher can give to this election only the signification circumscribed by responsibility for the other. This antecedence of responsibility to freedom would signify the Goodness of the Good: the necessity that the Good choose me first before I can be in a position to choose, that is, welcome its choice. That is my pre-originary *susceptiveness*. It is a passivity prior to all receptivity, it is transcendent. It is an antecendence prior to all representable antecedence: immemorial. The Good is before being. There is diachrony: an unbridgeable difference between the Good and me, without simultaneity, odd terms. But also a non-indifference in this difference. The Good assigns the subject, according to a susception that cannot be assumed, to approach the other, the neighbour. This is an assignation to a non-erotic proximity,[26] to a desire of the non-desirable, to a desire of the stranger in the neighbour. It is outside of concupiscence, which for its part does not cease to seduce by the appearance of the Good. In a Luciferian way it takes on this appearance and thus claims to belong to the Good, gives itself out to be its equal, but in this very pretention which is an admission it remains subordinated. But this desire for the non-desirable, this responsibility for the neighbour, this substitution as a hostage, is the subjectivity and uniqueness of a subject.

From the Good to me, there is assignation: a relation that survives the 'death of God'. The death of God perhaps signifies only the possibility to reduce every value arousing an impulse to an impulse arousing a value. The fact that in its goodness the Good declines the desire it arouses while inclining it toward responsibility for the neighbour, preserves *difference* in the non-indifference of the Good, which chooses me before I welcome it. It preserves its *illeity* to the point of letting it be excluded from the analysis, save for the trace it leaves in words or the 'objective reality' in thoughts, according to the unimpeachable witness of Descartes' Third Meditation. That in the responsibility for another, the ego, already a self, already obsessed by the neighbour, would be unique and irreplaceable is what confirms its election. For the condition for, or the unconditionality of, the self does not begin in the auto-affection of a sovereign ego that would be, after the event, 'compassionate' for another. Quite the contrary: the uniqueness of the responsible ego is possible only *in* being obsessed by another, in the trauma suffered prior to any auto-identification, in an unrepresentable *before*. The one affected by the other is an anarchic trauma, or an inspiration of the one by the other, and not a causality striking mechanically a matter subject to its energy.[27] In this trauma the Good reabsorbs, or redeems, the violence of non-freedom. Responsibility is what first enables one to catch sight of and conceive of value.

What of the notion of finite freedom? No doubt the idea of a responsibility prior to freedom, and the compossibility of freedom and the other such as it shows itself in responsibility for another, enables us to confer an irreducible meaning to this notion, without attacking the dignity of freedom which is thus conceived in finitude. What else can finite freedom mean? How can a will be partially free? How can the Fichtean free ego undergo the suffering that would come to it from the non-ego? Does the finitude of freedom signify the necessity by which a will to will finds itself in a given situation which limits the arbitrariness of the will? That does not cut into the infinity of freedom beyond what the situation determines. In finite freedom, there can then be disengaged an element of pure freedom, which limitation does not affect, in one's will. Thus the notion of finite freedom rather poses than resolves the problem of a limitation of the freedom of the will.

The responsibility for another, an unlimited responsibility which the strict book-keeping of the free and non-free does not measure, requires subjectivity as an irreplaceable hostage. This subjectivity it denudes under the ego in a passivity of persecution, repression and expulsion outside of essence, into oneself. In this self, outside of essence, one is in a deathlike passivity! But in responsibility for the other for life and death, the adjectives unconditional, undeclinable, absolute take on meaning. They serve to qualify freedom, but wear away the substrate, from which the free act arises in essence. In the accusative form, which is a modification of no nominative form, in which I approach the neighbour for whom, without having wished it, I have to answer, the irreplaceable one is brought out (*s'accuse*). This finite freedom is not primary, is not initial; but it lies in an infinite responsibility where the other is not other because he strikes up against and limits my freedom, but where he can accuse me to the point of persecution, because the other, absolutely other, is another one (*autrui*). That is why finite freedom is not simply an infinite freedom operating in a limited field. The will which it animates wills in a passivity it does not assume. And the proximity of the neighbour in its trauma does not only strike up against me, but exalts and elevates me, and, in the literal sense of the term, inspires me. Inspiration, heteronomy, is the very pneuma of the psyche. Freedom is borne by the responsibility it could not shoulder, an elevation and inspiration without complacency. The for-the-other characteristic of the subject can be interpreted neither as a guilt complex (which presupposes an *initial* freedom), nor as a natural benevolence or divine 'instinct', nor as some love or some tendency to sacrifice. This is quite the opposite of the Fichtean conception, where all suffering due to the action of the non-ego is first a positing of this action of the non-ego by the ego.

But in the irreplaceable subject, unique and chosen as a responsibility and a substitution, a mode of freedom, ontologically impossible, breaks the unrendable essence. Substitution frees the subject from ennui, that is, from the enchainment to itself, where the ego suffocates in itself due to the tautological way of identity, and ceaselessly seeks after the distraction of games and sleep in a movement that never wears out. This liberation is not an action, a commencement, nor any vicissitude of essence and of ontology, where the equality with oneself would be established in the form of self-consciousness. An anarchic liberation, it emerges, without being assumed, without turning into a beginning, in inequality with oneself. It is brought out without being assumed, in the undergoing by sensibility beyond its capacity to undergo. This describes the suffering and vulnerability of the sensible as *the other in me*. The other is in me and in the midst of my very identification. The ipseity has become at odds with itself in its return to itself. The self-accusation of remorse gnaws away at the closed and firm core of consciousness, opening it, fissioning it. In consciousness equality and equilibrium between the trauma and the act is always reestablished. Or at least this equilibrium is sought in reflection and its *figures*, although the possibility of total reflection and of the unity of Mind, beyond the multiplicity of souls, is not effectively ensured. But is not that the way an other can of itself be in the same without alienating it, and without the emancipation of the same from itself turning into a slavery to anyone? This way is possible because, since an 'immemorial time', anarchically, in subjectivity the by-the-other is also the for-the-other. In suffering by the fault of the other dawns suffering for the fault of others, supporting. The for-the-other keeps all the patience of undergoing imposed by the other. There is substitution for another, expiation for another. Remorse is the trope of the literal sense of the sensibility. In its passivity is effaced the distinction between being accused and accusing oneself.

The recurrence in the subject is thus neither freedom of possession of self by self in reflection, nor the freedom of play where I take myself for this or that, traversing avatars under the carnival masks of history. It is a matter of an exigency coming from the other, beyond what is available in my powers, to open an unlimited 'deficit', in which the self spends itself without counting, freely. All the suffering and cruelty of essence weighs on a point that supports and expiates for it.

Essence, in its seriousness as *persistence in essence*, fills every interval of nothingness that would interrupt it. It is a strict book-keeping where nothing is lost nor created. Freedom is compromised in this balance of accounts in an order where responsibilities correspond exactly to liberties taken, where they compensate for them, where time relaxes and then is tightened again after having allowed a decision in the interval opened up. Freedom in the genuine sense can be only a contestation of this book-keeping by a gratuity. This gratuity could be the absolute *distraction* of a play without consequences, without traces or memories, of a pure pardon. Or, it could be responsibility for another and expiation.

In expiation, on a point of the essence there weighs the rest of the essence, to the point of expelling it. The self, the subjection or subjectivity of the subject, is the very over-emphasis of a responsibility for creation. Responsibility for the other, for what has not begun in me is responsibility in the innocence of being a hostage. My substitution for another is the trope of a sense that does not belong to the empirical order of psychological events, an *Einfühlung* or a compassion which signifies by virtue of this sense.

My substitution – it is as *my own* that substitution for the neighbour is produced. The Mind is a multiplicity of individuals. It is in me - in me and not in another, in me and not in an individuation of the concept Ego – that communication opens. It is I who am integrally or absolutely ego, and the absolute is my business. No one can substitute himself for me, who substitutes myself for all. Or, if one means to remain with the hierarchy of formal logic – genus, species, individual – it is in the course of the individuation of the ego in me that is realized the elevation in which the ego is for the neighbour, summoned to answer for him. When this relation is really thought through, it signifies the wound that cannot heal over of the self in the ego accused by the other to the point of persecution, and responsible for its persecutor. Subjection and elevation arise in patience above non-freedom. It is the subjection of the allegiance to the Good.

The disinterestedness of the subject is a descent or elevation of the ego to me. This movement is not reducible to the formalism of the logical operation of generalization or specification. Philosophy, which is consigned in the said, converts disinterestedness and its signification into essence and, by an abuse of language, to be sure, says that of which it is but a servant, but of which it makes itself master by saying it, and then reduces its pretensions in a new said. The subject posited as deposed is me; I universalize myself. And that is also my truth, my truth of being mortal, belonging to generation and corruption, which the negativity of the universalization presupposes. But the concept of the ego can correspond to me only inasmuch as it can signify responsibility, which summons me as irreplaceable. That is, in my flight out of concepts, which is not the naivety or blindness of non-thought, for positively it is responsibility for my neighbour. (It is time the abusive confusion of foolishness with morality was denounced.) Thus there is true movement between the conceptuality of the ego and the patience of a refusal of concepts, between universality and individuation, between mortality and responsibility. The very diachrony of truth is in this alternation. This ambiguity puts concepts into question inasmuch as it shakes the very idea of truth as a result, truth abiding in the present with an as it were mono-syllabic sense. The ego involved in responsibility is me and no one else, me with whom one would have liked to pair up a sister soul, from whom one would require substitution and sacrifice. But to say that the other has to sacrifice himself to the others would be to preach human sacrifice! 'Me' is not an inimitable nuance of *Jemeinigkeit* that would be added on to a being belonging to the genus 'soul' or 'man' or 'individual', and would thus be common to several souls, men and individuals, making reciprocity possible among them from the first. The uniqueness of the ego, overwhelmed by the other in proximity, is the other in the same, the psyche. But is it I, I and no one else, who am a hostage for the others. In substitution my being that belongs to me and not to another is undone, and it is through this substitution that I am not 'another', but me. The self in a being is exactly the not-being-able-to-slip-away-from an assignation that does not aim at any generality. There is no ipseity common to me and the others; 'me' is the exclusion from this possibility of comparison, as soon as comparison is set up. The ipseity is then a privilege or an unjustifiable election that chooses me and not the ego. I am unique and chosen; the election is in the subjection. The conceptualization of this last refusal of conceptualization is not contemporaneous with this refusal; it transcends this conceptualization. The transcendence separating itself from the consideration that conceptual-izes it, the diachrony of subjectivity, is my entry into the proximity of the neighbour.

Subjectivity is being hostage. This notion reverses the position where the presence of the ego to itself appears as the beginning or as the conclusion of philosophy.[28] This coinciding in the same, where I would be an origin, or, through memory, a covering over of the origin, this presence, is, from the start, undone by the other. The subject resting on itself is confounded by wordless accusation. For in discourse it would have already lost its trauma-tic violence. The accusation is in this sense persecuting; the persecuted one can no longer answer it. More exactly, it is accusation which I cannot answer, but for which I cannot decline responsibility. Already the position of the subject is a deposition, not a *conatus essendi*. It is from the first a substitution by a hostage expiating for the violence of the persecution itself. We have to conceive in such terms the de-substantiation of the subject, its de-reification, its disinterestedness, its subjection, its subjectivity. It is a pure self, in the accusative, responsible before there is freedom. Whatever be the ways that lead to the superstructure of society, in justice the dissymmetry that holds me at odds with regard to the other will find again law, autonomy, equality.

To say that the ego is a substitution is then not to state the universality of a principle, the quiddity of an ego, but, quite the contrary, it is to restore to the soul its egoity which supports no generalization. The way by which, from this situation, the logos arises to the concept of the ego passes through the third party.[29] The subject as an ego is not an entity provided with egoity as an eidetic structure, which should make it possible to form a concept of it, and make the singular entity be its realization.

Modern antihumanism, which denies the primacy that the human person, free and for itself, would have for the signification of being, is true over and beyond the reasons it gives itself. It clears the place for subjectivity positing itself in abnegation, in sacrifice, in a substitution which precedes the will. Its inspired intuition is to have abandoned the idea of person, goal and origin of itself, in which the ego is still a thing because it is still a being. Strictly speaking, the other is the end; I am a hostage, a responsibility and a substitution supporting the world in the passivity of assignation, even in an accusing persecution, which is undeclinable. Humanism has to be denounced only because it is not sufficiently human.

Will it be said that the world weighs with all its suffering and all its fault on the ego because this ego is a free consciousness, capable of sympathy and compassion? Will it be said that only a free being is sensitive to the weight of the world that weighs on it? Let us admit for a moment a free ego, capable of deciding for solidarity with others. At least it will be recognized that this freedom has no time to assume this urgent weight, and that consequently it is as checked or undone under the suffering. It is impossible to evade the appeal of the neighbour, to move away. One approaches the other perhaps in contingency, but henceforth one is not free to move away from him. The assumption of the suffering and the fault of another nowise goes beyond the passivity: it is a passion. This condition or unconditionality of being a hostage will then at least be an essential modality of freedom, the first, and not an empirical accident of the freedom, proud in itself, of the ego.

To be sure – but this is another theme – my responsibility for all can and has to manifest itself also in limiting itself. The ego can, in the name of this unlimited responsibility, be called upon to concern itself also with itself.

The fact that the other, my neighbour, is also a third party with respect to another, who is also a neighbour, is the birth of thought, consciousness, justice and philosophy. The unlimited initial responsibility, which justifies this concern for justice, for oneself, and for philosophy can be forgotten. In this forgetting consciousness is a pure egoism. But egoism is neither first nor last. The impossibility of escaping God, the adventure of Jonah indicates that God is at least here not a value among values. (I pronounce the word God without suppressing the intermediaries that lead me to this word, and, if I can say so, the anarchy of his entry into discourse, just as phenomenology states concepts without ever destroying the scaffoldings that permit one to climb up to them.) The impossibility of escaping God lies in the depths of myself as a self, as an absolute passivity. This passivity is not only the possibility of death in being, the possibility of impossibility. It is an impossibility prior to that possibility, the impossibility of slipping away, absolute susceptibility, gravity without any frivolity. It is the birth of a meaning in the obtuseness of being, of a 'being able to die' subject to sacrifice.

The self inasmuch as, in an approach, it abrogates the egoism of perseverance in being, which is the imperialism of the ego, introduces meaning into being. There could be no meaning in being which could not be measured to being. Mortality renders senseless any concern that the ego would have for its existence and its destiny. It would be but an evasion in a world without issue, and always ridiculous. No doubt nothing is more comical than the concern that a being has for an existence it could not save from its destruction, as in Tolstoy's tale where an order for enough boots for twenty-five years is sent by one that will die the very evening he gives his order. That is indeed as absurd as questioning, in view of action, the stars whose verdict would be without appeal. But through this image one sees that the comical is also tragic, and that it belongs to the same man to be a tragic and a comical personage.

The approach, inasmuch as it is a sacrifice, confers a sense on death. In it the absolute singularity of the responsible one encompasses the generality or generalization of death. In it life is no longer measured by being, and death can no longer introduce the absurd into it. Death gives lie to pleasure, in which for the space of an instant the tragi-comedy is forgotten, and which would be defined by this forgetting. But despite all its adversity, it is accorded with the for-the-other of approach. No one is so hypocritical as to claim that he has taken from death its sting, not even the promisers of religions. But we can have responsibilities and attachments through which death takes on a meaning. That is because, from the start, the other affects us despite ourselves.

If one had the right to retain one trait from a philosophical system and neglect all the details of its architecture (even though there are no details in architecture, according to Valéry's profound dictum, which is eminently valid for philosophical construction, where the details alone prevent collapse), we would think here of Kantism, which finds a meaning to the human without measuring it by ontology and outside of the question 'What is there here . . . ?' that one would like to take to be preliminary, outside of the immortality and death which ontologies run up against. The fact that immortality and theology could not determine the categorical imperative signifies the novelty of the Copernican revolution: a sense that is not measured by being or not being; but being on the contrary is determined on the basis of sense.

NOTES

This chapter was the germ of *Otherwise than Being*. Its principal elements were presented in a public lecture at the Faculté Universitaire Saint-Louis in Brussels, on 30 November 1967. That talk was a continuation of the lecture entitled 'Proximity' given the previous day, and which was substantially the same text as the study entitled 'Langage et Proximité' subsequently published in the second edition of our book *En découvrant l'existence avec Husserl et Heidegger* (Paris: Vrin, 1967). The two lectures 'La Proximité' and 'La Substitution' were given the general title 'Au-delà de l'Essence.'. The text of the second lecture published in the *Revue Philosophique de Louvain* (August, 1968) represented a finished version of the lecture. Certain developments have been formulated in a more severe manner for the reader, who can go further than the listener. Notes were also added. In its present form that text has been further modified.

1 If the anarchical were not signalled in consciousness, it would reign in its own way. The anarchical is possible only when contested by language, which betrays, but conveys, its anarchy, without abolishing it, by an abuse of language.

2 Cf. the pages Bergson has written, in *Creative Evolution*, concerning the notion of disorder, which deserve close attention. Subversion and revolution remain within order. This is to be compared with Hegel: what in the experience of a 'new object' appears to consciousness as the 'annihilation of a prior object', the philosopher, who can see what is 'behind consciousness', sees as the result of a genesis, something coming to birth in the same dialectical order (cf. Hegel, *Phenomenology of Spirit*, p. 120). The movement of genesis traverses the State and issues in absolute knowledge, which fulfills consciousness. The notion of anarchy we are introducing here has a meaning prior to the political (or antipolitical) meaning currently attributed to it. It would be self-contradictory to set it up as a principle (in the sense that anarchists understand it). Anarchy cannot be sovereign, like an *arche*. It can only disturb the State – but in a radical way, making possible moments of negation *without any* affirmation. The State then cannot set itself up as a Whole. But, on the other hand, anarchy can be stated.

Yet disorder has an irreducible meaning, as refusal of synthesis. Cf. p. 191, note 6.

3 Yet this is an inability which is *said*. Anarchy does not *reign*, and thus remains in ambiguity, in enigma, and leaves a trace which speech, in the pain of expression, seeks to state. But there is only a trace.

4 It is a relationship without any a priori which arises from a spontaneity, not from that which ontology requires in a finite thought. For, in order to welcome entities finite thought, a pure receptivity, must operate as a transcendental imagination, formative of the imaginary.

5 It is not a question here of descending toward the unconscious, which, defined in a purely negative way with reference to the conscious, preserves the structure of self-knowledge (whatever be the unexpected ramifications that would then complicate this structure), of a quest of self, though it be led astray on obstructed byways. The unconscious remains a play of consciousness, and psychoanalysis means to ensure its outcome, against the troubles that come to it from repressed desires, in the name of the very rules of this game. The play of consciousness does indeed involve rules, but irresponsibility in the game is declared to be a sickness. The play of consciousness is a game par excellence, 'transcendental imagination', but as such source of phantasms.

6 We continue to use the term *essence*, underscored, as an abstract noun of action for being as distinguished from entities in the amphibology of being and entities.

7 Cf. *En découvrant l'existence avec Husserl et Heidegger*, 2nd edn. pp. 217–23.

8 The singularity of the subject is not the uniqueness of an *hapax*. For it is not due to some distinctive quality, like fingerprints, that would make of it an incomparable *unicum*, and, as a principle of individuation, make this unity deserve a proper noun, and hence a place in discourse. The identity of the oneself is not the inertia of a quiddity individuated by an ultimate specific difference inherent in the body or in character, or by the uniqueness of a natural or historical conjuncture. It is in the uniqueness of someone summoned.

9 Heidegger's analysis describes anxiety over the limitation of being. Inasmuch as this analysis is not to be read as simply psychological or anthropological, it teaches us that form (which in our philosophical tradition defines a being) is always too small for a being. Definition, which, as form, 'formosity', is beauty, lustre and appearing, is also strangulation, that is, anguish. The disproportion between Being and its phenomenality, the fact that Being is cramped in its manifestation, would then be produced in anthropological form in a finite being understood as being-existing-for-death. The measure of a determination would thus be the evil measurement of a Nessus tunic. But anxiety as being-for-death is also the hope to reach the deep of non-being. The possibility of deliverance (and the temptation to suicide) arises in death anxiety: like nothingness, death is an openness into which, along with a being, the anxiety over its definition is engulfed. But, on the other hand, anxiety as the tightness of the 'going forth into fullness', is the recurrence of the oneself, but without evasion, without shrinking, that is, a responsibility stronger than death – which Plato in the *Phaedo* affirms in his own way, in condemning suicide (62b).

10 The notion of the hither side is indeed justified by this text from the *Parmenides*.

There is question of a withdrawal, a reclusion, which does not go outside of the world in a chimerical effort to set itself up as a force freed from the world and endowed with spiritual powers which may triumph or fail – which would still be to be a presence in the world and in the history of a state or a church. That would amount to a hyperbole of ontological, logical and archic relations, an amplification of order, even though the hyperbole resorts to the superlative of the beyond being. Triumphs and failures presuppose personal freedom, and, consequently, an I endowed with political and religious sovereignty or political principality. On the hither side of that, the I is itself, does not belong to Being or history, is neither an effect at rest nor a cause in movement. The reclusion 'in one's own skin', the present essay wishes to suggest, is a movement of the ego into itself, outside of order. The departure from this subterranean digs, from the plenum into the plenum, leads to a region in which all the weight of being is borne and supported in the other.

11 The body is neither an obstacle opposed to the soul, nor a tomb that imprisons it, but that by which the self is susceptibility itself. Incarnation is an extreme passivity; to be exposed to sickness, suffering, death, is to be exposed to compassion, and, as a self, to the gift that costs. The oneself is on this side of the zero of inertia and nothingness, in deficit of being, in itself and not in being, without a place to lay its head, in the no-grounds, and thus without conditions. As such it will be shown to be the bearer of the world, bearing it, suffering it, blocking rest and lacking a fatherland. It is the correlate of a persecution, a substitution for the other.

12 This freedom enveloped in a responsibility which it does not succeed in shouldering is the way of being a creature, the unlimited passivity of a self, the unconditionality of a self.

13 Lamentations, 3: 30.

14 In Otrepiev's dream, thrice repeated, in Pushkin's *Boris Godunov*, the false Dmitri catches sight of his future sovereignty in the equivocal laughter of the people: '. . . from above Moscow appeared to me like an anthill, below the people were boiling and pointed to me and laughed. I was overcome with shame and fear and in throwing myself down head first, I awoke.' Laughter at the bottom of the gesture that points me out, shame and fear of the ego, the 'accusative' where everything designates me and assigns me, awakening in a headlong fall – all this is the unconditionality of the subject behind its sovereignty.

15 Every idea of evasion, as every idea of malediction weighing on a destiny, already presupposes the ego constituted on the basis of the self and already free.

16 The passivity of the self in the in-itself does not enter into the framework of the distinction between attitude and category. The category, as Eric Weil wishes, is obtained by reflection on an attitude, which is a liberation from the attitude and its particularity. By comparison with the passivity or patience of the Self, the attitude is already freedom and position. The passivity of the self precedes the voluntary act that ventures toward a project, and even the certainty which in truth is coinciding with itself. The oneself is prior to self-coinciding.

17 Identity not of a soul in general, but of me, for in me alone innocence can be

accused without absurdity. To accuse the innocence of the other, to ask of the other more than he owes, is criminal.

18 All the descriptions of the face in the three final studies of the second edition of our book *En découvrant l'existence avec Husserl et Heidegger* which describe the very ambiguity or enigma of anarchy – the illeity of infinity in the face as the trace of the withdrawal which the infinite *qua* infinite effects before coming, and which addresses the other to my responsibility – remain descriptions of the non-thematizable, the anarchical, and, consequently, do not lead to any theological thesis. Language can none the less speak of it, if only by an abuse of language, and it thus confirms the fact that it is impossible for the anarchical to be constituted as a sovereignty – which implies the unconditionality of anarchy. But the hold of language on the anarchical is not a mastery, for otherwise anarchy would be subordinate to the *archè* of consciousness. This hold is the struggle and pain of expression. Whence comes discourse and the necessity of the *archè* of sovereignty and of the State; we shall speak of that further (chapter V of *Otherwise than Being*, pp. 156ff). It is clear also that in our way of interpreting signifyingness, the practical order (and the religious which is inseparable from the practical) is defined by the anarchical. Theology would be possible only as the contestation of the purely religious, and confirms it only by its failures or its struggles.

19 One could be tempted to take substitution to be the being of the entity that is the ego. And, to be sure, the hither side of the ego lends itself to our speaking only by referring to being, from which it withdraws and which it undoes. The said of language always says being. But in the moment of an enigma language also breaks with its own conditions, as in a sceptical saying, and says a signification before the event, a before-being. Events happen to subjects that undergo or provoke them. The verbs by which the events are said and the nouns by which the subjects are said are formalized, even the verb being, even the noun being. The homonym is here an extreme amphibology in which the difference rests not on a common genus, but uniquely on the commonness of the word. Language thus shows itself to be something quite different from a doubling up of thoughts. The oneself and substitution do not enter into this framework. The defection or already the defeat of the identity of the ego, which can finally be said to be the event of the oneself, precedes every event undergone or conducted by a subject. On the hither side is expressed precisely in the term anarchy. It is identity undone to the limit, without being remade in the other, prior to a transubstantiation into another avatar and prior to the putting in place of an other. For it does not rest in the other, but remains in itself without rest. There is a requisition with no escape possible, which, as the irreplaceable one itself is uniqueness.

20 The vortex – suffering of the other, my pity for his suffering, his pain over my pity, my pain over his pain, etc. – stops at me. The I is what involves one movement more in this iteration. My suffering is the cynosure of all the sufferings – and of all the faults, even of the fault of my persecutors, which amounts to suffering the ultimate persecution, suffering absolutely. This is not a purifying fire of suffering, which magically would count here. This element of a 'pure born', for nothing, in suffering, is the passivity of suffering which prevents its

reverting into suffering assumed, in which the for-the-other of sensibility, that is, its very sense, would be annulled. This moment of the 'for nothing' in suffering is the surplus of non-sense over sense by which the sense of suffering is possible. The incarnation of the self and its possibilities of gratuitous pain must be understood in function of the absolute accusative characteristic of the self, a passivity prior to all passivity at the bottom of matter becoming flesh. But in the anarchic character of suffering, and prior to all reflection, we have to catch sight of a suffering of suffering, a suffering because of what is pitiful in my suffering, which is a suffering 'for God' who suffers from my suffering. There is an anarchic trace of God in passivity.

21 Substitution operates in the entrails of the self, rending its inwardness, putting its identity out of phase and disrupting its recurrence. Yet this occurs in the impossibility for me to evade substitution, which confers uniqueness on this ever failing identity of the oneself. Substitution is a communication from the one to the other and from the other to the one without the two relations having the same sense. It is not like the reversibility of the two-way road open to the circulation of information, where the direction is indifferent. We have shown above this dissymmetry of communication in the analysis of proximity. It is the proximity of the third party (cf. chapter V of *Otherwise than Being*) that introduces, with the necessities of justice, measure, thematization, appearing and justice. It is on the basis of the self and of substitution that being will have a meaning. Being will be non-indifferent, not because it would be living or anthropomorphic, but because, postulated by justice which is contemporaneousness or copresence, space belongs to the sense of my responsibility for the other. The everywhere of space is the from everywhere of faces that concern me and put me in question, despite the indifference that seems to present itself to justice. Being will have a meaning as a universe and the unity of the universe will be in me as subject to being. That means that the space of the universe will manifest itself as the dwelling of the others. It is inasmuch as it is inhabited by the others that look at me that the pre-geometrical eidos of space is described. I support the universe. The self does not only form the unity of human society, which is one in my responsibility. The unity of being has to do with the self.

22 Cf. chapter V, 2.

23 Here one has to denounce the suspicion that objectivism casts over all philosophy of subjectivity, and which consists in measuring and controlling the ego by what is objectively observable. Such a position is possible, but arbitrary. Even if the ego were but a reflection forming an illusion and contenting itself with false semblances, it would have a signification of its own precisely as this possibility of quitting the objective and universal order and abiding in itself. Quitting the objective order is possible in the direction of a responsibility beyond freedom as well as toward the freedom without responsibility of play. The ego is at the crossroads. But to quit the objective order to go in oneself toward the privatissime of sacrifice and death, to enter upon the subjective ground, is not something that happens by caprice, but is possible only under the weight of all the responsibilities.

24 Thus theological language destroys the religious situation of transcendence. The

infinite 'presents' itself anarchically, but thematization loses the anarchy which alone can accredit it. Language about God rings false or becomes a myth, that is, can never be taken literally.

25 Proximity, obsession and subjectivity as we have expressed them are not reducible to phenomena of consciousness. But their un-consciousness, instead of giving evidence of a preconscious stage or a repression which would oppress them, is one with their exception from totality, that is, their refusal of manifestation. Inasmuch as essence is not separable from exposition, and thus from the ideality of the logos and the kerygmatic principality, this exception is non-being or anarchy, prior to the still ontological alternative of being and nothingness, prior to essence. Non-consciousness is to be sure characteristic of mechanical phenomena or the repression of psychic structures. From this comes the pretension of mechanism or psychologism to universality. But the non-conscious can be read in a different way on the basis of its traces, and undo the categories of mechanism. The non-conscious is understood as the non-voluntary event of persecution, which *qua* persecution breaks off every justification, every apology, every logos. This reduction to silence is a passivity beneath every material passivity. This absolute passivity beneath the neutrality of things takes on the form of incarnation, corporeity – susceptibility to pain, outrage and unhappiness. It hears in its susceptibility the trace of this *hither side* of things, as the responsibility for that of which there was no will, in the persecuted one, in ipseity, that is, as responsibility for the very persecution it suffers.

26 If obsession is suffering and contrarity, it is that the altruism of subjectivity-hostage is not a tendency, is not a natural benevolence, as in the moral philosophies of feeling. It is against nature, non-voluntary, inseparable from the possible persecution to which no consent is thinkable, anarchic. The persecution reduces the ego to itself, to the absolute accusative in which there is imputed to the ego a fault it has not committed or willed, and which confounds it in its freedom. Egoism and altruism and posterior to responsibility, which makes them possible. Egoism is not a term of the alternative of which altruism would be the other term, freedom choosing in indifference. The terms are not of the same order, but only the ethical qualification here distinguishes the equivalents. But values are valid before freedom: responsibility precedes it. Persecution is a trauma, violence par excellence without warning or a priori, without possible apology, without logos. Persecution leads back to a resignation not consented to, and consequently crosses a night of unconsciousness. That is the sense of the unconscious, night in which the reverting of the ego into itself under the trauma of persecution occurs, a passivity more passive still than every passivity on the side of identity, responsibility, substitution.

27 Perhaps the notion of anarchy accounts for the notion of worth, whose dimension is so difficult to distinguish from the being of entities. To be worth is to 'weigh' on the subject, but otherwise than the way a cause weighs on an effect, a being on the thought to which it presents itself, an end on the tendency or the will it solicits. What does this 'otherwise' mean? We think that worth gives rise to a susceptibility incapable of thematizing it, that is, a susceptibility which cannot assume what it receives, but which, in spite of itself, becomes responsible

for it. Value in its original radiation renders 'pure' or 'impure' before any intentional movement, without there being a free attitude toward value that could be taken up. The death of the other makes me impure through its proximity, and explains the *Noli me tangere*. That is not a phenomenon of the mystical mentality, but an ineffaceable moment which the notion of value brings us back to.

28 Cf. 'Enigme et phénomène' in *En découvrant l'existence avec Husserl et Heidegger*, 2nd edn, pp. 203–16.

29 Cf. chapter V, sect. 3. I cannot detach myself from the self, that is, suspend the responsibility that is incumbent on me and on no one else, independently of the questions and answers of free dialogue, which persecution paralyzes without annulling responsibility, whereas I can pardon others in their alterity inasmuch as they are subsumed under the concept of the ego. Here there is a priority of the self before all freedom (or non-freedom).

Translated by Alphonso Lingis

PART II

Reading, Writing, Revolution
or Aesthetics, Religion, Politics

7

Reality and Its Shadow

Published in *Les Temps Modernes*, 38 (1948), 771–89 and included in the English-language volume of *Collected Philosophical Papers* edited by Alphonso Lingis (Dordrecht: Martinus Nijhoff, 1987), pp. 1–13, Levinas's most controversial application of ethical responsibility to the field of aesthetics is famous for the extraordinary riposte which it provoked from the editorial board of *Les Temps Modernes*, who actually prefaced the article with their own Sartrean objections, on pp. 769–70.

In Levinas's view, art offers images, whereas criticism speaks through concepts. These images are interesting in the literal sense (inter-esse) without being useful. The way in which the closed world of art therefore freezes time within images doubles and immobilizes being: characters suffer an eternal anxiety, imprisoned in an inhuman interval. The disengagement this encourages means that art is an evasion of responsibility, since it offers consolation rather than a challenge. Only criticism relates this irresponsibility to real history once more by measuring the distance between the myth proposed by art, and real being. Levinas appears to be replying to Heidegger's 'poetically man dwells' (in *Poetry, Language, Thought*, translated and introduced by Albert Hofstadter (London and New York: Harper and Row, 1971), pp. 211–29) with the view that *criticism* is the basic capacity for human dwelling in so far as the term signifies a primordial relation with the other.

The preface in *Les Temps Modernes* claims that Levinas has ignored Sartre's treatment of this subject. It is true that, in François Poirié's book, Levinas admits (on p. 88) that he merely flicked through *Being and Nothingness* after returning from captivity during the war. But Levinas's article surely reveals a knowledge of, and disagreement with, the notion of the analogon proposed by Sartre in *L'Imaginaire*, a phenomenological study of the imagination produced in 1940. The *Temps Modernes* preface itself reminds us how *L'Imaginaire* reveals a deep mistrust of the word-image which can lure us into a state of hypnotic inertia, producing a degraded form of knowledge and thought. The preface then goes on to show how in *Situations II* Sartre is anxious to isolate literature and the possibility of commitment which it represents from those arts which do not convey conceptual meaning, adding that philosophical expression in any case is faced with no less a task than artistic expression when it comes to making real contact with the world.

Sartre's theory of literature is summarized in *Literature and Existentialism* (cited in note 2) and his *Literary and Philosophical Essays* (taken from *Situations II* and III), translated by Annette Michelson (New York: Collier, 1955, 1965 and London:

Hutchinson, 1968). For further reading one may also usefully consult Christina Howells, *Sartre's Theory of Literature* (London: Modern Humanities Research Association, 1979).

S.H.

———————

Art and Criticism

It is generally, dogmatically, admitted that the function of art is expression, and that artistic expression rests on cognition. An artist – even a painter, even a musician – tells. He tells of the ineffable. An artwork prolongs, and goes beyond, common perception. What common perception trivializes and misses, an artwork apprehends in its irreducible essence. It thus coincides with metaphysical intuition. Where common language abdicates, a poem or a painting speaks. Thus an artwork is more real than reality and attests to the dignity of the artistic imagination, which sets itself up as knowledge of the absolute. Though it be disparaged as an aesthetic canon, realism nevertheless retains all its prestige. In fact it is repudiated only in the name of a higher realism. Surrealism is a superlative.

Criticism too professes this dogma. It enters into the artist's game with all the seriousness of science. In artworks it studies psychology, characters, environments, and landscapes – as though in an aesthetic event an object were by the microscope or telescope of artistic vision exposed for the curiosity of an investigator. But, alongside of difficult art, criticism seems to lead a parasitic existence. A depth of reality inaccessible to conceptual intelligence becomes its prey. Or else criticism substitutes itself for art. Is not to interpret Mallarmé to betray him? Is not to interpret his work faithfully to suppress it? To say clearly what he says obscurely is to reveal the vanity of his obscure speech.

Criticism as a distinct function of literary life, expert and professional criticism, appearing as an item in newspapers and journals and in books, can indeed seem suspect and pointless. But it has its source in the mind of the listener, spectator or reader; criticism exists as a public's mode of comportment. Not content with being absorbed in aesthetic enjoyment, the public feels an irresistible need to speak. The fact that there might be something for the public to say, when the artist refuses to say about artwork anything in addition to the work itself, the fact that one cannot contemplate in silence, justifies the critic. He can be defined as the one that still has something to say when everything has been said, that can say about the work something else than that work.

One then has the right to ask if the artist really knows and speaks. He does in a preface or a manifesto, certainly; but then he is himself a part of the public. If art originally were neither language nor knowledge, if it were therefore situated outside of 'being in the world' which is coextensive with truth,[1] criticism would be rehabilitated. It would represent the intervention of the understanding necessary for integrating the inhumanity and inversion of art into human life and into the mind.

Perhaps the tendency to apprehend the aesthetic phenomenon in literature, where speech provides the material for the artist, explains the contemporary dogma of knowledge through art. We are not always attentive to the transformation that speech undergoes in literature. Art as speech, art as knowledge, then brings on the problem of committed art, which is a problem of committed literature.[2] The completion, the indelible seal of artistic production by which the artwork remains essentially disengaged, is underestimated – that supreme moment when the last brush stroke is done, when there is not another word to add to or to strike from the text, by virtue of which every artwork is classical. Such completion is different from the simple interruption which limits language and the works of nature and industry. Yet we might wonder if we should not recognize an element of art in the work of craftsmen, in all human work, commercial and diplomatic, in the measure that, in addition to its perfect adaptation to its ends, it bears witness to an accord with some destiny extrinsic to the course of things, which situates it outside the world, like the forever bygone past of ruins, like the elusive strangeness of the exotic. The artist stops because the work refuses to accept anything more, appears saturated. The work is completed *in spite of* the social or material causes that interrupt it. It does not give itself out as the beginning of a dialogue.

This completion does not necessarily justify the academic aesthetics of art for art's sake. The formula is false inasmuch as it situates art *above* reality and recognizes no master for it, and it is immoral inasmuch as it liberates the artist from his duties as a man and assures him of a pretentious and facile nobility. But a work would not belong to art if it did not have this formal structure of completion, if at least in this way it were not disengaged. We have to understand the value of this disengagement, and first of all its meaning. Is to disengage oneself from the world always to go *beyond*, toward the region of Platonic ideas and toward the eternal which towers above the world? Can one not speak of a disengagement on the hither side – of an interruption of time by a movement going on on the hither side of time, in its 'interstices'?

To go beyond is to communicate with ideas, to understand. Does not the function of art lie in not understanding? Does not obscurity provide it with its very element and a completion sui generis, foreign to dialectics and the life of ideas? Will we then say that the artist knows and expresses the very obscurity of the real? But that leads to a much more general question, to which this whole discussion of art is subordinate: in what does the *non-truth* of being consist? Is it always to be defined by comparison with truth, as what is left over after *understanding*? Does not the commerce with the obscure, as a totally independent ontological event, describe categories irreducible to thsoe of cognition? We should like to show this event in art. Art does not know a particular type of reality; it contrasts with knowledge. It is the very event of obscuring, a descent of the night, an invasion of shadow. To put it in theological terms, which will enable us to delimit however roughly our ideas by comparison with contemporary notions: art does not belong to the order of revelation. Nor does it belong to that of creation, which moves in just the opposite direction.

The Imaginary, the Sensible, the Musical

The most elementary procedure of art consists in substituting for the object its image. Its image, and not its concept. A concept is the object *grasped*, the intelligible object. Already by action we maintain a living relationship with a real object; we grasp it, we conceive it. The image neutralizes this real relationship, this primary conceiving through action. The well-known disinterestedness of artistic vision, which the current aesthetic analysis stops with, signifies above all a blindness to concepts.

But the disinterestedness of the artist scarcely deserves this name. For it excludes freedom, which the notion of disinterestedness implies. Strictly speaking, it also excludes bondage, which presupposes freedom. An image does not engender a *conception*, as do scientific cognition and truth; it does not involve Heidegger's 'letting be', *Sein-lassen*, in which objectivity is transmuted into power.[3] An image marks a hold over us rather than our initiative, a fundamental passivity. Possessed, inspired, an artist, we say, harkens to a muse. An image is musical. Its passivity is directly visible in magic, song, music, and poetry. The exceptional structure of aesthetic existence invokes this singular term magic, which will enable us to make the somewhat worn-out notion of passivity precise and concrete.

The idea of rhythm, which art criticism so frequently invokes but leaves in the state of a vague suggestive notion and catch-all, designates not so much an inner law of the poetic order as the way the poetic order affects us, closed wholes whose elements call for one another like the syllables of a verse, but do so only insofar as they impose themselves on us, disengaging themselves from reality. *But they impose themselves on us without our assuming them.* Or rather, our consenting to them is inverted into a participation. Their entry into us is one with our entry into them. Rhythm represents a unique situation where we cannot speak of consent, assumption, initiative or freedom, because the subject is caught up and carried away by it. The subject is part of its own representation. It is so not even despite itself, for in rhythm there is no longer a oneself, but rather a sort of passage from oneself to anonymity. This is the captivation or incantation of poetry and music. It is a mode of being to which applies neither the form of consciousness, since the I is there stripped of its prerogative to assume, its power, nor the form of unconsciousness, since the whole situation and all its articulations are in a dark light, *present*. Such is a waking dream. Neither habits, reflexes, nor instinct operate in this light. The particular automatic character of a walk or a dance to music is a mode of being where nothing is unconscious, but where consciousness, paralyzed in its freedom, plays, totally absorbed in this playing. To listen to music is in a sense to refrain from dancing or stepping; the movement or gesture is of little import. It would be more appropriate to talk of interest than of disinterestedness with respect to images. An image is interesting, without the slightest sense of utility, interesting in the sense of *involving*, in the etymological sense – to be *among* things which should have had only the status of objects. To be 'among things' is different from Heidegger's 'being-in-the-world'; it constitutes the pathos of the imaginary world of dreams – the subject is among things not only by virtue of its density of being, requiring a 'here', a 'somewhere', and retaining its freedom; it is among things as a thing, as part of the spectacle. It is exterior to itself, but with an exteriority which is not that of a body, since the pain of the I-actor is felt by the I-spectator, and not through compassion. Here we have really an exteriority of the inward. It is surprising that phenomenological analysis never tried to apply this fundamental paradox of rhythm and dreams, which describes a sphere situated outside of the conscious and the unconscious, a sphere whose role in all ecstatic rites has been shown by ethnography; it is surprising that we have stayed with metaphors of 'ideomotor' phenomena and with the study of the prolongation of sensations into actions. Here we shall use the terms rhythm and musical while thinking of this reversal of power into participation.

Then we must detach them from the arts of sound where they are ordinarily envisioned exclusively, and draw them out into a general aesthetic category. Rhythm certainly does have its privileged locus in music, for the musician's element realizes the pure deconceptualization of reality. Sound is the quality most detached from an object. Its relation with the substance from which it emanates is not inscribed in its quality. It resounds impersonally. Even its timbre, a trace of its belonging to an object, is submerged in its quality, and does not retain the structure of a relation. Hence in listening we do not apprehend a 'something', but are without concepts: musicality belongs to sound naturally. And indeed, among all the classes of images distinguished by traditional psychology, the image of sound is most akin to real sound. To insist on the musicality of every image is to see in an image its detachment from an object, that independence from the category of substance which the analyses of our textbooks ascribe to pure sensation not yet converted into perception (sensation as an adjective), which for empirical psychology remains a limit case, a purely hypothetical given.

It is as though sensation free from all conception, that famous sensation that eludes introspection, appeared with images. Sensation is not a residue of perception, but has a function of its own – the hold that an image has over us, a function of rhythm. What is today called being-in-the-world is an existence with concepts. Sensibility takes place as a distinct ontological event, but is realized only by the imagination.

If art consists in substituting an image for being, the aesthetic element, as its etymology indicates, is sensation. The whole of our world, with its elementary and intellectually elaborated givens, can touch us musically, can become an image. That is why classical art which is attached to objects – all those paintings, all those statues representing *something*, all those poems which recognize syntax and punctuation – conforms no less to the true essence of art than the modern works which claim to be pure music, pure painting, pure poetry, because they drive objects out of the world of sounds, colours and words into which those works introduce us – because they break up representation. A represented object, by the simple fact of becoming an image, is converted into a non-object; the image as such enters into categories proper to it which we would like to bring out here. The disincarnation of reality by an image is not equivalent to a simple diminution in degree. It belongs to an ontological dimension that does not extend between us and a reality to be captured, a dimension where commerce with reality is a rhythm.

Image and Resemblance

The phenomenology of images insists on their transparency. The intention of one who contemplates an image is said to go directly through the image, as through a window, into the world it represents, and aims at an *object*.[4] Yet nothing is more mysterious than the term 'world it represents' – since representation expresses just that function of an image that still remains to be determined.

The theory of transparency was set up in reaction to the theory of mental images, of an inner tableau which the perception of an object would leave in us. In imagination our gaze then always goes outward, but imagination modifies or neutralizes this gaze: the real world appears in it as it were between parentheses or quote marks. The problem is to make clear what these devices used in writing mean. The imaginary world is said to present itself as unreal – but can one say more about this unreality?

In what does an image differ from a symbol, a sign, or a word? By the very way it refers to its object: resemblance. But that supposes that thought stops on the image itself; it consequently supposes a certain opacity of the image. A sign, for its part, is pure transparency, nowise counting for itself. Must we then come back to taking the image as an independent reality which resembles the original? No, but on condition that we take resemblance not as the result of a comparison between an image and the original, but as the very movement that engenders the image. Reality would not be only what it is, what it is disclosed to be in truth, but would be also its double, its shadow, its image.

Being is not only itself, it escapes itself. Here is a person who is what he is; but he does not make us forget, does not absorb, cover over entirely the objects he holds and the way he holds them, his gestures, limbs, gaze, thought, skin, which escape from under the identity of his substance, which like a torn sack is unable to contain them. Thus a person bears on his face, alongside of its being with which he coincides, its own caricature, its picturesqueness. The picturesque is always to some extent a caricature. Here is a familiar everyday thing, perfectly adapted to the hand which is accustomed to it, but its qualities, colour, form, and position at the same time remain as it were behind its being, like the 'old garments' of a soul which had withdrawn from that thing, like a 'still life'. And yet all this is the person and is the thing. There is then a duality in this person, this thing, a duality in its being. It is what it is and it is a stranger to itself, and there is a relationship between these two moments. We will say the thing is itself and is its image. And that this relationship between the thing and its image is resemblance.

This situation is akin to what a fable brings about. Those animals that portray men give the fable its peculiar colour inasmuch as men are seen *as* these animals and not only *through* these animals; the animals stop and fill up thought. It is in this that all the power and originality of allegory lies. An allegory is not a simple auxiliary to thought, a way of rendering an abstraction concrete and popular for childlike minds, a poor man's symbol. It is an ambiguous commerce with reality in which reality does not refer to itself but to its reflection, its shadow. An allegory thus represents what in the object itself doubles it up. An image, we can say, is an allegory of being.

A being is that which is, that which reveals itself in its truth, and, at the same time, it resembles itself, is its own image. The original gives itself as though it were at a distance from itself, as though it were withdrawing itself, as though something in a being delayed behind being. The consciousness of the absence of the object which characterizes an image is not equivalent to a simple neutralization of the thesis, as Husserl would have it, but is equivalent to an alteration of the very being of the object, where its essential forms appear as a garb that it abandons in withdrawing. To contemplate an image is to contemplate a picture. The image has to be understood by starting with the phenomenology of pictures, and not the converse.

In the vision of the represented object a painting has a density of its own: it is itself an object of the gaze. The consciousness of the representation lies in knowing that the object is not there. The perceived elements are not the object but are like its 'old garments', spots of colour, chunks of marble or bronze. These elements do not serve as symbols, and in the absence of the object they do not force its presence, but by their presence insist on its absence. They occupy its place fully to mark its removal, as though the represented object died, were degraded, were disincarnated in its own reflection. The painting then does not lead us beyond the given reality, but somehow to the hither side of it. It is a symbol in reverse. The poet and painter who have discovered the 'mystery' and 'strangeness' of the world they inhabit every day are free to think that they have gone beyond the real. The mystery of being is not its myth. The artist moves in a universe that precedes (in what sense we will see below) the world of creation, a universe that the artist has already gone beyond by his thought and his everyday actions.

The idea of shadow or reflection to which we have appealed – of an essential doubling of reality by its image, of an ambiguity 'on the hither side' – extends to the light itself, to thought, to the inner life. The whole of reality bears on its face its own allegory, outside of its revelation and its truth. In utilizing images art not only reflects, but brings about this allegory. In art allegory is introduced into the world, as truth is accomplished in cognition. These are two contemporary possibilities of being. Alongside of the simultaneity of the idea and the soul – that is, of being and its disclosure – which the *phaedo* teaches, there is the simultaneity of a being and its reflection. The absolute at the same time reveals itself to reason and lends itself to a sort of erosion, outside of all causality. Non-truth is not an obscure residue of being, but is its sensible character itself, by which there is resemblance and images in the world. Because of resemblance the Platonic world of becoming is a lesser world, of appearances only. As a dialectic of being and non-being, becoming does indeed, since the *Parmenides*, make its appearance in the world of Ideas. It is through imitation that participation engenders shadows, distinct from the participation of the Ideas in one another which is revealed to the understanding. The discussion over the primacy of art or of nature – does art imitate nature or does natural beauty imitate art? – fails to recognize the simultaneity of truth and image.

The notion of shadow thus enables us to situate the economy of resemblance within the general economy of being. Resemblance is not a participation of a being in an idea (the old argument of the third man shows the futility of that); it is the very structure of the sensible as such. The sensible is being insofar as it resembles itself, insofar as, outside of its triumphal work of being, it casts a shadow, emits that obscure and elusive essence, that phantom essence which cannot be identified with the essence revealed in truth. There is not first an image – a neutralized vision of the object – which then differs from a sign or symbol because of its resemblance with the original; the neutralization of position in an image is precisely this resemblance.

The *transdescendence* Jean Wahl speaks of, when separated from the ethical significance it has for him and taken in a strictly ontological sense, can characterize this phenomenon of degradation or erosion of the absolute which we see in images and in resemblance.

The Meanwhile

To say that an image is a shadow of being would in turn be only to use a metaphor, if we did not show *where* the hither side we are speaking of is situated. To speak of inertia or death would hardly help us, for first we should have to say what the ontological signification of materiality itself is.

We have envisioned the image as the caricature, allegory or picturesque element which reality bears on its own face. All of Giraudoux's work effects a casting of reality into images, with a consistency which has not been fully appreciated, despite all Giraudoux's glory.[5] But up to now we seemed to be basing our conception on a fissure in being between being and its essence which does not adhere to it but masks and betrays it. But this in fact only enables us to approach the phenomenon we are concerned with. The art called classical – the art of antiquity and of its imitators, the art of ideal forms – corrects the caricature of being – the snub nose, the stiff gesture. Beauty is being dissimulating its caricature, covering over or absorbing its shadow. Does it absorb it completely? It is not a question of wondering whether the perfect forms of Greek art could be still more perfect, nor if they seem perfect in all latitudes of the globe. The insurmountable caricature in the most perfect image manifests itself in its stupidness as an idol. The image *qua* idol leads us to the ontological significance of its unreality. This time the work of being itself, the very *existing* of a being,[6] is doubled up with a semblance of existing.

To say that an image is an idol is to affirm that every image is in the last analysis plastic, and that every artwork is in the end a statue – a stoppage of time, or rather its delay behind itself. But we must show in what sense it stops or delays, and in what sense a statue's existing is a semblance of the existing of being.

A statue realizes the paradox of an instant that endures without a future. Its duration is not really an instant. It does not give itself out here as an infinitesimal element of duration, the instant of a flash; it has in its own way a quasi-eternal duration. We are not thinking just of the duration of an artwork itself as an object, of the permanence of writings in libraries and of statues in museums. Within the life, or rather the death, of a statue, an instant endures infinitely: eternally Laocoon will be caught up in the grip of serpents; the Mona Lisa will smile eternally. Eternally the future announced in the strained muscles of Laocoon will be unable to become present. Eternally, the smile of the Mona Lisa about to broaden will not broaden. An eternally suspended future floats around the congealed position of a statue like a future forever to come. The imminence of the future lasts before an instant stripped of the essential characteristic of the present, its evanescence. It will never have completed its task as a present, as though reality withdrew from its own reality and left it powerless. In this situation the present can assume nothing, can take on nothing, and thus is an impersonal and anonymous instant.

The immobile instant of a statue owes its acuteness to its non-indifference to duration. It does not belong to eternity. But it is not as though the artist had not been able to give it life. It is just that the life of an artwork does not go beyond the limit of an instant. The artwork does not succeed, is bad, when it does not have that aspiration for life which moved Pygmalion. But it is only an aspiration. The artist has given the statue a lifeless life, a derisory life which is not master of itself, a caricature of life. Its presence does not cover over itself and overflows on all sides, does not hold in its own hands the strings of the puppet it is. We can attend to the puppet in the personages of a tragedy and laugh at the Comédie-Française. *Every image is already a caricature.* But this caricature turns into something tragic. The same man is indeed a comic poet and a tragic poet, an ambiguity which constitutes the particular magic of poets like Gogol, Dickens, Tchekov – and Molière, Cervantes, and above all, Shakespeare.

This present, impotent to force the future, is fate itself, that fate refractory to the will of the pagan gods, stronger than the rational necessity of natural laws. Fate does not appear in universal necessity. It is a necessity in a free being, a reverting of freedom into necessity, their simultaneity, a freedom that discovers it is a prisoner. Fate has no place in life. The conflict between freedom and necessity in human action appears in reflection: when action is already sinking into the past, man discovers the motifs that necessitated it. But an antinomy is not a tragedy. In the instant of a statue, in its eternally suspended future, the tragic, simultaneity of necessity and liberty, can come to pass: the power of freedom congeals into impotence. And here too we should compare art with dreams: the instant of a statue is a nightmare. Not that the artist represents being crushed by fate – beings enter their fate because they are represented. They are enclosed in their fate but just this is the artwork, an event of darkening of being, parallel with its revelation, its truth. It is not that an artwork reproduces a time that has stopped: in the general economy of being, art is the falling movement on the hither side of time, into fate. A novel is not, as Jean Pouillon thinks, a way of reproducing time; it has its own time, it is a unique way for time to temporalize.

We can then understand that time, apparently introduced into images by the non-plastic arts such as music, literature, theatre and cinema, does not shatter the fixity of images. That the characters in a book are committed to the infinite repetition of the same acts and the same thoughts is not simply due to the contingent fact of the narrative, which is exterior to those characters. They can be narrated because their being *resembles* itself, doubles itself and immobilizes. Such a fixity is wholly different from that of concepts, which initiates life, offers reality to our powers, to truth, opens a dialectic. By its reflection in a narrative, being has a non-dialectical fixity, stops dialectics and time.

The characters of a novel are beings that are shut up, prisoners. Their history is never finished, it still goes on, but makes no headway. A novel shuts beings up in a fate despite their freedom. Life solicits the novelist when it seems to him as if it were already something out of a book. Something somehow completed arises in it, as though a whole set of facts were immobilized and formed a series. They are described between two well-determined moments, in the space of a time existence had traversed as through a tunnel. The events related form a *situation* – akin to a plastic ideal. That is what myth is: the plasticity of a history. What we call the artist's choice is the natural selection of facts and traits which are fixed in a rhythm, and transform time into images.

This plastic issue of the literary work was noted by Proust in a particularly admirable page of *The Prisoner*. In speaking of Dostoyevsky, what holds his attention is neither Dostoyevsky's religious ideas, his metaphysics, nor his psychology, but some profiles of girls, a few images: the house of the crime with its stairway and its *dvornik* in *Crime and Punishment*, Grushenka's silhouette in *Brothers Karamazov*. It is as though we are to think that the plastic element of reality is, in the end, the goal of the psychological novel.

Much is said about atmosphere in novels. Criticism itself likes to adopt this meteorological language. Introspection is taken to be a novelist's fundamental procedure, and one supposes that things and nature can enter into a book only when they are enveloped in an atmosphere composed of human emanations. We think, on the contrary, that an exterior vision – of a total exteriority, like the exteriority in rhythm we have described above, where the subject itself is exterior to itself – is the true vision of the novelist. Atmosphere is the very obscurity of images. The poetry of Dickens, who was surely a rudimentary psychologist, the atmosphere of those dusty boarding schools, the pale light of London offices with their clerks, the antique and second-hand clothing shops, the very characters of Nickleby and Scrooge, only appear in an exterior vision set up as a method. There is no other method. Even the psychological novelist sees his inner life on the outside, not necessarily through the eyes of another, but as one participates in a rhythm or a dream. All the power of the contemporary novel, its art-magic, is perhaps due to this way of seeing inwardness from the outside – which is not all the same as the procedures of behaviorism.

Since Bergson it has become customary to take the continuity of time to be the very essence of duration. The Cartesian teaching of the discontinuity of duration is at most taken as the illusion of a time grasped in its spatial trace, an origin of false problems for minds incapable of conceiving duration. And a metaphor, one that is eminently spatial, of a cross-section made in duration, a photographic metaphor of a snapshot of movement, is accepted as a truism.

We on the contrary have been sensitive to the paradox that an instant can stop. The fact that humanity could have provided itself with art reveals in time the uncertainty of time's continuation and something like a death doubling the impulse of life. The petrification of the instant in the heart of duration – Niobe's punishment – the insecurity of a being which has a presentiment of fate, is the great obsession of the artist's world, the pagan world. Zeno, cruel Zeno – that arrow . . .

Here we leave the limited problem of art. This presentiment of fate in death subsists, as paganism subsists. To be sure, one need only give oneself a constituted duration to remove from death the power to interrupt. Death is then sublated. To situate it in time is precisely to go beyond it, to already find oneself on the other side of the abyss, to have it behind oneself. Death *qua* nothingness is the death of the other, death for the survivor. The time of *dying* itself cannot give itself the other shore. What is unique and poignant in this instant is due to the fact that it cannot pass. In *dying*, the horizon of the future is given, but the future as a promise of a new present is refused; one is in the interval, forever an interval. The characters of certain tales by Edgar Allen Poe must have found themselves in this empty interval. A threat appears to them in the approach of such an empty interval; no move can be made to retreat from its approach, but this approach can never end. This is the anxiety which in other tales is prolonged like a fear of being buried alive. It is as though death were never dead enough, as though parallel with the duration of the living ran the eternal duration of the interval – the *meanwhile*.

Art brings about just this duration in the interval, in that sphere which a being is able to traverse, but in which its shadow is immobilized. The eternal duration of the interval in which a statue is immobilized differs radically from the eternity of a concept; it is the meanwhile, never finished, still enduring – something inhuman and monstrous.

Inertia and matter do not account for the peculiar death of the shadow. Inert matter already refers to a substance to which its qualities cling. In a statue matter knows the death of idols. The proscription of images is truly the supreme command of monotheism, a doctrine that overcomes fate, that creation and revelation in reverse.

For Philosophical Criticism

Art then lets go of the prey for the shadow.

But in introducing the death of each instant into being, it effects its eternal duration in the meanwhile, has there its uniqueness, its value. Its value then is ambiguous – unique because it is impossible to go beyond it, because, being unable to end, it cannot go toward the *better*. It does not have the quality of the living instant which is open to the salvation of becoming, in which it can end and be surpassed. The value of this instant is thus made of its misfortune. This sad value is indeed the beautiful of modern art, opposed to the happy beauty of classical art.

On the other hand, art, essentially disengaged, constitutes, in a world of initiative and responsibility, a dimension of evasion.

Here we rejoin the most common and ordinary experience of aesthetic enjoyment. It is one of the reasons that bring out the value of art. Art brings into the world the obscurity of fate, but it especially brings the irresponsibility that charms as a lightness and grace. It frees. To make or to appreciate a novel and a picture is to no longer have to conceive, is to renounce the effort of science, philosophy, and action. Do not speak, do not reflect, admire in silence and in peace – such are the counsels of wisdom satisfied before the beautiful. Magic, recognized everywhere as the devil's part, enjoys an incomprehensible tolerance in poetry. Revenge is gotten on wickedness by producing its caricature, which is to take from it its reality without annihilating it; evil powers are conjured by filling the world with idols which have mouths but do not speak. It is as though ridicule killed, as though everything really can end in songs. We find an appeasement when, beyond the invitations to comprehend and act, we throw ourselves into the rhythm of a reality which solicits only its admission into a book or a painting. Myth takes the place of mystery. The world to be built is replaced by the essential completion of its shadow. This is not the disinterestedness of contemplation but of irresponsibility. The poet exiles himself from the city. From this point of view, the value of the beautiful is relative. There is something wicked and egoist and cowardly in artistic enjoyment. There are times when one can be ashamed of it, as of feasting during a plague.

Art then is not committed by virtue of being art. But for this reason art is not the supreme value of civilization, and it is not forbidden to conceive a stage in which it will be reduced to a source of pleasure – which one cannot contest without being ridiculous – having its place, but only a place, in man's happiness. Is it presumptuous to denounce the hypertrophy of art in our times when, for almost everyone, it is identified with spiritual life?

But all this is true for art separated from the criticism that integrates the inhuman work of the artist into the human world. Criticism already detaches it from its irresponsibility by envisaging its technique. It treats the artist as a man at work. Already in inquiring after the influences he undergoes it links this disengaged and proud man to real history. Such criticism is still preliminary. It does not attack the artistic event as such, that obscuring of being in images, that stopping of being in the meanwhile. The value of images for philosophy lies in their position between two times and their ambiguity. Philosophy discovers, beyond the enchanted rock on which it stands, all its possibles swarming about it. It grasps them by interpretation. This is to say that the artwork can and must be treated as a myth: the immobile statue has to be put in movement and made to speak. Such an enterprise is not the same as a simple reconstruction of the original from the copy. Philosophical exegesis will measure the distance that separates myth from real being, and will become conscious of the creative event itself, an event which eludes cognition, which goes from being to being by skipping over the intervals of the meanwhile. Myth is then at the same time untruth and the source of philosophical truth, if indeed philosophical truth involves a dimension of intelligibility proper to it, not content with laws and causes which connect beings to one another, but searching for the work of being itself.

Criticism, in interpreting, will choose and will limit. But if, *qua* choice, it remains on the hither side of the world which is fixed in art, it reintroduces that world into the intelligible world in which it stands, and which is the true homeland of the mind. The most lucid writer finds himself in the world bewitched by its images. He speaks in enigmas, by allusions, by suggestion, in equivocations, as though he moved in a world of shadows, as though he lacked the force to arouse realities, as though he could not go to them without wavering, as though, bloodless and awkward, he always committed himself further than he had decided to do, as though he spills half the water he is bringing us. The most forewarned, the most lucid writer none the less plays the fool. The interpretation of criticism speaks in full self-possession, frankly, through concepts, which are like the muscles of the mind.

Modern literature, disparaged for its intellectualism (which, none the less goes back to Shakespeare, the Molière of *Don Juan*, Goethe, Dostoyevsky) certainly manifests a more and more clear awareness of this fundamental insufficiency of aristic idolatry. In this intellectualism the artist refuses to be only an artist, not because he wants to defend a thesis or cause, but because he needs to interpret his myths himself. Perhaps the doubts that, since the renaissance, the alleged death of God has put in souls have compromised for the artist the reality of the henceforth inconsistent models, have imposed on him the onus of finding his models anew in the heart of his production itself, and made him believe he had a mission to be creator and revealer. The task of criticism remains essential, even if God was not dead, but only exiled. But we cannot here broach the 'logic' of the philosophical exegesis of art; that would demand a broadening of the intentionally limited perspective of this study. For one would have to introduce the perspective of the relation with the other without which being could not be told in its reality, that is, in its time.

NOTES

All notes are by the translator unless otherwise indicated.
1 Cf. Martin Heidegger, *Being and Time*, trans. John Macquarrie and Edward Robinson (New York and Evanston: Harper and Row, 1962), p. 44.
2 Cf. Jean-Paul Sartre, *Literature and Existentialism*, trans. Bernard Frechtman (New York: Citadel, 1964).
3 Martin Heidegger, *Being and Time*, p. 405. Also 'On the Essence of Truth', trans. John Sallis in *Basic Writings*, ed. David Farrell Krell, pp. 127–30.
4 Jean-Paul Sartre, *Imagination, a Psychology of Imagination*, trans. Bernard Frechtman (New York: Washington Square Press, 1966).
5 Editor: Jean Giraudoux (1882–1944) wrote modern versions of classical tragedy which emphasized the human qualities inherent in classical myth.
6 Cf. *Existence and Existents*, p. 17.

Translated by Alphonso Lingis

8

The Transcendence of Words

First published in *Les Temps Modernes*, 44 (1949), 1090–5, and reprinted in a special volume of *L'Ire des Vents*, 3–4 (1981), devoted to Michel Leiris, the recent reissue of 'The Transcendence of Words' in *Hors sujet* (Montpellier: Fata Morgana, 1987), pp. 213–22, indicates the abiding interest of this early reading of one of France's most important writers.

Michel Leiris (b. 1901) has been associated with every decisive intellectual current since World War I. He has been a surrealist, a member of the *Collège de sociologie* which included Georges Bataille and Roger Caillois, an editor of *Les Temps Modernes* and an important ethnographer and art critic. Above all, in *La Règle du jeu* Leiris has produced what is arguably the most revolutionary autobiography of the twentieth century. The first volume, *Biffures* (1948), elaborates a sinuous and precise narrative that shows how the childhood past, the sense of self, and the recognition of the objective, adult world are created and confronted by language. The title *Biffures* is in itself a reference to this linguistic construction and deferral: a *bifur* is a bifurcation, and a *biffure* an erasure.

Having recognized the surrealist foundations in such a practice, Levinas stresses how the notion of an original bifurcation prohibits the reduction of multiple meanings to a single origin. An original bifurcation means that any static identity or representation overflows from the beginning. The primary *space* which this creates is one filled with infinite anxiety for Levinas, unless it includes a relation with someone, that is the necessity of critique. This necessary communication means that there is no pure sound prior to the word: sound, or words, produce a transcendence by breaking the world of self-sufficiency. Speech situates the self in relation to the other in a way that shows us how being for the other is the first fact of existence. The way in which language reveals this relation prior to self-consciousness leads Levinas to conclude that Leiris's word associations still accept the primacy of thought in relation to language. For Levinas, however, the saying and the said, the act of expression and the thing expressed are never correlative, as noesis and noema, since in the saying there is always the trace of alterity that goes beyond anything that can be measured in terms of its thought content.

For a full outline of the linguistic nature of Leiris's autobiography, see Seán Hand, 'The Sound and the Fury: language in Leiris', *Paragraph*, 7 (1986), 102–20. One may also usefully compare Levinas's view of Leiris to the 'marginal' use made of *Biffures* by Jacques Derrida in the 'Tympan' section of *Margins of Philosophy* (Brighton: Harvester and Chicago: University of Chicago Press, 1982), pp. ix–xxix.

S.H.

Surrealism's aims go well beyond those of a literary school. It seeks to identify metaphysical freedom with poetic freedom. Because of their absurd and capricious nature, dreams do not tie us to a fate that negates all human dignity, but present themselves as emancipatory. Nor are they the privilege of genius. Non-sense is the most evenly distributed thing in the world. None the less, in Breton's first manifesto we have on the one hand a naive confidence placed in the secret and miraculous energy of the Unconscious, his references to Freud being no more than allusions to some mythological region that promises to yield up buried treasure, and on the other hand a critique of the conscious mechanisms of thought, where he is not so much analysing them as prospecting the dead end into which they lead.

Michel Leiris, who for a while belonged to the surrealist group, also exalts the power of dreams in his book *Biffures*. But he does so very much in his own way. Instead of exploiting some mysterious power possessed by the Unconscious, he finds reasons for his dreams in the conscious world. The richness and apparently unexpected nature of the images initially derive from an association of ideas whose 'latent birth' is in each case patiently described by Leiris.

Up until the middle of the book what we are in fact given is a prodigious amplification of Rimbaud's famous sonnet. The only difference is that the correspondences evoked are no longer mysterious, since their genesis is given. Michel Leiris is more of a chemist than an alchemist of the Word. From page 128 on, this chemistry stretches to facts, situations and memories. It becomes the very content of the narrative, which presents itself simultaneously as a work of art and as a reflection on the essence of this art. This is after all very much the tradition in French poetry from Mallarmé to Blanchot: the emotion that constitutes the subject matter of the work is the very emotion that forms such matter.

In the very last part of his work, Leiris reveals how his art is constructed from bifurcations (*bifurs*) or erasures (*biffures*) which give the book its title and also lend meaning to this astonishing rehabilitation of the association of ideas. Bifurcations – since sensations, words and memories continually turn a train of thought from the path it seemed to be taking towards some unexpected direction; erasures – since the univocal meaning of each element is continually corrected and altered. But in these bifurcations and erasures Leiris is less concerned to go down the new paths opened up or to latch onto the corrected meaning than he is to capture thought at that special moment when it turns into something other than itself. It is because of this inherent ambiguity in bifurcation that the very phenomenon of the association of ideas becomes possible.

While we are used to reducing the function of signifying to the association of ideas, and to thinking that the multiplicity of meanings in some verbal sign or other can be explained by the network of associations to which it belongs, with the notion of bifurcation the process of association of ideas loses its inherent role. Thought is originally erasure – that is to say a symbol. And because thought is symbolic, ideas can link up to form a network of associations. From then on, whether due to the circumstances in which the word was learned, or the way it resembles other words in terms of sound or even in its written form, this network, further enriched by all that the signs of writing can then evoke, is important not for the way it displaces one idea onto another, but because it assures the presence of one idea *in* another. As animals in a fable are not just there to suggest morality but through their physical presence enrich the idea put forward, so a thought at the moment of its erasure still influences through its erased meaning; its different meanings participate with one another. Surrealist freedom is not opposed to other mechanisms of thought – it is their supreme principle.

Taken at the level of erasure, the association of ideas thus becomes a thought that lies beyond the classical categories of representation and identity. This overflowing of thought naturally makes us think of Bergsonian duration, but Bergson's conception represents this negation of identity as a process of evolution. The primordial status of the notion of erasure affirms the simultaneity of multiplicity, and the irreducibly ambiguous nature of consciousness. Leiris's memories, as they are presented by his 'rule of the game', curiously enough do not leave an impression of a temporal rhythm. Instead the ambiguity of erasures forms a space.

It would be interesting to compare the operations of erasure with the work of modern painters. I recently saw an exhibition of paintings by Charles Lapicque. By breaking down perspective and the practical access it gives to objects, Lapicque creates a space that is above all a realm of simultaneity. This resembles a literary description which produces a picture not by reproducing the continuity of duration but by assembling certain details in a particular order that is determined by the nature of those details, and their powers of suggestion. Space does not accommodate things; instead, through their erasures, things delineate space. The space of each object in turn is divested of its volume, and from behind the rigid line there begins to emerge the line as ambiguity. Lines shed the function of providing a skeleton and become the infinite number of possible connections. Forms vary according to their essential themes, as with those pictures of foaming seas on which Lapicque now works, where all perceptible matter is reduced to the infinite suggestions relating one form to another. There is a variation on themes, but not of a musical kind, since there is no sense of duration; it is precisely simultaneous and spatial. This means the very form of a single painting would halt the game of erasures. So in Lapicque the painting is accompanied by variations which do not play the role of *études* that progress towards the *ne varietur* completion of the work, but are all situated on the same plan. An incomplete, rather than complete state, paradoxically is the fundamental category of modern art.

But isn't the spatial dimension of this game of erasures related to the visual dimension? The proliferation of erasures is of course like the return of consciousness to its perceptible existence, and the return of the perceptible to its aesthetic essence. But the particular symbolism entailed in the aesthetic essence of reality can be explained by the very nature of visual experience to which Western civilization ultimately reduces all spiritual life. It is concerned with ideas, it is light, it looks for clarity and evidence. It culminates in an unveiling and in the phenomenon. Everything is immanent to it.

To see is to be in a world that is entirely *here* and self-sufficient. Any vision beyond what is given remains within what is given. The infinity of space, like the infinity of the signified referred to by the sign, is equally absent from the here below. Vision is a relation with a being such that the being attained through it precisely appears as the world. Sound, for its part, appeals to intuition and can be given. This naturally involves the primacy of vision with respect to the other senses. And on the primacy of vision rests the universality of art. By creating beauty out of nature, art calms and quietens it. All the arts, even those based on sound, create silence.

This silence may be the result of a bad conscience, or it may weigh heavy, or cause dread. This need to enter into a relation with someone, in spite of or over and above the peace and harmony derived from the successful creation of beauty is what we call the necessity of critique.

In sound, and in the consciousness termed hearing, there is in fact a break with the self-complete world of vision and art. In its entirety, sound is a ringing, clanging scandal. Whereas, in vision, form is wedded to content in such a way as to appease it, in sound the perceptible quality overflows so that form can no longer contain its content. A real rent is produced in the world, through which the world that is *here* prolongs a dimension that cannot be converted into vision. It is in this way, by surpassing what is given, that sound is the symbol *par excellence*. If none the less it can appear as a phenomenon, as a *here*, it is because the transcendence it brings about operates only in verbal sound. The sounds and noises of nature are failed words. To really hear a sound, we need to hear a word. Pure sound is the word.

Contemporary philosophy and sociology have accustomed us to underestimating the direct social link between persons who speak, and to prefer silence or the complex relations, such as customs or law or culture, laid down by civilization. This scorn for words certainly has to do with the way language can degenerate into a prattle that reveals nothing but social unease. But this scorn cannot triumph over the situation Robinson Crusoe is privileged to experience when, in a magnificent tropical landscape, where he has continued to maintain civilization through his tools and his morality and his calendar, he still finds in his encounter with Man Friday the greatest event of his insular life. It is the moment when finally a man who speaks replaces the inexpressible sadness of echoes.

Naturally, this is a way of saying that in social relations the real presence of the other is important; but above all it means that this presence, far from signifying pure and simple coexistence with me, or expressing itself through the romantic metaphor of 'living presence', is fulfilled in the act of hearing, and derives its meaning from the role of transcendent origin played by the word that is offered. It is to the extent that the word refuses to become flesh that it assures a presence amongst us. The presence of the Other (*Autre*) is a presence that teaches us something; this is why the word, as a form of education, amounts to more than the experience of reality, and why the master of the word is more than a spiritual obstetrician. The use of the word wrenches experience out of its aesthetic self-sufficiency, the *here* where it has quietly been lying. Invoking experience transforms it into a creature. It is in this sense that I have been able to say elsewhere that criticism, which is the word of a living being speaking to a living being, brings the image in which art revels back to the fully real being. The language of criticism takes us out of our dreams, in which artistic language plays an integral part. Certainly, in its written form, it in turn generates new criticism. Books call up books – but this proliferation of writings halts or culminates at the moment when the living word is installed and criticism blossoms into teaching.

This privilege of the living word, which is destined to be heard, in contrast to the word that is an image and already a picturesque sign, appears equally when we contemplate the act of expression.

Is self-expression merely the manifestation of a thought by a sign? This is something suggested by writing. Words are disfigured or 'frozen', when language is transformed into documents and vestiges. The living word struggles against this transfer of thought into vestige, it struggles with the letter that appears when there is no-one there to hear. The act of expression makes it impossible to remain within oneself (*en soi*) or keep one's thought for oneself (*pour soi*) and so reveals the inadequacy of the subject's position in which the ego has a given world at its disposal. To speak is to interrupt my existence as a subject and a master, but without offering myself up as a spectacle. I am simultaneously a subject and an object. My voice carries the element in which this dialectical situation is realized in concrete terms. The subject who speaks does not situate the world in relation to himself, nor situate himself purely and simply at the heart of his own spectacle, like an artist. Instead he is situated in relation to the Other (*Autre*). This privilege of the Other (*Autre*) ceases to be incomprehensible once we admit that the first fact of existence is neither being in-itself (*en soi*) nor being for-itself (*pour soi*) but being *for the other* (*pour l'autre*); in other words that human existence is a creature. By offering a word, the subject putting himself forward lays himself open and, in a sense, prays.

In these remarks, which are too cursory for such a serious subject, the real event taking place with an expression lies outside its traditional subordination to thought. The conception of a word serving only to communicate a thought, or to dissimulate it, rests on a tradition that is so ancient and venerable that we scarcely dare touch it. I believe that the erasures of Michel Leiris magnificently exhaust every possibility of thought, when he shows a thought, at the actual moment of thinking, make contact with the perceptible matter of words. But these erasures still accept the primacy of thought in relation to language expressed by the classic notion of 'what is well conceived'. The riches offered up by language are finally measured by Michel Leiris only in terms of their counterpart, the thought content.

NOTE

1 Michel Leiris, *Biffures* (Paris: Gallimard, 1948).

Translated by Seán Hand

9

The Servant and her Master

First published in *Critique*, 229 (1966), 514–22 and reprinted in *Sur Maurice Blanchot* (Montpellier: Fata Morgana, 1975), pp. 27–42, 'The Servant and her Master' is one of the clearest explications of Levinas's admiration for the work of Maurice Blanchot (b. 1907). In Levinas's view, Blanchot's writings embody a 'moral elevation, an aristocracy of thought'. Blanchot and Levinas met while both were students in Strasbourg. Though their political positions were very different – Blanchot was at that time a monarchist and during the thirties was published in antisemitic journals – the two writers felt drawn to one another intellectually. It was Blanchot, for example, who introduced Levinas to the work of Proust and Valéry. Later, Blanchot's political position shifted: during the Occupation he refused to collaborate, and he saved Levinas's wife from being captured by the Nazis.

In Blanchot's fiction, an anonymous witness attempts to convey, in a cold, neutral language, the one and only truth, that of absence and death. It is a truth which, of course, is precisely inexpressible. The 'neutral' or 'outside' zone in which this language moves resembles the experience of 'there is': one bears witness to an event that is neither being nor nothingness, but a disaster in the literal sense. Objectivizing consciousness is replaced by a sense of being that is detached from cosmological existence, from any fixed reference to a star (dis-aster), a being that strains towards obliteration in an inaccessible nonlanguage.

Levinas reads Blanchot's work as the continual attempt to have noesis without noema, a poetic saying which exceeds the said, transforming words as moments of a totality into signs of infinity. The movement of this poetic language is radically opposed to that of ontology: instead of confirming itself in discourse, it unfolds as a sovereign waiting and forgetting. This activity 'loosens up' the ontological field by reintroducing duration in a way that cannot be subordinated to intentionality. It is a primordial waiting that is not *for* something, a primordial forgetting of self that undoes ipseity. Blanchot's speakers therefore become detached from themselves only to join up again in a way that leads beyond being, through sensuous communication, a first concern for justice, and the transcendence revealed by the surpassing of the said.

Garth Gillon has translated an interview with Levinas in which he discusses the work of Blanchot in *SubStance*, 14 (1976), 54–7. For a different, fascinating use of Blanchot see Jacques Derrida's essay 'Living On' in *Deconstruction and Criticism* (New York: Seabury, 1979), pp. 75–176. For a full phenomenological account of the relations between Levinas and Blanchot the best book to consult is Joseph Libertson, *Proximity, Levinas, Blanchot, Bataille and Communication* (The Hague: Martinus Nijhoff, 1982).

S.H.

I

Artistic activity makes the artist aware that he is not the author of his works. The efficient causality which, in day-to-day activity, binds the worker quite unambiguously to what he produces – while at the same time allowing an estimate of the part played by the material used, by the desired end and by the formal and legal exigencies of the undertaking in hand – turns out, in the artist, to be at the service of a vocation which penetrates it to its very core; to be under the influence of voices that are mysterious insofar as they cannot be compared to those resorted to in usual forms of collaboration; to be consumed by summonses which even deflect its propulsion from true.

This awareness of a foreign interference in human causality, this age-old experience of inspiration (with which *Waiting Forgetting*[1] opens perhaps), an experience to which the artist joyfully surrenders and which so many of the optimistic philosophies of art in our time hail as a self-transcendence (even though Valéry felt humiliated by it), takes on exceptional weight when one asks oneself whether enthusiasm or possession are not concealed at the heart of all activity, even beneath the primordial activity of consciousness and language; whether a delirium more profound than thought does not support thought; whether language which claims to be act and origin, 'the decisive word', and as it were the possibility, if such there be, of finishing and interrupting, is not an inveterate passivity, the endless reiteration of an old old story, without beginning or end, a turbulence, impersonal and profound, which sensation traverses only as a surface ripple.

The discredit affecting the supernatural in the thought and customs of the West does not extend to the mystery of inspiration. Not so long ago, we still distinguished, in the production of poetry, the role of the intellect as master of its intentions, of the thinker controlling his thoughts (one perhaps devoid of interest but inalienable); and on the other hand what was deemed the better role, that of genius, the demon, the muse, the unconscious. Surrealism, despite its audacity, remained typical of that stage of things with its theory of an automatic writing which had to be freed from conscious thought. But it did thereby acknowledge that inspiration had a vigilant rival which had, as a preliminary, to be rendered dormant. In Blanchot's *Amindab*, Thomas is chained to a companion whose prisoner he is or else who is his prisoner. Similarly, in *Waiting Forgetting*: 'He began to hear alongside what she was saying, and somehow behind it ... another language with which hers had almost nothing in common' (p. 25).[2] As if people, through being identical, became double; as if consciousness, despite its freedom, exercised a function it had never assumed.

'And yet all remains unchanged' (p. 29). The other is merely a repetition of the same, and the other language echoes the first in spite of its difference. Absurdity at the heart of absurdity: the alienation of consciousness does not free it from itself. Nothing *extra*-ordinary occurs. Language is obliged to continue on the terms under which it was first undertaken. Its movement outside is for ever paralyzed by the undertakings entailed by those first words, and which each new word tacitly renews. The idea that God has withdrawn from the world, or that God is dead, is perhaps the expression of that monotony multiplying and extending through infinite variations, and of the Self, incapable of staying still in its identity. 'It is endlessly restless' (p. 40). Blanchot's writings seek to undo the double knot of non-sense, the monstrosity, never before expressed, of the identical beginning to prolifer-ate like a cancerous cell, producing nothing other than repetition and tautology. 'Is there still the same light, even though it is night?' (p. 35).

The fate of our world which has lost the use of speech is proffered in its intensity (*se tend*) in this work. 'Arrange for me to be able to speak to you': that is the invocation which dominates the entire first part of *Waiting Forgetting*. We can no longer speak not only because of that foreign inter-ference, but also because of the tautological rhythm which punctuates dialogue itself, because of the monotonous droning which immediately closes off the avenues of communication. As if everything was, from time immemorial, finished. To speak, to write is to attempt to disrupt the definitiveness of eternity; but does the last word belong to discourse? Does it not belong to the ontological act which is accomplished by discourse and which immures discourse in advance? Speech turns into being, which does not draw its significance from a discursive intention. 'She spoke the truth, but not in what she said' (p. 36). 'They were always conversing', says another essential passage, 'about the instant when they would no longer be there, and while aware that they would always be there conversing about such an instant, they thought that there was nothing more worthy of their eternity than to spend it evoking its end' (p. 35). Is it possible to get out of this circle otherwise than by expressing the impossibility of getting out of it, by speaking the inexpressible? Is not poetry, of itself, the Exit? In that case, Blanchot would disagree with the Hegelian doctrine of the death of art since the end of the Classical period, of its subordination to Religion in the

Middle Ages and to philosophy in our age. This is of course no noble revolt against the prose of the technological age. We have here an audacious idea. Blanchot calls into question the seemingly incontestable claim of a certain sort of language to be the privileged bearer of what is meaningful, to be its well-spring, its mouth and its riverbed. Does the meaningful depend on a certain order of propositions, constructed according to a certain grammar so as to constitute a logical argument? or does meaning cause language to explode and then signify amidst these fragments (grammar remaining intact in Blanchot's case!) – but already in spirit and in truth in advance of any subsequent interpretation? *Waiting Forgetting* refuses to grant the philosophical language of interpretation, which 'speaks without a stop' (and with which Blanchot the literary critic complies), the dignity of the ultimate language. To call in the logos, gathering together above and beyond the language of poetry which, in its dispersal, speaks the impossible outcome of language, is to block off the opening in which the going round in circles of coherent discourse is announced, but also denounced – and hence transcended. Can we not in that case venture further and argue that the presuppositions of coherent speaking can no longer refute what speaking has to say? And perhaps we are wrong to name art and poetry that exceptional event – that sovereign forgetfulness – which frees language from its servitude towards the structures in which the *said* prevails. Perhaps Hegel was right as far as art is concerned. What matters – call it poetry or whatever – is that a meaning should be utterable beyond the confines of Hegel's completed discourse, that a meaning forgetful of the presuppositions of that discourse should become *fable*.

II

Blanchot's literary writing proper provides above all a new sensation; a 'new thrill' or, more exactly, a new tingling in the skin as it brushes against things. Everything begins at this tangible level: those places – hotel bedrooms, kitchen, corridors, windows, walls – where space weighs down by its very transparency, 'exerting the same continuous pressure not exerting it' (p. 31); the resonance which dies away across this space, interminably dying away on the edge of a silence from which it emerges, as out of a distant buzzing from which silence is at first indistinguishable: 'in place of the beginning, a sort of initial void, an energetic refusal to let the story begin' (p. 22); the remoteness and the strangeness of things heavy with their insignificance: a glass of water, a bed, a table, an armchair, each of them exiled and abstract; the transparency of a dialogue between initiates, reduced to the verbal markers between which there creeps an implied argument, devoid of mystery for the speakers, but opaque through its own emptiness. This constant condensation in opposition to erosion, occurring where there is, at the same time, nothing. 'The innumerable peopling of the void' (p. 54) like the upsurge of a numb suffering, the dull slow tumefaction of Nothing. The panting of nothingness and so to speak its way of labouring, struggling and 'coming to pass' (*'se passe'*) and departing from its identity as void: 'the voices echo in the immense void, the void of the voices and the void of these empty places' (pp. 18–19). The silence which occurs does not put a stop to the rustling. Already it can be heard coming from the other side of the wall, and no negation could possibly silence this commotion: is not the other sound the same as the one that has just been silenced on this side? Was it so as to hear it that they endeavoured to be silent? Was it so as to hear 'the same words returning to themselves' (pp. 38–9) that they sought to speak? 'Those old words which want to be there once again without speaking . . . a rumour without trace . . . nowhere straying, everywhere dwelling' (p. 13). 'Once again, once again walking yet always on the spot, another country, other towns, the same country' (p. 14). Language is closed like that bedroom. 'How stifling it was for both of them in this enclosed place where the words she spoke could no longer mean anything but that enclosure. Did she not say this, only this: "We are shut away, we shall never leave this place again"' (pp. 28–9). The words succeed each other and interrupt those which preceded them, *they cannot get away from getting away*: 'Poor room . . . how little I inhabit you. Do I not live here solely in order to wipe out every trace of my stay?' (pp. 13–14). An eternal present, an eternity of tautology or of iteration.

III

'Is there a door he hasn't noticed? Is there a bare wall where two windows open?' (p. 35). Is an exit possible or on the contrary is even the light that seems to illuminate this abode artificial, and does our consciousness of the situation become lost in the same interminable game played by language, without leading to any *cogito*? Poetic language will break through the wall while preserving itself against the rubble from that very breakthrough, which threatens to bury and immobilize its advance by breaking it down into projects and memories that are synchronous and eternally contemporaneous in significance. The game which consists in staying in a place so as to efface all trace of a stay must not be allowed to recommence. She struggled, says Blanchot, 'against certain words which had so to speak been deposited in her and which she endeavoured to maintain in a relation to the future, or to something which had not yet happened, yet already present all the same, yet already past all the same' (p. 17). It is perhaps this movement, which undoes words reduced to the present, that Blanchot names Waiting, Forgetting.

Forgetting against reminiscence, waiting that is not waiting for something. 'Waiting, waiting that is the refusal to wait for anything, a calm expanse unfurled by steps' (p. 20). Waiting, Forgetting which are juxtaposed without having been brought together structurally by any conjunction. They do not refer to moods or attitudes whose intentionality, by its innumerable threads, might be seen as consolidating further the inextricable web of being as it twists and closes in on itself. Subjectivity infiltrates the world's core (*noyaute*) and reinforces its fabric: someone in the fabric of being makes a nest and then 'feathers' it (*'fait son beurre'*). Waiting, forgetting loosen up the ontological field, let drop a stitch, core (*dénoyautent*), crumble, relax, erase. 'An initial distraction'! (p. 20). The instant 'heavy with all its past and big with its future', the present instant whose taut dynamism renders everything contemporary and eternal, reverts to tranquillity in waiting. Neither anticipation nor impatience, 'waiting waits for nothing' (p. 51). And forgetting turns away from the past instant, but keeps up a relation to what it turns away from when it 'abides in words' (p. 69). Thus is diachrony restored to time. A nocturnal time: 'night in which nothing is waited for represents this movement of waiting' (p. 50). But primordial forgetting is forgetfulness of self. Is not *ipseity* both absolute origin and an insatiable turning back upon oneself, an imprisoning of self by self just as language is? Reflection brings to the surface the old stones of the foundations and mixes them in with things of the moment. This simultaneity of conditioner and conditioned is called coherent discourse. But once they become attentive to their condition, words come to a stop and turn into pillars of salt. Here again, Forgetting restores diachrony to time. A diachrony without protension or retention. To wait for nothing and to forget everything, the opposite of subjectivity, 'absence of all centre' (p. 45). A relaxing of the Self, and its tension in upon itself (*tension sur soi*), of that 'existence for which in its existence it is a question of that existence itself'. 'With what melancholy, but what calm certainty, he felt that he could never again say: "I"' (p. 34). 'She has ... detached from him, himself' (p. 44). The speakers, in the second part of the book, which is so calm, often cheerful and triumphant, instead of flexing in upon (*se tendre sur*) themselves, deny their identity without losing it, become detached from themselves like butterflies from their chrysalises, shed a garment so to speak, only to be caught up in it again immediately, make moves, within themselves, out to meet Others, abandon themselves, join up again, stripped of self and present to self – so many new relations between self and self! – find a door, in this loosened self, leading beyond being and, in an expression epitomizing equality, justice, caressing, communication and transcendence, an expression admirable in its precision and its grace, 'are together, but not yet' (p. 76).

IV

This language of poetry becomes for Blanchot a language which contradicts itself. The beauty, the quasi-tangible beauty, taken on in his writing, and especially in *Waiting Forgetting*, by this contradictory alternation of utterance, is well-known. Affirmation is followed, often in the same proposition, by its negation. Saying lets go of what it grasps. The thing which is given – being – is out of proportion to Waiting and its hyperbolic intention beyond Being, whereas subjectivity asks only to be absorbed into its object, which 'the intentionality of consciousness' puts within its reach. Saying is Desire which the approach of the Desirable exacerbates and whets, and where the approach of the Desirable withdraws in the process. Such is the scintillating modality of transcendence, of what truly *comes to pass*.[3]

A discontinuous and contradictory language of scintillation. A language which can give sign (*faire signe*) above and beyond all signification. A sign made from afar, from beyond and in the beyond. Poetic language gives sign without the sign being a bearer of signification through relinquishing signification. But it is absolutely 'in clear' both this side of and beyond the inevitable conventions of languages. Though lying outside of the coded system of languages, it leads to it, like the metalanguage referred to in logistics, which 'unlocks' the symbolism of writing.

Giving sign, without this being for something. Blanchot speaks admirably about that. 'It is the voice which has been imparted and entrusted to you, and not what it says. What it says, the secrets which you obtain and which you transcribe so as to exhibit and bring out the best in them, must be led back gently by you, in spite of their attempt at seduction, towards the silence which you derived from them in the first place' (p. 11). Poetry can be said to transform words, the tokens of a whole, the moments of a totality, into unfettered signs, breaching the walls of immanence, disrupting order. Two beings locked in a bedroom struggle with a fatality which draws them together or separates them too much (p. 42) for them to find a door. No novel, no poem – from the *Iliad* to *Remembrance of Things Past* – has thus perhaps done anything else. To introduce meaning into Being is to go from the Same to the Other (*Autre*), from Self to Other (*Autrui*), it is to give sign, to undo the structures of language. Without this, the world would know only the meanings which inspire official records or the minutes of the board meetings of Limited Companies.

V

The poetic word (*verbe*) itself can, however, betray itself, become engulfed in order and take on the appearance of a cultural product, a document or testimony. It becomes encouraged, applauded and rewarded, sold, bought, consumed and consoling, talking to itself in the language of a whole people. This can be explained by the precise place in which it surfaces (and there is no other), between knowledge which embraces All and culture with which it identifies, two pincers which threaten to close around it. It is precisely that moment between seeing and saying, when the pincers have not quite closed, that Blanchot watches out for.

Between seeing and saying. This is already an abandonment of the eternally present order of vision. But it is still signs, 'words which evoke nothing' (p. 19), still falling short of cultural and historical order. The latter undeniably will have unsettled the intuitive simultaneity of its completed world and have drawn it into history. None the less, it will still solidify into a narrative, still envelop itself in the totality of the *said*, which alone will have the power to confer meaning on what is said, even if every instance of discourse were to produce, in its own way, that illuminating totality, and possessed its own way of taking things to their conclusion. 'No-one here wishes to be bound by a story' (p. 22). 'Arrange for me not to be able to speak to you (*vous*)' is a prayer like 'Arrange for me to be able to speak to you (*te*)'. It preserves the movement located between seeing and saying, that language of pure transcendence without correlative, like waiting which nothing awaited has yet destroyed, noesis without noema. This is a language of pure extra-vagance, moving from one singularity to another without there being anything in common between them ('there is still too much in common between the speakers', a language without words which gives sign before signifying anything, a language of pure complicity, but a complicity for nothing: 'she gave the impression, when she spoke, of being unable to connect words to the richness of a prior language. They were without history, without links with a common past, unrelated even to her own life, or indeed the life of anyone' (p. 24). Could that be the language, stronger than prayer and combat, to which Lermontov responds in that mysterious poem which can be translated (in bad prose) as follows:

There are utterances – their meaning / is obscure or negligible – / but without emotion / we cannot possibly understand them. / How full their sounds are /

of the madness of desire! / In them are the tears of separation / in them are the thrill of reunion. / No reply whatsoever / in the noise of the world / to the world which was born / of flame and light. / But in the temple, in battle / and wherever I may be / as soon as I have heard it / I will recognize it everywhere / Without finishing my prayer / I shall answer it / And out of battle / I shall rush to meet it. /

But language which gives sign without establishing itself in the eternity of the idea it signifies, discontinuous language, is circumvented by that ancillary language which follows in its tracks and never stops speaking. The coherent language in which being (and even 'the Being of beings') stretches and extends, is all memory, all anticipation, all eternity. It is never-fading, and always has the last word. It contaminates with logic the ambiguity inscribed in the trace of forgotten discourse and never gives itself up to enigma. As the speaker of truth, how can she be silenced? She recounts, in a consistent manner, the extravagances of her master and is reputed to love wisdom. She derives triumph and presence from narrating the failures, the absences and the escapades of him she serves and spies upon. She has taken stock of the secret places she cannot open and holds the keys to doors which have been destroyed. She is an utterly reliable housekeeper, who supervises the house she rules over and disputes the existence of secret locks.

Housekeeper or Mistress? A marvellous hypocrite! For she loves the madness she keeps watch over.

NOTES

1 Perhaps. We are not dealing with allegorical characters. Though spare and so to speak abstract, these figures are fully tangible. We find ourselves at grips with densities and masses which extend through dimensions and belong to an order peculiar to them, giving rise, as in delirium, to problems which are scarcely communicable once fever has subsided and day has dawned. That is the sole relief to Blanchot's literary space. The meaning of his world concerns our own. But interpretation is something this kind of work resists. It is perhaps exclusively a breaching of that envelopment which non-contradictory *saying* attempts around all movement. Ought we to attempt to capture some of these shimmerings, regardless of whether we extinguish them in the process? Everything here must be said in the mode of a *'perhaps'*, after the fashion of Blanchot himself when he wants to explain what has been said in his books.
2 The figures given in brackets refer to *L'attente L'oubli* (Paris: Gallimard, 1962).
3 No ethical element comes into play in Blanchot's work so as to constitute this modality. It is not owing to its impoverished nature, nor to persecution or contempt, that it acquires the privilege of disappearing from the horizon, of transcending it, and then responding from the depths of its absence only to the

call of the best. And yet every now and then, transcendence in Blanchot consists of the very uncertainty of presence, 'as if she were only present so as to prevent herself from speaking. Then came the moments when, the thread of their relationship having been broken, she recovered her calm reality. It was at those moments that he saw better in how extraordinary a state of weakness she was, one from which she drew that authority which sometimes made her speak' (pp. 25–6). We said earlier that the word poetry referred to the disruption of immanence to which language is condemned in becoming its own prisoner. There is no question of considering this disruption as a purely aesthetic event. But the word poetry does not after all name a species whose genus is referred to by the word art. Inseparable from speech (*le verbe*), it overflows with prophetic meanings.

Translated by Michael Holland

10

The other in Proust

First published in *Deucalion*, 2 (1947), 117–23 and reprinted in *Noms propres* (Montpellier: Fata Morgana, 1976), pp. 149–56, 'The other in Proust' ('L'autre dans Proust') seeks to move us beyond the dominant images of the Proust industry: Proust the Freudian, Proust the Bergsonian, Proust the snob and sociologist. Again Levinas begins with the central view of art articulated in 'Reality and Its Shadow': namely, that the artist differs from the philosopher in creating the object through images whose hypnotic quality has no sense of utility. This creates an ambiguous and indeterminate interpretation of the world, as each thought or act is a reality that is accompanied in the Proustian world by counter-acts or shadows. This structure of appearances, which provides infinite possibilities, has the effect of nullifying every choice with its strange amorality. Henceforth the ego in Proust has to struggle to attain what it previously felt was its natural sovereignty. The mystery at the heart of Proustian research is therefore the mystery of the other. What the self seeks is itself, and it is therefore the way in which the often banal event is seized upon and thought marvellous by this self that constitutes the event itself. It is marvellous and strange because of the way the self encounters the other in itself. The story of Marcel and Albertine is therefore not about solitude and the breakdown of communication. This common reading of Proust is based on the idea that one struggles towards a unity in which being is identified with knowledge. For Levinas, Marcel did not ever love Albertine, if love is still to be thought of as fusion with the Other. But to the extent that Marcel struggles with her presence as absence in the narrative, this struggle is love, in that it is directed not by being-toward-death but by the death of the Other, not by *Dasein*, but by the responsibility for the Other's death which *creates* his infinitely answerable 'I'. In this way, the agonies of solitude which unfold in Proust situate reality not in a generous project that moves towards meaning, but in the relation with the other that forever remains other. Proust's work should stand not as a monument to the apotheosis of being, but as the relational space in which I am hostage to the Other.

An interesting comparison can be drawn between Levinas's ethical reading of Proust, and Deleuze's view of 'the opposition of Athens and Jerusalem' in the same writer in *Proust and Signs* (New York: Braziller, 1972).

The timeless qualities of a masterpiece do not in any way lift it out of time.

The unconscious and capricious concerns of the present try to find a reason and a grounding for themselves in the works of the past. Despite being complete in themselves, these works consequently change in significance as they are given a new lease of life. Proust, who no longer belongs to the present in the sense that he already acts as its guide, enjoys the magnificent fate of surviving in countless ways.

How was he seen between the two wars by those readers who, around 1933, became attracted to the literature of action, heroism and the soil, and so began to forget him? For them he was a master at the differential calculus of souls, the psychologist of the infinitesimal, and a wizard of inexpressible rhythm. He was the writer who, through a miracle of language, rediscovered and recreated a world and a time that had been lost through being dispersed into tiny moments. He emulated Freud and Bergson, and really canonized himself by giving critics the endless task of tracing influences. Dusty textbooks were already capturing the aroma of a madeleine soaked in tea, a madeleine that became the schoolboy's provisions as he set out into the unknown world of exams.

There was also Proust the sociologist. He was the new Saint-Simon of a nobility without a Versailles, the analyst of a world of artifice and affectation, that was frozen in history, and caught up in conventions more concrete than reality itself. Remarkably, he used this world's abstractions to place its inhabitants in the profound, dramatic situations which question man's very humanity in a Shakespeare or Dostoyevsky.

We have not done away with all of that. But the minute analysis which we once thought so marvellous is no longer enough in our eyes, while the 'explanations' often added by Proust to his analyses are no longer always so convincing. No doubt this reasoning or set of 'theories' about the soul's mechanism which abound in *Remembrance of Things Past* is what Sartre was referring to in 1938 when he wrote: 'Proust's psychology isn't even that of Bergson, it's more like Ribot'. This judgement may be harsh, but it indicates all the same the disrepute into which a whole area of Proust has fallen for a generation who were nourished on it.

This disrepute brings us to the essential point. The theory put forward by a scholar or philosopher refers unequivocally to the object that stands as its theme. The theory put forward by a poet, like everything he says, harbours an ambiguity, for it is concerned not to express but to create the object. Like images or symbols, reasoning is called on to produce a certain rhythm in which the reality that is sought will appear by magic. The truths or errors articulated are of no value in themselves. They are spells and incantations. To recognize in Proust's psychology the mainsprings of empiric psychology is not to destroy Proust's work, for which theory is only a means, but to allow its charm to emerge.

It is clear that this ambiguity characterizes the way Proust's poetry throws light on a subject. Despite the precision of line and the depth of character type, the contours of events, persons and things remain absolutely indeterminate. We never know right until the end what exactly has happened in this world which is none the less the same as our own and historically and geographically precise. It is a world that is never definitive and where one course of action does not preclude other possibilities. These press at the gates of being, and, like Banquo's ghost, rise and sit in the royal place. Like thoughts accompanied by reservations, acts are shadowed by unpredictable 'counter-acts', and things by 'counter-things' that reveal unsuspected perspectives and dimensions. This is the real interiorization of the Proustian world. It stems not from a subjective vision of reality, nor even from interior coordinates that exclude objective references in explaining all events that appear to come from nowhere, nor to a metaphysical base that can be sensed behind allegorical, symbolical or enigmatic appearances; but from the very structure of appearances which are both what they are and the infinity of what they exclude. Like the soul itself which, in the universe of formulable legalities and fulfilled choices, is perpetually turned into an 'outlaw', a compossibility of contradictory elements, and a nullification of every choice. It is curious to note the extent to which Proust's amorality fills his world with the wildest freedom, and confers on definite objects and beings a scintillating sense of possibility undulled by definition. One would have thought that moral laws rid the world of such glittering extravaganzas more rigorously than natural laws and that magic begins, like a witches' sabbath, where ethics leave off. The change and development in characters, some of them highly unlikely, feel completely natural in a world that has reverted to Sodom and Gomorrah, and relations are established between terms that seemed not to permit them. Everything is giddily possible.

This movement, in which reality exceeds its definition, constitutes the very mystery that intrudes into Proustian reality. This mystery is in no way nocturnal; it does not prolong the world into an invisible realm. The power of being to be incomparably more than what it is comes not from assuming some symbolic function or other, nor from some dynamism that would progressively expand this power, but from the way it continues to sparkle beneath the gaze of reflection. Reality is recalled in innumerable ways and derives the sharpness of reality from such recalls. Joy, grief and emotion are facts in Proust that are worth nothing in themselves. Within the intimate relation that it normally maintains with itself, the ego has already been split off from its own state, like a stick immersed in water which appears broken while remaining whole. All spiritual striving henceforth takes place on a plane where the ego must assume that which it quite naturally felt was already its own. True emotion in Proust is always the emotion of emotions. The former lends the latter all its warmth and all its anxiety. In spite of Lachelier's principle, which distinguishes between grief and reflection on grief, the one being grievous, the other merely true or false, Proustian reflection, which is governed by a sort of refraction, a gap existing between the ego and its state, puts its own stress on the inner life. Everything takes place as if the self were constantly doubled by another self, with a friendship that cannot be matched, but equally with a cold strangeness that life struggles to overcome. The mystery in Proust is the mystery of the other.

From this, Proust gives us something unique and without precedent in literature. His analyses, even when they do recall Ribot, which happens rarely, no matter what Sartre might say, translate only that strangeness of self to self which is a spur to the soul. The rarefied atmosphere in which events take place confers an aristocratic air on even the most mundane realities, and gives simple phrases like 'I suffered' or 'I savoured a pleasure' an intangible resonance, a mark of the nobility of a rare and precious social relation. It is not the inner event that counts, but the way in which the self seizes it and is bowled over by it, as though it were encountered in another. It is this way of grasping an event that constitutes the very event. Psychological life thus trembles in inimitable fashion. Behind the mainsprings of the soul lies the shiver through which the self takes possession of self, the dialogue in the self with the other, the soul of the soul.

In this sense Proust is a poet of social reality, though not one who portrays the manners of the day. The emotion provoked by a reflection on emotion is entirely contained within this reflection. Places and things arouse this emotion which exists through others (*les autres*), through Albertine, his grandmother, or his own past self. To know what Albertine does, what Albertine sees, who sees Albertine, is of no interest in itself as a form of knowledge, but is infinitely exciting because of its fundamental strangeness in Albertine, this strangeness which mocks knowledge.

The story of Albertine, as a prisoner and as someone who disappears, into which Proust's vast work throws itself, and all this searching down memory lane, is the account of the way the inner life looms forth from an insatiable curiosity about the alterity of the Other that is both empty and inexhaustable. The reality of Albertine is her evanescence within her very captivity, a reality made of nothingness. She is a prisoner although she has already vanished and has vanished despite being a prisoner, since despite the strictest surveillance she possesses the ability to withdraw into herself. The objective facts which Proust will manage to gather about his subject after her death will not destroy the doubt that surrounded her when her deceit masked her various escapes. When she is no longer there to defend her absence, when the accumulation of evidence no longer leaves room for any doubt, this doubt survives in full. The nothingness of Albertine discovers its total alterity. Here death is the death of the Other, contrary to the view of contemporary philosophy which remains attached to the self's solitary death. Only the death of the Other lies at the crossroads of the journey to rediscover the past. But the perpetual daily death of the Other that withdraws into the Other does not throw beings into incommunicable solitude, for it is precisely this death that nurtures love. Ontologically pure, this Eros is not a relation built on a third term, such as tastes, common interests, or the conaturality of souls, but has a direct relation to something that both gives and refuses to give itself, namely to the Other as Other, the mystery.

The theme of solitude and the breakdown in human communication are viewed by modern literature and thought as the fundamental obstacle to universal brotherhood. The pathos of socialism breaks against the eternal Bastille in which each person remains his own prisoner, locked up with himself when the party is over, the crowd gone and the torches extinguished. The despair felt at the impossibility of communication, one that fills the somewhat unfairly neglected 'solitudes' of Estaunié, for example, marks the limits of all pity, generosity and love. Collectivism in general shares this same despair. It searches for a term outside people to which each person can contribute so as to found a community that cannot be formed face to face. An ideal, a collective representation, a common enemy will reunite individuals who cannot touch or endure one another.

But if communication bears the mark of failure or inauthenticity in this way, it is because it is sought as a fusion. One begins with the idea that duality must be transformed into unity, and that social relations must culminate in communion. This is the last vestige of a conception that identifies being with knowledge, that is, with the event through which the multiplicity of reality ends up referring to a single being and where, through the miracle of clarity, everything that encounters me exists as coming from me. It is the last vestige of idealism. The breakdown of communication is the breakdown of knowledge. One does not see that the success of knowledge would precisely abolish the proximity of the Other. A proximity that, far from meaning less than identification, precisely opens up the horizons of social existence, making the whole surplus of our experience of friendship and love burst forth, and introducing the definitive quality of our identical existence to all the non-definitive possibilities.

Marcel did not love Albertine, if love is a fusion with the Other, the ecstasy of one being over the perfections of the other, or the peace of possession. Tomorrow he will break with the young woman who bores him. He will make that journey he has been planning for so long. The account of

Marcel's love is doubled by confessions that are seemingly destined to put in question the very consistency of that love. But this non-love is precisely love, the struggle with what cannot be grasped (possession, that absence of Albertine), her presence.

Through this, the theme of solitude in Proust acquires a new meaning. Its occurrence lies in the way it turns back into communication. Its despair is an inexhaustible source of hope. This is a paradox in a civilization which, in spite of the progress made since the Eleatic philosophy still sees unity as the very apotheosis of being. But Proust's most profound lesson, if poetry can contain lessons, consists in situating reality in a relation with something which for ever remains other, with the Other as absence and mystery, in rediscovering this relation in the very intimacy of the 'I', and in inaugurating a dialectic that breaks definitively with Parmenides.

Translated by Seán Hand

11

God and Philosophy

Published in *Le Nouveau Commerce*, 30–31 (1975), 97–128, 'God and Philosophy' was incorporated into *De Dieu qui vient à l'idée* (Paris: Vrin, 1982), pp. 93–127. The translation by Richard A. Cohen, first published in *Philosophy Today*, 22 (1978), 127–47 has been included in the *Collected Philosophical Papers* (Dordrecht: Martinus Nijhoff, 1987), pp. 153–73. Over the years 'God and Philosophy' has evolved into a key text by Levinas. The definitive version published here is based on the core of a lecture delivered in six very different contexts: at the University of Lille; at the annual congress of the Association des professeurs de philosophie des Facultés Catholiques de France; at the University of Jerusalem, in Hebrew; at the Facultés Universitaires Saint-Louis in Brussels; at the Centre Protestant d'Etudes, and the Faculté de Théologie Protestante, at Geneva. This has given it an ecumenical character. Indeed, on its first publication, Levinas paid homage in a preliminary note to Hugo Bergman, a professor in the philosophy department of the University of Jerusalem, who 'was always faithful to Israel's universal vocation which the state of Zion ought to serve only, to make possible a discourse addressed to all men in their human dignity, so as then to be able to answer for all men, our neighbours'.

The text itself is largely in answer to Derrida's famous essay on Levinas, 'Violence and Metaphysics' in *Writing and Difference*, and so begins by quoting (without direct reference) Derrida's concluding remark (attributed to 'a Greek') that 'if one has to philosophize, one has to philosophize; if one does not have to philosophize, one still has to philosophize'. Derrida here reads Levinas as a form of empiricism, or 'thinking *by* metaphor without thinking the metaphor *as such*' (p. 139). In reply, Levinas repeats certain ideas we have already encountered in order to show that philosophy does not contain every kind of meaning. In order to avoid a relapse into the mere *alternatives* of opinion or faith, Levinas reminds us of the vigilance of insomnia, a category we have already seen in chapter 2. This wakefulness without intentionality does not contain a theme; rather, it signifies through the introduction into discourse of infinity, which overturns the primordial character of intentionality. This infinity both includes and negates the finite: the *in* of infinity means both *non* finite and *in* the finite. Such a transcendence reveals what is beyond being: the good, and the limitless 'empirical event of obligation to another'. This responsibility is announced by the phrase: 'Here I am!', an exposure to the other where this sincere saying will for ever exceed what is said. It is a cry of ethical revolt, bearing witness to responsibility and a beyond in such a way that Levinas concludes with his denial: not to philosophize *would not be* to philosophize still.

For a full account of this distinction between Levinas and Derrida, which is so fundamental to the future of philosophy, see three excellent articles by Robert Bernasconi, which form part of a forthcoming book: 'Levinas: Philosophy and Beyond' in *Philosophy and Non-Philosophy since Merleau-Ponty*, edited by Hugh J. Silverman (London and New York: Routledge, 1988), pp. 232–58; 'The Trace of Levinas in Derrida' in *Derrida and Difference*, edited by David Wood and Robert Bernasconi (University of Warwick: Parousia Press, 1985), pp. 17–44; and 'Levinas and Derrida: The Question of the Closure of Metaphysics' in *Face to Face with Levinas* (New York: State University of New York Press, 1986), pp. 181–202.

The Priority of Philosophical Discourse, and Ontology

'Not to philosophize is still to philosophize.' The philosophical discourse of the West claims the amplitude of an all-encompassing structure or of an ultimate comprehension. It compels every other discourse to justify itself before philosophy.

Rational theology accepts this vassalage. If, for the benefit of religion, it reserves a domain from the authority of philosophy, one will know that this domain will have been recognized to be philosophically unverifiable.

The dignity of being the ultimate and royal discourse belongs to Western philosophy because of the strict coinciding of thought, in which philosophy resides, and the idea of reality in which this thought thinks. For thought, this coinciding means not having to think beyond what belongs to 'being's move' ('geste d'être'), or at least not beyond what modifies a previous belongingness to 'being's move', such as formal or ideal notions. For the being of reality, this coinciding means: to illuminate thought and the conceived by showing itself. To show oneself, to be illuminated, is just what having meaning is, what having intelligibility par excellence is, the intelligibility underlying every modification of meaning. Then we should have to understand the rationality of 'being's move' not as some characteristic which would be attributed to it when a reason comes to know of it. That a thought comes to know of it is intelligibility. Rationality has to be understood as the incessant emergence of thought from the energy of 'being's move' or its manifestation, and reason has to be understood out of this rationality. Meaningful thought, and thought about being, would be pleonasms and equivalent pleonasms, which, however, are justified by the vicissitudes and privations to which this identification of the thought of the meaningful and of being is de jure exposed.

Philosophical discourse therefore should be able to include God, of whom the Bible speaks – if this God does have a meaning. But as soon as he is conceived, this God is situated within 'being's move'. He is situated there as the *entity* par excellence. If the intellectual understanding of the biblical God, theology, does not reach to the level of philosophical thought, this is not because it thinks of God as *a being* without first explicating the 'being of this being', but because in thematizing God it brings God into the course of being. But, in the most unlikely way – that is, not analogous with an idea subject to *criteria*, or subject to the demand that it show itself to be true or false – the God of the Bible signifies the beyond being, transcendence. It is not by chance that the history of Western philosophy has been a destruction of transcendence. Rational theology, fundamentally ontological, strives to take account of transcendence in the domain of being by expressing it with adverbs of height applied to the verb being; God is said to exist eminently or par excellence. But does the height, or the height above all height, that is thus expressed belong to ontology? And does not the modality which this adverb, borrowed from the dimension of the sky over our heads, expresses modify the verbal meaning of the verb to be to the point of excluding it from the thinkable as something inapprehendable, excluding it from the *esse* showing itself, that is, showing itself meaningfully in a theme?

One can also, to be sure, claim that the God of the Bible does not have meaning, that is, is not properly speaking thinkable. This would be the other term of the alternative. 'The concept of God is not a problematical concept; it is not a concept at all,' writes Mme Delhomme in a recent book, continuing a major tradition of philosophical rationalism which refuses to accept the transcendence of the God of Abraham, Isaac, and Jacob among the concepts without which there would be no thought. What the Bible puts above all comprehension would have not yet reached the threshold of intelligibility!

The problem which is thus posed, and which will be ours, is whether the meaning that is equivalent to the *esse* of being, that is, the meaning which is meaning in philosophy, is not already a restriction of meaning. Is it not already a derivative or a drifting of meaning? Is not the meaning equivalent to essence – to being's move, to being *qua* being – first broached in presence, which is the time of the same? This supposition can be justified only through the possibility of going back from this allegedly conditioned meaning to a meaning which could no longer be put in terms of being or in terms of beings. We must ask if beyond the intelligibility and rationalism of identity, consciousness, the present, and being – beyond the intelligibility of immanence – the signifyingness, rationality, and rationalism of transcendence are not understood. Over and beyond being does not a meaning whose priority, translated into ontological language, would have to be called *antecedent* to being, show itself? It is not certain that in going beyond the terms and beings one necessarily relapses into speaking of opinion or faith.

In fact, in staying or wanting to be outside of reason, faith and opinion speak the language of being. Nothing is less opposed to ontology than opinion and faith. To ask, as we are trying to do here, if God can be expressed in a rational discourse which would be neither ontology not faith is implicitly to doubt the formal opposition, established by Yehouda Halevy and taken up by Pascal, between the God of Abraham, Isaac, and Jacob, invoked in faith without philosophy, and the god of philosophers. It is to doubt that this opposition constitutes an alternative.

The Priority of Ontology and Immanence

We said that for Western philosophy meaning or intelligibility coincide with the manifestation of being, as if the very doings of being led to clarity, in the form of intelligibility, and then became an intentional thematization in an experience. Pressing toward or waiting for it, all the potentialities of experience are derived from or susceptible to such thematization. Thematic exposition concludes the business of being or truth. But if being *is* manifestation, if the exertion of being amounts to this exhibition, the manifestation of being is only the manifestation of this 'exertion', that is, the manifestation of manifestation, the truth of truth. Philosophy thus finds in manifestation its matter and its form. In its attachment to being, to beings or the being of beings, it would thus remain a movement of knowledge and truth, an adventure of experience between the clear and the obscure. It is certain that this is the sense in which philosophy is the bearer of the spirituality of the West, where spirit is taken to be coextensive with knowing. But knowing – or thought, or experience – is not to be understood as a kind of reflection of exteriority in an inner forum. The notion of reflection, an optical metaphor taken from thematized beings and events, is not the proper trope for knowing. Knowing is only understood in its proper essence when one begins with consciousness, whose specificity is lost when it is defined with the concept of knowing, a concept which presupposes consciousness.

It is as a modality or modification of *insomnia* that consciousness is consciousness of . . . , a gathering into being or into presence, which, at a certain depth of vigilance where vigilance has to clothe itself with justice, is essential to insomnia.[1] Insomnia, wakefulness or vigilance, far from being definable as the simple negation of the natural phenomenon of sleep, belongs to the categorial, antecedent to all anthropological attention and stupor. Ever on the verge of awakening, sleep communicates with vigilance; while trying to escape, sleep stays tuned in, in an *obedience to the wakefulness* which threatens it and calls to it, which *demands*. The categorial proper to insomnia is not reducible to the tautological affirmation of the same, dialectical negation, or the ecstasy of thematizing intentionality. Here being awake is not equivalent to *watching over* . . . , where already the identical, rest, sleep, is sought after. It is in consciousness alone that the *watching*, already petrified, bends over toward a content which is identified and gathered into a presence, into a 'move of being', and is absorbed in it. Insomnia as a category – or as a meta-category (but the *meta-* becomes meaningful through it) – does not get inscribed in a table of categories from a determining activity exercised on the other as *given* by the unity of the same (and all activity is but the identification and crystallization of the same against the other, upon being affected by that other), in order to ensure to the other, consolidated into a being, the gravity of being. Insomnia – the wakefulness in awakening – is disturbed in the core of its formal or categorical *sameness* by the *other*, which tears away at whatever forms a nucleus, a substance of the same, identity, a rest, a presence, a sleep. Insomnia is disturbed by the other who breaks this rest, breaks it from this side of the state in which equality tends to establish itself. The irreducible categorial character of insomnia lies precisely in that. The other is in the same, and does not alienate the same but awakens it. Awakening is like a demand that no obedience is equal to, no obedience puts to sleep; it is a 'more' in the 'less'. Or, to use an obsolete language, it is the spirituality of the soul, ceaselessly aroused from its state of soul, in which wakefulness itself already closes over upon itself or falls to sleep, resting within the boundaries it has as a state. We find here the passivity of inspiration, or the subjectivity of the subjectivity of the subject aroused, sobered up, out of its being. There is a formalism in insomnia, a formalism more formal than that of any defining, delimiting, confining form, more formally formal than that of a form that closes into a presence and an *esse*, filling with content. Insomnia is wakefulness, but a wakefulness without intentionality, dis-interested. Its indeterminatedness does not call for a form, is not a material-ity. It is a form that does not *terminate* the drawing out of a form in it, and does not condense its own emptiness into a content. It is uncontained – infinity.

Consciousness has already broken with this dis-interestedness. It is the identity of the same, the presence of being, the presence of presence. We must think of consciousness beginning with the emphasis of presence.[2] Presence is only possible as a return of consciousness to itself, outside of sleep – and consciousness thus goes back to insomnia. That is so even though this return to itself, in the form of self-consciousness, is only a forgetting of the other which awakens the same from within, and even if the freedom of the same is still only a waking dream. Presence is only possible as an incessant taking up of presence again, an incessant re-presentation. The incessance of presence is a repetition, its being taken up again an apperception of representation. Representation is not to be described as a taking up again. Representation is the very possibility of a return, the possibility of the *always*, or of the presence of the present. The unity of apperception, the 'I think', which is discovered and acquired its role in re-presentation, is not a way to make presence purely subjective. The synthesis effected by the unity of the *I think* behind experience constitutes the act of presence, presence as an act, or presence in act. This encompassing movement is accomplished by the unity formed into a nucleus in the 'I think', a synopsis which is a structure necessary for the actuality of the present. The 'activity of the mind', the operative concept of transcendental idealism, is not based on an empirical experience of the deployment of intellectual energy. It is rather the extreme purity – to the point of tension – of the presence of presence, which is Aristotle's being in act, a presence of presence, an extreme tension breaking up *presence* into an 'experience of a subject', where precisely presence returns upon itself and is filled up and fulfilled. The psychic nature of consciousness is this emphasis of being, this presence of presence, a presence outdoing itself, without loopholes, without hedging, without any possible forgetting in the folds of what would be only implicit and could not be unfolded. The 'incessance' is an explication without any possible shading off; it refers to an awakening that would be lucidity, but also to a watching over being, an attention to . . . and not an exposedness to the other (and already a modification of the formalism without intentionality of insomnia). It is always true that because of consciousness nothing can be dissimulated in being. Consciousness is a light which illuminates the world from one end to the other; everything which goes off into the past is recalled or recovered by history. Reminiscence is the extreme consciousness which is also the universal presence and the universal ontology; whatever is able to fill the field of consciousness was, in its time, received or perceived, had an origin. Through consciousness the past is only a modification of the present. Nothing can happen and nothing could have happened without presenting itself, nothing could be smuggled by without being declared, without being shown, without being inspected as to its truth. Transcendental subjectivity is the figure of this presence; no signification precedes that which I give to myself.

Thus the process of the present unfolds through consciousness like a 'held note' held in its *always*, in its identity of being the same, in the simultaneity of its moments. The process of the subjective does not come from the outside; the presence of the present involves consciousness. And philosophy, then, in search of the transcendental operations of the apperception of the *I think*, is not some unhealthy and accidental curiosity; it is representation, the reactualization of representation, that is, the emphasis of presence, being's remaining-the-same in the simultaneity of its presence, in its always, in its immanence. Philosophy is not merely the knowledge of immanence; it is immanence itself.[3]

Immanence and consciousness, as gathering up the manifestation of manifestation, are not disturbed by the phenomenological interpretation of affective states or of the voluntary psyche, which puts in the very heart of consciousness the emotion or the anxiety which upset its imperturbability – nor by that interpretation that starts from fear or trembling before the sacred, and understands them as primary lived states. It is not accidental that the axiological and practical strata in Husserl cover over a representational ground.

The axiological and the practical strata remain experiences – experiences of values, or experiences of the willed *qua* willed. The representational ground, which Husserl brings out in them, consists, moreover, less in some serenity of the theoretical intention than in the identification of the identical in the form of ideality, in the assembling, in the representation in the form of a presence, a lucidity which allows nothing to escape. In short, it consists in immanence.

But let us take note of this: the interpretation of affectivity as a modification of representation, or as founded on a representation, succeeds in the measure that affectivity is taken at the level of a tendency, or concupiscence, as Pascal would say – at the level of an aspiration which can be satisfied in pleasure or, when unsatisfied, remains a pure lack which causes suffering. Beneath such an affectivity is found the ontological activity of consciousness – wholly investment and comprehension, that is, presence and representation (of which the specifically theoretical thematization is but a modality). This does not exclude the possibility that, in another direction besides that of a tendency going to its term, there may break out an affectivity which breaks with the form and purpose of consciousness, and leaves immanence, is a transcendence. We are going to try to speak of this 'elsewhere'.

A religious thought which appeals to religious experiences allegedly independent of philosophy already, inasmuch as it is founded on experience, refers to the 'I think', and is wholly connected on to philosophy. The 'narration' of religious experience does not shake philosophy and cannot break with presence and immanence, of which philosophy is the emphatic completion. It is possible that the word God has come to philosophy out of religious discourse. But even if philosophy refuses this discourse, it understands it as a language made of propositions bearing on a theme, that is, as having a meaning which refers to a disclosure, a manifestation of presence.

The bearers of religious experience do not conceive of any other signification of meaning. Religious 'revelation' is therewith already assimilated to philosophical disclosure; even dialectical theology maintains this assimilation. That a discourse can speak otherwise than to say what has been seen or heard on the outside, or previously experienced, remains unsuspected. From the start then a religious being interprets what he lived through as an experience. It spite of himself he already interprets God, of whom he claims to have an experience, in terms of being, presence and immanence.

Then the first question has to be: can discourse signify otherwise than by signifying a theme? Does God signify as the theme of the religious discourse which names God – or as the discourse which, at least to begin with, does not name him, but says him with another form of address than denomination or evocation?

The Idea of the Infinite

The thematization of God in religious experience has already avoided or missed the inordinate plot that breaks up the unity of the 'I think'.[4]

In his meditation on the idea of God, Descartes, with an unequalled rigour, has sketched out the extraordinary course of a thought that proceeds on to the breakup of the *I think*. Although he conceives of God as a being, he conceives of him as an eminent being or being that *is* eminently. Before this rapprochement between the idea of God and the idea of being, we do indeed have to ask whether the adjective *eminent* and the adverb *eminently* do not refer to the elevation of the sky above our heads, and whether they do not go beyond ontology. Be that as it may, interpreting the immeasurability of God as a superlative case of existing, Descartes maintains a substantialist language. But for us this is not what is unsurpassable in his meditation. It is not the proofs of God's existence that matter to us here, but the breakup of consciousness, which is not a repression into the unconscious, but a sobering up or an awakening, jolting the 'dogmatic slumber' which sleeps at the bottom of every consciousness resting on its object. The idea of God, the *cogitatum* of a *cogitatio* which *to begin with* contains that *cogitatio, signifies the non-contained par excellence.* Is not that the very absolution of the absolute? It overflows every capacity; the 'objective reality' of the *cogitatum* breaks up the 'formal reality' of the *cogitatio.* This perhaps overturns, in advance, the universal validity and primordial character of intentionality. We will say that the idea of God breaks up the thought which is an investment, a synopsis and a synthesis, and can only enclose in a presence, re-present, reduce to presence or let be.

Malebranche knew how to gauge the import of this event; there is no idea of God, or God is his own idea. We are outside the order in which one passes from an idea to a being. The idea of God is God in me, but God already breaking up the consciousness which aims at ideas, and unlike any content. This difference is certainly not an emergence, which would be to imply that an inclusion of God in consciousness had been possible, nor some sort of escaping the realm of consciousness, which is to imply that there could have been *comprehension*. And yet there is an idea of God, or God is in us, as though the being-not-includable were also an ex-ceptional relationship with me, as though the difference between the Infinite and what ought to include and comprehend it were a non-indifference of the Infinite to this impossible inclusion, a non-indifference of the Infinite to thought. There is a putting of the Infinite into thought, but this is wholly different from what is structured as a comprehension of a *cogitatum* by a *cogitatio*. This putting is an unequalled passivity, because it is unassumable. (It is perhaps in this passivity – beyond all passivity – that we should recognize awakening.) Or, conversely, it is as though the negation of the finite included in In-finity did not signify any sort of negation resulting from the formal structure of negative judgement, but rather signified the *idea of the Infinite*, that is, the Infinite in me. Or, more exactly, it is as though the psyche in subjectivity were equivalent to the negation of the finite by the Infinite, as though – without wanting to play on words – the *in* of the Infinite were to signify both the *non* and the *within*.[5]

The actuality of the *cogito* is thus interrupted by the unincludable, not thought but undergone in the form of the idea of the Infinite, bearing in a second moment of consciousness what in a first moment claimed to bear it. After the certainty of the *cogito*, present to itself in the second Meditation, after the 'halt' which the last lines of this Meditation mark, the third Meditation announces that 'in some way I have in me the notion of the infinite earlier than the finite – to wit, the notion of God before that of myself.' The idea of the Infinite, *Infinity in me*, can only be a passivity of consciousness. Is it still consciousness? There is here a passivity which cannot be likened to receptivity. Receptivity is a collecting that takes place in a welcome, an assuming that takes place under the force of the blow received. The breakup of the actuality of thought in the 'idea of God' is a passivity more passive still than any passivity, like the passivity of a trauma through which the idea of God would have been put into us. An 'idea put into us' – does this stylistic turn suit the subjectivity of the cogito? Does it suit consciousness and its way of holding a content, which is always to leave some traces of its grasp on it? Does not consciousness, in its present, get its origin and its contents from itself? Can an idea be put into a thought and abjure its letters patent of Socratic nobility, its immanent birth in remini-scence, that is, its origin in the very presence of the thought that thinks it, or in the recuperation of this thought by memory? But in the idea of the

Infinite there is described a passivity more passive still than any passivity befitting consciousness: there is the surprise or susception of the unassumable, more open still than any openness – wakefulness – but suggesting the passivity of someone created.[6] The putting into us of an unincludable idea overturns that presence to self which consciousness is, forcing its way through the barrier and checkpoint, eluding the obligation to accept or adopt all that enters from the outside. It is then an idea signifying with a signifyingness prior to presence, to all presence, prior to every origin in consciousness and thus an-archical, accessible in its trace. It signifies with a signifyingness from the first older than its exhibition, not exhausting itself in exhibiting itself, not drawing its meaning from its manifestation, and thus breaking with the coinciding of being with appearance in which, for Western philosophy, meaning or rationality lie, breaking with synopsis. It is more ancient than the rememberable thought which representation retains in its presence. What can this signification more ancient than exhibition mean? Or, more exactly, what can the antiquity of a signification mean? In exhibition, can it enter into another time than that of the historical present, which already annuls the past and its dia-chrony by re-presenting it? What can this antiquity mean if not the trauma of awakening – as though the idea of the Infinite, the Infinite in us, awakened a consciousness which is not awakened enough? As though the idea of the Infinite in us were a demand, and a signification in the sense that an order is signified in a demand.

Divine Comedy

We have already said that it is not in the negation of the finite by the Infinite, understood in its abstraction and logical formalism, that the idea of the Infinite, or the Infinite in thought, is to be interpreted. On the contrary, the idea of the Infinite, or the Infinite in thought, is the proper and irreducible figure for the negation of the finite. The *in* of infinity is not a *not* like any other; its negation is the subjectivity of the subject, which is behind intentionality. The difference between the Infinite and the finite is behind intentionality. The difference between the Infinite and the finite is a non-indifference of the Infinite to the finite, and is the secret of subjectivity. The figure of the Infinite put in me, and, according to Descartes, contemporaneous with my creation,[7] would mean that the not being able to comprehend the Infinite by thought is somehow a positive relationship with this thought – but with this thought as passive, as a *cogitatio* as though dumbfounded and no longer, or not yet, commanding the *cogitatum*, not yet hastening toward adequation between the term of the spontaneous teleology of consciousness and this term given in being. Such an adequation is the destiny of the essential teleology of consciousness, which proceeds to its intentional term, and conjures up the presence of representation. Better yet, the not-being-able-to-comprehend-the-Infinite-by-thought would signify the condition – or the unconditionality – of thought, as though to speak of the non-comprehension of the Infinite by the finite did not amount to simply saying that the Infinite is not finite, and as though the affirmation of the difference between the Infinite and the finite had to remain a verbal abstraction, without consideration of the fact that through the non-comprehension of the Infinite by thought, thought is posited as thought,[8] as a posited subjectivity, that is, is posited as self-positing. The Infinite has nothing to add on to itself so as to affect subjectivity; its very in-finity, its difference from the finite, is already its non-indifference to the finite. This amounts to a *cogitatio not comprehending the cogitatum* which affects it utterly. The Infinite affects thought by devastating it and at the same time calls upon it; in a 'putting it back in its place' it puts thought in place. It awakens it. The awakening of thought is not a welcoming of the Infinite, is not a recollecting, not an assuming, which are necessary and sufficient for *experience*. The idea of the Infinite puts these in question. The idea of the Infinite is not even taken up as love, which is awakened when the arrow strikes, but then the subject stunned by the trauma finds himself forthwith in the immanence of a state of soul. The Infinite signifies precisely prior to its manifestation; here the meaning is not reducible to manifestation, the representation of presence, or teleology. Here meaning is not measured by the possibility or impossibility of the truth of being, even if this antecedent signification should, in one way or another – and if only through its trace – show itself in the enigmas involved in saying.

What then is the plot of meaning, other than that of re-presentation and of empirical experience, which is hatched in the idea of the Infinite – in the monstrosity of the Infinite *put* in me – an idea which in its passivity over and beyond all receptivity is no longer an idea? What is the meaning of the trauma of awakening, in which the Infinite can neither be posited as a correlate of the subject, nor enter into a structure with it, nor become its contemporary in a co-presence – but in which it transcends him? How is transcendence as a relationship thinkable if it must exclude the ultimate and the most formal co-presence which a relationship guarantees to its terms?

The *in* of the Infinite designates the depth of the affecting by which subjectivity is affected through this 'putting' of the Infinite into it, without prehension or comprehension. It designates the depth of an undergoing that no capacity comprehends, that no foundation any longer supports, where every process of investing fails and where the screws that fix the stern of inwardness burst. This putting in without a corresponding recollecting devastates its site like a devouring fire, catastrophying its site, in the etymological sense of the word.[9] It is a dazzling, where the eye takes more than it can hold, an igniting of the skin which touches and does not touch what is beyond the graspable, and burns. It is a passivity or a passion in which desire can be recognized, in which the '*more* in the *less*' awakens by its most ardent, noblest and most ancient flame a thought given over to thinking more than it thinks.[10] But this desire is of another order than the desires involved in hedonist or eudaemonist affectivity and activity, where the desirable is invested, reached, and identified as an object of need, and where the immanence of representation and of the exterior world is restored. The negativity of the *in* of the Infinite – otherwise than being, divine comedy – hollows out a desire which cannot be filled, nourishes itself with its very augmentation, and is exalted as a desire, withdraws from its satisfaction in the measure that it approaches the desirable. It is a desire that is beyond satisfaction, and, unlike a need, does not identify a term or an end. This endless desire for what is beyond being is dis-inter*estedness*, transcendence – desire for the Good.

But if the Infinite in me means a desire for the Infinite, is one certain of the transcendence which *passes* there? Does not desire restore the contemporaneousness of desiring and the desirable? Or, in other words, does not the desiring being derive from the desirable a complacency in desiring, as though it had already grasped it by its intention? Is not the disinter*estedness* of the desire for the Infinite an inter*estedness*? We have spoken of a desire for the Good beyond being, a transcendence, without giving our attention to the way interestedness is excluded from the desire for the Infinite, and without showing how the transcendent Infinite deserves the name Good, when its very transcendence can, it seems, only mean indifference.

Love is possible only through the idea of the Infinite – through the Infinite put in me, through the 'more' which devastates and awakens the 'less', turning away from teleology, destroying the moment and the happiness of the end. Plato forces out of Aristophanes an admission which, coming from the lips of the master of comedy, is striking indeed: 'These are the people who pass their whole lives together; yet they could not explain what they desire of one another.'[11] Hephaestus will say that they want to become 'one instead of two',[12] and he thus assigns an end to love and reduces it to a nostalgia for what was in the past. But why can the lovers themselves not say what they ask from one another beyond pleasure? Diotima will put love's intention beyond this unity, but will find love to be indigent, needy, and subject to vulgarity. The celestial and the vulgar Venus are sisters. Love is complacent in waiting for the lovable, that is, it enjoys the lovable through the representation which fills up the waiting. Perhaps pornography is that, arising in all eroticism, as eroticism arises in all love. Losing in this enjoyment the inordinateness of desire, love is concupiscence in Pascal's sense of the term, an assuming and an investing by the *I*. The *I think* reconstitutes presence and being, inter*estedness* and immanence, in love.

Is a transcendence of the desirable beyond the inter*estedness* and eroticism in which the beloved abides possible? Affected by the Infinite, desire cannot proceed to an end which it would be equal to; in desire the approach distances, and enjoyment is but the increase of hunger. Transcendence or the disinter*estedness* of desire 'passes' in this reversal of terms. How? And in the transcendence of the Infinite what dictates to us the word Good? For dis-inter*estedness* to be possible in the desire for the Infinite, for the desire beyond being, or transcendence, not to be an absorption in immanence, which would thus make its return, it is necessary that the desirable or God remain separated in the desire; as desirable it is near but different: holy. This can only be if the desirable orders me to what is the non-desirable, the undesirable par excellence – the other. The reference to the other is an awakening, an awakening to proximity, and this is responsibility for the neighbour, to the point of substituting for him. Elsewhere[13] we have shown that substitution for another lies in the heart of responsibility, an undoing of the nucleus of the transcendental subject, the transcendence of goodness, the nobility of a pure *supporting*, an ipseity of pure election. Such is love without Eros. Transcendence is ethics, and subjectivity which is not, in the last analysis, the 'I think' (which it is at first) or the unity of 'transcendental apperception' is, as a responsibility for another, a subjection to the other. The I is a passivity more passive still than any passivity because it is from the first in the accusative – oneself (*soi*) – and never was in the nominative; it is under the accusation of the other, even though it be faultless. It is a hostage for the other, obeying a command before having heard it, faithful to a commitment that it never made, to a past that has never been present. This wakefulness or openness to oneself is completely exposed, and sobered up from the ecstasy of intentionality. We have designated this way for the Infinite, or for God, to refer, from the heart of its very desirability, to the non-desirable proximity of others, by the term 'illeity'; it is the extraordinary reversal of the desirability of the desirable, the supreme desirability, calling to itself the rectilinear straightforwardness of desire. Through this reversal the desirable escapes desire. The goodness of the Good – the Good which never sleeps or nods – inclines the movement it calls forth, to turn it from the Good and orient it toward the other, and only thus toward the Good. Here is an obliqueness that goes higher than straightforwardness. The desirable is intangible and separates itself from the relationship with desire which it calls for; through this separation or holiness it remains a third person, the *he* in the depth of the you. He is good in just this eminent sense; He does not fill me up with goods, but compels me to goodness, which is better than goods received.[14]

To be good is a deficit, waste and foolishness in a being; to be good is excellence and elevation beyond being. Ethics is not a moment of being; it is otherwise and better than being, the very possibility of the beyond.[15] In this ethical reversal, in this reference of the desirable to the non-desirable, in this strange mission that orders the approach to the other, God is drawn out of objectivity, presence and being. He is neither an object nor an interlocutor. His absolute remoteness, his transcendence, turns into my responsibility – non-erotic par excellence – for the other. And this analysis implies that God is not simply the 'first other', the 'other par excellence', or the 'absolutely other', but other than the other (*autre qu'autrui*), other otherwise, other with an alterity prior to the alterity of the other, prior to the ethical bond with another and different from every neighbour, transcendent to the point of absence, to the point of a possible confusion with the stirring of the *there is*.[16] In this confusion the substitution for the neighbour gains in dis-inter*estedness*, that is, in nobility, and the transcendence of the Infinite arises in glory. Such transcendence is true with a dia-chronic truth and without any synthesis, higher than the truths that are without enigma.[17] For this formula 'transcendence to the point of absence' not to mean the simple explicitation of an ex-ceptional word, this word itself has to be put back into the significance of the whole plot of the ethical or back into the divine comedy without which it could not have arisen. That comedy is enacted equivocally between temple and theatre, but in it the laughter sticks to one's throat when the neighbour approaches – that is, when his face, or his forsakenness, draws near.

Phenomenology and Transcendence

The exposition of the ethical signification of transcendence and of the Infinite beyond being can be worked out beginning with the proximity of the neighbour and my responsibility for the other.

Until then a passive subjectivity might seem something constructed and abstract. The receptivity of finite knowledge is an assembling of a dispersed given in the simultaneity of presence, in immanence. The passivity 'more passive still than any passivity' consisted in undergoing – or more exactly in having already undergone, in a non-representable past which was never present – a trauma that could not be assumed; it consisted in being struck by the '*in*' of infinity which devastates presence and awakens subjectivity to the proximity of the other. The non-contained, which breaks the container or the forms of consciousness, thus *transcends* the essence or the 'move' of knowable being which carries on its being in presence; it transcends the

inter*estedness* and simultaneity of a representable or historically reconstitut-
able temporality; it transcends immanence.

This trauma which cannot be assumed, inflicted by the Infinite on presence, or this affecting of presence by the Infinite – this affectivity – takes
shape as a subjection to the neighbour. It is thought thinking more than it
thinks, desire, the reference to the neighbour, the responsibility for
another.

This abstraction is nevertheless familiar to us in the empirical event of
obligation to another, as the impossibility of indifference – impossible
without fail – before the misfortunes and faults of a neighbour, the
unexceptionable responsibility for him. It is impossible to fix limits or
measure the extreme urgency of this responsibility. Upon reflection it is
something completely astonishing, a responsibility that even extends to the
obligation to answer for another's freedom, to be responsible for his responsibility, whereas the freedom which would demand an eventual commitment or even the assuming of an imposed necessity cannot find a present
that includes the possibilities which belong to the other. The other's freedom can neither constitute a structure along with my freedom, nor enter
into a synthesis with it. Responsibility for the neighbour is precisely what
goes beyond the legal and obliges beyond contracts; it comes to me from
what is prior to my freedom, from a non-present, an immemorial. A difference gapes open between me and the other that no unity of transcendental apperception can undo. My responsibility for the other is precisely
the non-indifference of this difference – the proximity of the other. An
absolutely extra-ordinary relation, it does not reestablish the order of
representation in which every past returns. The proximity of a neighbour
remains a dia-chronic break, a resistance of time to the synthesis' of simultaneity.

The biological human brotherhood – conceived with the sober coldness of
Cain – is not a sufficient reason for me to be responsible for a separated
being. The sober coldness of Cain consists in conceiving responsibility as
proceeding from freedom or in terms of a contract. But responsibility for
another comes from what is prior to my freedom. It does not come from the
time made up of presences, nor presences that have sunk into the past and
are representable, the time of beginnings or assumings. It does not allow me
to constitute myself into an *I think*, substantial like a stone, or, like a heart
of stone, existing in and for oneself. It ends up in substitution for another,
in the condition – or the unconditionality – of being a hostage. Such
responsibility does not give one time, a present for recollection or coming
back to oneself; it makes one always late. Before the neighbour I am
summoned and do not just appear; from the first I am answering to an
assignation. Already the stony core of my substance is dislodged. But the

responsibility to which I am exposed in such a passivity does not apprehend me as an interchangeable thing, for here no one can be substituted for me; in calling upon me as someone accused who cannot reject the accusation, it obliges me as someone unreplaceable and unique, someone chosen. Inasmuch as it calls upon my responsibility it forbids me any replacement. Unreplaceable in responsibility, I cannot, without defaulting, incurring fault or being caught up in some complex, escape the face of a neighbour; here I am pledged to the other without being able to take back my pledge.[18] I cannot evade the face of the other, naked and without resources. The nakedness of someone forsaken shows in the cracks in the mask of the personage, or in his wrinkled skin; his being 'without resources' has to be heard like cries not voiced or thematized, already addressed to God. There the resonance of silence – *Gelaut der Stille* – certainly sounds. We here have come upon an imbroglio that has to be taken seriously: a relationship to ... that is not represented, without intentionality, not repressed; it is the latent birth of religion in the other, prior to emotions or voices, prior to 'religious experience' which speaks of revelation in terms of the disclosure of being, when it is a question of an unwonted access, in the heart of my responsibility, to an unwonted disturbance of being. Even if one says right away, 'It was nothing.' 'It was nothing' – it was not being, but otherwise than being. My responsibility in spite of myself – which is the way the other's charge falls upon me, or the way the other disturbs me, that is, is close to me – is the hearing or understanding of this cry. It is awakening. The proximity of a neighbour is my responsibility for him; to approach is to be one's brother's keeper; to be one's brother's keeper is to be his hostage. Immediacy is this. Responsibility does not come from fraternity, but fraternity denotes responsibility for another, antecedent to my freedom.

To posit subjectivity in this responsibility is to catch sight of a passivity in it that is never passive enough, that of being consumed for the other. The very light of subjectivity shines and illuminates out of this ardour, although the ashes of this consummation are not able to fashion the kernel of a being existing in and for itself, and the I does not oppose to the other any form that protects itself or provides it with a measure. Such is the consuming of a holocaust. 'I am dust and ashes', says Abraham in interceding for Sodom.[19] 'What are we?' says Moses more humbly still.[20]

What is the meaning of this assignation in which the nucleus of the subject is uprooted, undone, and does not receive any form capable of assuming this? What do these atomic metaphors mean, if not an I torn from the concept of the ego and from the content of obligations for which the concept rigorously supplies measure and rule, and thus left to an unmeasured responsibility, because it increases in the measure – or in the immeasurableness – that a response is made, increasing gloriously. This is the I that is not designated, but which says 'here I am'. 'Each of us is guilty before everyone, for everyone and for each one, and I more than others,' writes Dostoyevsky in *The Brothers Karamazov*. The I which says I is not that which singularizes or individuates a concept or a genus. It is I, unique in its genus, who speaks to you in the first person. That is, unless one could maintain that it is in the individuation of the genus or the concept of the ego that I myself awaken and expose myself to others, that is, begin to speak. This exposedness is not like self-consciousness, the recurrence of the subject to himself, confirming the ego by itself. The recurrence in awakening is something one can describe as a shudder of incarnation through which *giving* takes on meaning, as the primordial dative of the *for another*, in which a subject becomes a heart, a sensibility, and hands which give. But it is thus a position already deposed of its kingdom of identity and substance, already in debt, 'for the other' to the point of substitution for the other, altering the immanence of the subject in the depths of its identity. This subject unreplaceable for the responsibility assigned to him finds in that very fact a new identity. But in extracting me from the concept of the ego, the fission of the subject is a growth of obligation in proportion as obedience grows, the augmentation of guilt that comes with the augmentation of holiness, the increase of distance proportionate to the approach. Here there is no rest for the self sheltered in its form, in its ego-concept! There are no conditions, not even those of servitude. There is an incessant solicitude for solicitude, the extreme of passivity in responsibility for the responsibility of the other. Thus proximity is never close enough; as responsible, I am never finished with emptying myself of myself. There is infinite increase in this exhausting of oneself, in which the subject is not simply an awareness of this expenditure, but is its locus and event and, so to speak, its goodness. The *glory of a long desire*! The subject as a hostage has been neither the experience nor the proof of the Infinite, but a witness borne of the Infinite, a modality of this glory, a testimony that no disclosure has preceded.

This growing surplus of the Infinite that we have ventured to call *glory* is not an abstract quintessence. It has a signification in the response to the summons which comes to me from the face of a neighbour, and which could not be evaded; it is the hyperbolic demand which at once exceeds that response. This comes as a surprise for the respondent himself by which, ousted from his inwardness as an ego and a 'being with two sides', he is awakened, that is, exposed to the other without restraint or reserve. The passivity of such an exposure to the other is not exhausted in some sort of being open to the other's look or objectifying judgement. The openness of the ego exposed to the other is the breakup or turning inside out of inwardness. Sincerity is the name of this extra-version.[21] But what else can this inversion or extra-version mean but a responsibility for others such that I keep nothing for myself? A responsibility such that everything in me is debt and donation and such that my being-there is the ultimate being-there where the creditors find the debtor? It is a responsibility such that my position as a subject in its *as for me* is already my substitution or expiation for others. Responsibility for the other – for his distress and his freedom – does not derive from any commitment, project or antecedent disclosure, in which the subject would be posited for itself before being-in-debt. Here passivity is extreme in the measure (or inordinateness) that the devotion for the other is not shut up in itself like a state of soul, but is itself from the start given over to the other.

This excess is *saying*. Sincerity is not an attribute which eventually receives the saying; it is by saying that sincerity – exposedness without reserve – is first possible. Saying makes signs to the other, but in this sign signifies the very giving of signs. Saying opens me to the other before saying what is said, before the said uttered in this sincerity forms a screen between me and the other. This saying without a said is thus like silence. It is without words, but not with hands empty. If silence speaks, it is not through some inward mystery or some sort of ecstasy of intentionality, but through the hyperbolic passivity of giving, which is prior to all willing and thematization. Saying bears witness to the other of the Infinite which rends me, which in the saying awakens me.

Language understood in this way loses its superfluous and strange function of doubling up thought and being. Saying as testimony precedes all the said. Saying, before setting forth a said, is already the testimony of this responsibility – and even the saying of a said, as an approach to the other, is a responsibility for him. Saying is therefore a way of signifying prior to all experience. A pure testimony, it is a martyr's truth which does not depend on any disclosure or any 'religious' experience; it is an obedience that precedes the hearing of any order. A pure testimony, it does not testify to a prior experience, but to the Infinite which is not accessible to the unity of apperception, non-appearing and disproportionate to the present. Saying could neither include nor comprehend the Infinite; the Infinite concerns and closes in on me while speaking through my mouth. And the only pure testimony is that of the Infinite. This is not a psychological wonder, but the modality in which the Infinite *comes to pass*, signifying through him to whom it signifies, understood inasmuch as, before any commitment, I answer for the other.

Like someone put under leaden skies that suppress every shadowy corner in me, every residue of mystery, every mental reservation, every 'as for

me...' and every hardening or relaxing of the plot of things by which
escape would be possible, I am a testimony, or a trace, or the glory of the
Infinite, breaking the bad silence which harbours Gyges's secrecy. There is
extra-verting of a subject's inwardness; the subject becomes visible before
becoming a seer! The Infinite is not 'in front of' me; I express it, but
precisely by giving a sign of the giving of signs, of the 'for-the-other' in
which I am dis-interested; here I am (*me voici*)! The accusative (*me* voici!)
here is remarkable: here I am, under your eyes, at your service, your
obedient servant. In the name of God. But this is without thematization; the
sentence in which God gets mixed in with words is not 'I believe in God.'
The religious discourse that precedes all religious discourse is not dialogue.
It is the 'here I am' said to a neighbour to whom I am given over, by which
I announce peace, that is, my responsibility for the other. 'Creating ... the
fruit of the lips. Peace, peace to the far and to the near, says the Lord.'[22]

In the description which has been elaborated up to now there has been no
question of the transcendental condition for some sort of ethical experience.
Ethics as substitution for the other, giving without reserve, breaks up the
unity of transcendental apperception, that condition for all being and all
experience. Disinter*estedness* in the radical sense of the term, ethics designates the improbable field where the Infinite is in relationship with the finite
without contradicting itself by this relationship, where on the contrary it
alone *comes to pass* as Infinity and as awakening. The Infinite transcends
itself in the finite, it *passes* the finite, in that it directs the neighbour to me
without exposing itself to me. This order steals into me like a thief, despite
the outstretched nets of consciousness, a trauma which surprises me absolutely, always already *passed* in a past which was never present and remains
un-representable.

  One can call this plot of infinity, where I make myself the author of what
I understand inspiration. It constitutes, prior to the unity of apperception,
the very psyche in the soul. In this inspiration, or prophesying, I am the
go-between for what I set forth. God has spoken 'that you shall not
prophesy', says Amos,[23] comparing the prophetic reaction to the passivity
of the fear which takes hold of him who hears the roaring of wild beasts.
Prophesying is pure testimony, pure because prior to all disclosure; it is
subjection to an order before understanding the order. In the recoverable
time of reminiscence, this anachronism is no less paradoxical than a prediction of the future. It is in prophesying that the Infinite passes – and
awakens. As a transcendence, refusing objectification and dialogue, it signifies in an ethical way. It *signifies* in the sense in which one says *to mean an
order*; it *orders*.

In sketching out, behind philosophy where transcendence is always reduced, the outlines of prophetic testimony, we have not entered into the
shifting sands of religious experience. To say that subjectivity is the temple
or the theatre of transcendence, and that the understanding of transcendence takes on an ethical meaning, does indeed not contradict the idea of the
Good beyond being. This idea guarantees the philosophical dignity of an
undertaking in which the signifyingness of meaning is separated from the
manifestation or the presence of being. But one can only wonder if Western
philosophy has been faithful to this Platonism. It discovered intelligibility in
terms in conjunction, posited by relation with one another, signifying one
another; for Western philosophy being, thematized in its presence, is illuminated in this way. The clarity of the visible signifies. The appropriate
trope for the signifyingness of signification is: the one-for-the-other. But
signifyingness becomes visibility, immanence and ontology, inasmuch as the
terms unite into a whole, and even their history is systematized, so as to be
clarified.

On the pages of this study transcendence as the ethical structure, the-
one-for-the-other has been formulated in terms of signifyingness and intelligibility.[24] The trope of intelligibility takes form in the ethical
one-for-the-other, a signifyingness prior to that which terms in conjunction
in a system acquire. But does this signifyingness more ancient than all
patterns really *take form*? We have shown elsewhere the latent birth of
systems and philosophy out of this august intelligibility; we shall not return
to that here.[25]

The intelligibility of transcendence is not something ontological. The
transcendence of God cannot be stated or conceived in terms of being, the
element of philosophy, behind which philosophy sees only night. But the
break between philosophical intelligibility and the beyond being, or the contradiction there would be in com-prehending infinity, does not exclude God
from signifyingness, which, if it is not ontological, does not simply amount
to thoughts bearing on being in decline, to views lacking necessity and
word-plays.

In our times – is this its very modernity? – a presumption of being an
ideology weighs on philosophy. This presumption cannot claim to be a part
of philosophy, where the critical spirit cannot content itself with suspicions,
but owes it to itself that it bring forth proofs. This presumption, which is
irrecusable, draws its force from elsewhere. It begins in a cry of ethical
revolt, bearing witness to responsibility; it begins in prophecy. Philosophy
does not become suspect at just any moment in the spiritual history of the
West. To recognize with philosophy – or to recognize philosophically – that
the real is rational and that the rational is alone real, and not to be able to

smother or cover over the cry of those who, the morrow after this recognition, mean to transform the world, is already to move in a domain of meaning which the inclusion cannot comprehend and among reasons that 'reason' does not know, and which have not begun in philosophy. A meaning thus seems to bear witness to a beyond which would not be the no-man's-land of non-sense where opinions accumulate. *Not to philosophize would not be 'to philosophize still'*, nor to succumb to opinions. There is meaning testified to in interjections and outcries, before being disclosed in propositions, a meaning that signifies as a command, like an order that one signifies. Its manifestation in a theme already devolves from its signifying as ordering; ethical signification signifies not *for* a consciousness which thematizes, but *to* a subjectivity, wholly an obedience, obeying with an obedience that precedes understanding. Here is a passivity still more passive than that of receptivity in knowing, the receptivity that assumes what affects it. In this signification the ethical moment is not founded on any preliminary structure of theoretical thought, on language or on any particular language. Language then has over signification only the hold a form has, clothing matter. This recalls the distinction between form and signification, which shows itself in that distinction and through its references to a linguistic system. The distinction holds even if this *said* has to be *unsaid* – and it will have to so as to lose its linguistic alternation. The signification will indeed have to be reduced and lose the 'stains' to which it owed its exposition to the light or its sojourn in shadow. An alternating rhythm of the said and the unsaid, and the unsaid being unsaid in its turn, will have to be substituted for the unity of discourse. There is here a breakup of the omnipotence of the logos, that of system and simultaneity. The logos breaks up into a signifier and a signified which is not *only* a signifier. This negates the attempt to amalgamate signifier and signified and to drive transcendence from its first or last refuge, in consigning all thought to language as a system of signs. Such an attempt was elaborated in the shadow of a philosophy for which meaning is equivalent to the manifestation of being, and manifestation equivalent to being's *esse*.

Transcendence as signification, and signification as the signification of an order given to subjectivity before any statement, is the pure one-for-the-other. Poor ethical subjectivity deprived of freedom! Unless this would be the trauma of a fission of the self that occurs in an adventure undergone with God or through God. But in fact this ambiguity also is necessary to transcendence. Transcendence owes it to itself to interrupt its own demonstration and monstration, its phenomenality. It requires the blinking and dia-chrony of enigma, which is not simply a precarious certainty, but breaks up the unity of transcendental apperception, in which immanence always triumphs over transcendence.

NOTES

1 Cf. *Otherwise than Being, or Beyond Essence*, pp. 153–62.
2 Which is required by justice, itself required by vigilance, and thus by the Infinite in me, by the idea of infinity.
3 The notion of experience is inseparable from the unity of presence, or simultaneity. It thus refers to the unity of apperception which does not come from the outside and 'become conscious' of simultaneity. It belongs to the very 'way' of presence, for presence, being, is only possible as a thematization or gathering of the transitory, and thus as a phenomenon, which is thematic exhibition itself. But all signification does not derive from experience, does not resolve into a manifestation. The formal structure of signifyingness, the-one-for-the-other, does not from the first amount to a 'showing oneself'. Suffering for another, for example, has a meaning in which knowing is adventitious. The adventure of knowledge which is characteristic of being, ontological from the first, is not the only mode, nor the preliminary mode, of intelligibility or meaning. Experience as the souce of meaning has to be put into question. It is possible to show that meaning *qua* knowing has its motivation in a meaning that at the start is not a knowing at all. This is not to deny that philosophy is itself knowledge. But the possibility for knowing to take in all meaning does not reduce all meaning to the structures that its exhibition imposes. This then suggests the idea of a dia-chrony of truth in which the said has to be unsaid, and the unsaid unsaid in its turn. In this sense the sceptical essence of philosophy can be taken seriously: scepticism is not an arbitrary contestation; it is a doctrine of inspection and testing, although not reducible to testing of the scientific sort.
4 This possibility of conjuring away or missing the division of truth into two times – that of the *immediate* and that of the *reflected* – deserves consideration and prudence. It does not necessarily lead to the subordination of one to the other. Truth as *dia-chrony*, as refusal of synchronization and synthesis, is perhaps proper to transcendence.
5 The latent birth of negation occurs not in subjectivity, but in the idea of the Infinite. Or, if one prefers, it is in subjectivity *qua* idea of the Infinite. It is in this sense that the idea of the infinite, as Descartes affirms, is a 'genuine idea' and not merely what I conceive 'by the negation of what *is* finite'.
6 Translator's Note. Inquiring after the 'manner in which I have acquired this idea', the sense of this receptivity, Descartes says in the third Meditation: 'For I have not received it through the senses, and it is never presented to me unexpectedly, as is usual with the ideas of sensible things when these things present themselves, or seem to present themselves, to the external organs of my senses . . . ' In the ideas of sensible things, the surprise of the experience is taken up by the understanding, which extracts from the sense the clear and distinct intelligible, and this allows one to say that the sensible things 'seem to present themselves to the external organs of my senses'. This is the very process of receptivity! 'Nor is it [the idea of infinity]', Descartes continues, 'likewise a fiction of my mind, for it is not in my power to take from or add anything to it;

and consequently the only alternative is that it is innate in me, just as the idea of myself is innate in me'. (*The Philosophical Works of Descartes*, vol. 1, trans. E.S. Haldane and G.R.T. Ross (Cambridge: Cambridge University Press, 1969), p. 170).

7 Cf. preceding note.

8 Or, as Descartes says, 'which is *created*'.

9 'For behold, the Lord is coming forth out of his place, and will come down and tread upon the high places of the earth. And the mountains will melt under him, and the valleys will be cleft, like wax before the fire, like waters poured down a steep place' (Micah 1: 3–4). 'What sustains yields to what is sustained', is overwhelmed or gives way. This 'structure' (which is, so to speak, destructure itself) is what is announced and expressed in this text, which we cite independently of considerations of its authority and 'rhetoric' as Holy Writ.

10 Cf. *Totality and Infinity*, pp. 33–104 and passim.

11 *Symposium*, 192c.

12 Ibid. 192e.

13 Cf. *Otherwise than Being, or Beyond Essence*, ch. 4.

14 Franz Rosenzweig interprets the *response* given by man to the love with which God loves him as the movement unto the neighbour (*The Star of Redemption*, trans. William W. Hallo (Boston: Beacon, 1964), Part III. This takes up the structure which commands a homiletic theme in Jewish thought. The 'fringes' on the corners of their garments, whose sight should remind the faithful of 'all the commandments of the Lord' (Numbers 15: 38–40), are in Hebrew called *tzitzit*. The ancient rabbinical commentary *Siphri* connects this word with the verb *tsouts* of which one form, in the Song of Songs 2: 9, means 'to observe' or 'to look' as in 'My beloved . . . looking through the lattice'. The faithful looking at the 'fringes' which remind him of his obligations, thus returns the gaze of the beloved who observes him. This would be the vis-à-vis or the face-to-face with God!

15 It is the meaning of the beyond, of transcendence, and not ethics, that our study is pursuing. It finds this meaning in ethics. There is *signification*, for ethics is structured as the-one-for-the-other; there is signification of the beyond being, for one finds oneself outside of all finality in a responsibility which ever increases, in a dis-interestedness where a being undoes itself of its being.

16 Trace of a past which was never present, but this absence still disturbs.

17 Dia-chronic truth; that is, the dia-chrony of truth that is without any possible snythesis. Contrary to what Bergson teaches us, there would be 'a disorder' which is not another order, there where the elements cannot be made contemporary, in the way, for example (but is this an example or the ex-ception?), in which God contrasts with the presence of re-presentation.

18 A devotedness as strong as death, and in a sense stronger than death. In *finitude* death outlines a destiny which it interrupts, but there can be no dispensation from the response which I am *passively* held to. The tomb is not a refuge; it is not a pardon. The debt remains.

19 Genesis 18: 27.

20 Exodus 16: 7.

21 The-one-for-the-other, the formal structure of signification, the signifyingness of rationality of signification, here does not begin by being exposed in a theme. It is my openness to the other, my sincerity or *veracity*.

22 Isaiah 57: 18–19.

23 Amos 2: 12.

24 It is quite remarkable that the word signifyingness (*signifiance*) has empirically the meaning of a mark of attention given to someone.

25 Cf. *Otherwise than Being, or Beyond Essence*, pp. 46 and 153.

Translated by Richard A. Cohen and Alphonso Lingis

12

Revelation in the Jewish Tradition

First published in the collected volume of essays entitled *Révélation* (Bruxelles: Editions des Facultés universitaires Saint-Louis 1977), pp. 55–77, and subsequently incorporated into *L'Au–Delà du Verset* (Paris: Editions de Minuit, 1982), pp. 158–81, 'Revelation in the Jewish Tradition' is one of Levinas's most important articles on the relevance of Law, or *Torah*, to the Jewish tradition. The fact of revelation (which has been contrasted with reason ever since the medieval writings of Saadya, often called the father of Jewish philosophy) leads Levinas to present the Bible as the model of ethical transcendental philosophy. The book is an *espace vital* (the importance of Levinas's use of this phrase is discussed in note 2) whose form and structure emphasize the polysemy and ambiguity of the message, obliging the reader to become an active interpreter, within the context of history's readings. This structure of oral and written law is further divided into *Halakhah* and *Aggadah* (see Glossary). The prescriptive approach which this adds up to confers a sense of unity that encourages rather than silences further discussion. In content also, the obligation to follow the Most-High which is related must be interpreted by each unique reader in terms of his or her responsibility for the other. Given that, in both structure and content, the prescription of prescriptions is the actual study of the written or oral Law, this obedience to the Most-High confers freedom on the individual. At the same time, this face-to-face response to God's commandment breaks open immanence. Being-there is transcended by the responsibility of interpretation; the closed order of totality is opened up by a different rationality, one based on an unfilfillable obligation.

As the chapters in this section discuss Jewish identity in terms of reading and saying, we have sought to preserve their more oral and discursive tone, and have retained all references to conferences or papers which have provided the starting-point for Levinas. All quotations from the Talmud are taken from *The Babylonian Talmud*, under the editorship of I. Epstein (London: Soncino Press, 1948).

Levinas's concept of Law is dealt with in a fascinating way in an article by Jean-François Lyotard, 'Levinas' Logic' in *Face to Face with Levinas*, edited by Richard A. Cohen (Albany: State University of New York Press, 1986), pp. 117–58, especially sections VI to VIII.

S.H.

The Content and its Structure

THE PROBLEM

I think that our fundamental question in this conference is less concerned with the content attributed to revelation than with the actual fact – a metaphysical one – referred to as the Revelation. This fact is itself the first content, and the most important, to be revealed by any revelation. From the outset we are told that it is an abnormal and extraordinary relationship, able to connect the world we inhabit to something which is no longer of this world. How is it thinkable? Which model can we appeal to? Our world lies before us, enabling us, in its coherence and constancy, to perceive it, enjoy it (*jouissance*), and think about it; it offers us its reflections, metaphors and signs to interpret and study. Within this world, it appears that the opening of certain books can cause the abrupt invasion of truths from outside – from where? – dated according to the 'chronology' of Sacred History, the history related by the Bible! And, in the case of the Jews, this sacred history leads, without any break in continuity, to the 'historian's history', which is profane history. Herein lies without doubt the originality of Israel and its relationship to the Revelation, whether that relationship be one of reading the Bible, forgetting it, or harbouring memories or feelings of remorse even after it is forgotten: most of the history which, to the Christian West, is 'sacred' is the ancient history of a people still here today, retaining a unity, however mysterious, in spite of its dispersion among the nations or perhaps in spite of its integration within them. In contrast to the mythical status – degradation or sublimation – which always threatens to befall the 'far distant times' of the Revelation, there is the astonishing fact of Judaism's continuing existence today as a collective human reality. And even if this entity is small in number, constantly eroded by persecution, enfeebled by half-heartedness, temptation and apostasy, it remains capable, even in its irreligiosity, of founding its political life on truths and rights drawn from the Bible. And, in actual fact, chapters of sacred history have been reproduced in the course of profane history by ordeals which constitute another Passion, the Passion of Israel. For many Jews, those who who have long since forgotten or never learned the narrative and the message of the Scriptures, the only available signs of the received Revelation – and the muffled calling of its exaltation – are to be found in the traumatism of events experienced long after the point at which the Biblical canon ends, long after the Talmud was put into writing. (The Talmud is the other form of the Revelation, distinct from the Old Testament which Christians and Jews have in common.) For many Jews, the only meaning of sacred history and the Revelation it brings us is to be found in their memories of the stake, the gas chambers, and even the snubs dealt to them publicly in international assemblies or implicitly in the refusal to allow them to emigrate. Their experience of the Revelation is transmitted through persecution!

We have heard Paul Ricoeur take up Emil Fackenheim's expression and talking of 'history making events'.[1] But surely these events must refer us to the Bible, which remains their *espace vital?*[2] It is through reading that references take on reality; through reading, in a way, we come to inhabit a place. The volume of a book can provide the *espace vital!* In this sense, too, the people of Israel are the people of the Book, whose relationship to the Revelaton is unique. Even their land rests on the Revelation. Their nostalgia for the land is nourished by texts, and owes nothing to any organic attachment to a particular piece of soil. Clearly, this kind of presence to the world makes the paradox of transcendence less anomalous.

For many Jews today, both as individuals and communities, the Revelation is still understood in terms of a communication between Heaven and Earth and corresponds, therefore, to the most obvious interpretation of the Biblical accounts. Many excellent souls have accepted this view, as they travel through the desert of today's religious crisis, finding fresh water in the literal expression of the Epiphany at Sinai, in God's Word calling upon the prophets, and in their trust in an uninterrupted tradition, to which a prodigious history bears witness. Orthodox Jews, individually or in communities, untouched by the doubts of the modern age even though they sometimes participate, in their professional lives, in the feverish world of industry, remain – despite the simplicity of the metaphysics involved – spiritually attuned to the highest virtues and most mysterious secrets of God's proximity. This enables these men and communities to live, in the literal sense of the word, outside History, where events neither come to pass, nor join those that belong to the past. For modern Jews, however – and they are the majority – whose concern with the intellectual destiny of the West and its triumphs and crises is not simply borrowed, the problem of the Revelation remains pressing, and demands the elaboration of new modes of thought. How can we make sense of the 'exteriority' of the truths and signs of the Revelation which strike the human faculty known as reason? It is a faculty which, despite its 'interiority', is equal to whatever the world confronts it with. But how can these truths and signs strike our reason if they are not even of this world?

These questions are indeed urgent ones for us today, and they confront anyone who may still be responsive to these truths and signs but who is troubled to some degree – as a modern person – by the news of the end of metaphysics, by the triumphs of psychoanalysis, sociology and political economy; someone who has learnt from linguistics that meaning is produced by signs without signifieds and who, confronted with all these intellectual splendours – or shadows – sometimes wonders if he is not witnessing the magnificent funeral celebrations held in honour of a dead god. The ontological status or *régime* of the Revelation is therefore a primordial concern for Jewish thought, posing a problem which should take precedence over any attempt to present the contents of that Revelation.

THE STRUCTURE OF A REVELATION: THE CALL TO EXEGESIS

None the less, we shall devote this first section to an exposition of the contents of the Revelation, and the structure they present within Judaism. Some of the inflections of this structure already suggest a way in which the transcendence of its message can be understood. I think that this exposition is also useful because the general public is unfamiliar with the forms in which the Revelation appears to Jews. Ricoeur has given a magisterial account of the origins of the Old Testament which Judaism and Christianity have in common.[3] This dispenses me from the need to talk further about the various literary genres of the Bible: its prophetic texts, the narration of historical founding events, prescriptive texts, the Wisdom literature, hymns and forms of thanksgiving. Each genre has its own revelatory function and power.

But perhaps, for a Jewish reading of the Bible, these distinctions cannot be established quite as firmly as in the pellucid classification we have been offered. Prescriptive lessons – found especially in the Pentateuch, the part of the Torah known as the Torah of Moses – occupy a privileged position within Jewish consciousness, as far as the relationship with God is concerned. Every text is asked to produce such lessons; the psalms may allude to characters and events, but they also refer to prescriptions: Psalm 119: 19 says, notably, 'I am a sojourner on earth: hide not thy commandments from me!'. The texts of the Wisdom literature are prophetic and prescriptive. Cutting across the 'genres' in all directions, then, are allusions and references which are visible to the naked eye.

I would also like to add this: our studies must take us, in every case, beyond the obvious or most immediate meaning of the text. Of course, we can know that meaning, and recognize it as the obvious one, completely valid at that level of investigation. But it may be less easy to establish what that meaning is than the translations of the Old Testament lead us to suppose. We must leave the translations, however worthy of respect they may be, and return to the Hebraic text to reveal the strange and mysterious ambiguity or polysemy which the Hebrew syntax permits. In this syntax the words co-exist, rather than falling immediately into structures of co-ordination and sub-ordination, unlike the dominant tendency in the 'developed' or functional languages. The return to the Hebraic text certainly makes it harder than people think – and the difficulty is legitimate – to decide on the ultimate intention of a verse, *a fortiori* of a book, of the Old Testament. And indeed, the specifically Jewish exegesis of the Scriptures is punctuated by these concerns: the distinction between the obvious meaning and the one which has to be deciphered, the search for this buried meaning and for one which lies deeper still, contained within the first. There is not one verse, not one word, of the Old Testament, if the reading is the religious one that takes it as Revelation, that does not open up an entire world, unsuspected at first, in which the text to be read is embedded. 'Rabbi Akiba used to interpret even the decorations on the letters of the Holy text' says the Talmud. These scribes and doctors known as slaves to the letter, would try to extort from the letters all the meanings they can carry or can bring to our attention, just as if the letters were the folded wings of the Holy Spirit, and could be unfurled to show all the horizons which the flight of the Spirit can embrace. 'Once God has spoken; twice have I heard this': this fragment of verse 11 of Psalm 62 proclaims that God's Word contains innumerable meanings. That is, at least, if we are to believe the rabbi who, in the name of this pluralism, is already exercising the right – to subject the text to scrutiny – which this very verse teaches him! This exegesis of the Old Testament is called *Midrash*, meaning exposition or research, or interrogation. It was well under way before grammatical investigations – which, arriving late on the scene, were nevertheless well received – joined in the deciphering of these enigmas, even though they are enclosed within the gramma of the Scriptures by means very different to those of grammar.

This lively attention to the text of the Old Testament did not overlook its diversity of style and its contradictions. They were the pretext for new, more penetrating interpretations, for renewals of meaning which could match the acuteness of the reading. Such is the breadth of the Scriptures. Their Revelation can also be called mystery, not the kind of mystery which banishes clarity, but one which demands greater intensity.[4]

But this invitation to seek, to decipher, to the *Midrash*, already marks the reader's participation in the Revelation, in the Scriptures. The reader is, in his own fashion, a scribe. This provides a first indication of what we may call the 'status' of the Revelation: its word comes from elsewhere, from outside, and, at the same time, lives within the person receiving it. The only 'terrain' where exteriority can appear is in the human being, who does far more than listen. Which means, surely, that the person, the uniqueness of the 'self', is the necessary condition of the breach and the manifestation which enter from outside? Surely it is the human, fracturing the identity of substance, which can, 'by itself', enable a message to come from outside? Not in order to collide with a reason which is 'free', but to assume instead a unique shape, which cannot be reduced to a contingent 'subjective impression'. The Revelation has a particular way of producing meaning, which lies in its calling upon the unique within me. It is as if a multiplicity of persons – and it is this multiplicity, surely, that gives the notion of 'person' its sense – were the condition for the plenitude of 'absolute truth', as if each person, by virtue of his own uniqueness, were able to guarantee the revelation of one unique aspect of the truth, so that some of its facets would never have been revealed if certain people had been absent from mankind. I do not mean that truth is anonymously produced within History, where it finds its own 'supporters'! On the contrary, I am suggesting that the totality of truth is made out of the contributions of a multiplicity of people: the uniqueness of each act of listening carries the secret of the text; the voice of Revelation, in precisely the inflection lent by each person's ear, is necessary for the truth of the Whole. The fact that God's living word can be heard in a variety of ways does not only mean that the Revelation adopts the measure of the people listening to it; rather, that measure becomes, itself, the measure of the Revelation. The multiplicity of people, each one of them indispensable, is necessary to produce all the dimensions of meaning; the multiplicity of meanings is due to the multiplicity of people. We can now appreciate in its full weight the reference made by the Revelation to exegesis, to the freedom attaching to this exegesis and to the participation of the person listening to the Word, which makes itself heard now, but can also pass down the ages to announce the same truth in different times.

A passage in Exodus (25: 15) prescribes the way in which the Holy Ark of the Tabernacle is to be constructed, and anticipates the poles on which the Ark will be transported: 'The poles shall remain in the rings of the ark; they shall not be taken from it'. The Law carried in the Ark is always ready to move; it is not attached to a particular point in space and time but is transportable at all times, ready to be transported at any moment. This is also brought to our attention by the famous Talmudic apologue about Moses's return to earth in the time of Rabbi Akiba. He enters the Talmudic doctor's school, understands nothing of the lesson being given by the master, but a voice from heaven tells him that this teaching, so poorly understood, was none the less received from him: it was given 'to Moses at Sinai'. This contribution of the readers, listeners and pupils to the open-ended work of the Revelation is so essential to it that I was recently able to read, in a very remarkable book written by a rabbinical doctor at the end of the eighteenth century, that the slightest question put to the schoolmaster by a novice constitutes an ineluctable articulation of the Revelation which was heard at Sinai.

The individual person, unique in his historical position, is called upon: this means no less than that the Revelation requires History, which means, whatever theosophical 'wisdom' may have to say, that our God is a personal

God – for surely the first characteristic of any God calling upon persons must be that he is personal? By what means, however, can this calling upon a diversity of people guard against the arbitrariness of subjectivism? But perhaps it is essential that a certain risk of subjectivism, in the pejorative sense of the term, should be taken by the truth . . .

That does not at all mean that in the Jewish spiritual tradition the Revelation is left to arbitrary and subjective fantasms, that it has no authority and no definite characteristics of its own. Fantasms are not the essence of subjectivity, even if they are a by-product. Without any need for a magisterium, an authority on doctrinal matters, the 'subjective' interpretations of the Jewish Revelation have managed to maintain, in this people, the consciousness of their unity, despite their geographical dispersion. There is, moreover, a means of discriminating between personal originality brought to bear upon the reading of the Book and the play of the fantasms of amateurs (or even charlatans): this is provided by the necessity of referring subjective findings to the continuity of readings through history, the tradition of commentaries which no excuse of direct inspiration from the text allows one to ignore. No 'renewal' worthy of the name can dispense with these references; nor, equally, can it fail to refer to what is known as the oral Law.

Oral Law and Written Law

This allusion to the oral Law leads us to point out another essential feature of the Revelation in Judaism: the role of the oral tradition as recorded in the Talmud. It is presented in the form of discussions between the rabbinical doctors. These took place in the period which begins with the first centuries before the Christian era and ends with the sixth century after Christ. From the historians' point of view, these discussions are an extension of more ancient traditions and reflect the shift which was taking place in the centre of Jewish spirituality, away from the Temple towards the house of study, from worship to study. The discussions and teachings relate, in the main, to the prescriptive part of the Revelation – matters of ritual, morality and law – although, in the guise of apologues about man's entire spiritual universe, they are also concerned, in their own way, with philosophy and religion. The keystone of it all is prescription. The image which people outside Judaism – or within a Judaism which has lost its Jewish character – have of the prescriptive, assimilating it to the mean-spiritness of a regulation that demands respect, or to the 'yoke of the law', does not portray it accurately.

On the other hand, and contrary to what is often thought, the oral Law cannot be reduced to a commentary on the Scriptures, however important its role in this area may be. In religious thought, it is traced back to its own source in the Revelation at Sinai. We have, therefore, alongside the written Torah, an oral Torah whose authority is at least equal.[5] The Talmud itself claims this authority, which is acknowledged by religious tradition and granted by the philosophers of the Middle Ages, including Maimonides. For the Jews, it constitutes a Revelation which completes that of the Old Testament. It is able to articulate principles and provide information, things which are missing from the written text or passed over in silence. The Tannaim, the earliest doctors of the Talmud, whose generation ends towards the close of the second century after Christ, speak with sovereign authority.

It remains true, of course, that the oral teaching of the Talmud is inseparable from the Old Testament. It is a guide to the interpretation of the Old Testament. Its way of reading, scrutinizing the text in the literal manner described above – something to which the Hebrew of the original Bible lends itself so wonderfully – defines the entire Talmudic approach. All the prescriptive part of the Torah is 'reworked' by the rabbinical doctors, and the narrative part is amplified and placed in a particular light. Thus it is the Talmud which allows us to distinguish the Jewish reading of the Bible from the Christian or 'scientific' reading of historians or philosophers. Judaism is indeed the Old Testament, but read through the Talmud.

In reality, the guiding spirit of this reading, which is naively called 'literal', is perhaps one that tries to keep each particular text within the context of the whole. The comparisons which can seem merely verbal, to depend upon the letter of the text, actually demonstrate this attempt to make the 'harmonics' of a particular verse resound within other verses. The aim is also to keep the passages which are entirely to our taste – in their talk of spiritualization and interiorization – in contact with the tougher texts, in order to extract from these, too, their own truth. And, by developing those remarks which seem most severe to us, we may also bring the most generous moments of the text closer to its hardest realities. The language of the Old Testament is so suspicious of any rhetoric which never stammers that it has as its chief prophet a man 'slow of speech and of tongue'. In this disability we can see more than the simple admission of a limitation; it also acknowledges the nature of this kerygma, one which does not forget the weight of the world, the inertia of men, the dullness of their understanding.

The freedom of exegesis is upheld at this Talmudic school. Tradition, running through history, does not impose its conclusions upon us, but it does demand that we make contact with what it sweeps before it. Does it constitute an authority on doctrinal matters? Tradition is the expression, perhaps, of a way of life thousands of years old, which conferred unity upon a collection of texts, however disparate historians say they were in their origins. The miracle of this confluence is as great as the miracle of the common origin attributed to the texts – and it is the miracle of that life. Just as the strings of a violin are stretched across its wood, so is the text stretched across all the amplifications brought by tradition. The Scriptures are therefore far from being a source of exercises for grammarians, in complete submission to the philologists; rather, their mode of being is such that the history of each piece of writing is less important than the lessons it contains, and its inspiration is measured in terms of what it has inspired. These are some aspects of the 'ontology' of the Scriptures.

We said that the oral Torah is committed to writing in the Talmud. So the oral Torah is in fact written. But it was put into writing belatedly. This event can be explained by contingent and dramatic circumstances in Jewish history, extrinsic to the true nature and manner of its message. However, the style of the oral Torah retains, even in its written form, the character of oral teaching; the direction and energy of the teacher addressing his disciples, who listen and ask questions. In its written form it reproduces the variety of opinions expressed, always taking great care to give the name of the person contributing or commenting upon them. It records the multiplicity of views and the disagreements between the doctors. The big disagreement which runs throughout the Talmud between the school of Hillel and the school of Shammai (in the first century BCE) is called a discussion or disagreement 'for the glory of heaven'. Despite its anxious concern to find agreement, the Talmud repeatedly applies the well-known formula both to the disagreement between Hillel and Shammai and to the divergent currents of ideas which stem from it, through successive generations of doctors: 'These words and the others are all words of the living God'. The discussion or dialectic remains open to its readers, who are only worthy of the name if they enter into it on their own account. The consequence – which is reflected even in the typography – is that the texts of the Talmud are accompanied by commentaries, and by commentaries on and discussion of those commentaries. Through these continuously overlaid pages the life of the text – which may be weakened or reinforced but still remains 'oral' – is prolonged. In this way the religious act of listening to the revealed word can take on the form of a discussion, which aims always to be open, however daring the problems it raises may be. So true is this that the messianic age is often referred to as the epoch of conclusions. Which does not prevent discussion, even of this point! A text from *Berakoth* (64a) says: 'R. Hiyya b. Ashi said in the name of Rab: The disciples of the wise have no rest either in this world or in the world to come, as it says, *They go from strength to strength; the God of gods will be seen in Zion.*' (Psalm 84: 7).[6] This movement of ever increasing strength is attributed by the sovereign authority of R. Hiyya to the doctors of the Law. And the eleventh-century French commentator Rashi, whose explanations guide all readers, even modern ones, through the sea of the Talmud, adds by way of comment: 'They are advancing from one house of study to another, from one problem to another.' The Revelation is this continual process of hermeneutics, discovering new landscapes in the written or oral Word, uncovering problems and truths locked within each other. As such, it is not only a source of wisdom, the path of deliverance and elevation; it is also the food of the life of knowledge, and the object of the enjoyment (*jouissance*) which goes with it. Thus Maimonides, in the twelfth century, could attach the same pleasure and happiness to the hermeneutics of the Revelation that Aristotle attaches to the contemplation of pure essences in Book 10 of the *Nicomachean Ethics*.

If Israel is the 'people of the Book' by virtue of its land, an extension of its in-folio manuscripts and scrolls, it also earns this title in another way: it is books that have nourished Israel, almost in the physical sense of the term, like the prophet who swallows the scroll in chapter 3 of Ezekiel. A strange diet, indeed, of celestial foods! As we have said, this does not involve the existence of a doctrinal authority. The strict formulations which – in the form of dogmas – could unify the multiple and sometimes disparate traces of the Revelation in the Scriptures are absent from the spirit of Judaism. No Credo influences the reading of the texts or dictates its method, in which even those discoveries which renew the reading and lend new meanings to the verses resemble, in their effect, the pouring of new wine into old goatskins, where it retains its ancient shape and even its former bouquet. The formulation of articles of faith is a philosophical or theological genre which came to Judaism late. It only appears in the Middle Ages, when religious life had already been ordered and was two thousand years old (if we believe historical research, which is continually bringing forward the date at which the spiritual role of texts developed, even as it continues to push their genealogy further back, rooting them in myth). Two thousand years already divide the first formulations of the Jewish Credo – in which even the number of essential points varied – from the flowering of the prophetic message of Israel in the eighth century BCE (when much of the Mosaic content of the Pentateuch was written down); and these formulations are separated by more than one thousand years from the end of the Biblical canon, and by several centuries from the writing down of the Talmudic teachings.

HALAKHAH AND AGGADAH

But if the contents of the Revelation are not summed up in the dogmatism of a Credo, there is another form in which the unity of the revelation is expressed for the Jews. Cutting across the distinction – specific to Judaism –

between the written Revelation and the oral Revelation, there is a second distinction, to which we have already alluded. This distinction separates the *Halakhah* – those texts and teachings which relate to conduct and formulate practical laws, which constitute the real Torah, and are recognizably 'prescriptive' in Ricoeur's sense – from those texts and teachings of homiletic origin which, in the form of apologues, parables and amplifications of Biblical tales represent the theological and philosophical part of the tradition, and are grouped together under the concept of *Aggadah*. The first of these gives the Jewish Revelation, written and oral, its characteristic physiognomy and, like a physician, has kept the Jewish body from fragmentation, even in its dispersion, and down through history. From the outset the Jewish revelation is one of commandment, and piety lies in obedience to it. But this form of obedience, while it accepts the practical decrees, does not bring to a halt the dialectic which is called upon to fully determine them. This dialectic continues, and is intrinsically valuable for its style of open discussion.

The distinctions between oral Law and written Law, on the one hand, and *Aggadah* and *Halakhah* on the other constitute, as it were, the four compass points of the Jewish Revelation. The real motivation of the *Halakhah*, let me repeat, is still under debate. This is because its discussion of rules of conduct is shot through with thought of the most searching kind. Its concern with obedience and casuistry leads to more intellectual issues. This is very important: the thought generated by prescriptive problems goes beyond the question of which material act should be carried out, although, true to its dialectical nature, it does also state which conduct is the correct one, the *Halakhah*. The decision it makes cannot, therefore, be strictly seen as a conclusion. It is, rather, as if the decision rested with a specific tradition, although it could never have been reached without discussion, and does not nullify that discussion in any way. In company with the dialectical antinomies, which cause the waves in the 'Talmudic sea', there are the 'decisions' or 'decrees'. And, shortly after the completion of the Talmud, the 'decision manuals' made their appearance, and fixed the form of the *Halakhah*. This project lasted several centuries and culminated in the definitive code entitled *Shulhan Arukh*, the 'prepared table', which fixes the life of the faithful Jew to the last detail.

The Jewish revelation is based on prescription, the *Mitzvah*, whose rigorous execution seemed to Saint Paul to impose the yoke of the Law. In any case, the unity of Judaism depends on the Law, which is never experienced as some kind of stigma or mark of enslavement. The unity it brings is quite distinct, in its consequences for the religion, from any doctrinal unity, and in any case is the source for all formulations of doctrine. Rashi's first rabbinical commentary, with which all 'Jewish' editions of the Pentateuch begin, expresses astonishment at the first verse of the Torah: why does it begin with the account of Creation, when the prescriptions only begin in verse 2 of Exodus 12: 'This month shall be for you the beginning of months'? In response, Rashi tries to explain the religious value of the account of the Creation. The Jewish people are united by their practice. This unity still exerts an influence on the consciousness of contemporary Judaism, which recognizes its antiquity and continues to acord it great respect, even when the Law, in the strict sense, is poorly observed. One would not be wrong in claiming that it is the unity conferred on the Jews by the Law – which at one time was observed by everyone – which sustains, although they are unaware of this, those Jews who have ceased to practise but still feel a sense of solidarity with the Jewish destiny. Finally, it is worth remarking that the study of the commandments – the study of Torah, the resumption of the rabbinical dialectic – is equal in religious value to actually carrying them out, just as if man, through this process of study, came into mystical contact with the divine will itself. The highest action in the practice of the prescriptions, the prescription of prescriptions which equals all of them, is the actual study of the (written or oral) Law.

Beside these Halakhic texts we have just discussed, which unify the prescriptions of the Law, and in which one can find ethical laws side by side with ritual prescriptions – texts which define Judaism, from the outset, as an ethical monotheism – there are the apologues and parables known as *Aggadah* which constitute the metaphysics and philosophical anthropology of Judaism. In the Talmudic texts, the *Aggadah* alternates with the *Halakhah*. The *Aggadah* also contains special collections of texts, of varying age and quality, which have given life to Judaism, and which are treated – without any awareness of historical perspective – as if the wisdom they offered were equal to that of the *Halakhah* which unifies the religion. To know the system of thought with which Judaism survived as a unity, retaining its religious integrity throughout the centuries (which is not the same as knowing its historical development), it is necessary to consider these texts from different epochs as if they were contemporary. The lucid research of historians and critics – both Jewish and non-Jewish – which explains the miracle of the Revelation *or* that of the national spirit of the Jews by means of the multiplicity of influences which they underwent has no spiritual significance when the hour of crisis strikes – as it has frequently struck in the course of two thousand years – for post-exile Judaism. The voice which speaks out then, and is immediately recognized, belongs to what we referred to earlier as the miracle of confluence; and the thought and sensibility through which it reverberates understand it at once, just as if they were already expecting it.

THE CONTENTS OF THE REVELATION

But so far we have talked only about the form or structure of the Revelation in Judaism without saying anything about its contents. Our task here is not to provide a body of dogma, a task which resisted the Jewish philosophers of the Middle Ages. We want to set out, quite empirically, some of the relationships which are established between, on the one side, Him whose message is carried by the Bible and, on the other, the reader, when he agrees to place the verse he is examining in the context of the entire Biblical text – that is, when he takes the oral tradition as the point of departure for his reading of the Bible.

Of course, the invitation extended is to follow the highest path at all times, to keep faith with the Unique alone, and to distrust the myths which force upon us the *fait accompli*, the grip of custom and of terror, and the Machiavellian state with its 'state reasons'. But to follow the Most High is to know, also, that nothing is of greater importance than the approach made towards one's neighbour, the concern with the fate of the 'widow and the orphan, the stranger and the poor man', and that no approach made with empty hands can count as an approach. The adventure of the Spirit also unfolds on earth among men. The traumatism of my enslavement in Egypt constitutes my very humanity, that which draws me closer to the problems of the wretched of the earth, to all persecuted people. It is as if I were praying in my suffering as a slave, but with a pre-oratorial prayer; as if the love of the stranger were a response already given to me in my actual heart. My very uniqueness lies in my responsibility for the other; nobody can relieve me of this, just as nobody can replace me at the moment of my death. Obedience to the Most High is defined for me by precisely this impossibility of running away; through this, my 'self' is unique. To be free is simply to do what nobody else can do in my place. To obey the Most High is to be free.

But man is also the irruption of God within Being, or the bursting out of Being towards God; man is the fracture in Being which produces the act of giving, with hands which are full, in place of fighting and pillaging. This is where the idea of being chosen comes from, an idea which can deteriorate into pride, but originally expresses the awareness of an appointment which cannot be called into question; an appointment which is the basis of ethics and which, through its indisputability, isolates the person in his responsibility. 'You only have I known of all the families of the earth; therefore I will punish you for your iniquities.' (Amos 3: 2). Man is questioned at his judgment by a justice which recognizes this responsibility; mercy – the *rahamim* –, the trembling of the uterus in which the Other (*L'Autre*) gestates within the Same,[7] God's maternity, if we can call it that, attenuates the rigours of the Law (without ever suspending it in principle, although it can go so far as to suspend it in fact). Man can what he must; he shall master the hostile forces of History and bring into being the messianic reign foretold by the prophets. The awaiting of the Messiah is the duration of time itself – waiting for God – but here the waiting no longer attests to the absence of Godot, who will never come, but rather to a relationship with that which is not able to enter the present, since the present is too small to contain the Infinite.

But perhaps it is in the ritual which regulates every action of everyday life, in that famous 'yoke of the Law' that we find the most characteristic aspect of Judaism's difficult freedom. There is nothing numinous about ritual, no element of idolatry; in ritual a distance is taken up *within* nature, *towards* nature, which constitutes perhaps the very act of awaiting the Most High. An awaiting which is a relationship to Him; or, if one prefers, a deferring to Him, a deferring to the beyond (*l'au-delà*) which has given rise, here, to our concept of a beyond (*au-delà*) or a towards-God (*à-Dieu*).

The Fact of the Revelation and Human Understanding

I come now to the main question: how does a Jew 'explain' to himself the very fact of the Revelation, in all its extraordinariness, which tradition – in keeping with the literal interpretation of the Scriptures – presents as coming from outside this world, and belonging to another order? It will not have escaped the reader's attention that the account of the contents, and especially of the structure of the Revelation given so far has enabled us to make some progress towards answering this question.

SOME PARTICULARS

Let us stay, for the moment, with the literal sense. We may note a few significant facts. The Bible itself tells us that its origin is supernatural. Some men heard the voice from heaven. The Bible also warns us against false prophets. Thus prophecy is suspicious of prophecy, and the person who commits himself to the Revelation runs a risk. We can see here a warning to be vigilant; this is an essential part of the Revelation, which does not leave worry behind. There is a further important point: when Moses recalls the Epiphany at Sinai in Deuteronomy 4: 15, he says: 'Therefore take good heed to yourselves. Since you saw no form on the day that the Lord spoke to you at Horeb out of the midst of the fire'. The Revelation is a saying (*dire*) in which the uprightness of the relationship between man and God is drawn without mediation. In Deuteronomy 5: 4, we read: 'The Lord spoke with you face to face.' These sentences allow the rabbinical doctors to confer prophetic status on all the Israelites that were present at the foot of Sinai, and to suggest by this that, in principle, the human mind is inherently open to inspiration and that man is inherently able to become a prophet! Let us look, too, at Amos 3: 8: 'The Lord God has spoken; who can but prophesy?' The receptivity of the prophet already lies within the human soul. Can we not see, in this possibility of listening – of obeying, that is – that subjectivity is the very fracturing of immanence? But the Master of the Revelation emphasizes, in the text quoted from Deuteronomy, that the Revelation is of words and offers no image to the eyes. And if the words which describe the Revelation in the Scriptures borrow from the vocabulary of visual perception, what you perceive of God is a divine verbal message (*devar elohim*) which is, more often than not, an order. It is commandment rather than narration which marks the first step towards human understanding and is, therefore, the beginning of language.

The Old Testament honours Moses as the greatest of the prophets. Moses has the most direct relationship with God, described (in Exodus 33: 11) as 'face to face'. And yet, the vision of the divine face is refused and, according to Exodus 33: 23, only God's 'back' is shown to Moses. It may be of some interest, if we are to reach an understanding of the true spirit of Judaism, to mention the way in which the rabbinical doctors interpret this text about the Epiphany: the 'back' which Moses saw from the cleft in the rock where he stood to follow the passage of the divine Glory was nothing other than the knot formed by the straps of the phylacteries on the back of God's neck. The prescriptive teaching appears even here! Which demonstrates how thoroughly the entire Revelation is bound up with the ritual practices of each day. And this ritualism confirms the conception of God in which He is welcomed in the face-to-face with the Other, in the obligation towards the Other. It confirms it to the extent that, by suspending the immediacy of one's contact with Nature's given, it can determine, against the blinding spontaneity of Desire, the ethical relationship with the other person.

The Talmud affirms the prophetic and verbal origin of the Revelation, but lays more emphasis on the voice of the person listening. It is as if the Revelation were a system of signs to be interpreted by the auditor and, in this sense, already handed over to him. The Torah is no longer in heaven, it is given to men; henceforth, it is at their disposal. There is a famous apologue in the tractate *Baba Mezi'a* (59b) which is telling on this point: Rabbi Eliezer, disagreeing with his colleagues about a problem arising from the *Halakhah*, finds his opinion is lent support by miracles and, finally, by a voice from heaven, or the echo of such a voice. His colleagues reject all these signs, and the echo of the voice, with the irrefutable argument that, since Sinai, the heavenly Torah has been on earth and calls upon man's exegesis, which thereafter deprives all echoes of voices from heaven of their power. Man is not therefore a 'being' (*étant*) among 'beings' (*étants*), a mere receiver of sublime messages. He is, at the same time, the person to whom the word is said, and the one through whom there *is* a Revelation. Man is the site of transcendence, even if he can be described as 'being there' or *Dasein*. Perhaps, in the light of this situation, the standing accorded to subjectivity and reason should be entirely revised. In the event which constitutes the Revelation, the prophets are succeeded by the *hakham*; the sage, or doctor, or man of reason, who is also inspired, in his own way, since he bears the oral teaching. As someone who is both taught and teaching, he is sometimes given the suggestive name of *Talmid-hakham*; the disciple of a sage, or disciple-sage, who receives, but also subjects what he receives to scrutiny. The Jewish philosophers of the Middle Ages, notably Maimonides, do trace back the Revelation to the prophetic gifts. But, rather than thinking of these in terms of a heteronomous inspiration, they assimilate them – to various degrees – to the intellectual faculties described by Aristotle. The Maimonidean man, like the Aristotelian man, is a 'being' situated *in his place* in the cosmos; he is a part of being which never leaves being behind, in which there never occurs any fracture of the same (*même*), that radical transcendence which the idea of inspiration and the whole traumatism of prophesy seem to involve in the Biblical texts.

REVELATION AND OBEDIENCE

Now we come to the main problem. It is not at all a problem of apologetics, the defence of a religion, which would require the authentification of the various contents revealed or confessed within the religions which are called 'revealed'. The problem lies in the possibility of a fracture or opening in the closed order of totality, of the world, or equally in the self-sufficiency of reason which is its correlative. This fracture would be produced by a movement from outside but, paradoxically, it would not entail the loss of that rational self-sufficiency. If the possibility of a fissure of this kind within the hard core of reason were thinkable, the main part of the problem would be solved. Our difficulty here stems from our habit of thinking of reason as the correlative of the possibility of the world, the counterpart to its stability and identity. Could it be otherwise? Could we account for intelligibility in terms of a traumatic upheaval in experience, which confronts intelligence with something far beyond its capacity, and thereby causes it to break? Surely not. Unless, perhaps, we consider the possibility of a command, a 'you must', which takes no account of what 'you can'. In this case, the exceeding of one's capacity does make sense. In other words, the type of reason corresponding to the fracture we have spoken of is practical reason.

Surely, then, our model of revelation must be an ethical one?

This makes me wonder if many aspects of Judaism might not, equally, point to this type of 'rationality', a reason far less turned in upon itself than the reason of the philosophical tradition. For example, there is the primordial importance in Judaism of the prescriptive, which is the keystone of the entire Revelation (even the narrative), according to both the written teaching (the Pentateuch) and the oral teaching. There is also the fact that the attitude in which the revealed is received is one of obedience, so that the phrase in Exodus 24: 7: 'All that the Lord has spoken we will do and we will be obedient (listen to it)', in which the expression for obedience is placed before the expression referring to understanding, exemplifies, in the eyes of the Talmudic doctors, Israel's greatest merit, the 'wisdom of an angel'. The rationality appearing here is not that of a reason 'in decline'; to understand it in its plenitude the irreducible 'intrigue' of obedience must be taken as the starting point. This obedience cannot be assimilated to the categorical imperative, where a universal suddenly finds itself in a position to direct the will; it derives, rather, from the love of one's neighbour, a love without eros, lacking self-indulgence, which is, in this sense, a love that is obeyed. Or equally, it stems from responsibility for one's neighbour, the taking upon oneself of the destiny of the other, fraternity. The relationship with the other is placed right at the beginning! Moreover, it is towards a relationship of this kind that Kant hastens, when he formulates the second version of the categorical imperative by a deduction – which may be valid or not – from the universality of the maxim. This obedience, which finds its concrete realization in the relationship with the Other, points to a reason which is less nuclear than the reason of the Greeks, which is seen from the outset as the correlative of stability, the law of the Same (*Même*).

The rational subjectivity bequeathed to us by Greek philosophy (and the fact that I have not begun with this legacy does not mean that I am rejecting it, nor that I will not have recourse to it later, nor that I am caught up in 'mystical slumbers') does not feature that passivity which, in other philosophical essays, I have identified with the responsibility for the Other. A responsibility which is not a debt that can be limited by the extent of one's active commitment, for one can acquit oneself of a debt of that sort, whereas, unless we compromise our thought, we can never be clear of our debts to the Other. It is an infinite responsibility, a responsibility which does not suit my wishes: the responsibility of a hostage.[8]

We are not suggesting, of course, that the actual contents of the Bible – Moses and the prophets – can be deduced from this responsibility. We are concerned, rather, to formulate the possibility of a heteronomy which does not involve servitude, a receptive ear which still retains its reason, an obedience which does not alienate the person listening, and to recognize, in the ethical model of the Bible, the transcendence of understanding. No such move towards acknowledging an irreducible transcendence can occur within the dominant conception of reason held by the philosophical profession today; a reason which is solid and positive, with which all meaning (*sens*) begins and to which all meaning must return, to become assimilated to the Same (*Même*), whatever appearance it may give of having come from outside. Nothing can fissure the nuclear solidity of this power of thought, which is the correlative of the positivity of the world, whose starting point is the vast repose of the cosmos; a thought which freezes its object as a theme, always adopts its measure, which thinks *knowingly*. I have already wondered whether this reason, refusing to be moved by the excessive disproportion of transcendence, can adequately express the irruption of man within Being, or the interruption of Being by man – or, more exactly, the interruption of the alleged correlation of man and Being in essance,[9] where the figure of the Same (*Même*) appears; just as I have wondered if the worry generated in the Same by the Other (*l'Autre*) might not be the meaning of reason, its very rationality. This worry is induced in man by God's Infinity, which he can never contain, but which inspires him – inspiration being the original mode of worry, the inspiration of man by God constituting man's humanity; and the 'within' of this 'disproportionate within the finite' only becomes possible through the 'here I am' of the man welcoming his neighbour. Listening to the muse dictating one's songs is not the original form of inspiration; instead, it lies in obedience to the Most High by way of the ethical relationship with the Other.

We said this right at the beginning: the subject of our enquiry is the very fact of the Revelation, and the relation it establishes with exteriority. This exteriority – unlike the exteriority which surrounds man whenever he seeks knowledge – cannot be transformed into a content within interiority; it remains 'uncontainable', infinite (*infinie*), and yet the relation is maintained. The path I am led to follow, in solving the paradox of the Revelation, is one that claims we may find a model for this relation in the attitude of non-indifference towards the Other, in the responsibility towards him; and that it is precisely through this relation that man becomes his 'self' (*moi*), designated without any possibility of escape, chosen, unique, not inter-changeable, and – in this sense – free.[10] Ethics provides the model worthy of transcendence and it is as an ethical kerygma that the Bible is Revelation.

THE RATIONALITY OF TRANSCENDENCE

What we should also like to suggest and, albeit very briefly, to justify, is the idea that the openness to transcendence shown in ethics does not entail the loss of rationality, that which makes sense (*sens*) significant. Rational theology is a theology of Being which equates the rational with the identity of the Same, and is suggested by the firmness and positivity of the firm ground beneath the sun. It belongs to the ontological adventure which, adopting the standpoint of the positivity of the world, swept along the God and man of the Bible and dragged them towards the 'death' of God and the end of the humanism – or the humanity – of man. The notion of a subjectivity which coincided with the identity of the Same, and the rationality which went with it entailed the gathering together of the world's diversity within the unity of a single order that left nothing out; an order produced or reproduced by the sovereign act of Synthesis. The idea of a passive subject who, in the heteronomy of his responsibility for the Other, differs (*différant*) from every other subject, is a difficult one. The Subject who does not return to himself, who does not meet up with himself in order to establish himself triumphantly, in the absolute repose of the earth beneath the canopy of heaven is unfavourably regarded as the product of Romantic subjectivism. The opposites of repose – worry, questioning, seeking, Desire – are all taken to be a waste of repose, an absence of response, a privation, a pure insufficiency of identity, a mark of self-inequality. We have wondered if the Revelation might not lead us to precisely this idea of inequality, difference and irreducible alterity which is 'uncontainable' within gnoseological intentionality, a mode of thought which is not knowledge but which, exceeding knowledge, is in relation with the Infinite or God. May we not see, in the intentionality which - through the noetic–noematic correlation – can 'measure' its object, a sign, on the contrary, of its insufficiency, of a psychic structure more impoverished than the question, which, in its purity, addresses a demand to the other and thereby enters into relation with an object which can never offer an *investment?* And perhaps the attitudes of seeking, desiring and questioning do not represent the emptiness of need but the explosion of the 'more within the less' which Descartes called the idea of Infinity, and demonstrate a psyche which is more alert than that of intentionality, or a knowledge adequate to its object.

The Revelation, described in terms of the ethical relation or the relation with the Other, is a mode of the relation with God and discredits both the figure of the Same and knowledge in their claim to be the only site of meaning (*signification*). This figure of the Same, this knowledge only reflect a certain level of intelligence, where it is prone to become *embourgoisé*, and fall asleep, satisfied with its own presence. Reason, here, is continually led back to seek repose, appeasement and conciliation – all of which imply the ultimate status or priority of the Same – and has already resigned from life. Not that the lack of plenitude, or the non-adequacy of the self is more valuable than self-coincidence. If we were only concerned with the self (*soi*) in its substantiality, equality would be better than lack. We are not recommending the Romantic ideal of unsatisfaction in preference to a full self-possession. But does the Spirit reach its limit in self-possession? Are there not grounds for imagining a relation with an Other (*Autre*) that would be 'better' than self-possession? Is there not a certain way of 'losing one's soul' which comes from deference to something greater or better or 'higher' than the soul? Perhaps it is only in this act of deference that the very notions of 'better' or 'higher' are articulated and manifest their sense (*sens*), and that seeking, desire and questioning are therefore better than possession, satisfaction and answers.

Should we not go beyond the consciousness which is equal to itself, seeking always to assimilate the Other (*l'Autre*), and emphasize instead the act of deference to the other in his alterity, which can only come about through the awakening of the Same – drowsy in his identity – by the Other? The form of this awakening, we have suggested, is obedience. And, surely, the way to think about the consciousness which is adequate to itself is as a mode or modification of this awakening, this disruption which can never be absorbed, of the Same by the Other, in his difference. Surely we should think of the Revelation, not in terms of received wisdom, but as this awakening?

These questions concern the nature of the ultimate and put into question the rationality of reason, and the very possibility of the ultimate. Faced with a thought which aspires, as if to its repose, to the identity of the Same, should we not be wary of stupor and petrifaction? The idea that the other is the enemy of the Same is an abuse of the notion; its alterity does not bring us to the play of the dialectic, but to an incessant questioning, without any ultimate instance, of the priority and tranquillity of the Same, like an inextinguishable flame which burns yet consumes nothing. And the form of this flame, surely, is the prescription of the Jewish Revelation, with its unfulfillable obligation. An unfulfillable obligation, a burning which does not even leave any ash, since ash would still be, in some respect, a substance resting on itself. The 'less' is forever bursting open, unable to contain the 'more' that it contains, in the form of 'the one for the other'. Here the word 'forever' (*toujours*) keeps its native force, its sense of great patience, diachrony, temporal transcendence. There is a sobering of the spirit which reaches 'forever' deeper and is, in this way (*sens*), the spirituality of obedience. We may ask questions about the manifestation of these things within what is said (*dit*). But can we convert transcendence as such into answers without losing it in the process? And in the question, which also calls into question, do we not hear the true resonance of the voice commanding from beyond?

NOTES

1 Paul Ricoeur, 'Herméneutique de l'idée de la Révélation', in Paul Ricoeur, Emmanuel Levinas, et al., *La Révélation*, (Bruxelles: Facultés universitaires Saint-Louis, 1984), p 20.

2 '*Espace vital*', means, literally, 'living space'. The term reflects the German word '*Lebensraum*' and is also used, in French, with the sense of that term: to refer to territory believed by a people or State to be essential to its development and well-being. There is no word for this concept in English, which simply borrows the German word rather than translate it. We have left the term in French, rather than impose the connotations of German expansionism which '*Lebensraum*' brings, connotations which are not necessarily, or not as inescapably, implied by the French. This has been confirmed by Levinas in a private correspondence with the editor: 'The expression "*espace vital*" ... evokes the "nourishing terrain" of the book to which the land, in the geographical sense of the term, refers in Judaism, and so draws out its spiritual meaning. It does not necessarily refer to the biological *Lebensraum*'.

3 Paul Ricoeur, 'Herméneutique ... '.

4 It invites our intelligence and protects it, at the same time, by the mystery which is its source, from the 'dangers' of its truth. A Talmudic apologue, commenting on Exodus 33: 21–2 ('And the Lord said: "Behold, there is a place by me where you shall stand upon the rock; and while my glory passes by I will put you in a cleft of the rock, and I will cover you with my hand until I have passed by"') says: 'Protection was needed, because the destructive powers had been given full powers to destroy.' The moment of truth is when all interdicts are lifted, when the questioning spirit is forbidden nothing. At this supreme instant, only the truth of the Revelation can protect against evil, for it is in the nature of all truth to risk giving evil, too, its freedom.

5 *Torah* is the name given to the twenty-four books of the Jewish Biblical canon; in its narrower sense, the *Torah of Moses* is the Pentateuch. In its widest meaning, *Torah* refers to the Bible and the Talmud together, including their commentaries and even the collected pieces and homiletic texts known as the *Aggadah*.

6 *Tractate Berakoth*, translated by Maurice Simon, in *The Babylonian Talmud*.

7 On this theme, see also ch. 3 of my *Otherwise than Being, or Beyond Essence*, and the essay entitled 'Sans identité' in my *Humanisme de l'autre homme* (Fata Morgana, 1972), pp. 85–101.

8 See *Otherwise than Being, or Beyond Essence*.

9 I write this as 'essance', an abstract noun used to indicate the verbal sense of the word 'être' (*Being*).

10 Freedom means, therefore, the hearing of a vocation which I am the only person able to answer – or even the power to answer right there, where I am called.

Translated by Sarah Richmond

13

The Pact

Published in *L'Au-Delà du Verset* (Paris: Editions de Minuit, 1982), pp. 82–106, 'The Pact' is a particularly good example of the Talmudic reading which Levinas produces virtually every year. It complies with all the criteria laid down in the previous chapter: its formal presentation of the material is an exemplary model of an ethical transcendental philosophy at work; while the content concerns precisely a contemporary reaction to the way in which the covenants are handed down in the Bible, and the sense of community they establish. The subtlety of analysis and the skill with which its insights are revealed to us as a community of readers manage to bring us together into an adherence to the Law of the text that in no sense subjugates each concrete response to a single, universal reading. Levinas therefore even manages to show here how, in one's ethical response, one is responsible for the other's responsibility.

S.H.

They turned their faces towards Mount Gerizim and opened with the blessing etc. Our Rabbis taught: There was a benediction in general and a benediction in particular, likewise a curse in general and a curse in particular. (Scripture states): *to learn, to teach,* to *observe* [keep] and to *do*; consequently there are four (duties associated with each commandment). Twice four are eight and twice eight are sixteen. It was similar at Sinai and the plains of Moab; as it is said, *These are the words of the covenant which the Lord commanded Moses* etc., and it is written, *Keep therefore the words of this covenant* etc. Hence there were forty-eight covenants in connection with each commandment. R. Simeon excludes (the occasion of) Mount Gerizim and Mount Ebal and includes that of the Tent of Meeting in the wilderness. The difference of opinion here is the same as that of the teachers in the following: R. Ishmael says: General laws were proclaimed at Sinai and particular laws in the Tent of Meeting. R. Akiba says: Both general and particular laws were proclaimed at Sinai, repeated in the Tent of Meeting, and for the third time in the plains of Moab. Consequently there is not a single precept written in the Torah in connection with which forty-eight covenants were not made. R. Simeon b.

Judah of Kefar Acco said in the name of R. Simeon: There is not a single precept written in the Torah in connection with which forty-eight times 603,550 covenants were not made. Rabbi said: According to the reasoning of R. Simeon b. Judah of Kefar Acco who said in the name of R. Simeon that there is not a single precept written in the Torah in connection with which forty-eight times 603,550 covenants were not made, it follows that for each Israelite there are 603,550 commandments. (And forty-eight covenants were made in connection with each of them.) What is the issue between them? – R. Mesharsheya said: The point between them is that of personal responsibility and responsibility for others [*the responsibility of responsibility*].[1] (Tractate *Sotah* 37a–b)

The Formal Law

The problem that concerns us in this conference – that of the community – is, without doubt, a topical one, due to the unease felt by man today within a society whose boundaries have become, in a sense, planetary: a society in which, due to the ease of modern communications and transport, and the worldwide scale of its industrial economy, each person feels simultaneously that he is related to humanity as a whole, and equally that he is alone and lost. With each radio broadcast and each day's papers one may well feel caught up in the most distant events, and connected to mankind everywhere; but one also understands that one's personal destiny, freedom or happiness is subject to causes which operate with inhuman force. One understands that the very progress of technology – and here I am taking up a commonplace – which relates everyone in the world to everyone else, is inseparable from a necessity which leaves all men anonymous. Impersonal forms of relation come to replace the more direct forms, the 'short connections' as Ricoeur calls them, in an excessively programmed world.

Certainly, the context of State and nation is less abstract than that of the planet, but it is still too broad, and the universal ties of the law guarantee a condition in which men find themselves side by side rather than face to face. Even within the family, human relationships are less alive and less direct, because of the multiplicity of systems in which each person is involved. But perhaps the parental structure has never fully satisfied man's social vocation, and thus gives rise to the search for a more circumscribed society than today's, one whose members would know each other. Some think that to achieve this it is necessary to spend time together in personal encounters. Is this really the solution? The achievement of a concrete but marginal society, existing only on the edge of real society which, despite its impersonal structure, is definitely founded in 'the nature of things'? Will our social nature really be fulfilled by a leisure culture, a Sunday society, the temporary society of the club?

If the structure of a more intimate social life is to give people a sense of community, one which exults in the recognition of each person by his fellows, surely this structure cannot be artificial? A healthy society is one which reflects the vitality of its contact with the world. Modern professional life, with the points of focus it imposes, its towns, industry and crowds – as well as its intercontinental dispersion – retains an understanding of the things which matter today. It is not the result of an aberration or an error. It is the very essence of modernity. The cohesive nature of the modern world, planned by means of Law and regulation, and all the 'remote connections' it sets up are constitutive of today's reality, even if these relationships make us march forward together rather than turn our faces towards each other. And this brings us back, does it not, to the point from which we set out?

Our Talmudic Passage

But perhaps we have not properly considered all the implications of the Law, which may have got lost in the over-formal approach of Western society. This is what brings me to the Talmud.

We may have, here, good reason to study one of Israel's ancient texts. The Talmudic text I have chosen is relatively simple, although, as always, unusual. It concerns the problem we have raised. It is about a covenant. It interprets it in its own way, which appears to be one of not touching upon the matter at all. It interprets the covenant made between the Eternal God of Israel, and Israel's children. A covenant by which the society of Israel is founded, through the legislation of the Torah. I have entitled the passage 'The Pact'. It comes from the Babylonian Talmud, tractate *Sotah*, 37a–b. It is very short, half a page.

I must place it in its context. The *Gemara* sequence from which it is drawn follows on from a *Mishnah* which is related to a completely different theme. This *Mishnah* discusses the question of whether, for certain liturgical formulae, such as 'blessings', 'oaths', etc., it is fitting to use Hebrew or the profane languages. The *Mishnah* is followed by several pages of *Gemara*. It is from these pages that the short sequence distributed to you has been taken. It is, in fact, a digression from the main theme, language, an area where the problem of Greek continually arises. The theme of language will emerge at a certain point in our passage. It is in no way a neutral or irrelevant theme. It introduces – perhaps in disguise – the problem of the relationship between the particular case of Israel and the universal state of mankind. We will find this echoed in the commentary of our passage.

From the Bible to the Talmud

The text presents itself as a commentary to chapter 27 of Deuteronomy, but it also refers to chapter 7 of Joshua. By looking at these texts, along with the *Mishnah* which refers to them (at greater length than the first sentence of our extract), we will be able, from this example, to appreciate the distance which can separate the written Law from the oral Law.

Chapter 27 of Deuteronomy expounds the recommendations made by Moses to the people of Israel for a ceremony which will take place at a later date, when, after Moses's death, at the end of their peregrinations in the desert, the people shall enter the Holy Land. Here are some of its verses. From the end of verse 2: 'And on the day you pass over the Jordan . . . you shall set up large stones, and plaster them with plaster; and you shall write upon them all the words of this law.' These 'words' being the entire Torah. Verse 4: 'And . . . you shall set up these stones, concerning which I command you this day, on Mount Ebal.' The place where the ceremony is to be performed is indicated; two mountains stand there, Mount Ebal and, beside it, Mount Gerizim. After the stones have been set up there, and the Torah inscribed, there is a second recommendation, in verse 5: 'And there you shall build an altar to the Lord your God, an altar of stones; you shall lift up no iron tool upon them.' We should attend to this suggestive symbol: unbroken stones, intact, stones which no iron tool has touched. Iron, probably the basis of all industry, is in any case fundamental to all war. On this altar burnt offerings will be given, and peace offerings will be sacrificed. Verse 8 returns to the initial theme of the inscription of the Torah on the stones, but specifies how it should be done. The question of language is not raised at this point; for the moment, it is the graphic quality of the inscription that is described: 'And you shall write upon the stones all the words of this law "very plainly" (*be'er hetev*).' From verse 11, Moses's recommendations concern the positioning of the people on Mounts Ebal and Gerizim 'for the ceremony of the Covenant' being planned. Six tribes are to stand on Mount Gerizim 'to bless the people' and six others 'shall stand upon Mount Ebal for the curse'. In this way, will not everybody, blessed or cursed, be visible to everybody else? Throughout the ceremony anticipated here, all the members of society will be able to see each other. This is an extremely important point for our conference, dedicated as it is to the problem of the community. In verse 14 we have: 'And the Levites shall declare to all the men of Israel with a loud voice', then the verses of curses forbidding the transgression of various interdicts, followed by 'And all the people shall say, "Amen"'. From verse 15 to verse 26, the interdicts in question are enumerated – there are eleven of them – to which is added the general interdict against transgressing 'this law' (verse 26). These interdicts certainly represent the most important principles of the pact, but they only partially coincide with the Ten Commandments of Sinai. We find here the prohibition of idolatry, of dishonouring father and mother, the interdict on moving the boundaries of a field (one must not encroach upon a neighbour's property), the order not to lead the blind astray, not to pervert the justice due to the sojourner, the widow and the orphan; the prohibition of various forms of incest, the interdict on 'slaying one's neighbour in secret' (in this way calumny, notably, is outlawed); the interdict on taking a bribe that allows an innocent life to be lost. No doubt these are founding principles of society. However, they do not exhaust the contents of the Torah; hence the last verse of the chapter, which alludes to the principles in their entirety. The mention of both blessings and curses in the opening verses of Deuteronomy 27 is surely meant to suggest that those who respect the interdict will be blessed, and those who fail to respect it will be cursed. But in actual fact, only the negative side, the cursing, is given in this passage. The people, after each curse from the Levites, shall all reply: 'Amen'. The words of the Levites will reach everyone's ears: each person here is in the presence of all the others. Each person shall say: 'Amen'. The pact concluded, then, is an authentic one, made in the presence of all the people, members of a society in which – I continue to emphasize this point – everyone can observe everyone else.

Admittedly, Deuteronomy leaves vague many details concerning the staging of the ceremony of the pact – which seems to be the pact that is referred to, or at least presupposed, by the first sentence of the Talmudic text on which I am giving a commentary.

Indeed, this sentence: 'They turned their faces towards Mount Gerizim and opened with the blessing . . . ' mentions a 'blessing' which Deuteronomy fails to explain. The sentence refers to another description of the scene enacted between Mounts Ebal and Gerizim, the account given in the Book of Joshua, 8: 30–5. I will read it to you, and indicate the points at which the two versions differ. This second account is more precise, and shorter; I reproduce it unabridged. It presents itself as a record of the ceremony which Joshua carried out, faithfully following the recommendations given by Moses in Deuteronomy 27. It refers explicitly to these recommendations.

Then Joshua built an altar in Mount Ebal to the Lord the God of Israel, as Moses the servant of the Lord had commanded the people of Israel, as it is written in the book of the law of Moses, 'an altar of unhewn stones, upon which no man has lifted an iron tool'; and they offered on it burnt offerings to the Lord, and sacrificed peace offerings. And there, in the presence of the people of Israel, he wrote upon the stones a copy of the law of Moses, which he had written. And all Israel, sojourner as well as home-born, with their elders and officers and their judges, stood on opposite sides of the ark before the Levitical priests who carried the ark of the covenant of the Lord, half of them in front of Mount Gerizim and half of them in front of Mount Ebal, as Moses the servant of the Lord had commanded at the first, that they should bless the people of Israel. And afterwards he read all the words of the law, the blessing and the curse, according to all that is written in the book of the law.

For each prescription in the Book of the Law the formula for cursing and the formula for blessing are repeated! 'There was not a word of all that Moses commanded which Joshua did not read before all the assembly of Israel, and the women and the little ones, and the sojourners who lived among them.'

Take note: they were all there, the twelve tribes with women and children, excluding nobody, not even the foreigners, the *gerim* among our people. You can see that the pact has grown in significance since the version we looked at in Deuteronomy. The scene looks a bit different, the positioning of the actors is more precise, the 'staging' is not quite the same: but there remain the stones untouched by any tool of iron, stones which represent the reign of peace, not of war; and above all there is the remarkable insistence on the totality of people present at the ceremony, women, children and foreigners. Together with the insistence on the Mosaic text, to be read *in full*, beyond the eleven verses mentioned in Deuteronomy 27. And finally, the insistence on the absolute fidelity to the words of Moses, the servant of the Lord: any departure here from the contents of Deuteronomy is to be ascribed to Moses. Even if Moses did not quite say these things!

Allow me now to give you the last version of this scene, taken from the *Mishnah* itself (32a) to which the *Gemara* which contains our text is attached. The first sentence of my translation, ending in 'etc.' comes from that *Mishnah*. As I mentioned earlier, the theme of this *Mishnah* is the languages which are authorized or prohibited for certain ritual or liturgical formulae – a topic which so far has merely offered a shadowy pretext for our discussion of the pact. Here it is:

Six tribes ascended the summit of Mount Gerizim, six tribes ascended the summit of Mount Ebal and the priests [the *Cohanim*] and Levites with the Ark were stationed below in the centre [as in Joshua], the priests surrounding the Ark, the Levites (surrounding) the priests, and all Israel on this side and that side; as it is said [the *Mishnah* makes it clear that it is following the account in Joshua], and all Israel, and their elders and officers, and their judges stood on this side the Ark and on that side etc. They turned their faces towards Mount Gerizim [Joshua 8] and opened with the blessing: 'Blessed be the man that maketh not a graven or molten image', and both parties respond 'Amen' [a quotation from Deuteronomy]. Then they turned their faces towards Mount Ebal and opened with the curse: 'Cursed be the man that maketh a graven or molten image' and both parties respond 'Amen'. (So they continue) until they complete the blessings and curses. After that they brought the stones, built the altar and plastered it with plaster, and inscribed thereon all the words of the Torah in seventy languages, as it is said, very plainly [*be'er hetev*].[2]

A question that was about handwriting has been transformed into one about the language used! This third version of the pact refers to the account in Joshua but uses the formulae of Deuteronomy. The pact which, according to Deuteronomy, was concluded in the presence of all the tribes in front of an altar whose stones, from the very earliest texts – texts which belong to a civilization that aspires to have no wars – are untouched by any tool of iron; the pact which, in Joshua, includes women, children and foreigners, has, in this *Mishnah* become truly universal: its law is written in seventy languages. A message addressed to humanity as a whole! The real meaning of this apparently particular ceremony, performed by a people whose members can all look upon one another, a community which one gaze can encompass, is that *all* human beings are included in the legislation in whose name the pact is concluded.

This transition from Hebrew to the universality which I call 'Greek' is, then, very remarkable. The phrase *be'er hetev* 'very plainly', which recommends the clarity and distinctness of the Scriptures takes on the new meaning of complete translatability. This process of liberating and universalizing the texts must, therefore, be continued. We have still not finished translating the Bible. The Septuagint is incomplete. Nor have we finished the task of translating the Talmud. We have hardly begun. And, it must be said, where the Talmud is concerned the task is a tricky one! What was until recently a heritage reserved for oral teaching passes, perhaps too rapidly, into foreign languages without losing any of its unusual quality.

This universality is rooted, in some way, in a society which makes itself entirely visible to its members congregated on the two mountain tops, visible as if on stage. From the outset the society which values the intimacy of its twelve tribes looking at each other, and which aims to be one community, is already available or reaching out to humanity as a whole.

I have offered you here a precise example of the way an idea can develop as it passes from the written Law to the oral Law. The oral Law claims to discuss the contents of the written Law. But the actual knowledge of the oral Law is greater still. It goes beyond the obvious meaning of the passage studied, but remains within the spirit of the global meaning of the Scriptures.

The Various Dimensions of the Law

Let us return to our text. It is about to reveal to us the various dimensions of this pact concerning the Torah, those aspects which are there to ensure that a community whose members are practically face to face retains these interpersonal relations when its members turn their gaze towards humanity as a whole. The distinction between community and society belongs to an immature stage of social thought. The adoption of the Law which is the foundation of this society brings with it, for those men who adopt it in the proper manner, the possibility of remaining in contact, face to face with each other.

> Our Rabbis taught: There was a benediction in general and a benediction in particular, likewise a curse in general and a curse in particular. (Scripture states): *to learn, to teach,* to *observe* and to *do*; consequently there are four (duties associated with each commandment). Twice four are eight and twice eight are sixteen.

The arithmetic is undeniable! But what is the passage talking about? In Deuteronomy, the same laws are proclaimed with curses for the man who transgresses them and blessings for the man who obeys them. Curse and blessing, that makes two: two independent ways of adhering to the same Law, for the man who undertakes to keep it. In the Covenant made on Mounts Ebal and Gerizim there were, then, two acts of will made to the same Law, 'Yes' was said twice over. Looking again at Deuteronomy 27, we find that the interdicts are enumerated separately, but also, by means of the last verse, included in the invocation of 'all the words of this Law'. The Torah is expressed, therefore, in both a general form and a particular one. That makes two more acts of adherence. Two acts of adherence in the curses and two acts of adherence consenting to the blessings. That makes four acts of adherence. Four, not as two plus two, but four as two times two.

But we also know – if we refer to Deuteronomy 5: 1 and Deuteronomy 11: 19 – that the Torah brings with it four general obligations: to learn it (*lilmod*), to teach it (*lelammed*), to observe it (*lishmor*), to carry it out (*la'asot*). Four covenants are included within the Covenant, sixteen pacts within the pact. Such arithmetic can be astonishing. I will return to this point later. Let us say, speaking generally, that in what we simply call the adherence to the Law the rabbinical doctors distinguish sixteen dimensions.

Sixteen dimensions! But there are still more! If the rabbinical calculations are correct, the Torah was handed down on three different occasions. According to Exodus, the first time was at Sinai; the second time, according to Deuteronomy, was in the plains of Moab; and the third time – we have just seen – was between Ebal and Gerizim. And each time, we have said, there were sixteen acts of adherence, which makes forty-eight altogether. You will see that there are still more.

I will try to explain the significance of these distinctions and calculations.

I am sure that some people must be surprised that, in the act of adhering to a law which involves a blessing for the man who obeys it and a curse on the man who transgresses it, one can discern two separate acts, as if the blessing and the curse were not simply the two sides – positive and negative – of the sanction which accompanies every law. In concrete terms there is a real difference between these two sides. It is possible to acknowledge a law and reckon, at the same time, that its transgression would be met with forgiveness. One tells oneself that something can always be worked out! Thank God, forgiveness is not unknown in Israel. Only, in Israel, it is not already taken into account at the moment at which the Law is adopted. In order for forgiveness to have any sense, it cannot already be included at the moment of adhering to the law. We know about Judaism's mistrust of any pardon acquired in advance. We know where that can lead.

Can the adherence to the Law as a whole, to its general tenor, be distinguished from the 'yes' which is said to the particular laws it spells out? Naturally, there has to be a general commitment. The spirit in which a piece of legislation is made has to be understood. And we must deepen this understanding of the spirit of the Law. Philosophy is not forbidden here – the participation of the faculty of reason is not unwelcome! For there to be true inner adherence, this process of generalization is indispensable. But why is it necessary to distinguish between this knowledge of the general spirit, and the knowledge of its particular forms of expression? Because we cannot understand the spirit of any legislation without acknowledging the laws it contains. These are two distinct procedures, and the distinction is justified from several particular points of view. Everyone responds to the attempt to encapsulate Judaism in a few 'spiritual' principles. Everyone is seduced by what might be called the angelic essence of the Torah, to which many verses and commandments can be reduced. This 'internalization' of the Law enchants our liberal souls and we are inclined to reject anything which seems to resist the 'rationality' or the 'morality' of the Torah. Judaism has always been aware, as rabbinical literature attests, of the presence within it – a necessary feature of any expression of great spirituality – of elements which can not be immediately internalized. Alongside the *mishpatim*, the laws we call all recognize as just, there are the *hukkim*, those unjustifiable laws in which Satan delights when he mocks the Torah. He claims the ritual of the 'red heifer' in Numbers 19 is tyrannical and demented. And what are we to make of circumcision? Can we explain it away with a little psychoanalysis? Such a solution was certainly never anticipated, and we may wonder if it really works. And what about the numerous other ritual or ceremonial arrangements described in the Torah? It can be seen that there are points in the law of Israel which demand, over and above the acceptance of the general or 'underlying' spirit of the Torah, a special consent to particular details which are too easily dismissed as having lost their relevance. There is a constant struggle within us between our two adherences; to the spirit and to what is known as the letter. Both are equally indispensable, which is why two separate acts are discerned in the acceptance of the Torah. Jacob's struggle with the Angel has the same meaning: the overcoming, in the existence of Israel, of the angelism or other-worldliness of pure interiority. Look at the effort with which this victory is won! But is it really won? There is no victor. And when the Angel's clasp is released it is Jacob's religion which remains, a little bruised. It is an unending struggle. But remember, the Angel is not the highest creature: as a purely spiritual being, he does not participate in that condition which the Torah considers to be inseparable from life; he has no need to eat, or take, or give, or work, or even not to work on the Shabbat! He is a principle of generosity, but no more than a principle. Of course, generosity demands an adherence. But the adherence to a principle is not enough; it brings temptation with it, and requires us to be wary and on our guard.

There is a further reason why the particular should be seen within the Law as a principle which is independent of the universality that every particular law reflects. It is precisely the concrete and particular aspect of the Law and the circumstances of its application which give rise to the Talmudic dialectic: the oral law is a system of casuistry. It is concerned with the passage from the general principle embodied in the Law to its possible execution, its concrete effects. If this passage were simply deducible, the Law, in its particular form, would not have demanded a separate adherence. But the fact is that general principles and generous principles can be inverted in the course of their application. All generous thought is threatened by its own Stalinism. The great strength of the Talmud's casuistry is that it is the special discipline which studies the particular case in order to identify the precise moment within it when the general principle is at risk of turning into its opposite; it surveys the general from the standpoint of the particular. This preserves us from ideology. Ideology arises out of the generosity and clarity of a principle, qualities which do not take into account the betrayal which lies in wait for this general principle at the moment of its application; to use our image of a moment ago, the Talmud is the struggle with the Angel. That is why the adherence to the particular law is an irreducible dimension of any allegiance, and you will see that Rabbi Akiba thinks this is not only of equal importance to the adherence to the Law in its general form, but that the place devoted to its study – the *yeshivah*, ultimately – is one of the three places where the pact was made, a place equal in dignity to Sinai where the Torah was revealed, and to the plains of Moab where Moses reiterated it.

In the apparently bizarre calculation of the forty-eight covenants which our text distinguishes within the pacts relating to the Law, the number four has figured repeatedly, representing the four undertakings which each act of adherence to the Law brings with it: the undertakings to learn it, to teach it, to observe it, and to carry it out. Without the theoretical activity of study, without the exacting regime of listening and reading, without the *lilmod*, we can absorb nothing. But it is also necessary to teach what one has learned, in order to hand it down. This transmission, the *lelammed*, is an obligation distinct from the simple receptivity of study. For the accumulated knowledge of humankind is always in danger of becoming fossilized, settling like inert matter within our consciousness, to be passed on in this rigid form from one generation to another. This congealment of the spirit is not the same as its true transmission, whose essence lies, rather, in the revival, vitality, discovery and renewal which come with the keeping of tradition, the lesson taught to the other and taken up by him. Without these qualities no revelation – no truly authentic thought – is possible. The activity of transmission therefore involves a teaching which begins to take shape even in the receptive attitude of study, and adds something to that attitude: true learning now consists in receiving a lesson so profoundly that the student is compelled to pass it on to another. The lesson of truth cannot be contained within the consciousness of a single man, it bursts out of those bounds, towards the Other. To study well, to read well, to listen well; all these already require one to speak, whether this be by asking questions which will teach, in turn, the master teaching you, or by teaching a third person.

In the four last books of the Pentateuch, there is a verse which constantly reappears: 'Speak to the children of Israel *le'mor* ("thus").' A renowned scholar who taught me just after the Liberation used to claim that he could give 120 different interpretations of this phrase, whose immediate meaning seems to contain no mystery. He only revealed one of these interpretations to me. I have tried to divine a second. The one which he revealed was the translation of *le'mor* by 'in order not to say'. This produced 'Speak to the children of Israel in order not to say.' The idea is that there must be something unsaid (*non-dit*) if listening is to remain thoughtful; or perhaps that the word must also be unsaid if truth (or God's word) is not to consume the people listening to it; or that God's word must be able to reside, without danger to men, within their language and speech. In my own reading of this verse, *le'mor* would mean 'in order to say'. This gives us: 'Speak to the children of Israel in order that they speak', teach them so profoundly that they themselves begin to speak, let them listen till they reach the point of speaking. The 118 other meanings of the verse remain to be discovered. My teacher took their secret with him to his grave.

Let us move on to the third obligaton: to observe, or keep. *Lishmor.*

There are two possibilities: *lishmor* may mean the observance of the negative commandments, the interdicts. At this point, where the distinction between negative and positive commandments has not been made, such an interpretation is impossible. Or *lishmor* may mean that new thing which becomes necessary once one has learned something: never to forget, that is, to repeat the lesson. The study involved here can never be finished; even at the moment of its first assimilation, it demands to be recommenced.

Finally, *la'asot*, 'to carry out'. This does not need explanation. The profundity of our text is shown in its reflection upon these four points as a group, susceptible to isolation rather than to perversion. Each of these moments of study demands a special adherence, special attention. So there were sixteen covenants within each pact. Now, the pact was concluded in these three places – at Sinai, in the plains of Moab, and between Mounts Ebal and Gerizim – which amounts to forty-eight covenants in connection with the Law. But this was a point of contention. Rabbi Akiba, you will see, does not agree that the ceremony between Mounts Ebal and Gerizim should be included among the three occasions. Speaking for myself, I am glad that Rabbi Akiba had doubts about this. I will tell you why later.

The Three Occasions

The account of the ceremony near Mount Gerizim given in the Talmudic text we are studying suggests that the pact of the Covenant was concluded three times, and the phrase 'It was similar at Sinai and the plains of Moab . . . ' confirms this. Here is the passage in full: 'It was similar at Sinai and the plains of Moab; as it is said, *These are the words of the covenant which the Lord commanded Moses.*' The covenant referred to here is independent of the one made at Horeb. Then we have: 'and it is written, *Keep therefore the words of this covenant.*' But here someone contests part of the calculation: 'R. Simeon excludes (the occasion of) Mount Gerizim and Mount Ebal and includes that of the Tent of Meeting in the wilderness'. Rabbi Simeon agrees that the covenant was made three times, but, in his opinion, the ceremony which took place between Mounts Gerizim and Ebal does not count. To arrive at the figure of three, Rabbi Simeon regards the meetings held between Moses and the people, alluded to in Exodus 33: 7, as the making of a covenant: 'Now Moses used to take the tent and pitch it outside the camp, far off from the camp; and he called it the tent of meeting. And everyone who sought the Lord would go out to the tent of meeting which was outside the camp.' The figure of forty-eight alliances is confirmed. But Rabbi Simeon prefers to accord the dignity of the making of a covenant not to the solemn event which took place between Mounts Ebal and Gerizim – which, in his view, is a mere ceremony – but rather to the discussion of the Law of the Lord which is supposed to have been held inside the 'tent of meeting in the desert' where Moses greeted those people who had questions or problems. Here the Covenant is not understood as an event staged so as to allow each person to see everyone else; rather, it is the questioning of the master by the pupils, on an individual basis. It was in precisely that tent of meeting, in Moses's *yeshivah*, that the voice of God was heard, and it was there, after Sinai and before the plains of Moab, that the Covenant was made for the second time.

Rabbi Simeon thinks, therefore, that the ceremony should be replaced by the activity of study. This is an important decision. As we shall soon see, Rabbi Akiba shared this opinion. What are Rabbi Simeon's motives? Rashi naturally raises this question. The answer must be that the passage in Deuteronomy 27 which announces the ceremony of Mount Gerizim only lists some of the laws of the Torah. The Torah does not appear in its entirety. Thus the ceremony cannot count as the making of a 'complete' covenant. I do not want to contest the words of Rashi. But surely – we may add – Rabbi Simeon would also have been shocked by the fact that, in Deuteronomy 27, the laws which are mentioned are given only in their repressive form? Only curses are listed. There were blessings too, of course, but they are not formulated here.

In any case, Rabbi Simeon's intervention, disputing the validity of the covenant at Mount Gerizim, raises an important question. It takes us back to a disagreement between those two giants of Talmudic scholarship, the Tannaim Rabbi Ishmael and Rabbi Akiba (who was Rabbi Simeon's teacher). Here is the passage:

> The difference of opinion here is the same as that of the teachers in the following: R. Ishmael says: General laws were proclaimed at Sinai and particular laws in the Tent of Meeting. R. Akiba says: Both general and particular laws were proclaimed at Sinai, repeated in the Tent of Meeting, and for the third time in the plains of Moab. Consequently there is not a single precept written in the Torah in connection with which forty-eight covenants were not made.

The disagreement expressed by Rabbi Simeon takes us back, then, to an earlier discussion held by the Tannaim, between Rabbi Ishmael and Rabbi Akiba. Rabbi Ishmael thought that the ceremony which took place between Mounts Ebal and Gerizim should be counted as one of the three occasions on which the pact was made. What did he mean by this? Perhaps he thought that apart from Sinai and the plains of Moab there was no further ceremony to mark the Covenant. In his view, it was only the particular details that were taught in the tent of meeting, while the principles were taught at Sinai, so that Sinai and the tent of meeting should be counted together as a single covenant. The plains of Moab are the second covenant, and Mounts Ebal and Gerizim the third. Perhaps Rabbi Ishmael also thought there was a further possible problem which ought to be discussed, which I shall not discuss here: he may have contested the absolute equality accorded to the study of the general principles and that of the particular cases of the Law. He believed, of course, that the particular and the general were both important. Without that belief, he could not be a great Talmudist. But all the same, he considered the general principles to be more important. Does this make him more liberal than Rabbi Akiba? You must ask the Talmudists in this hall who are more competent than I for a reply to that question. Perhaps Rabbi Ishmael thought that the ceremony in which everyone is able to see everyone else is of importance. Perhaps some of his ideas were close to the ones we have formulated here concerning the distinction between society and community, so that he believed the experience of the community was an essential part of the revelation.

Rabbi Akiba seems to be opposed to these ideas. He maintains that the general and the particular are absolutely equal in worth. He seems to rule out the ceremony in which everyone sees everyone else. Perhaps he thinks that a concrete situation in which men are present to each other does not constitute a true face-to-face.

So far we have counted forty-eight covenants. We have tried to understand this calculation in terms of the affirmation of the various dimensions of the Law. These dimensions cannot be accommodated by the formalism of today's law, which is utterly anonymous; a fact which may be regarded as the origin of the crisis facing modern society.

The Law and Interpersonal Relations

Forty-eight covenants? We can do better. 'Rabbi Simeon ben Judah of Kefar Acco said in the name of Rabbi Simeon:' – this is the same Rabbi Simeon that disputed the importance of the ceremony at Gerizim – 'There is not a single precept written in the Torah in connection with which forty-eight times 603,550 covenants were not made'. The number of covenants made in the course of these three ceremonies is said, then, to be 603,550 times 48. Where does this figure of 603,550 come from? It represents the number of Israelites standing at the foot of Sinai. But why do we multiply by that number? Because the Covenant concerning the revealed Law does not have the character of an abstract and impersonal juridical act; rather, its acceptance establishes living bonds with all those adopting the Law. Within this Covenant each person finds himself responsible for everyone else; each act of the Covenant expresses more than six hundred thousand personal acts of responsibility. The forty-eight dimensions of the pact become 48 × 603,550. This might, of course, raise a smile. It is a large number. But it is not an infinite one. The Israelites, more correctly described as men participating in a common humanity, answer for each other before a genuinely human law. In the making of this Covenant the relationship between one person and the other is not a matter of indifference. Everyone is looking at me! It is not necessary to gather on the mountains of Ebal or Gerizim, to gaze at length into each other's eyes, for there to be a situation in which everyone looks at everyone else. Everyone looks at me. Let us not forget the seventy languages in which the Torah is read out. The Torah belongs to everyone: everyone is responsible for everyone else. The phrase 'Love your neighbour as yourself' still assumes the prototype of love to be love of oneself. Here, the ethic is one which says: 'Be responsible for the other as you are responsible for yourself.' In this way we avoid the assumption about self-love which is often accepted as the very definition of a person. But we have not finished yet: 'Rabbi said . . . ' The Rabbi speaking at this point is Rabbenu Hakadosh, who gave the *Mishnah* its written form, the highest Talmudic authority after, or perhaps alongside, Rabbi Akiba. 'Rabbi said: According to the reasoning of R. Simeon b. Judah of Kefar Acco, who said in the name of R. Simeon . . . ' What a lot of references! Do not be surprised, those of you who may be attending your first Talmudic lesson, by this accumulation of names. In the Talmud it is always of great importance to specify, for each saying, who said it. A true teaching is one in which the universal nature of the truth it announces does not obliterate the name or the identity of the person who said it. The Talmudic scholars even believe that the Messiah will come at the moment when everyone quotes what they have learned, in the name of the person they learned it from. So the Rabbi says: 'there is not a single precept written in the Torah in connection with which forty-eight times 603,550 covenants were not made, it follows that for each Israelite there are 603,550 commandments. (And forty-eight covenants were made in connection with each of them.)' Doesn't this repeat what we heard a moment ago? The *Gemara* asks this question: 'What is the issue between them?' And R. Mesharsheya finds it: 'R. Mesharsheya said: The point between them is that of personal responsibility and responsibility for others [the responsibility of responsibility].' One is not only responsible for everyone else, but responsible also for the responsibility of everyone else. So forty-eight must be multiplied by 603,550, and the product multiplied by 603,550 again. This point is extremely important. A moment ago, we saw a part played by something resembling the recognition of the Other, the love of the Other. To such an extent that I offer myself as guarantee of the Other, of his adherence and fidelity to the Law. His concern is my concern. But is not my concern also his? Isn't he responsible for me? And if he is, can I also answer for his responsibility for me? *Kol Yisrael 'arevim zeh lazeh*, 'All Israel is responsible one for the other', which means: all those who cleave to the divine law, all men worthy of the name, are all responsible for each other.

This must also mean that my responsibility includes the responsibility taken up by other men. I always have, myself, one responsibility more than anyone else, since I am responsible, in addition, for his responsibility. And if he is responsible for my responsibility, I remain responsible for the responsibility he has for my responsibility. *Ein ladavar sof*, 'it will never end'. In the society of the Torah, this process is repeated to infinity; beyond any responsibility attributed to everyone and for everyone, there is always the additional fact that I am still responsible for that responsibility. It is an ideal, but one which is inseparable from the humanity of human beings. In the Covenant, when it is fully understood, in the society which fully deploys all the dimensions of the Law, society becomes a community.

NOTES

1 Square brackets indicate alternatives provided where necessary to fit Levinas's text more exactly.
2 In this extract, square brackets indicate Levinas's interpolations.

Translated by Sarah Richmond

14

Prayer Without Demand

Published in *Etudes philosophiques*, 38 (1984), 157–63, 'Prayer Without Demand' has recently attracted the attention of several philosophers, among them Derrida. It is essentially an explication of the *Nefesh ha'Hayyim*, reinforced by references to the Bible which, as ever, provides the ethical model.

The *Nefesh ha'Hayyim*, or Soul of Life, was the posthumously published work of Rabbi Hayyim Volozhiner (1759–1821). Quoting widely from Kabbalistic as well as rabbinic sources, it is addressed to 'the men of the yeshivah'. In reaction to Hasidism, it elevates the study of the Torah to the highest degree in terms of understanding rather than mystical ecstasy, and thus lays emphasis on textual criticism. It describes a cosmological hierarchy in which man's body lies at the bottom while man's soul exists at the highest point, next to God. The degree of soul to body displayed in man's behaviour therefore determines his being or nothingness.

Levinas interprets this cosmology in terms of a fidelity to the Law that shows how each person is responsible not only for his or her own death but for the possibility of life or death for everyone. The *reason* for being displayed here shows ethics preceding ontology. In this hierarchy, being must operate for the other rather than for itself. Such dis-inter-est is exemplified in prayer that makes no demands for itself. Individual supplication occurs, rather, when the 'I' in danger is Israel, the bearer of the revelation. The political questions which this obviously raises will be dealt with in the next section.

S.H.

Reflections on an Aspect of Judaism

In the second half of the eighteenth century, Jewish life and religious thought in Eastern Europe came under the influence of a movement which began in Lithuania, inspired by the moral and intellectual teaching of a renowned rabbinical scholar, Elijah Gaon of Vilna (1720–97), one of the last Talmudists of genius, an excellent Kabbalist, a man of strong and rounded personality. In particular he played a large part in the resistance to Hasidism, the popular mystical and sentimental movement which was stirring up the Jews of Poland. To Rabbi Elijah of Vilna, this movement seemed likely to harm a religious way of life which was dedicated, above all, to the study of the Torah. But the Gaon's influence, checked by that of Hasidism, only just preceded the tide of liberal and secular rationalism, known as *Haskalah*, which appeared to reject him, and which, in the course of the nineteenth century, was to introduce the Jewish communities throughout Eastern Europe to the values of the modern West, which had long since been absorbed and embraced by the Jews of Western Europe. Their aspiration to political emancipation and integration within the nation states of Europe, which began at the end of the eighteenth and continued throughout the nineteenth century, was the expression, in permanent and concrete terms, of their attachment to the European spirit. None the less, the Judaism of the Vilna Gaon and his disciples represents an important moment in Jewish consciousness, which still bears its mark – often unknowingly – even in its modern form. By the Gaon's time, Lithuanian Judaism was content to congratulate itself about its own authenticity and to glorify its traditional cultural and religious notions; somehow, it managed to feed on the religion of its forefathers, and to bypass any alien influences which might have seeped in at the time of, or since, its birth but which by now had long ceased to influence its spirit. This civilization rested squarely on the study of the Torah, as received through the learned rabbinical commentaries of the Talmud. Its wisdom was constantly renewed precisely through study and interpretation, an activity which naturally was conducted in the hope of discovering such opportunities for renewal, the 'hidoushims' and their creative surprises, but which, none the less, sought and obtained these findings through a method which itself was already tested by tradition. Such was the study of the Torah – motivated by more than just the need to know how to carry out the Law, or show pious obedience. The act of study constituted in itself the most direct communication with a transcendent, non-objectifiable God, whose word and will and commandments create an inexhaustible text which seems, with each new day, to present itself for the first time. At its greatest intellectual and dialectical moments, this discipline reaches heights as lofty as those of liturgy, surpassing even the transports of prayer, although, to meet the severe demands imposed by this wisdom, no life of study can dispense with either worship or ritual practices. It is a discipline which entails, of course, a particular worldview, a doctrine of the full meaning of Israel's destiny and its place within the structure of the universe and the unfolding of human history. But there were few works concerned to expound this philosophical aspect of the existence of Israel in a culture which expressed itself most successfully through the Talmud's own problematic – in terms of the legislation governing behaviour known as 'Halakhah', the study of which yielded infinitely more than a set of practical rules. In the light of this task, a distinctively philosophical system would appear to be already derivative, or implicit, but in any case something to be taken for granted.

There is a book called *Nefesh ha'Hayyim* (*The Soul of Life*), whose title probably comes from the expression '*Nefesh hayya*' which means 'living soul' in Genesis 2: 7 and refers there to the moment in man's creation when the divine breath entered the 'nostrils' of the body formed out of 'dust from the ground'. This book, which we may entitle, in effect, *Of Man* has always struck me as an attempt to lay out the philosophical ideas implicit in Rabbinical study. The book was published posthumously in Vilna in 1824, and was the work of Rabbi Hayyim Volozhiner (1759–1821), the Elijah Gaon's favourite disciple and himself endowed with exceptional intelligence and spirituality. He also founded a famous 'house of study', a *yeshivah*, in the small Lithuanian town of Volozhin whose name in some way he came to bear. His book is, of course, devotional, but it is also the work of a Talmudist and Kabbalist, and it is inspired by the desire to show the future pupils of the *yeshivah* – which the author had founded and directed – the metaphysical dimensions, if we can call them that, of the study of the Torah, which is seen not only as the vocation of Judaism, but also as the foundation of the very *Being* of reality. Perhaps the stealthy approach of a new society, the first rumblings of modernity, could already be sensed and were partly responsible for this literary project – which is not concerned with any strictly 'Halakhic' problems, but which already raises the question of the essence of Judaism. In any case, it provides some remarkable perspectives on the fundamental structure of Judaism, the religion of Study and the Law.

We will examine some of the notions which this presentation brings to our attention. To summarize this relatively short work would be impossible: it proceeds by way of allusion and reference to an entire tradition, and is built upon a Talmudic and Kabbalistic framework which cannot be neglected without impoverishing its meaning. We shall try to isolate certain strands of thought which, in our view, take us beyond the categories and colours of the particularism – the narrowness of focus – which forms their context.[1] Such a context is, of course, worthy of respect, since it is probably the only way in which these ideas could first be formulated; none the less, we will try here to free our discourse from it, even if we cannot entirely avoid the echoes of a bid for singularity which is an essential human possibility.

The existence of reality – the being of countless beings, as we say today – or, in the terminology of *Nefesh ha'Hayyim*, the being of creatures designated by the plural term 'worlds', is a sign of God's *association* with these worlds, which would return to nothingness or fall into decline if God withdrew from them. The worlds owe their being to this divine energy of association which creates them and preserves them by continually recreating them. In consequence, the being of the worlds becomes equivalent to their holiness, their light and their spirituality; it gives them life and is their *elevation* or *loftiness* (*hauteur*). Together, the worlds form a hierarchy. Each superior world gives life to the world beneath, governing, sanctifying and throwing light on it, and in turn receives movement, being and holiness from the world above it. This hierarchy is not, therefore, just a monumental piece of architecture. The worlds are emanations of the divine, and can only exist as such. God, whose 'throne' is at the highest point, inspires these worlds like a soul. God – God the creator – is the soul of these worlds.

This account of the cosmological hierarchy, with its apparent harmony, should not be taken as more than a rough outline. A complication presents itself at once: man, the last being to be created, plays a pre-eminent part. Although he was created in the shadow of the worlds, out of substance taken from those worlds, man – thereby related to the worlds – is the element on which the whole structure depends (!); his body is situated at the lowest point, at the level of *doing*, the level of *work*, but his soul occupies the highest point, beside the 'throne of the Lord' from whose breath it comes. And so it is that, through God's will, man's acts, words and thoughts – following or departing from the commandments of the Torah – condition or disturb or block the association of God with the world. They determine, in this way, the being or nothingness of all creatures. God needed man in his fidelity to the *Law* in order to give life to the worlds, to sanctify them, illuminate them, and thereby bring them into existence. But, in consequence, each man becomes responsible for the life and death of all the other worlds and men. 'Let nobody in Israel – God forbid!', wrote Volozhiner,

> ask himself: "what am I, and what can my humble acts achieve in the world?". Let him rather understand this, that he may know it and fix it in his thoughts: not one detail of his acts, of his words and of his thoughts is ever lost. Each one leads back to its origin, where it takes effect in the height of heights, in the worlds ... The man of intelligence who understands this in its truth will be fearful at heart and will tremble as he thinks how far his bad acts reach and what corruption and destruction even a small misdeed can cause.

This responsibility for others therefore comes to be for man the meaning of his own self-identity. His self (*son moi*) is not originally *for itself* (*pour soi*); 'through the will of God' it is 'for others'. In this way man becomes, in turn, the *soul* of the world, as if God's creative word had been entrusted to him to dispose of as he liked, to let it ring out, or to interrupt it. This is the ultimate meaning of Genesis 1: 27 which affirms that humanity was conceived 'in the image of God'; it is also the literal meaning – and, for all that, the most profound one – of the Hebraic verse of Genesis 2: 7, where man is called a 'living soul' (and not, as the modern translations would have it, a 'living being'); it is also the meaning of Isaiah 51: 16: 'And I have put my words in your mouth, and hid you in the shadow of my hand, stretching out the heavens and laying the foundations of the earth'. Another verse which should be taken literally! It tells us that God's creative word was placed in the mouth of man: the being or non-being of the universe depends upon his adherence to the Torah.

That the all-powerful Divinity, wishing to create and to secure the being of beings or worlds by his association with them, should depend on man's submission to the Torah demonstrates not only God's humility, alongside – or perhaps contributing to – his greatness. It also articulates, quite radically, the inability of being (*être*) *qua* pure being to provide beings (*étants*) with an adequate *raison d'être*. Onto-logy – that is, the intelligibility of being – only becomes possible when ethics, the origin of all meaning, is taken as the starting point. Humanity must irrupt into Being: behind the perseverance, in being, of the beings or worlds – of men, too, insofar as they are themselves simple worlds – behind their *conatus essendi* or their identity, affirming its own ego or egoism, there must figure, somewhere, in some form or other, the responsibility of *the one for the others*. The *for itself* must be inverted, and become the *for the other*, the immediate fear of the one *for* the other. We can see here – if we go beyond the terminology of our author – that we are already talking about love, the first value, which is that small amount of humanity by virtue of which alone the creation deserves to continue. Through this alone can the imperturbable existence of the worlds – or beings – be justified, in the disinterested attitude of one man answering for another. It is only at this point that the dimension of justification and justice appears, in which God's association with the worlds – which is the being (*être*) of these beings (*étants*) – reveals its divine dignity.

Can we see, in this possibility given to humanity – that of being responsible for the other – the foremost meaning of Israel's historical existence? Does it lie in this possibility, where the ultimate stake is being itself? Or should we understand this reversal of the self (*moi*) into the for-the-other as the Judaic endowment of all men? To answer such questions would take us, of course, beyond the scope of the doctrines of Rabbi Hayyim Volozhiner; I do not think these doctrines rule out, however, the most universal of answers. Our author's concern, clearly, is with man's fidelity to the commandments of the Torah insofar as it is this which makes God's association with the worlds possible. But, behind the local and particularistic purposes which one can be tempted to see in the religion or culture of the Torah, there is the affirmation of the idea that *being-for-itself* – and no doubt being-in-itself too – has as its condition the unconditioned responsibility of *being-for-the-other*. Within the subsistence of the worlds, it is necessary to seek their elevation, holiness and purity. To affirm the Torah's anteriority over being – the anteriority of God's word, as entrusted to man – is simply to affirm the ethical meaning of the creation, in accordance with Psalms 82: 5 where injustice is said to shake 'all the foundations of the earth'.

This reversal of human subjectivity which is no longer defined in terms of an *in itself*, nor by a *for itself*, but rather through a forgetting of the self in the 'fear and trembling' for the other, for the worlds and for other men, is given remarkable expression in Hayyim Volozhiner's book by his analysis of prayer. Prayer never asks for anything for oneself; strictly speaking, it makes no demands at all, but is an elevation of the soul. This describes true prayer, at least, or the prayer of the just man, prayer which conforms – if we are to believe *Nefesh ha'Hayyim* – to Jewish piety.

I will circumvent here the fine points of exegesis, the Kabbalistic and Talmudic details in which Hayyim Volozhiner's account is embedded. In his eyes, the essence of prayer lies in the moment of benediction, the generous act of offering that is necessary for God's association with the worlds. This offering 'feeds' the association – the existence or life of the worlds – in the same way as the food which guarantees the continued animation of living bodies even though the spiritual principle of animation has no need to consume this food. The prayer of Jewish ritual has its words carefully chosen by the 'men of the chief Synagogue', and is 'composed in the tradition of the wise men and prophets'. After the captivity of Babylon, such prayer restored the continuity of Jewish life, which had been interrupted by exile. Its words are endowed with an unparalleled spiritual force, 'bringing thought to an extreme purity of intention and elevation', 'a privilege of that marvellous refinement which annuls all those vain ideas weighing down and impeding purity of thought and intention'. To pray, our author tells us, is to 'strip the soul of the clothing of the body'. Better still, it is 'to pour out one's soul'. Indeed, in I Samuel 1: 15 do we not find Anne, the future mother of Samuel, describing her prayer in these terms: 'I have been pouring out my soul before the Lord'? Is prayer, then, the soul itself? At one point, Rabbi Hayyim makes this claim. Deuteronomy 6: 5 says: 'you shall love the Lord your God ... with all your soul.' All these verses we have been quoting demand to be taken literally – and in each case, the literal meaning yields far more than the figurative one! Far from being a demand addressed to God, prayer consists in the 'elevation, surrender and *adherence* of the soul to the heights'. The soul rises up, just as the smoke from a sacrifice does. One dis-inter-ests oneself (*se dés-inter-esser*), loosens the ties of that unconditional attachment to being. Adherence to the heights: the term used in verses such as Deuteronomy 4: 4 and Psalms 63: 4, '*devekut*', means attachment, adherence, the state of sticking to something . . .

God desires prayer in the manner of Proverbs 15: 8, where the verse is read for the most obvious meaning: 'the prayer of the upright is his delight (*désir*)'. He needs prayer, just as he needs man's fidelity to the Torah, to make his association with the worlds, their existence and elevation, possible. Here we return to the theme which seemed to be so central earlier on: it is not enough – and it is not possible – for the worlds to continue *to be*, by virtue of their power to subsist. They must be justified. The ethical must intervene! Man, and man's prayer are essential. In this way, prayer, which is called in Hebrew 'the service of the heart' or even 'the work of the heart' (once again, such an expression is not simply a metaphor) refers, in the true sense of the term, to the task of edifying the worlds, or 'repairing the ruins of creation'.[2] For the self (*moi*), prayer means that, instead of seeking one's own salvation, one secures that of others.

True prayer, then, is never for oneself, never 'for one's needs', and Rabbi Hayyim states this explicitly. Instituted as it was, by the 'men of the chief Synagogue', to replace the daily sacrifices made in the now destroyed or far-off temple, how could it contain any human demands? For were those daily sacrifices at the temple not burnt offerings, or holocausts? And was the flesh offered at the altar in this way, as a holocaust, not meant to be entirely consigned to the flames, leaving nothing behind for the man making the offering? How could any individual allude to his egoistic needs in his prayer, and so compromise the pure dis-inter-estedness of the holocaust?

Moreover, is it right for us to ask, in our prayers, for human suffering to be eased? The meaning of suffering is surely the expiation of sin.[3] Would we have the sick give up taking their medicine just because it tastes bitter? Would we have our sins remain unexpiated?

But doesn't the Talmud itself authorize the individual supplications of human beings, alongside the prayers which honour the glory of God? It does, but only in those circumstances where Israel as a whole is in danger, when its people are persecuted and held in contempt. This is not in the name of any nationalist egoism. The people of Israel, we must remember, are the bearers of the revelation; their role is to manifest the glory of God and His message among all the peoples of the earth. Israel's history is sacred history, the history related by the Bible. And it is for the sake of this sacred history, the glory of its message, that an act of supplication is permitted, provided it does not drag prayer down to a level of interest exclusively

concerned with the 'self' (*mon moi*). Is our human suffering, then, condemned to silence? Does the Talmud's ruling about prayer for oneself (*soi*)
absolutely exclude the claims of the unhappy 'I' (*moi*)?

According to *Nefesh ha'Hayyim*, no prayer whose basic concern is with
one's own unhappiness can be counted as pious. The prayers of the suffering just man are of a very different kind. The meaning of any prayer can be
found only in its relationship to God's need of the prayers of the just to
bring the worlds into existence, to sanctify and elevate them. But, insofar as
the suffering of any 'I' (*moi*) immediately becomes God's suffering – who
suffers in this suffering of 'mine' – there is a way in which the suffering self
can pray: by praying for the suffering of God who suffers through my
human suffering. I do not have to pray for my suffering. God, prior to any
demand, is already there with me. Does He not say in Psalms 91: 15: 'I will
be with him in trouble (*dans sa souffrance*)'? And Isaiah 63: 9 speaks of God
suffering in man's affliction, or suffering. The suffering self prays on behalf
of God's suffering, for the God who suffers both through man's transgression and through the suffering by which this transgression can be
expiated. Through his orisons, man is elevated and brought closer to this
divine suffering which exceeds his own. Confronted with this torture, he
finds his own suffering diminished – he can no longer feel it, in comparison
with the suffering of God which is so much greater than his own. The
transgression is expiated precisely through this surplus of God's suffering
over man's: God suffers in reparation for transgression, right up to the
moment when the suffering is brought to an end, and the transgression
expiated. By such holy means is 'bitterness sweetened by bitterness'!

NOTES

All notes are by the author, unless otherwise indicated.
1 I have devoted an essay to Rabbi Hayyim Volozhiner, entitled 'A l'image de Dieu'
  in my *L'au-delà du Verset* (Paris: Editions de Minuit, 1982), pp. 182–200.
2 Translator's note: Levinas is referring to the sense (now rare) of 'to build' which
  the verb 'to edify' can have, from the Latin root, 'aedificare'.
3 A phrase which, after Auschwitz, has become unacceptable. Preaching it to others
  is intolerable. But does this prevent one from saying it to oneself?

Translated by Sarah Richmond

15

Ideology and Idealism

'Ideology and Idealism' was originally published in *Démythisation et idéologie* (Actes du Colloque organisé par le Centre international d'Etudes humanistes et par l'Institut d'Etudes philosophiques de Rome), edited by E. Castelli (Paris: Aubier-Montaigne, 1973), pp. 135–45, and collected in *De Dieu qui vient à l'idée* (Paris: Vrin, 1982), pp. 17–33. The present text of this essay comes from the English-language version collected in *Modern Jewish Ethics*, edited by Martin Fox (Athens, Ohio: Ohio State University Press, 1975), pp. 121–38. This latter text is based on a combination of the original publication, a shorter French version, and a Hebrew version. The shorter French version was given as a paper to the 'Société de Philosophie de Fribourg' in June 1972, while the Hebrew version, entitled 'Ethics as Transcendence and Contemporary Thought' was originally presented in July 1972 to the 'Summer Institute on Judaism and Contemporary Thought' at Nir Etzion in Israel, before being offered again at a public conference organized by the Katholieke Theologische Hogeschool of Amsterdam in November 1972. Our text also includes the transcript of Levinas's responses to a series of questions raised at the end of his paper, when it was delivered at Nir Etzion.

I have chosen to begin the section entitled 'Politics' with this essay for the way in which Levinas explains his thinking in terms of the broad social and intellectual currents of the last two centuries, confronting in the process the political problem of nationhood: 'contemporary thought is the thought of the nations among whom we live.' He recognizes that traditional ethics has come to an end with the modern critique of ideology to be found in the work of Marx, Nietzsche and Freud. But he interprets this as one more refutation of the claim that 'not-to-philosophize is still to philosophize'. The way in which the validity of philosophizing is put in question by the struggle against ideology leads Levinas once more to a demand for justice and a better society, and in this he makes a direct appeal to the youth whom he hopes to remind of both Holocaust and Halakhah. And if ethics should be a victim of youthful rebellion, this is perhaps because rebellion is an eminently ethical activity. Finally, he sees in the responsibility for the other a refutation of the Derridean tendency to develop the critique of ideology to the point where dissemination delays the emergence of any signified. The Talmud itself works with the idea of proliferating interpretations; but ultimately shows how the ethical relation must couch the saying in justice, state, society and law.

For a reply to Levinas's essay, see Abner Weiss, 'Ethics as Transcendence and the Contemporary World: A Response to Emmanuel Levinas' in *Modern Jewish Ethics*, pp. 139–52.

S.H.

―――――――――

Contemporary thought is the thought of the nations among whom we live, even in Israel, which I do not view as a new ghetto or as a country separated from the world like those that in France are called 'underdeveloped'. Contemporary thought is the thought of a human society that is undergoing global industrial development, a fact that should not be treated lightly. Contemporary thought stands at a very great distance from the world of the Halakhah and from many problems that have been under consideration at the meeting of the Institute for Judaism and Contemporary Thought.

Contemporary thought does not know Joseph, or at least pretends not to know. Is there a bridge between the ethics of the Jewish people and contemporary thought, or between this thought and Jewish ethics? Do they have a common language? This question must be answered, but to do so we must begin from another point. We must speak, first of all, not of the relation between ethics and Halakhah, but rather of the passage from the non-ethical in general to the ethical, for this is truly the necessity of our time. This question must be answered on behalf of that Jewish youth which has forgotten the Holocaust, and which sees in the rejection of all morality an end to violence, an end to repression by all forms of authority. We must answer a youth that sees in the particularism of Judaism, in the world of the commandments and of true Jewish distinctiveness, only support for an anachronism, for a world that is passing away. For us, who live in the Diaspora that extends even to Israel, there is a special problem of Judaism. The problem of Judaism is the problem of opening a way to Judaism that will show it to those who being blinded are now outside. I speak of those who, unlike the wicked men of Sodom, are knocking at the gate and seeking to enter; and even those who are not yet seeking entrance.

The assimilation of these young people who stand outside and do not hear us as we deliberate within the framework of Halakhah (would that we were truly considering Halakhah!), this form of assimilaton in our time has a new motive that distinguishes it from that which was common a hundred years ago. Our young people today no longer assimilate for the sake of an easier life in the contemporary world. They take on the burden of participating in the building of a new world, a world that is difficult to build and to sustain.

So we turn to our topic, which seems to be metaphysics. Is this laudable or shameful? But all metaphysics in Europe is now both laudable and shameful. We are deep into the end of metaphysics, and at the end of metaphysics we are all occupied with it.

Ideology and Morality

Ideology pretends to be science, while the very admission of its concept leaves morality suspect. The least suspicion of ideology delivers to morality the most severe blow it has ever sustained. This suspicion probably signals the end of traditional ethics, and, in any case, overthrows the theory of duty and of value.

Morality understood as an ensemble of rules of conduct based upon the universality of a set of maxims, or upon a hierarchical system of values, contains its own rational justification within itself. It has its own kind of evidence and is apprehended in an intentional act analogous to knowing. Like the categorical imperative, axiology belongs to Logos. The relativity of morality in relation to history, its variation and variants according to social and economic structures, does not basically compromise this rationality. We may correctly interpret historical situations and social conditions as determining the subjective conditions under which we have accession to the moral Logos; they may also determine the time necessary for this accession. These are variable conditions of insight that does not fall full-blown from heaven, and that knows periods of obscurity. The relativism to which the experience of these conditions might seem to invite is mitigated in proportion as historical evolution is understood as the manifestation of Reason itself, as a progressive rationalization of the subject toward the absolute of a reason becoming free act or efficacious, practical reason.

In modern thought, at least in Western Europe, the morality that was understood as an actualization of rational understanding received a nearly fatal blow from the concept of ideology. The concept of ideology, which was Hegelian in origin, and which is used in the Marxist critique of bourgeois humanism, received much of its persuasive force from Nietzsche and Freud. This is the novelty of this concept: that the appearance of rationality could be more insinuating and more resistant than a paralogism, and that its powers of mystification could be so hidden that the art of logic would not be adequate for demystificaton, that proceeding from an unconscious intention, the mystification mystifies the mystifiers!

It is, however, permissible to think that the strange notion of a *suspect reason* did not arise in a mode of philosophical discourse that simply allowed itself to lapse into suspicions instead of furnishing proofs.[1] The notion of a suspect reason forced itself upon us in the 'spreading desert', in the increasing spiritual misery of the industrial era. It is a notion that finds its meaning in agonized groaning, or in a cry denouncing a scandal to which Reason –

that Reason which is capable of considering as ordered a world in which the poor man is sold for a pair of sandals[2] – would remain insensitive if there were not this cry.[3] A prophetic cry, scarcely discourse; a voice that cries out in the wilderness; the rebellion of Marx and some Marxists, beyond Marxist science! A meaning that is rent as a cry, which is not stifled by the system that absorbs it, where it does not cease to echo a voice other than that which bears coherent discourse. It is not always true that not-to-philosophize is still to philosophize. The forcefulness of the break with ethics does not evidence a mere slackening of reason, but rather a questioning of the validity of *philosophizing*, which cannot lapse again into philosophy. But what a strange reversal! On account of its historical relativity, on account of its normative aspects that are called repressive, ethics becomes the first victim of the struggle against ideology that it inspired. It loses its status as reason for the precarious condition of Ruse. It passes for an unconscious effort, but one susceptible of becoming conscious and, from then on, courageous or cowardly, in order to fool others, those faithful to it, or those who preach it. Its rationality, henceforth merely apparent, is a stratagem in the war of class against class, or a refuge for the frustrated, a bundle of illusions dominated by the class interests or by the needs of compensation.

Ideology and Disinterestedness

That ideology – like Reason in the transcendental dialectic of Kant – could be a *necessary* source of illusions is probably a still more recent view. If one were to believe Althusser, ideology always expresses the fashion in which consciousness experiences its dependence on the objective or material conditions that determine it, conditions that scientific reason grasps in their objectivity. One necessarily wonders if that does not, at the same time, teach us about a certain eccentricity of consciousness with regard to the order controlled by science and to which science, to be sure, belongs, a dislocation of the subject, a yawning gap, 'play' (*un 'jeu'*) between it and being.

If illusion is the modality of this play, it does not render illusory this play, this gap, this exile, or this ontological 'homelessness' of consciousness. Could this gap be simply the effect of the incompleteness of science, which, as it completed itself would gnaw away to the quick of the subject, the ultimate vocation of which would be only service of the truth and which, with science perfected, would lose its reason for being? But then this indefinite postponement of the perfection of science would itself signify the separation of the subject from being. Science would then have put ideology back in its place, and deprived it of the pretension of being a truthful kind of knowledge and of directing effective action. Meanwhile, this gap between the subject and being appears again in the possibility that the subject will forget the knowledge that would have returned it to the rank of a psychological factor to be modified by praxis, like any other factor of the real. The achievement of the perfection of science would not, however, have prevented this ideology, henceforth inoffensive, from continuing to assure the permanence of a subjective life that lives upon its own demystified illusions. In such a life, one commits follies under the nose of science, one eats and distracts oneself, one has ambitions and aesthetic tastes, one weeps and is indignant, all the while forgetting the certainty of death and all the physics, psychology, and sociology that, behind life's back, govern this life. The separation of the subject and reality, which is affirmed by ideology, would thus tend either to this completion of science that is always postponed, or to this forgetfulness of science that is always possible.

But does this separation come from the subject? Does it come from a becoming that is filled with concern for its *being* and for its persevering in being? Does it come from an interiority cloaked in the fixity of character, from a singularity revelling in its exception, solicitous of its own happiness – or its own health, having its private doubts, even in the heart of the universality of truth? Is it the subject himself who will have hollowed out an empty space for ideology between himself and being? Does not this empty space come from a previous break with the illusions and the ruses that filled it, from an interruption of essence, from a nonplace, from a utopia, from a pure interval of the *epoche*[4] opened by *disinterestedness*? Science would not yet have had either consoling dreams to interrupt, nor megalomania to restore to reason; it would only have found the necessary distance for its impartiality and objectivity. Ideology would thus have been the symptom or sign of a dismissal of charges by which the objectivity of science would refrain from taking sides. How can one decide between the terms of the alternative? Perhaps another moment of the modern spirit and a more complete analysis of disinterestedness will suggest the direction of the option to choose.

Science Interrupted

Modern epistemology pays little attention to this unconditioned condition, this necessity for extracting oneself from being in order to situate oneself, as subject, upon an absolute, or utopian, ground, on terrain that makes disinterestedness possible. Epistemology even distrusts this disinterestedness. In its eyes every step away from reality favours ideology. The conditions for rationality are all henceforth on the side of knowledge itself and of the technical activity that results from it. A kind of neo-scientism and neo-positivism dominates Western thought. It extends to the disciplines that have man for their object of study; it extends to ideologies themselves, dismantling their mechanisms and disengaging their structures. The mathematical formalization practiced by structuralism constitutes the objectivity of the new method, which is consistent to the extreme. Never, in the new science of man, will value serve as a basis for intelligibility. It is precisely in this new science that the great Lie would be concealed: impulse or instinct, a mechanical phenomenon objectively discernible in man gives, by its spontaneity, the illusion of being the subject and, by its extent, the appearance of a goal; the end is made to pass for a value, and the impulse, henceforth decked out as practical reason, is guided by a value promoted to the rank of a universal principle. What a drama! We would do well to recall Spinoza, the great demolisher of ideologies (though still ignorant of their name), and of knowledge of the first kind: it is the desirable that is valuable, not the valuable that arouses desires.

In the ambiguity of desire, which still allows itself to be understood, either as provoked by the value of its goal or as founding value by the movement that animates it, only the second term of the alternative is maintained. That is where the death of God began. It ended in our time in the subordination of axiology to desires, understood as impulses that arrange themselves according to certain formulas in the 'desiring machines' that men become. The new theory of knowledge no longer grants any transcendental role to human subjectivity. The subject's activity of knowing is interpreted as a roundabout way by which the various structures to which reality is reducible show themselves and are made into a balanced system. What was formerly called the effort of a creative intelligence would thus be only an objective event in the intelligible itself and, in a certain respect, a set of purely logical connections. According to structuralism, and contrary to Kantian teaching, true reason has no interests. Thus, theoretical reason is absolutely supreme.

Contemporary thought thus moves in a being without human traces, where subjectivity has lost its place in the middle of a mental landscape that one may compare to that which presented itself to the first astronauts who set foot on the moon, where the earth itself appeared as a dehumanized star. Enchanting sights, never before seen! Déjà vu – now, on to the next trip! Discoveries from which pounds of stones composed of the same chemical elements as our terrestrial minerals are carried away. Perhaps they will answer questions that until then seemed insoluble to the specialists; perhaps they will enlarge the horizons of particular problems. They will not erase the imaginary line that, of course, is no longer the meeting of heaven and earth, but that marks the boundary of the same. In the infinity of the cosmos presented to the travels of the cosmonaut or space-walker, man finds himself shut in without being able to set foot outside.

Has science produced the beyond-being disclosing the whole of being? Has it given itself the place (or the nonplace) necessary for its own birth, for the maintenance of its objective spirit? The question is open. The super-human adventure of the astronauts, to treat it as a parable, will certainly at some particular moment surpass all the knowledge that made it possible. This occurred when the ancient biblical verses were recited by Armstrong and Collins. Perhaps this *ideological* recitation expressed only the silliness of petit-bourgeois Americans, who were unworthy of their own courage, and also the infinite resources of rhetoric. This is rhetoric in the platonic sense, which according to *Gorgias* flatters the listeners and which 'is to the judicial art what cooking is to medicine' (465c); a rhetoric felt in all the fullness of its ideological essence, as 'an image of a kind of political art' (463d). Such is rhetoric according to the *Phaedrus*, a force of linguistic illusion, in-dependent of any flattery and of any interest: 'not only in connection with judicial debates, nor in connection with all those of the popular assembly . . . but . . . in connection with any use of speech . . . one will in the same way make anything resemble anything else' (261d–e). Such is the rhetoric that applies, not to speech that seeks to win a case or a position, but rhetoric that eats away the very substance of speech, precisely insofar as it 'functions in the absence of all truth'. Is this not already the possibility of signification that is reducible to a game of signs detached from meanings? From now on, we face an ideology more desolate than all ideology, one that no science could rehabilitate without running the risk of being bogged down in the very unproductive game that it sought to break up. This threatening ideology hides in the core of the Logos itself. Plato is confident that he can escape it by means of good rhetoric, but he soon hears within discourse the simian imitation of discourse.

In the parable of interstellar travel, however, there is also the silliness attributed to Gagarin; his statement that he did not find God in heaven. To take this seriously, we may hear in it a very important assertion: the new condition of existence in the weightlessness of a space 'without place' is still experienced by the first man sent there as a *here*, as the *same*, without genuine *otherness*. The marvels of technology do not open up the beyond where science, their mother, was born. In spite of all these movements, there is no outside here! What immanence! What a wretched infinite! Hegel expresses it with remarkable precision: 'something becomes an Other, but this Other is itself a Something, therefore it likewise becomes an Other, and soon *ad infinitum*. This infinity is the specious, or negative, infinity, insofar as it is nothing but the suppression of the finite which, however, is reborn again, and is, consequently, never completely suppressed.'[5]

The evil infinity originates in a thought incompletely thought out, a thought only of the intellect. But thought from beyond the intellect is necessary for the understanding itself. Does not a break with Essence become apparent in the objectively modern mind?

The Other Man

What, then, is ('objectively' manifest in modern times) this movement and this life, neither illusory ideology nor yet science, by which being appears as a dislocation, in the guise of subjectivity or of the humanity of the subject? Does not the visible face of this *ontologic interruption*, this epoche, coincide with the movement 'for a better society'? The modern world is even more shaken by this – shaken to the very depths of its religious sensibilities – than by the denunciation of ideologies, although, this movement, like Harpagon crying, 'Stop, thief!' is quick to suspect itself of ideology. To demand justice for the other man, is this not to return to morality? Indisputably, to the very core of morality. But the invincible concern for the other man in his destitution and in his lack of resources, in his nakedness, in his station or lack of station, as proletarian, this concern escapes the doubtful finality of ideologies. The seeking out of the other man, however distant, is already a relationship with this other man, a relation in all its directness, which is already proximity. How tautological it is to speak of 'drawing nigh to the neighbour' (*l'approche du prochain*)! What occurs in this case is something other than the complacency with ideas that suit the particularism and interests of a group. In that relationship with another man (who, in the nakedness of his face, as a proletarian, has no homeland) there emerges a transcendence, an exit from being, and, thus, impartiality itself, by which both science in its objectivity and humanity, as the 'I', become possible. Like the demand for scientific rigour, like the opposition to ideology, rebellion against an unjust society expresses the spirit of our age.[6] That spirit is expressed by rebellion against an unjust society. Even if in its injustice it is stable, ruled by law, submissive to a power and forming an order, a state, a city, a country, or a professional organization; a rebellion for another society, but a rebellion that begins where the other society is satisfied to leave off; a rebellion against injustice that begins once order begins; a new tonality, a tonality of youth, within the old Western progressism. As if it were a matter of a system of justice that accused itself of being senile and decrepit as soon as there were institutions to protect it; as if, in spite of all recourse to doctrine and to political, social, and economic sciences, in spite of all references to reason and to techniques of revolution, man had sought within revolution to the extent that it is disorder or permanent revolution, a breaking of frameworks, an obliteration of ranks, liberating man, like death, entirely, from everything and from the whole; as if the other man were sought – or approached – in an otherness where no administration could ever reach him; as if through justice a dimension opened up in the other man, that bureaucracy, even if it were of revolutionary origin, would block because of the very universality of the dimension, and by the admission in this new dimension, of the singularity of others that the notion of universality implies; as if in the guise of a relation with others denuded of all essence – with an *other*, thus irreducible to the individual of a species, and to an individual of humankind – the beyond of essence would open up an idealism of disinterestedness, in the strongest sense of the term, in the sense of a suspension of essence. The economic deprivation of the proletarian – to be sure, his condition as one who is exploited – constitutes this absolute stripping of the other as other, the de-formation to *formlessness*, beyond the simple changing of form. Is this idealism suspect of being ideological? We see here, however, a movement, so little ideological, so unlike the repose in an acquired situation, so unlike self-satisfaction, that it is the putting into question of the self, positing oneself from the start as 'de-posed', as for the other. Such a placing in question signifies not a fall into nothingness but a responsibility for the other, a resonsibility that is not assumed as a power but responsibility to which I am exposed from the start, like a hostage; responsibility that signifies, in the end, to the very foundation of my position in myself, my substitution for others. To transcend being through disinterestedness! Such a transcendence comes *under the species* of an approach to the neighbour without hesitation, even substitution for him!

Western thought does not learn of idealism behind ideology only from the century's youth movements. Plato sets forth a *beyond* of institutional justice, like that of the dead judging the dead (*Gorgias* 523e), as if the justice of the living could not pass beyond the clothing of men, that is, could not penetrate the attributes that in others, offer themselves to knowing, to knowledge, as if that justice could not pass beyond the qualities that mask men; as if the justice of the living judging the living could not strip the judges of their nature, which they always have in common with those qualities that hide the judges; as if justice could not, consequently, come near people who were not people of rank and, in the proximity to others, reach out towards the absolutely other. In the myth of the *Gorgias*, Zeus, with extreme precision, accuses the 'last judgment', which he intends to reform in the spirit worthy of a god, of remaining a tribunal where 'fully dressed' men are judged by men equally fully dressed, by judges who 'have placed in front of their own souls a veil made of their eyes and ears and their whole bodies.' A veil made entirely of eyes and ears! Essential point: dressed up, others lack unity.

In the social community, the community of clothed beings, the privileges of rank obstruct justice. The intuitive faculties, in which the whole body participates, are exactly what obstructs the view and separates like a screen the plasticity of the perceived, obscures the otherness of the other, the otherness precisely because of which the other is not an object under our control but a neighbour.

We must note that for Plato a relation may be possible between the one and the other, though they are 'dead to the world',[7] and lack, as a result, a shared other; that a relation might be possible without a common ground, that is to say, a relationship in difference; that the difference signifies a nonindifference; that this nonindifference might be developed by Plato as ultimate justice, and here, with all the approximations of myth, there is expressed in the *essence* of being an eccentricity, a dis-inter-*estedness*. It comes under the species of relation with others, under the species of the humanity of man; beyond essence, dis-inter-estedness; but as just judgement, not at all a nothingness. Ethics is not superimposed on essence as a second layer where an ideological gaze would hide, incapable of looking the real in the face. The commandment of the absolute, as Castelli states in a different context, is not 'in the system of a possible ideology' and, with regard to the rationality of knowledge, it 'constitutes a disorder'. The signification – each for the other – ethics, and the breaking of essence are the end of the illusions of its appearance. Plato speaks of a judgement bearing finally on merit. Would this merit be some real attribute underneath the apparent qualities, some preexisting attribute, which judgement could not do without, introducing in turn others by way of concepts and lacking any way of escape? Or, going from oneself to others, as if each of us were dead, the last judgement, is this not the manner in which a being puts himself in the place of another, contrary to any perseverance in being, to all *conatus essendi*, to all knowledge that receives from others only concepts?[8] And what can be the meaning of the movement to put oneself in another's place, if not literally drawing nigh to the neighbour (*l'approche du prochain*)?

The Other as the Other man

One may be surprised by the radicalism of an affirmation in which the breaking of the essence of being, irreducible to ideology, has meaning as responsibility for the other man approached in the nakedness of his visage, in his noncondition of proletarian, always 'losing his place', where the beyond of being has meaning as my disinterestedness, that of a dead man who expects nothing from a dead man. It is not difficult to see that the *for* in the 'for-the-other' of my responsibility for the other is not the *for* of finality; not difficult to see that the *for-the-other* of the one who is exposed to others without defence or covering, in an incessant disquiet of not being open enough, in the anxiety of being 'encapsulated in oneself', is an opening of the self, a disquiet to the point of denucleation. We shall not take up this theme again; it has frequently been developed elsewhere. This absolute 'otherness' of the 'beyond the being' (set forth by Plato and Plotinus), against the irrupturable identity of the Same, whose ontological stubbornness is incarnate, or comes to a head in Ego, would be produced nowhere if not in the substitution for another.

Nothing, in fact, is absolutely other in the Being served by knowing, in which variety turns into monotony. Is that not the thought of Proverbs 14: 13: 'Even in laughter the heart is sad, and the end of joy is grief.' The contemporary world, scientific, technical, and sensual, is seen to be without issue, that is to say, without God, not because everything is permitted and is possible by means of technology, but because everything is the same. The unknown immediately becomes familiar, the new, habitual. Nothing is new under the sun. The crisis described in Ecclesiastes is not of sin, but of boredom. Everything is absorbed, sunk, buried in sameness. In the enchantment of places, the hyperbole of metaphysical concepts, the artifice of art, the exaltation of ceremony, the magic of rites – everywhere one suspects and denounces theatricality, transcendence that is purely rhetorical, games. 'Vanity of vanities': the echo of our own voices, taken as answer to the few prayers that still remain with us; everywhere landing back on our own feet, as after the ecstasy of some drug. Except for others, whom, with all this boredom, one cannot drop.

The otherness of the absolutely other is not just some quiddity. Insofar as it is a quiddity, it exists on a plane it has in common with the quiddities that it cuts across. The notions of old and new, understood as qualities, are not adequate for the notion of the absolutely other. Absolute *difference* cannot itself delineate the plane common to those that are different. The other, absolutely other, is the Other (*L'autre, absolument autre, c'est Autrui*). The Other is not a particular case, a species of otherness, but the original exception to order. It is not because the Other is novelty that it 'gives room' for a relation of transcendence. It is because the responsibility for the Other is transcendence that there can be something new under the sun.

My responsibility for the other man, the paradoxical, contradictory responsibility for a foreign liberty – extending, according to the Talmud (*Sotah* 37b), even to responsibility for his responsibility – does not originate in a vow to respect the universality of a principle, nor in a moral imperative. It is the exceptional relation in which the Same can be concerned with the Other, without the Other's being assimilated to the Same, the relation in which one can recognize the inspiration, in the strict sense of the term, to bestow spirit upon man. What does it matter? At the heart of the rhetoric of all our enthusiasms, in the responsibility for others, comes a meaning from which no eloquence, not even poetry, can distract, a rupture of the Same without resumption by the Same of its sameness without aging, novelty, transcendence. All in all, it can be expressed in ethical terms. The crisis of meaning, which is evident in the dissemination of verbal signs that the signified no longer dominates (for it would only be illusion and ideological deception), is opposed by the meaning that is prior to the 'sayings', which spurns words and is unimpeachable in the nudity of its visage, which is felt in the proletarian destitution of another and in the offence he suffers. This is what the talmudic sages (who already knew a world in which language had corroded the meanings it was supposed to bear) probably had in mind when they spoke of a world in which prayers cannot penetrate to heaven, because all the heavenly gates are closed except those through which the tears of the sufferers may pass.[9]

That the Other as other is not an intelligible form bound to other forms in the process of an intentional 'unveiling', but is, rather, a visage, proletarian nakedness, destitution; that the Other is others; that the departure from the self is the approach to the neighbour; that transcendence is proximity, that proximity is responsibility for the Other, substitution for the Other, expiation for the Other; condition – noncondition – of serving as hostage; that responsibility, as response, is the prior speaking; that transcendence is communication, implying, beyond a simple exchange of signs, the 'gift,' 'the open house' – these are some ethical terms through which transcendence has meaning, in the guise of humanity, or of ecstasy as disinterestedness. Idealism confronts Science and Ideology.

In the discussion that followed the presentation of this paper by Professor Levinas a number of questions were raised. What follows is Professor Levinas's response, translated from Hebrew.

1   In my opinion, the problem of God is related to the problem of the Other. Divinity is not met as a great Other, as 'the absolute Thou' of Buber. It has within itself a sign of the Other, but the meaning of this sign is complete and requires philosophical analysis. One must be very careful here! The passage from the Other to divinity is a second step, and one must be careful to avoid stumbling by taking too large a step.

2   The philosophic status of the meaning of the word 'God', as best understood by the religious, by believers, has never been clarified properly, so that it is very difficult to establish any identity of what the believer understands with what the philosopher defines. I am not sure that one has the right to speak of 'divinity', rather than saying always 'God'. I am not sure that it is possible to distinguish between the property and the name. When God is spoken of as a being that is the Supreme Being, a superlative

is mentioned whose meaning does not have its source in Being, and is surely dependent on what Plato understood as 'beyond Being'. 'Beyond Being' – is this the Sinaitic revelation? I heard in this discussion the arguments of those who have the merit and the good fortune to stand at Mount Sinai. No philosopher (*qua* philosopher) has ever stood there. I shall not respond to the complaints of those people who do not understand why I need the ultimate Other to approach God. For them there are no problems at all, as is well known.

3   I shall respond to the serious and fundamental question of Professor Petuchowski who asks why I pass from ethics to divinity. Is morality possible without God? I answer with a question: is divinity possible without relation to a human Other? Is such a thing possible in Judaism? Consider Jeremiah, Chapter 22, or Isaiah 58: 7: 'to bring to your house the poor who are outcast.' The direct encounter with God, *this* is a Christian concept. As Jews, we are always a threesome: I and you and the Third who is in our midst. And only as a Third does He reveal Himself.

4   Is my discourse deficient in concern with concrete reality? Does all this metaphysics of mine have the ability to solve actual ethical problems? I have no ambition to be a preacher. I am neither a preacher nor the son of a preacher, and it is not my purpose to moralize or to improve the conduct of our generation. It is likely, in any case, that sermons have no power to raise the level of morals. I have been speaking about that which stands behind practical morality; about the extraordinary relation between a man and his neighbour, a relation that continues to exist even when it is severely damaged. Of course we have the power to relate ourselves to the other as to an object, to oppress and exploit him; nevertheless the relation to the other, as a relation of responsibility, cannot be totally suppressed, even when it takes the form of politics or warfare. Here it is impossible to free myself by saying, 'It's not my concern.' There is no choice, for it is always and inescapably my concern. This is a unique 'no choice', one that is not slavery.

Finally, I have never said that we must be satisfied with 'It doesn't concern me.' Indeed, if there were only two of us in the world, I and one other, there would be no problem. The other would be completely my responsibility. But in the real world there are many others. When others enter, each of them external to myself, problems arise. Who is closest to me? Who is the Other? Perhaps something has already occurred between them. We must investigate carefully. Legal justice is required. There is need for a state.

But it is very important to know whether the state, society, law, and power are required because man is a beast to his neighbour (*homo homini lupus*) or because I am responsible for my fellow. It is very important to

know whether the political order defines man's responsibility or merely
restricts his bestiality. It is very important, even if the conclusion is that all
of us exist for the sake of the state, the society, the law.

NOTES

1 The following lines are an attempt to respond to the stringent critique that Claude
 Bruaire makes of the idea of suspicion.
2 Cf. Amos 2: 6.
3 It is just in this way that Plato's denunciation of rhetoric presupposes the moral
 scandal of Socrates' condemnation.
4 We owe to a remark of Professor Filiasi Carcano the connection with the Husserlian step from the transcendental reduction that evokes the term, 'epoche'. The
 exception to being that we call disinterestedness will have (as will be seen further
 on) an ethical meaning. Ethics would thus be the possibility of a movement as
 radical as transcendental reduction.
5 *The Logic of Hegel* from the *Encyclopedia of the Philosophical Sciences*, trans.
 William Wallace (London, 1904), secs 93, 94, p. 174. We have adjusted the
 Wallace translation slightly to conform to the French version which Levinas used
 [Ed.].
6 It expresses the spirit of the age or, perhaps, already caricatures it. This strange
 destiny of revelation in a caricature deserves separate consideration. But the
 caricature is itself a revelation from which a meaning must be extracted; a
 meaning that requires correction, but which cannot be ignored or disregarded
 with impunity.
7 In talmudic literature, the burial of a human corpse, to which no one nearby is
 attending, is called 'mercy of truth' (*hesed shel emet*). Even the high priest, if he
 should find the corpse as he is on his way to the Temple to celebrate Yom Kippur
 must not hold back from burying this dead man out of concern that he will
 become impure and unclean and thus prevented from performing the sacred rites
 of the Holy Day. This is a symbol of mercy that is given absolutely without
 expectation of reward, mercy that one does to another 'as if he were dead', and
 not a law for the dead, for which the Gospel had a harsh phrase.
8 This is how we read, with forceful emphasis, the talmudic saying: 'Do not judge
 your neighbour until you have stood in his place' (*M. Abot* 2: 4).
9 *Berakhoth*, 32b, *Baba Meẓi'a*, 59b. The two passages should be read conjointly.

Translated by Sanford Ames and Arthur Lesley

16

Difficult Freedom

The title 'Difficult Freedom' covers four pieces, each of which has been taken from *Difficile liberté* (Paris: Albin Michel, 1963, 1976). 'Judaism' was originally an entry in the *Encyclopaedia Universalis* (Paris, 1968), vol. 2, first published in 1971, pp. 520–1; 'Judaism and the Present' was first published in *L'Arche*, 44 (1960), 32–6; 'The State of Israel and the Religion of Israel' first appeared in *Evidences*, 20 (1951), 4–6; and 'Means of Identification' was originally published in *Journées d'études sur l'identité juive* (1963), 63–5. An English translation of the complete work is forthcoming from Athlone Press.

Each of the extracts covers some aspect of the present-day political reality of Judaism. 'Judaism' assesses the several different concepts which the word embraces today: nationality; religion; civilization; or desire for justice. In all of these Jewish conscience and consciousness has most emerged in times of historical crisis, when its combination of textual exegesis and human endeavour has shown uniqueness to lie in responsibility for the other.

The Jewish revelation further confronts those rationalist epistemologies that have shaped modern society (including the Holocaust) in 'Judaism and the Present'. A modern Jewish consciousness is faced with a virtual coincidence of the religious and the profane. But the eternity of Israel is not simply built on a romantic subjectivism or doctrinaire inflexibility. 'It has a function in the economy of being' as a moral revelation sustained by individual study of the Torah. It allows one to commit oneself to the other while resisting doxa, and in this way to confront politics with morality.

'The State of Israel and the Religion of Israel' tests the religious privilege that Israel supposedly possesses against the sovereignty of the modern state. Humanist man is antagonistic towards religion within the State of Israel itself. But the essence of Judaism lies in a desire for justice which must be placed above the State since it has already achieved every spiritual aspiration that a State might embody. The ultimate opportunity for the State of Israel, therefore, is one in which it can carry out the social law of Judaism, and base itself on a study of the Talmud.

It is in these documents and their study that Levinas locates Jewish identity in 'Means of Identification'. The means referred to involve not merely political documentation, as identity cards; they provide above all an infinitely renewable means of moral examination that transcends all political rationale. In the latter even more than in the former case, the relation to History is vital.

S.H.

―――――――――――

Judaism

In the present day the word 'Judaism' covers several quite distinct concepts. Above all, it designates a religion, the system of beliefs, rituals and moral prescriptions founded on the Bible, the Talmud and Rabbinic literature, and often combined with the mysticism or theosophy of the Kabbalah. The principal forms of this religion have scarcely varied for two thousand years and attest to a spirit that is fully conscious of itself and is reflected in a religious and moral literature, while still being open to new developments. 'Judaism' thus comes to signify a culture that is either the result or the foundation of the religion, but at all events has its own sense of evolution. Throughout the world, and even in the state of Israel, there are people who identify with Judaism but who do not believe in God and who are not practising Jews. For millions of Israelites who have been assimilated into the civilization around them, Judaism cannot even be called a culture: it is a vague sensibility made up of various ideas, memories, customs and emotions, together with a feeling of solidarity towards those Jews who were persecuted for being Jews.

This sensibility, this culture and this religion are none the less seen from the outside as being aspects of a strongly characterized entity that cannot easily be classified. Is it a nationality or a religion, a fossilized civilization that somehow lives on, or the passionate desire for a better world? The mystery of Israel! This difficulty reflects a sense of presence to history that is unique in its kind. In fact, Judaism is the source of the great monotheistic religions, on which the modern world depends just as much as ancient Greece and Rome once did, and also belongs to the living present not only through the concepts and books it has supplied, but equally through real men and women who, as pioneers of various great ventures or as victims of great historical convulsions, form part of a direct and unbroken line of descent from the people of sacred History. The attempt to create a state in Palestine and to regain the creative inspiration of old whose pronouncements were of universal significance cannot be understood without the Bible.

Judaism has a special essence: it is something that is laid down in square letters and something that illuminates living faces; it is both ancient doctrine and contemporary history. But this runs the risk of favouring a mythical vision or a spirituality that can still none the less be analysed. Objective science, such as sociology, history or philology, tries to reduce the exception to the rule. Western Jews promoted this kind of research. At the end of the seventeenth century Spinoza's *Tractatus Theologico-Politicus* inaugurates a critical reading of the Scriptures. At the beginning of the nineteenth century in Germany, the founders of the famous 'science of Judaism' (*Wissenschaft des Judentums*) transformed the Holy Scriptures into pure documents. The paradoxes of an unequalled destiny and an absolute teaching slot easily into the scientific categories created for every spiritual reality and all other idiosyncrasies. Everything can be explained by its causes; and by methodically tracking down and logging every influence, many original features dissolve. Judaism emerges, perhaps, more aware of what it has received, but less and less sure of its own truth.

We may none the less ask whether the scientific categorization of a spiritual movement can ever reveal its real contribution and significance. Can wisdom ever bare its soul and reveal its secret without displaying a power that imposes itself on us as a message or appeals to us as a vocation? The Jewish conscience, in spite of its different forms and levels, regains its unity and unicity in moments of great crisis, when the strange combination of texts and men, who often cannot speak the language of these texts, is renewed in sacrifice and persecution. The memory of these crises sustains the quiet intervals.

During these extraordinary moments, the lucid work of the science of Judaism, which reduces the miracle of the Revelation or the national genius to a series of influences, loses its spiritual significance. In place of the miracle of the unique source, there shines the marvel of confluence. The latter is understood as a voice calling from the depths of converging texts and reverberating in a sensibility and a form of thought that are already there to greet it. What does the voice of Israel say and how can it be translated into a few propositions? Perhaps it announces nothing more than the monotheism which the Jewish Bible brought to humanity. At first, we might recoil from this hoary old truth or this somewhat dubious claim. But the word denotes a set of significations based on which the shadow of the Divine is cast beyond all theology and dogmatism over the deserts of Barbary. One must follow the Most High God and be faithful to Him alone. One must be wary of the myth that leads to the *fait accompli*, the constraints of customs or locale, and the Machiavellian State and its reasons of State. One follows the Most High God, above all by drawing near to one's fellow man, and showing concern for 'the widow, the orphan, the stranger and the beggar', an approach that must not be made 'with empty hands'. It is therefore on earth, amongst men, that the spirit's adventure unfolds.

The traumatic experience of my slavery in Egypt constitutes my very humanity, a fact that immediately allies me to the workers, the wretched, and the persecuted peoples of the world. My uniqueness lies in the responsibility I display for the other. I cannot fail in my duty towards any man, any more than I can have someone else stand in for my death. This leads to the conception of a creature who can be saved without falling into the egotism of grace. Man is therefore indispensable to God's plan or, to be more exact, man is nothing other than the divine plans within being. This leads to the idea of being chosen, which can degenerate into that of pride but which originally expresses the awareness of an indisputable assignation from which an ethics springs and through which the universality of the end being pursued involves the solitude and isolation of the individual responsible. Man is called before a form of judgement and justice which recognizes this responsibility, while the rigours of the Law are softened without being suspended by a sense of mercy. Man can do what he must do; he can master the hostile forces of history by helping to bring about a messianic reign, a reign of justice foretold by the prophets. The waiting for the Messiah marks the very duration of time.

This is the extreme humanism of a God who demands much of man. Some would say He demands too much! It is perhaps in a ritualism regulating all the gestures of the complete Jew's day-to-day life, in the famous yoke of the Law, which the pious experience as something joyful, that we find the most characteristic aspects of Jewish existence. This ritualism has preserved Jewish existence for centuries. While itself remaining completely natural, it keeps this existence alive by maintaining a distance from nature. But perhaps, for that very reason, it maintains a presence to the Most High God.

Translated by Seán Hand

Judaism and the Present

On the mean and petty level of day-to-day reality, a human community does not resemble its myth. It responds to a higher vocation, though, through its intellectuals (its elders), who are concerned with *raisons d'être* and its youth, who are ready to sacrifice themselves for an idea, who are capable, in other words, of extremist ideas. Western Jews between 1945 and 1960 will not have displayed their essence by converting, changing their names, economizing or forging a career for themselves. What they did do was carry on the Resistance, in the absolute sense of the term. A career is not incompatible with a rigorous intellect or a sense of courage, something that is always difficult to display. The young uprooted themselves and went to live in Israel as they had done in Orsay or Aix or Fublaines; or else, in other ways, they accepted whatever inhuman dogmatism promised to free Man. To situate Jews in the present is something that leads us, therefore, into a radical mode of thinking, one whose language is not always a lie. I should like to undertake such an analysis with all the due modesty and prudence dictated by the writing of a mere article on the subject. For, without even this brief study, the position of Judaism, in the latter half of this century, would be further reduced to the interminable question of antisemitism.

A religious age or an atomic age – these characterizations of the modern world, whether slogans or imprecations, hide a deeper trend. In spite of the violence and madness we see every day, we live in the age of philosophy. Men are sustained in their activities by the certainty of *being right* (*avoir raison*), of being in tune with the calculable forces that really move things along, of moving in the direction (*sens*) of history. That satisfies their conscience. Beyond the progress of science, which uncovers the predictable play of forces within matter, human freedoms themselves (including those thoughts which conceive of such a play) are regulated by a rational order. Hidden in the depths of Being, this order is gradually unveiled and revealed through the disorder of contemporary history, through the suffering and desire of individuals, their passions and their victories. A global industrial society is announced that will suppress every contradiction tormenting humanity. But it equally suppresses the hidden heart of man. Reason rises like a fantastic sun that makes the opacity of creatures transparent. Men have lost their shadows! Henceforth, nothing can absorb or reflect this light which abolishes even the interiority of beings.

This advent of reason as an offshoot of philosophy – and this is what is original about this age – is not the conquest of eternity promised to the Logos of ancient wisdom. Reason does not illuminate a thought which detaches itself from events in order to dominate them in a dialogue with a god, the only interlocutor of any work, according to Plato. There is nothing in reality that can be encountered in its wild or pure state, everything has already been formed, transformed or reflected by man, including nature, the sky and the forest. The elements show up on the surface through a civilization, a language, an industry, an art. Intelligibility is read in the mark left on things by the work of mortals, in the perspectives opened up by cities and empires that are doomed to fall. From that point, in the epic or drama of intelligence, man is an actor prior to being a thinker. Reality appears – that is to say radiates intelligible light – within the history in which each human undertaking takes its place, a work of finite freedoms which, by virtue of being finite, betray their projects even as they carry them out, and do not dominate their work. The individual's destiny consists in playing a role (which has not yet been assigned him) in the drama of reason and not of embracing this drama.

What matters is to be authentic and not at all to be true (*dans le vrai*), to commit oneself rather than to know. Art, love, action are more important than theory. Talent is worth more than wisdom and self-possession. Is it not the case that, a few years ago, a British Jewish intellectual conducted a very successful lecture tour throughout England in which he measured the value of Judaism in terms of the talent and originality of dejudaicized Jews?

Within the indulgent attitude towards mortality which we call the historical conscience, each of us has to wait for that unique if perishable moment in which it falls to our lot to rise to the occasion and recognize the call addressed to us. To respond to the call of the perishable instant! It must not come too late. Such was the case of the Angel who, according to the Midrash, had only one song to sing before the Throne of the Lord, at one single moment, which was his and his alone, in the whole of God's eternity. But this Angel, who was an antagonist of Israel, had a bad encounter, and his story took place on the night before the unique instant of his destiny.

In the wake of the Liberation, Jews are grappling with the Angel of Reason who often solicited them and who for two centuries now has refused to let go. Despite the experience of Hitler and the failure of assimilation, *the great vocation in life resounds like the call of a universal and homogenous society.* We do not have to decide here if the nature of modern life is compatible with respect for the Sabbath and rituals concerning food or if we should lighten the yoke of the Law. These important questions are put to men who have already chosen Judaism. They choose between orthodoxy and reform depending on their idea of rigour, courage and duty. Some are not necessarily hypocrites, others do not always take the easy way out. But it is really a domestic quarrel.

Jewish consciousness is no longer contained within these questions of choice. Like a house without a *muzuzah*, it exists as an abstract space traversed by the ideas and hopes of the world. Nothing can halt them, for nothing hails them. Interiority's act of withdrawal is undone before their unstoppable force. The Judaism of the Diaspora no longer has an interior. It enters deeply into a world to which it is none the less opposed. Or is it?

For the reason that shines forth from the Angel (or the Seducer) frees Judaism from all particularisms. Visions of ancient, crumbling things trouble our hazy dreams. Surely a greater, virile dream is born in this way. The cheap optimism of the nineteenth century, whose idealism was produced by isolated and ineffectual beings who had little grasp of reality, gives way to a transformation of being that derives its nobility from the attention it pays reality. It becomes an uncompromising logic that tolerates no exceptions and is universal like a religion. Our age is defined by the major importance which this transformation of things and societies takes on in the eyes of men and the attention that established religions pay to the transformations of life here below. The religious and the profane have perhaps never been so close. So how can one withstand the winds of change which threaten to sweep the Jewish personality away? When Reason tolls the knell for privileged revelations, isn't the sound as seductive as the song of the Sirens? Will Judaism raise the banner against what we tautologically term free thought, and the achievements of the concrete world? Is it not different from the religions it has spawned in that it questions whether personal salvation can be something distinct from the redemption of the visible world? And yet those other religions have every opportunity of doing the same. They offer supernatural truths and sacraments and consolations that no science can dispense. The reason that conquers the world leaves them with an extraterritoriality. Judaism unites men in an ideal of terrestrial justice in which the Messiah represents a promise and a fulfilment. Ethics is its primordial religious emotion. It does not found any church for trans-ethical ends. It insists on distinguishing between 'messianism' and a 'future world'. Every prophet has only ever announced the coming of the messianic age; as for the future world, 'no eye has seen it outside of You; God will bring it to those who wait' (*Synhedrin 99a*).

This struggle with the Angel is therefore strange and ambiguous. Isn't the adversary a double? Isn't this wrestling a twisting back on oneself, one that may be either a struggle or an embrace? Even in the most impressive struggle that Israel undertakes for the sake of its personality, even in the building of the State of Israel, even in the prestige it holds for souls everywhere, this sublime ambiguity remains: is one trying to preserve oneself within the modern world, or to drown one's eternity in it?

For what is at stake is Israel's eternity, without which there can be no Israel. The combat is a very real one. The modern reason which transforms the world threatens Judaism to an unparalleled degree, though Judaism has been threatened before. Cosmology and scientific history in their time had compromised the Bible's wisdom, while philology had questioned the special character of the Bible itself, dissolved in a sea of texts, pitching and rolling through its infinite undulations. Apologetics chose to reply to these attacks by discussing the arguments put forward. But believers have above all resisted them by interiorizing certain religious truths. Why worry about science's refutation of Biblical cosmology, when the Bible contains not cosmology but images necessary to an unshakable internal certainty, figures that speak to the religious soul that already dwells in the absolute? Why worry about philology and history challenging the supposed date and origin of the sacred texts, if these texts are intrinsically rich in value? The sacred sparks of individual revelations have produced the light needed, even if they were thrown up at different points in history. The miracle of their convergence is no less marvellous than the miracle of a unique source. Eternity was rediscovered within the fortress-like inner life which Israel built on an unshakeable rock.

At this point, modern thought denounces the eternity of Israel by questioning whether the inner life itself is a site of truth. Truth is henceforth manifested in the development of a society, which is the condition for every idea that arises in an individual brain. Only pipe dreams and ideologies have no social founding. Those elements in the Jewish revelation open to reason are obtained from economic and social determinism. Those ideas imbued with the force of inner conviction emerge as an impersonal and anonymous destiny that holds men in its grip. Reason just toys with them. They imagine they are thinking for themselves when they are really carrying out its plans. Prophecies are produced by the play of historical forces in the same way as synthetic oil and rubber are manufactured in the laboratory.

This time, the blades of reasonable History erode the very rock of Israel. This is what causes the erosion of the Absolute.

But this eternity of Israel is not the privilege of a nation that is proud or carried away by illusions. It has a function in the economy of being. It is indispensable to the work of reason itself. In a world that has become historical, shouldn't a person be as old as the world? Deprived of any fixed point, the modern world feels frustrated. It invoked reason in order to have justice, and the latter surely needs a stable base, an interiority, or a person, on which to rest. A person is indispensable to justice prior to being indispensable to himself. Eternity is necessary to a person, and even in our own day, it has been sought by the most lucid thinkers. Those who stress commitment (*engagement*) in Sartre's work forget that his main concern is to guarantee disengagement (*dégagement*) in the midst of engagement (*engagement*). This results in a nihilism that is given its most noble expression – a negation of the supreme commitment which in man's case is his own essence.

But dumping ballast in the face of the problems posed by existence, in order to gain even greater height over reality, leads ultimately to the impossibility of sacrifice, that is to say to the annihilation of self. Here, Judaism filters into the modern world. It does so by disengaging itself, and it disengages itself by affirming the intangibility of an essence, the fidelity to a law, a rigid moral standard. This is not a return to the status of thing, for such fidelity breaks the facile enchantment of cause and effect and allows it to be judged.

Judaism is a non-coincidence with its time, within coincidence: in the radical sense of the term, it is an *anachronism*, the simultaneous presence of a youth that is attentive to reality and impatient to change it, and an old age that has seen it all and is returning to the origin of things. The desire to conform to one's time is not the supreme imperative for a human, but is already a characteristic expression of modernism itself; it involves renouncing interiority and truth, resigning oneself to death and, in base souls, being satisfied with *jouissance*. Monotheism and its moral revelation constitute the concrete fulfilment, beyond all mythology, of the primordial anachronism of the human.

It lies deeper than history, neither receiving its meaning from the latter, nor becoming its prey. This is why it does not seek its liberation with respect to time, where time has the status of dead civilizations such as ancient Greece or Rome. Even in the grave, these do not escape the influence of events. When he lay dying, Rabbi Jose b. Kisma said to his disciples: 'Place my coffin deep (in the earth), for there is not one palm-tree in Babylon to which a Persian horse will not be tethered, nor one coffin in Palestine out of which a Median horse will not eat straw.'

Judaism, disdaining this false eternity, has always wished to be a simultaneous engagement and disengagement. The most deeply committed (*engagé*) man, one who can never be silent, the prophet, is also the most separate being, and the person least capable of becoming an institution. Only the false prophet has an official function. The Midrash likes to recount how Samuel refused every invitation he received in the course of his travels throughout Israel. He carried his own tent and utensils with him. And the Bible pushes this idea of independence, even in the economic sense, to the point of imagining the prophet Eli being fed by crows.

But this essential content, which history cannot touch, cannot be learned like a catechism or resumed like a credo. Nor is it restricted to the negative and formal statement of a categorical imperative. It cannot be replaced by Kantianism, nor, to an even lesser degree, can it be obtained from some particular privilege or racial miracle. It is acquired through a way of living that is a ritual and a heart-felt generosity, wherein a human fraternity and an attention to the present are reconciled with an eternal distance in relation to the contemporary world. It is an asceticism, like the training of a fighter. It is acquired and held, finally, in the particular type of intellectual life known as the study of the Torah, that permanent revision and updating of the content of the Revelation where every situation within the human adventure can be judged. And it is here precisely that the Revelation is to be found: the die is not cast, the prophets or wise men of the Talmud know nothing about antibiotics or nuclear energy; but the categories needed to understand these novelties are already available to monotheism. It is the eternal anteriority of wisdom with respect to science and history. Without it, success would equal reason and reason would be just the necessity of living in one's own time. Does this sovereign refusal of fashion and success come from the monks who render unto Caesar the things that are Caesar's? Or from the Left who do not dare carry through their political thought to its logical extremes, but are seized with an attack of vertigo and grind to a senseless halt at the edge of their own conclusions?

It is not messianism that is lacking in a humanity that is quick to hope and to recognize its hopes in everything that promises, builds and brings victory and presents itself as the fulfilment of a dream. Seen in this light, every nationalism carries a messianic message and every nation is chosen. Monotheism has not just a horror of idols, but a nose for false prophecy. A special patience – Judaism – is required to refuse all premature messianic claims.

These young people, who are eager to behave reasonably, and turn their backs on Judaism because, like a waking dream, it does not offer them sufficient enlightenment concerning contemporary problems, that 'vast reality taking place outside Judaism', forget that the strength needed to resist the importance that high society places on itself, is the privilege of Judaism and the absolutely pure teaching that it offers man; they forget that the revelation offers clarification but not a formula; they forget that commitment alone – commitment at any price, headlong commitment that burns its bridges behind it, even the commitment that ought to permit withdrawal into the self – is no less inhuman than the disengagement dictated by the desire to be comfortable which ossifies a society that has transformed the difficult task of Judaism into a mere confession, an accessory of bourgeois comfort.

No doubt the advocates of commitment resemble those disciples of Rabbi Jose b. Kisma who asked the Master: 'When will the Master come?.' They were already probably denouncing the sterility of Halakhah-style discussions, which remain aloof from the burning issues of messianism, of the meaning and end of history. Rabbi Jose shied away from the question: 'I fear lest ye demand a sign of me.' The disciples will continue to find the Master's wisdom too general and abstract. Already they are thinking that the messianic age is heralded by the events of history as the fruit is by the seed, and that the blossoming of deliverence is as predictable as the harvest of ripe plums. Will the Master speak?

The disciples will not ask for a sign. Rabbi Jose then speaks of the periodic structure of history, the alternating periods of greatness and decline from which the messianic age will ensue neither logically nor dialectically, but will enter from the outside: 'When this gate falls down, is rebuilt, falls again, and is again rebuilt, and then falls a third time, before it can be rebuilt the son of David will come'.

Does the Master perhaps bury himself in generalities in order to evade the issues? History is separated off from its achievements, as is politics from morality. The rigorous chain of events offers no guarantee of a happy outcome. No sign is inscribed here. So be it. But can the Master withold the signs necessary to those who reject the good if false news, and from which the Jew would derive the strength of his rejection, and the certainty of his *raison d'être*, in a world crossed by currents of energy and life in which he is nothing, overflowing with joyful waters which rise from the depths of the elements and which joyously sweep up the builders of States, regimes and Churches? A *No* demands a criterion. Rabbi Jose gives the required sign: '"let the waters of the grotto of Paneas turn into blood"; and they turned into blood'.

Paneas, the source of the Jordan, and one of the three legendary sources that remained open at the end of the flood. The waters from all the ends of history and from every nationalism (even the Jewish one) gushing forth like the irrepressible force of nature, the waters of every baptism and every effacement, the waters of every messianism! Those men who can see cannot turn their gaze from the innocent blood which these waters dilute.

Translated by Seán Hand

The State of Israel and the Religion of Israel

The idea that Israel has a religious privilege is one that ultimately exasperates everyone. Some see it as an unjustifiable pride, while to others it looks like an intolerable mystification which, in the name of a sublime destiny, robs us of earthly joys. To live like every other people on earth, with police and cinemas and cafes and newspapers – what a glorious destiny! Despite being scarcely established on our own land we are happy to emulate all the 'modern nations' and have our own little problem of the relationship between State and Church to resolve.

The satisfaction we can experience when, like a tourist, we can see a Jewish uniform or a Jewish stamp, is certainly one of our lesser delights. But it is difficult to resist. It imposes itself by way of contrast. It places great value on the very presence of the past which we refuse. It reveals both the obsessions of the traditional Jewish ideal and everything that is phoney about its by now literary perfection. It also reveals the prestige that men, whether or not they are Jews, attach today to anything bearing the stamp of the State.

The point is not that people are free to denounce such idolatry. We need to reflect on the nature of the modern State. The State is not an idol because it precisely permits full self-consciousness. Human will is derisory. It wishes to be of value but cannot evaluate the universe it repulses. The sovereignty of the State incorporates the universe. In the sovereign State, the citizen may finally exercise a will. It acts absolutely. Leisure, security, democracy: these mark the return of a condition, the beginning of a free being.

This is why man recognizes his spiritual nature in the dignity he achieves as a citizen or, even more so, when acting in the service of the State. The State represents the highest human achievement in the lives of western peoples. The coincidence of the political and the spiritual marks man's maturity, for spiritual life like political life purges itself of all the private, individual, sentimental chiaroscuro on which religions still nurture themselves. Elevation to the spiritual no longer equals possession by the Sacred. A spiritual life with no sacred dimension! Only a superficial analysis could claim that when men forget God, they are merely changing gods. The decline of church-constituted religions is an undeniable historical phenomenon. It stems not from man's mendacity but from the advent of States. When set against the universality of the political order, the religious order inevitably takes on a disordered or clerical air. Modern humanist man is a man in a State. Such a man is not merely vulgar; he is religion's true antagonist within the State of Israel itself.

But is it enough to restore the State of Israel in order to have a political life? And even if it were a life of the spirit, could it contain Judaism? A small state – what a contradiction! Could its sovereignty, which, like the light of satellites, is merely borrowed, ever raise the soul to a state of full self-possession? It is obvious that Israel asserts itself in a different way.

Like an empire on which the sun never sets, a religious history extends the size of its modest territory, even to the point where it absorbs a breath-taking past. But, contrary to national histories, this past, like an ancient civilization, places itself above nations, like a fixed star. And yet we are the living ladder that reaches up to the sky. Doesn't Israel's particular past consist in something both eternal and ours? This peculiar right, revealed by an undeniable Jewish experience, to call our own a doctrine that is none the less offered to everyone, marks the true sovereignty of Israel. It is not its political genius nor its artistic genius nor even its scientific genius (despite all they promise) that forms the basis of its majority, but its religious genius! The Jewish people therefore achieves a State whose prestige none the less stems from the religion which modern political life supplants.

The paradox would be insoluble if this religious genius did not consist entirely in struggling against the intoxication of individual forms of enthusiasm for the sake of a difficult and erudite work of justice. This religion, in which God is freed from the Sacred, this modern religion was already established by the Pharisees through their meditations on the Bible at the end of the Second Temple. It is placed above the State, but has already achieved the very notion of the spirit announced by the modern State.

In an anthology of essays written in Hebrew which appeared in New York, Chaim Grinberg, the head of the Cultural Section of the Jewish Agency, brought together articles by several Israeli authors on the relation between religion and State. Reading these texts, which are above all eye-witness accounts, one is struck by the ease with which the move from religion to ethics is carried out. We do not get the impression of a morality being added to the dogma, but of a 'dogma' that is morality itself. The grand terms 'love' or 'the presence of God' achieve a true grandeur even as they are given concrete expression in the sordid questions of food, work and shelter. Contrary to all the fervent mysticism that overexcites the orthodox or liberal tendencies of the Diaspora living alongside Christianity, an Israeli experiences the famous touch of God in his social dealings. Not that belief in God *incites* one to justice – it *is* the institution of that justice. Moreover, is this justice just an abstract principle? Doesn't religious inspiration ultimately aim to bring about the very possibility of Society, the possibility for a man to see the face of an other?

The thing that is special about the State of Israel is not that it fulfils an ancient promise, or heralds a new age of material security (one that is unfortunately problematic), but that it finally offers the opportunity to carry out the social law of Judaism. The Jewish people craved their own land and their own State not because of the abstract independence which they desired, but because they could then finally begin the work of their lives. Up until now they had obeyed the commandments, and later on they fashioned an art and a literature for themselves, but all these works of self-expression are merely the early attempts of an overlong adolescence. The masterpiece has now finally come. All the same, it was horrible to be both the only people to define itself with a doctrine of justice, and to be the meaning incapable of applying it. The heartbreak and the meaning of the Diaspora. The subordination of the State to its social promises articulates the significance of the resurrection of Israel as, in ancient times, the execution of justice justified one's presence on the land.

It is in this way that the political event is already outstripped. And ultimately, it is in this way that we can distinguish those Jews who are religious from those who are not. The contrast is between those who seek to have a State in order to have justice and those who seek justice in order to ensure the survival of the State.

But surely the religious Jews are those who practise their faith, while the irreligious Jews are those who do not? Such a distinction was valid during the Diaspora, when religious rites, isolated from the work sustaining them, miraculously preserved Judaism, but is it still valid at this dawning of a new age? Is it not the case that a revolt against ritualism stems from a rejection of any magical residue it may still possess, and so opens up the way to its real essence? We cannot doubt the absolute link that exists between justice and the fully developed civilization of Jewish ritualism, which represents the extreme conscience of such justice. It is in the justice of the kibbutz that the nostalgia for ritual is once again to be felt. This is provided that we wish to think of this sort of justice, because of our suspicions regarding any unconscious fervour. Religious liberalism moved back from ritual to a feeling of vague religiosity, hoping to move History back. It happens in the best families. But if ritual is valuable, it will only be reborn in the virility of action and thought.

Religion and religious parties do not necessarily coincide. Justice as the *raison d'être* of the State: that is religion. It presupposes the high science of justice. The State of Israel will be religious because of the intelligence of its great books which it is not free to forget. It will be religious through the very action that establishes it as a State. It will be religious or it will not be at all.

But how are we to read these books? The studies collected by Chaim Grinberg in the aforementioned volume show that the spirit of the Torah proclaims the essential values of democracy and socialism and can inspire an avant-garde State. We had had slight misgivings. But why, after all, should we get lumbered with the Torah? And how can we apply it to a contemporary situation that is so different politically, socially and economically from the order envisaged by the Law? This is a question put by one of the contributors, Dr Leibovitz, in an article entitled 'Religion and State'. Carrying out the Law does not involve the precondition of restoring outmoded institutions; nor does it allow you to ignore the modern forms of life that exist outside Judaism. The social and political situation described by the Bible and the Talmud is the example of a given situation that is rendered human by the Law. From it we can deduce the justice required for any and every situation.

This is an idea which we consider fundamental. The great books of Judaism do not in fact express themselves as parables that are open to the whims of a poetic imagination or as concepts that are always schematic, but as examples that betray nothing of the infinite relations that make up the fabric of the social being. They offer themselves up as an interpretation that is as rigorous as parables are vague and as rich as concepts are poor. Whosoever has encountered the Talmud, especially if the encounter is with a real master, notices this immediately. Others call this splitting hairs! We must isolate the ancient examples and extend them to the new situations, principles and categories which they contain. This means that between the Jewish State and the doctrine which should inspire it, we must establish a science, a formidable one. The relationship between the Jewish State and the Jewish religion – we do not dare to say Church – is that of study.

The progressive drying-up of Talmudic and Hebraic studies in the West in the course of the nineteenth century broke just such a secular contact between Judaism and this prophetic morality to which Judaism claimed an exclusive right. Separated from the Rabbinic tradition which already guaranteed this contact through the miracle of its very continuity, and then absorbed into the so-called scientific mechanisms of the prestigious Western universities, through the philosophies and philologies of the day, this morality, like a translated poem, certainly lost its most typical and perhaps its most virile features. By reducing it to what everyone knows, we lost what it had to teach us.

Henceforth we must return to what was strongest in Rabbinical exegesis. This exegesis made the text speak; while critical philology speaks *of* this text.

The one takes the text to be a source of teaching, the other treats it as a thing. Despite its method and its apparent modesty, critical history already claims to have gone beyond the archaeological curiosities which have been exhumed, and no more invites us to use these ancient truths than it asks us to cut wood with a stone-age axe. On the other hand, the apparent artifice and ingeniousness of the other method consists in saving the text from being turned into a mere book, that is to say just a thing, and in once more allowing it to resonate with the great and living voice of teaching.

Translated by Seán Hand

Means of Identification

The very fact of questioning one's Jewish identity means it is already lost. But, by the same token, it is precisely through this kind of cross-examination that one still hangs on to it. Between *already* and *still* Western Judaism walks a tightrope.

What identity does it cling to? One that refers only to itself and ignores all attributes: one is not a Jew by being this or that. Ideas, characters and things can be identified insofar as they differ from other ideas, characters and things. But people do not produce evidence in order to identify themselves. A person is not who he is because he was born here rather than there, and on such and such a day, or because he has blond hair, a sharp tongue or a big heart. Before he starts comparing himself to anyone else, he

just is who he is. In the same way, one just is a Jew. It is not even something one adheres to, for that already suggests the possibility of estrangement.
It is not something one is possessed by, for adherence to a doctrine soon
turns into fatalism. Through the ill that it inflicts on itself, this extreme
intimacy linking the Jew to Judaism is like a day-to-day expression of
happiness or the sense of having been chosen. 'You are born a Jew; you
don't become one.' This half-truth bears out the ultimate feeling of intimacy. It is not a racist remark, thank God. For one can indeed become a Jew,
but it is as if there had been no conversion. Can one subscribe to whatever
is human? Certain Jews have a way of saying 'Jew' instead of the word
'mankind', as if they took Judaism to be the subject and humanity the
predicate.

But this absolute and unshakable sense of identity, which is founded on
an adherence that preexists any form of allegiance, is not expressed in
uncontrollable terms, as being a subject that is stirred by unfathomable
feelings. On the contrary, it is alien to any sense of introspection or complacency. Instead of just paying attention to the outside world, it exhibits
a perpetual attentiveness that is exclusive and monotheist. It listens and
obeys like a guard who never expects to be relieved (*relève*). This was
recognized by Rabbi Hayyim Volozhiner, the favourite disciple of the Gaon
of Vilna, when, in 1824, in the *Nefesh ha'Hayyim* (a work little known in
the West but one in which the living elements of Judaism converge) he
wrote that a Jew is accountable and responsible for the whole edifice of
creation. There is something that binds and commits (*engage*) man still
more than the salvation of his soul. The act, word and thought of a Jew
have the formidable privilege of being able to destroy and restore whole
worlds. Far from being a serene self-presence, therefore, Jewish identity is
rather the patience, fatigue and numbness of a responsibility – a stiff neck
that supports the universe.

This primordial experience is expressed in a more tolerable way by
Zionism, even if it gets turned into politics and nationalism in the process.
For many Israelis, their identity card is the full extent of their Jewish
identity, as it is, perhaps, for all those potential Israelis who are still in the
Diaspora. But here Jewish identity runs the risk of becoming confused with
nationalism, and from that point on, a loss of Jewish identity is probably
the price to be paid in order to have it renewed.

The western mentality to which the Jew became assimilated, to such a
degree that henceforth he touched only the surface of Judaism, is perhaps
defined by its refusal to adhere to anything unless it performs an act of
adhesion. In the nationalist movements which it has promoted, this mentality uncovers something savage. Any special attachment is marked by the
feeling that it is shared by all. From that point on, one must not simply

accept one's own nature spontaneously; instead, one begins by stepping back, looking at oneself from the outside, pondering about oneself. To compare oneself to others involves analysing and weighing oneself up, reducing the personal identity that one *is* to a series of signs, attributes, contents, qualities and values. The institution that embodies such a mentality is called the University.

To the extent that the loss of an immediate Jewish identity proceeds from such a feeling and such demands, it does not represent a merely regrettable moment in the evolution of Judaism. A Western Jew must still pretend, as Descartes puts it, that he has still to be converted to Judaism. He feels duty bound to approach it as a system of concepts and values that are being presented for his judgement; even the exceptional fate of being the man who supports the universe is one he sees petrified in the statue of Atlas. It is his duty, then, to reformulate everything in the language of the University. Philosophy and philology are the two daughters of this universal speech (wherein we must guard against the younger devouring the elder). It is up to Judaism to support this language, even if it was important one day to turn this language back on the civilization nurturing (and nurtured by) the University.

But this legitimate demand for a system or doctrine – in short, for a conscience – is shown to be completely naive when it proceeds as though it were drawing up an inventory of values in the attempt to discover something original in Judaism. A great civilization does not make an inventory of itself, but opens itself up to study through grammar, the dictionary and scholarship. It does not define itself in a cut-and-dried manner on the basis of a few facile antitheses which are inevitably going to be fallacious. It is universal, that is to say it is precisely capable of whatever can be found in any other civilization, of whatever is humanly legitimate. It is therefore fundamentally non-original, stripped of all local colour. Only those civilizations labelled exotic (or the exotic and perishable elements of civilizations) can be easily distinguished from one another. To the extent that they lose their 'curiosity' value, they find it increasingly difficult to define themselves, since it is only through them that everything is defined. It is not to originality that civilizations owe their excellence, but to their high degree of universality, to their coherence, that is to say to the lack of hypocrisy in their generosity. We can tolerate the pluralism of great civilizations and even understand why they cannot merge. The very nature of truth explains how this is impossible: truth manifests itself in a way that appeals to an enormous number of human possibilities and, through them, a whole range of histories, traditions and approaches. But even when this multiplicity is acknowledged, it does not absolve the individual from a rational choice. Such a choice cannot be based on the vagaries of subjective taste or some sudden whim. At such moments the amateur and the brute come together again. The only criteria on which we can base the rational examination that is required are those of the maximum degree of universality and the minimum degree of hypocrisy.

This examination cannot be reduced to the level of testimony: it is not enough to take stock of what 'the rest of us as Jews' are, and what we feel these days. We should run the risk of taking a compromised, alienated, forgotten, ill-adapted or even dead Judaism to be the essence of Judaism. We cannot be conscious of something in whatever way we wish! The other path is steep but the only one to take: it brings us back to the source, the forgotten, ancient, difficult books, and plunges us into strict and laborious study.

Jewish identity is inscribed in these old documents. It cannot be annulled by simply ignoring these means of identification, just as it cannot be reduced to its simplest form of expression without entering into the discourse of the modern world. One cannot refute the Scriptures without knowing how to read them, or muzzle only philology without doing the same to philosophy, or put a halt, if necessary, to philosophical discourse, without still philosophizing.

Is this worm-eaten old Judaism to be preferred to the Judaism of the Jews? Well, why not? We don't yet know which of the two is the more lively. Are the true books just books? Or are they not also the embers still glowing beneath the ashes, as Rabbi Eliezer called the words of the Prophets? In this way the flame traverses History without burning in it. But the truth illuminates whoever breathes on the flame and coaxes it back to life. More or less. It's a question of breath. To admit the effect that literature has on men is perhaps the ultimate wisdom of the West in which the people of the Bible may recognize themselves. King Josiah ordered a kingdom to be established around an old lost book which was rediscovered by his clerks (*The Book of the Torah* in 622 BCE). It is the perfect image of a life that delivers itself up to the texts. The myth of our Europe as being born of a similar inspiration was called the Renaissance.

Translated by Seán Hand

17

Zionisms

The following three essays are taken from 'Zionisms', the final section of *L'Au-Delà du Verset* (Paris: Editions de Minuit, 1982), pp. 209–34.

'The State of Caesar and the State of David' was first published in *La théologie de l'histoire, Révélation et histoire* (Actes du Colloque organisé par le Centre international d'Etudes Humanistes et par l'Institut d'Etudes Philosophiques de Rome), edited by E. Castelli (Paris: Aubier-Montaigne, 1971), pp. 71–80; 'Politics After!' appeared originally in *Les Temps Modernes*, 398 (1979), 521–8; while the first publication of 'Assimilation and New Culture' was in *Les Nouveaux Cahiers*, 60 (1980), 4–7.

For a general definition of Zionism, see the Glossary.

'The State of Caesar' examines the tense relationship which historically Judaism has had to endure between political power and divine order. Levinas shows how key passages in the Bible and the Talmud constitute a charter for political power, while seeking to safeguard the moral principles and particular identity of Israel against the corruption and idolatry of the State. The monetheist politics that would ideally result is therefore one that can only be constructed by a patient and vigilant practice. The culmination of Zionism, since based on my ethical responsibility for the other, is therefore also the moral goal of all History.

In 'Politics After!' Levinas views the Palestinian conflict through the Diaspora of the Jewish people. Such an historical fact already calls into question any political policy of exclusivism, and in particular recalls the horrors of Hitlerism. This ethical heritage has to be borne today by Israel and Zionism. Both are therefore more than a purely political doctrine, since self-affirmation from the outset must entail a responsibility for the other. The powerful Israel, confronting a weak Palestinian people, is hostage to the other's vulnerability, for it is a state that must embody a prophetic morality transcending any purely political thinking.

'Assimilation and New Culture' considers the future of Jewish culture in the face of European structures of life which have become the social, institutional and democratic norm (again including Fascism and the Holocaust). Judaism is not seen as an extra dimension to be added to such a state, or part of a universal civilization, but rather an excess of responsibility towards humanity whose singularity leads beyond any universal value. A withdrawal into itself on the part of Jewish identity or a Jewish State would therefore be the prelude to the exemplification of a Jewish singularity revealing a moral beyond to the universal. As such the State of Israel will mark the end of assimilation by bringing us far beyond the concept in a spiritual, and so in a political, sense.

The quotations from Maimonides in 'The State of Caesar and the State of David' come from Treatise Five: Kings and Wars, chapter XI 'The Messiah' and chapter XII 'The Messianic Age' in *The Code of Maimonides, Book Fourteen: The Book of Judges*, translated from the Hebrew by Abraham M. Hershman (New Haven: Yale University Press and London: Oxford University Press, 1949), pp. 238–42. The quotations from the Bible in these extracts differ from the Collins version used elsewhere in this Reader. I have left the quotations as they stand but changed the verse numbers to accord with the Collins version.

S.H.

––––––––––––––

The State of Caesar and the State of David

Yes to the State

In the Judaism of the rabbis, during the centuries immediately preceding the birth of Christianity, as in post-Christian rabbinical doctrine, the distinction made between the political and the spiritual orders – between the terrestrial City and the City of God – is not so clear-cut as is suggested by the evangelical formula: 'Render to Cæsar the things that are Cæsar's, and to God the things that are God's.' (Luke 20: 25). In Christianity, the kingdom of God and the earthly kingdom remain separate, bordering each other without touching and, in principle, without dispute between them. They divide up the human between themselves, giving rise to no conflict. This political sense of indifference may be the reason why Christianity has so often served as a State religion.

Certainly it would not be true to say that, for Israel, political power and the divine order are identified. Nor is it because they were unable to expect of God anything other than their nation's salvation and the deliverance of Judea from Roman oppression that the Jews remained untouched by the message of Christianity. Being beyond the State was an era which Judaism could foresee without having to accept, in an age of States, that a State would be free from the rule of Law, or believe that the State was not a necessary path, even as it led beyond the State. The doctrine of the prophets was perhaps no more than such an anti-Machiavellism, anticipated in their refusal of anarchy.

It is the idea of kingship that, in the biblical texts, expresses the principle of the State. Deuteronomy 17: 14–20 and I Samuel 8 constitute a charter for political power. The institution of kingship is claimed as common to Israel and to Gentiles. The prophet does not so much recommend it as

consent to it, and does so with better grace in Deuteronomy than in I
Samuel. In Deuteronomy the king shall be the chosen of the Eternal,
faithful to the Torah in which he shall 'read all the days of his life', in order
that his heart may not be lifted up above his brethen. Little money; few
wives, lest his heart turn away from the Law; few horses, lest the people use
them to return to Egypt. This is an idea of power without the abuse of
power, of a power safeguarding the moral principles and particular identity
of Israel, which an institution common to Israel and all the nations might
compromise. It is an idea to which the image of Saul would seem to
conform when, at the beginning of his reign, hiding himself among the
baggage, he continues to work his field.

On the other hand, the text from I Samuel is an impassioned indictment.
The prophet foresees the ruler's enslavement of his subjects, and the attack
on their property, persons and family. This power eventually becomes
tyranny: 'And in that day you will cry out because of your king, whom you
have chosen for yourselves; but the Lord will not answer you in that day' (I
Samuel 8: 18). It is impossible to escape the State.

The Talmud then presents as royal prerogatives what in the text of I
Samuel 8 are exactions.[1] And the commentary on Deuteronomy 17: 14–20
attenuates the severity of the Bible's remarks.[2] The king should not have
too many horses (Deuteronomy 17: 16), but only enough to meet the needs
of his cavalry; nor should he have silver and gold in excess (Deuteronomy
17: 17), but just enough to pay his troops. Are the excesses of power
legitimate, then, when they are used to ensure the survival of a people
amongst other nations or of an individual amongst his fellow men? It would
appear so.

But can an absolute law be suspended? Can it be seen in Judaism purely
and simply as a yoke which we are authorized to throw off by the necessities
of life? Does opting for the State amount to choosing life over Law, when
that Law claims to be a Law of life (*Loi de vie*)? Unless it is the case that the
divinity of the Law consists only in entering the world as 'a great and strong
wind, rending the mountains and breaking in pieces the rocks', only as 'an
earthquake', as 'a fire';[3] unless its sovereignty or even its spirituality consists only in an extreme humility, soliciting in a 'voice of fine silence' an
entry to the hearts of the just,[4] unless these, the just, form a minority;
unless this minority is at every moment on the point of succumbing; unless
the spirit-in-the-world is fragility itself;[5] unless the entry of the Law into
the world requires education and protection and, consequently, a history
and a State; unless politics is the channel of this long patience and these
great precautions. This is a cautious attempt to return to the philosophical
presuppositions of the 'concession' that religion grants to political necessities, of the 'provisional abdication' that the 'spirit of the absolute' pro-

nounces before the spirit that is attentive to the variety of circumstance and the necessities of place and time to which politics belongs. This 'provisional abdication' is thinkable only if the temporal order wherein it is pronounced itself receives some justification in the absolute. The ultimate elevation in Revelation would consist in its requiring a response, and its quest for interiority. In this respect it is, precisely, a teaching, or Torah. But, as such, it needs time. The weakness of something that needs time to develop should not be looked upon abstractly: here it indicates, positively, an order superior to the eternity of Platonic Ideas or Aristotelian forms. This order consists in a spirit in contact with the Other (*l'Autre*), which brings to the spirit more than it can achieve alone. It is an order in which limits are surpassed; but this exposes it to danger. What is taught can be forgotten, to the point of total forgetting. Hence, the security of the times, favourable to a pedagogical continuity, and the politics capable of guaranteeing that security must of course be measured on a metaphysical scale, but these are principles of 'concession' and of 'provisional abdication' that derive from no suspect opportunism. The 'necessities of the moment' to which they are a response are those of the entry of eternity into the moment, that is to say those of the essence of Revelation. It is in this very precise sense that the treatise *Temurah* declares: 'It is better that one letter of the Torah should be uprooted than that the whole Torah should be forgotten.'[6] Does a political act not place itself in the void left by such a sacrifice of the letter? It does not see itself belonging to an order that is autonomous and freed from its original finality. According to the ideal doctrine, the Sanhedrin installs and controls the king.[7] Above the order that entails war, taxes, expropriation, is placed the Law of the Absolute, which does not raise up a political authority only to disappear and leave unconditionally to Cæsar that which it rendered to Cæsar.

Taking up the text of Deuteronomy, the Talmud says:

> The king shall write in his own name a Sefer Torah. When he goes forth to war he must take it with him; on returning, he brings it back with him; when he sits in judgement it shall be with him, and when he sits down to eat, before him, as it is written: and it shall be with him, and he shall read therein all the days of his life.[8]

And, to show the closeness of the prince's relationship to the Torah, here is the commentary:

> And he must not take credit for one belonging to his ancestors. Rabbah said: Even if one's parents have left him a *Sefer Torah*, yet it is proper that he should write one of his own, as it is written: 'Now therefore write ye this song

for you.'... The (scroll) which is to go in and out with (the king) [he shall write in the form of an amulet and fasten it to his arm, as it is written of David (Psalms 16: 8): 'I have set God always before me, surely He is at my right hand, I shall not be moved].

These precise ritual prescriptions, these scrupulous recommendations, are also means of expression: the State, in accordance with its pure essence, is possible only if penetrated by the divine word; the prince is educated in this knowledge; this knowledge is taken up by each person on his own account; tradition is renewal.

What is important above all is the idea that not only is the essence of the State not in contradiction with the absolute order, but that it has been called up by that order. Thus the Talmud thinks through radically something that, in fact, is in Samuel I & II, and in Kings I & II: in the midst of troubles, wars and political assassinations, the House of David is affirmed, in accordance with the will of God, as an eternal dynasty, the bearer of promises. Through the books of the prophets, it enters little by little into eschatology. The Messiah founds a just society and delivers humanity after having delivered Israel. These messianic times are the period of a kingship. The Messiah is king. The divine empowers History and State, it does not suppress them. The end of History retains a political form.[9] But the Messiah is descended from David. A genealogical tree of David's stock can matter little to the Messiah, who is justified by his own justice. But it is of the highest importance to David himself and to the political structure signified by his name. The Davidic State resides in the finality of Deliverance. The epoch of the Messiah can and must result from the political order that pretends to be indifferent to eschatology and preoccupied solely with the problems of the day. This political world must therefore remain related to the ideal world. The talmudic apologue is here singularly suggestive: king David wars and governs by day; at night when men rest, he gives himself up to the Law:[10] a double life designed to remake the unity of life. The political actions of each passing day begin in an eternal midnight, they derive from a nocturnal·contact with the Absolute.

In a famous passage of his *Yad ha-Hazakah* concerning the State, Maimonides characterizes the messianic age in a way that omits the haunting supernatural element. This non-apocalyptic messianism, where philosophical and Rabbinic thought merge once more, certainly does not absorb everything that waiting for the Messiah means to a Jewish sensibility. Yet it does permit us to gauge the importance attached in Jewish thought to moving beyond beautiful dreams in order to accomplish an ideal in real terms which are set out by a State. The extracts that follow indicate a distinction between messianism and the ultimate religious promises ('future world'), but also the extremely platonist confidence in the possibility that a rational political order might ensure the end of all exile and violence and bring about the happy peace of contemplation. Here are a few elements of this text which is remarkable for its rationalist sobriety:

> King Messiah will arise and restore the Kingdom of David to its former state and original sovereignty. He will rebuild the sanctuary and gather the dispersed of Israel . . . Do not think that King Messiah will have to perform signs and wonders, bring anything new into being, revive the dead, or do similar things . . . The general principle is: this Law of ours with its statutes and ordinances [is not subject to change]. It is for ever and all eternity; it is not to be added to or to be taken away from . . . If there arise a king from the House of David who meditates on the Torah, occupies himself with the commandments, as did his ancestor David, observes the precepts prescribed in the written and the oral Law, prevails upon Israel to walk in the way of the Torah and to repair its breaches, and fights the battles of the Lord, it may be assumed that he is the Messiah. If he does these things and succeeds, rebuilds the sanctuary on its site, and gathers the dispersed of Israel, he is beyond all doubt the Messiah. He will prepare the whole world to serve the Lord with one accord, as it is written: 'For then will I turn to the peoples a pure language, that they may all call upon the name of the Lord to serve Him with one consent' (Zephaniah, 3: 9).

Then Maimonides interprets the prophecies on the cohabitation of the wolf and the lamb as the reconciliation of peoples, who are like wild animals:

> Said the Rabbis: 'The sole difference between the present and the messianic days is delivery from servitude to foreign powers' (B. Sanhedrin 91b). Taking the words of the prophets in their literal sense, it appears that the inauguration of the messianic era will be marked by the war of Gog and Magog; that prior to that war, a prophet will arise to guide Israel and set their hearts aright, as it is written: 'Behold, I will send you Elijah the prophet' (Malachi 4: 5). He (Elijah) will come neither to declare the clean unclean, nor the unclean clean . . . but to bring peace in the world, as it is said: 'And he shall turn the hearts of the fathers to the children' (Malachi 4: 6).
>
> Some of our Sages say that the coming of Elijah will precede the advent of the Messiah. But no one is in a position to know the details and similar things until they have come to pass . . . No one should ever occupy himself with the legendary themes or spend much time on midrashic statements bearing on this and like subjects. He should not deem them of prime importance, since they lead neither to the fear of God nor to the love of Him. Nor should one calculate the end . . . In the days of King Messiah, when his kingdom will be established and all Israel will gather around him, their pedigrees will be determined by him through the Holy Spirit which will rest upon him . . . The Sages and Prophets did not long for the days of the Messiah that Israel might

exercise dominion over the world, or rule over the heathens, or be exalted by the nations, or that it might eat and drink and rejoice. Their aspiration was that Israel be free to devote itself to the Law and its wisdom, with no one to oppress or disturb it, and thus be worthy of life in the world to come.

In that era there will be neither famine nor war, neither jealousy nor strife. Blessings will be abundant, comforts within the reach of all. The one pre-occupation of the whole world will be to know the Lord. Hence Israelites will be very wise, they will know the things that are now concealed and will attain an understanding of their Creator to the utmost capacity of the human mind, as it is written: 'For the earth shall be full of the knowledge of the Lord, as the waters cover the sea' (Isaiah 11: 9).

But, if the Messianic City is not beyond politics, the City in its plainest sense is never this side of the religious. 'Pray for the welfare of the government', teaches the tractate on Principles (*Aboth*, ch. III), 'for were it not for the fear thereof, one man would swallow up alive his fellow-man.'[11] A passage from the *Bereschit Rabah*[12] declares paradoxically:

> Rabbi Shimon, son of Laquich, said: 'And God saw every thing he had made, and, behold, it was very good' (Genesis 1: 31). 'Behold it was good', is the rule of God, and 'Behold, it was very good', is the rule of the Romans. – What? The rule of the Romans is very good? – Yes, because the rule of the Romans asserts the Law and the rights of persons (*dikan chel brioth*).

This hyperbole expresses the importance attached to a grasp of the real world and a mistrust of being satisfied with dreams. The tractate *Shabbath* (11, a) offers a similar opinion:

> (It has been said) in Rab's name: If the seas were ink, reeds pens, the heavens parchment, and all men writers, they would not suffice to write down the intricacies of government.... What verse [teaches this]? (Proverbs 25: 3): 'The heaven for height, and the earth for depth, and the heart of kings is unsearchable.'

Homage is hereby paid to the State represented by Rome, one of the four powers (along with Babylonia, the Parthians and the Seleucid Empire) that, according to Jewish historical wisdom, incarnate the alienation or the paga-nization of History, political or imperial oppression, *chiboud malkhouyoth*. The rabbis cannot forget the organizing principle of Rome and its law! So they anticipate, with a remarkable independence of spirit, modern political philosophy. Already the City, whatever its order, guarantees the rights of humans against their fellow-creatures, imagined as still in a state of nature, men as wolves to other men, as Hobbes would have had it. Although Israel sees itself born of an irreducible fraternity, it is not ignorant of the temptation, within itself and surrounding it, of war between all.

Beyond the State

But the State of Caesar, despite its participation in the pure essence of the State, is also the site of corruption par excellence and, perhaps, the last refuge of idolatry.

According to certain doctors of the Talmud, oppression by great States, the *chiboud malkhouyoth*, constitutes the sole difference between the Messianic epoch and our own. The State of Caesar reaches its apogee, or a state of hypertrophy that is in some sense natural, without any hindrance to its growth, developing from the form it received from the Graeco-Roman world, the pegan State, jealous of its sovereignty, the State in pursuit of hegemony, the conquering, imperialist, totalitarian, oppressive State, attached to a realist egoism. As such it separates humanity from its deliverance. Unable to exist without adoring itself, it is pure idolatry. This striking vision arises independently of any text: in a world of scruples and of respect for man derived from monotheism, the Chancellory, with its *realpolitik*, comes from another universe, sealed off from sensibility, or protest by 'beautiful souls', or tears shed by an 'unhappy consciousness'.

Talmudic wisdom is entirely aware of the internal contradiction of the State subordinating some men to others in order to liberate them, whatever the principles embodied in those who wield power. This is a contradiction against which even the person who refuses the political order has no protection, since, by abstaining from any collaboration with power, he makes himself a party to the obscure powers repressed by the State. A subtle page of the Talmud[13] describes the way in which R. Eleazar participated in Rome's struggle against wrongdoers. The narrative derives its sense of drama from the fact that R. Eleazar was the son of R. Simeon b. Yohai to whom Israel's mystical tradition attributes the authorship of the Zohar and who is supposed to have spent fourteen years in a cave, with this very son, hiding from the Romans. A mystic in the service of the oppressive State! 'How long will you deliver up the people of our God for slaughter?' he is asked by R. Joshua, son of Karḥah. This people is, of course, Israel, but to be read as humanity conscious of its original resemblance to God. To serve the State is to serve oppression; to serve oppression is to belong to the police. Unless we ignore: 'in the service of the State yourself, O son of our God, you lose your soul.' R. Eleazar, beyond any doubt one of the just, replies: 'I weed out thorns from the vineyard.' There are thorns in the vineyard of the good Lord! Whereupon R. Joshua retorts: 'Let the owner of the vineyard himself (God) come and weed out the thorns!' It is not in terms of political action that the contradiction opposing monotheism and the State can be resolved.

The owner of the vineyard, not his agent! Behind the Davidic State, preserved from the corruption that already alienates the State of Caesar, we can glimpse what lies beyond the State. In certain texts, Israel is conceived of as a human society that has gone beyond Messianism, which is still political and historical. In others the future world or 'world to come' is announced – Messianism and this 'world to come' being radically distinct. The messianic state that seems to be entirely incorporated within the destiny of Israel (although this, to go by the letter of I Samuel 8, could have been avoided) is therefore only a stage, a transition. In effect, a number of talmudic passages assign a finite duration to the messianic era.[14] The future world is the true end of eschatology. It comprises possibilities that cannot be structured according to a political schema. In the interpretation that Jewish mysticism gives to the spiritual life – the Kabbalah – among the ten *sephirot* or categories of the presence of God in a creature, royalty is the lowest. There is no proof, though, that elevation allows us to leap over the intermediaries!

'All the prophets prophesied only in respect of the messianic era; but as for the world to come, "no eye has seen a God besides thee, who works for those who wait for him" (Isaiah 64: 4).' Texts that can certainly be taken as strictly religious, separating salvation from all earthly reference; but which can also be read as the announcement of new possibilities for the human Spirit, a new distribution of its centres, a new meaning to life, new relations with the Other.[15] Going beyond Messianism in this way is affirmed in terms that are even more precise: 'R. Hillel said: There shall be no Messiah for Israel, because they have already enjoyed him in the days of Hezekiah.'[16] This is a remark which the Talmud quotes in order to refute it: 'May God forgive him [for saying so].' But the editors of the Talmud did not judge it useful to omit this remark and thereby commit it to oblivion. For Israel, Messianism might well be a stage that has been surpassed. It suited a very archaic Israel! How do the commentators interpret this daring remark? If, for Israel, the Messiah has already come, it is because Israel is awaiting the deliverance that will come from God himself. This doesn't enter into the idea of royalty. It is there, the highest hope, separated forever from political structures! If the Messiah is still King, if Messianism is a form of political existence, then salvation by the Messiah is salvation by an other, as if, in my full maturity, I could be saved by an other, or as if, on the other hand, the salvation of all the others were not incumbent upon me, depending on the exact significance of my personal existence! As if the ultimate end of a person were not the possibility of listening to my own conscience, and of refusing the reasons of State! A point which modern man believes he has attained and which is probably the best definition of modernity, but which is perhaps more difficult than the 'spontaneism' with which it is confused. It is a dangerous and tempting confusion which is no doubt the reason why the doctors condemned Rev Hillel's daring thesis.

Towards a Monotheistic Politics

The culmination of the State of David in the messianic state, and the going beyond the State implied in the notion of the 'world to come' may appear utopian, and, at any rate, premature. Is the political philosophy of monotheism just a summary improvisation, even if – as seems obvious – utopia has claims to make of any thinking worthy of the name? This indiscreet question is put, paradoxically, in certain religious circles to be found in the State revived in the Holy Land, for which the tradition of Israel is the source of all meaning. The question is not put in order to lay claim to the idolatrous politics of the world, the only politics, actually, that exists and one which Christian monotheism has been unable to destroy. Instead, the question is put to obtain from Zion the formulation for a political monotheism that no one yet has managed to formulate. Not even the doctors of the Talmud. Only the responsibilities of the modern State, exercised over the promised land for Abraham's posterity, should allow his heirs to confront the formulae with the facts, and so patiently to construct a political doctrine that will suit monotheists.

Recently, in Paris, I attended a lecture given by Dan Avni-Segré,[17] an Israeli of Italian origin, professor at the law faculty in Haifa, where he conducts a seminar on the new politics with the participation, notably, of several Arab students. Let the testimony given there serve as a conclusion to the present note. Professor Avni-Segré sees the whole return to Zion in a perspective that restores it to sacred History. He emphasizes not the achievements of the young State but the possibilities for political innovation that it opens up. In the midst of daily conflict, the lived experience of the government – and even the painful necessities of the occupation – allow us to derive lessons as yet untaught in the ancient Revelation. Is a monotheistic politics a contradiction in terms? Or is this, on the contrary, the culmination of Zionism? Beyond the concern to guarantee a refuge to the persecuted, is this not the great task? Is there nothing to be found somewhere between having recourse to the methods of the Caesars, an unscrupulous idolatry whose model is the 'imperial oppression', the *chiboud malkhouyoth*, and the facile eloquence of an incautious moralism, that seems blinded by its own words and dreams, and condemns those dispersed people who had been brought together to a rapid destruction and a new diaspora. For two thousand years, Israel did not engage with History. Innocent of any political crime, pure with a victim's purity, a purity whose sole merit is perhaps its patient endurance, Israel had become unable to conceive of a politics that would put the finishing touches to its monotheistic message. Now such a commitment does exist. Since 1948. But all this is only a beginning. Israel is no less isolated in its struggle to complete its incredible task than Abraham was, four thousand years ago, when he began it. Beyond solving any particular problem, whether national or familiar, therefore, this return to the land of our forefathers marks one of the greatest events of internal history and, indeed, of all History.

NOTES

1 Tractate *Sanhedrin*, 20b.
2 Ibid., 21b.
3 Cf. I Kings 19: 11 and 19: 12.
4 Cf. *Sifre* of Deuteronomy 32: 2, cited by Rashi: 'He has knocked at the doors of all the nations . . . '
5 Unless – as has been said in a different context, in confusing the Spirit with its presence-in-the-world – civilizations know themselves to be mortal.
6 *Temurah*, 14b.
7 *Shabbath*, 15a.
8 *Sanhedrin*, 21b.
9 *Sanhedrin*, 99a–b: the Messianic era has a finite duration.
10 *Berakoth*, 3b.
11 Curiously, the formula 'swallow up alive' can be found in Psalms, 124: 2–3: 'If it had not been the Lord who was on our side . . . then they would have swallowed us up alive.' The State, and even the Roman State, is worthy of expressions praising the glory of God.
12 One of the earliest anthologies of Midrashic parables and sayings.
13 *Baba Meẓi'a*, 83b.
14 *Sanhedrin*, 99a–b.
15 'No eye has seen' recalls curiously the strange passages where Marx expects socialist society to bring about a change in the human condition, and frustrates a specific forecast by virtue of the revolutionary essence of such a change.
16 *Sanhedrin*, 99a.
17 At the IXth Colloquium of Francophone Jewish Intellectuals, held in Paris on 25–26 October 1970.

Translated by Roland Lack

Politics After!

The origins of the conflict between Jews and Arabs go back to Zionism. This conflict has been acute since the creation of the State of Israel on a small piece of arid land which had belonged to the children of Israel more than thirty centuries before and which, despite the destruction of Judea in 70 CE, has never been abandoned by the Jewish communities. During the Diaspora they continued to lay claim to it and since the beginning of this century their labours have made it flower again. But it also happens to be on a small piece of land which has been inhabited for centuries by people who are surrounded on all sides and by vast stretches of land containing the great Arab people of which they form a part. They call themselves Palestinians. This conflict, which, for the moment, dominates all other Jewish–Arab questions, has always been treated in political terms by men of State, public opinion and even intellectuals: for everyone it has been a matter of collectivities which deserve or usurp the name of 'nation', of the extent of powers exercised over territories, of their confrontation in war, and of their strategic role among the great world powers. This approach offers no clarification, nor pays sufficient attention to the dimensions that these political problems might derive from their spatio-temporal, psychological and moral premisses. As these premisses are capable of destroying the prefabricated categories of sociology and political science, no regard has been shown for their extraordinary nature or for the remarkable human adventure played out within them. Instead, the unshakable conviction remains that nature never departs from the order of things, that the extraordinary is a religious notion, a source of mystificaton and the refuge of ideologies, that the human is never so singular and that to invoke the human is only to appeal to the pity conceded, if need be, to the victims of the camps. But the reasonable course of action – so it is put – would be political first of all, even if the facts engaged with accommodate diverse and incompatible analyses.

We believe that, 'for men purely as men', independently of any religious consideration deriving from a confession or a set of beliefs, the sense (*sens*) of the human, between peoples as between persons, is exhausted neither by the political necessities that hold it bound nor by the sentiments that relax that hold. We believe that what moves outside the order of things can be brought into the general picture without having recourse to any supernatural or miraculous dimension and, demanding an approach irreducible to the established precedents, can authorize proper projects and models to which every mind, that is to say reason, can none the less gain access.

A Jew need be 'no prophet, neither a prophet's son' to wish and hope for a reconciliation between Jew and Arab, and to perceive it, beyond mere peace between neighbours, as a fraternal community. The peace concluded between Israel and Egypt, and the strange conditions in which it had been brought about by the visit of President Sadat to Jerusalem on 19 November 1977 must have seemed on the small screen like the first steps of mankind on the moon, though no more irrational. Despite the many peripheral details that threatened, in the reality of things, to make the agreement fail, despite all the obstacles that perhaps still await it and threaten to reduce it to nothing, this peace in our view represents the only path along which reconciliation had a chance of coming about. This is not because of the incomplete nature of the solution or the supposed excellence of progressing 'by little steps', but because peace had come through pursuing a path that lay beyond politics, whatever the actual role of the political route may have been in the itinerary of this peace.

Already the place – or the Diaspora, or the migrations – of the Jewish people among the nations, its antiquity as *one people* across the diverse and contradictory periods of History, should call into question the excluding nature of political conceptualization. Interiority is perhaps simply this. An interiority that would no longer be the imaginary dimension of 'beautiful souls' should no doubt be measured in terms of this antiquity, whether it is founded on fidelity to memories or a book. A prophetic book, in the event, made up of subversive discourses that defy kings and the grandees without fleeing into clandestinity. A book that bears within it this disputed land more deeply than do the geological strata of its depths. A fidelity that encourages, certainly, but, more surely, denotes an impassiveness in the face of the world's clamorous outbursts, its wars, glories and hegemonies. This guarantees that, in the melée of men and events, hypothetical imperatives do not conceal their conditioning nor impose themselves categorically. This represents an ethical destiny, one without anachoresis, or isolation, the distance necessary for judgement. It is the difficult freedom of Israel, which is not to be treated as an ethnographic curiosity but as one extreme limit of human potential. Such a potential disturbs and irritates the awareness of sovereignty that is assumed by well-settled nations firmly installed on their lands, whose self-affirmation is sustained by the firmness of the land beneath their feet, by this certainty, this original experience of the immovable.

Irritation and disturbance, an allergy less pardonable, whatever sociologists may say, than any simply quantitative or qualitative difference. Antisemitism is not simply the hostility felt by a majority towards a minority, nor only xenophobia, nor any ordinary racism, even if it were the ultimate rationale of these phenomena that are derived from it (throughout her work, Eliane Lévy-Amado argues for this quasi-ontological structure of antisemitism). It is a repugnance felt for the unknown within the psyche of the Other, for the mystery of its interiority or, beyond any agglomeration within an ensemble or any organization within an organism, a repugnance felt for the pure proximity of the other man, for sociality itself.

National socialism and the dramatic events of this century that have overturned the liberal world upon which, with more or less success, the existence of the Jews relied, have dragged antisemitism's apocalyptic secret out into the open and allowed us to see the extreme, demanding and dangerous destiny of humankind that, by antiphrasis, antisemitism denotes. The antisemitism of today, both on the left and on the right, defines itself through the traces left in all minds by Hitlerism, even if it is hidden behind different names. There are no more Jews privileged in the way those of Western Europe were in the eyes of the Jewish masses exterminated in Eastern Europe, the national minorities of the past who, often unconsciously, envied and hoped for that exceptional fate.

But there are no more unremarked – or unmarked – Jews as such in the so-called socialist countries. 'Internationalism is when the Russian, the Georgian, the Ukrainian, the Tchouvak and the Usbek come together to strike the Jews', notes Alexander Zinoviev in *The Radiant Future*. And that is the final test. Stalinism and post-stalinist antisemitism – or, if you prefer, the antisemitism that sixty years of applied Marxism have not eradicated from the Slavic soul and whose influence on the third world is reflected in the votes cast against Israel by the progressive nations at the UN – these constitute one of the greatest traumas ever to have struck modern Jewish consciousness. They condemn any hope on its part of a new and liberated humanity that might have been conceived in terms of a 'forgetting of Jerusalem'. The Zionism of this last quarter-century has been lived as a remembrance of Psalm 137.

This is an inverted experience of universality latent in a universal rejection, lived as a second self-consciousness. But it is an experience touching the essence of the human at least as deeply as it is touched by the condition of the proletariat. This experience is inverted into choosing life, a will-to-be, and even political initiatives. But it has its back to the wall, or the sea, and is loaded down with the burden of Israel's ethical heritage, since it is a love of life *to that end*, a resurrection *to that end*. This is what is signified by the first syllable of 'Zionism': the primary message. 'For out of Zion shall go forth the law', according to Micah 4: 2, a verse known to all from the Jewish liturgy. Reference to the Bible, as a doctrine of justice, counts for as much and for more than the documentation of imprescriptibe rights. Self-affirmation means from the outset a responsibility for all. Zionism is a politics and already a non-politics. An epic and a Passion. Wild energy and extreme vulnerability. Zionism, after the realism of its first political formulations, is finally revealed, in the terms of a Judaism of substance, to be a great ambition of the Spirit.

At all events, it has certainly been understood as such, since its first message, by the vast strata of Jews in Eastern Europe who had not yet entered the liberal society of the nineteenth century and had remained exposed to persecution and the pogroms. For, behind Herzl's political ideas, which seemed so Western, what counted above all was the identification he established between the *Judenstadt*[1] and the Promised Land, reopening eschatological perspectives, that were still global, on Sacred History.

Paradoxically, it was this universalist finality of the Jew that came into play in the opposition of Jews to Zionism in Europe prior to Hitler. The rehabilitation of Captain Dreyfus became in the West the symbol of the triumph of justice as expressed in the ideas of 1789 and 1848. Zionism seemed inadequate to the prophetic ideal whose accomplishments the Jew imagined he could perceive at the heart of the great democratic nations and in the brilliance of their sciences and arts.

Soon, even in Eastern Europe, the expansion of Marxist ideas, situated within the prolongation of those revolutions whose final struggles they seemed to announce, subordinated the fate of the Jew to that of all of the earth's disinherited. The vision of this disinheritance, of these hopes and of the mission they produced seemed to answer the human vocation as understood on a Biblical scale, even if it was one stripped of confessional, scriptural and geographical memories. Zionism's search for a Jewish State, and the development of colonies in Palestine, was interpreted for a long time, despite the new forms of collective life arising within the kibbutz, in terms of nationalism; at best as a nationalism for the poor. It was seen by some as a quasi-philanthropic, humanitarian operation; others viewed it as a secular survival of an outdated religious phenomenon, displaying its folklore in the manner of a self-motivated petty bourgeois ideology.

None the less, a small elite felt the true essence of the movement, without waiting for Hitlerism or Soviet antisemitism. I would like to refer in this context to the autobiographical writings of the great and admirable Israeli scholar Gershom Scholem, who describes his journey from Weimar Germany to Jerusalem, and offers a remarkable analysis of the spiritual dimension – which is not simply a religious dimension – of Zionism, as he has understood it since the end of the first world war.

Zionism, allegedly a purely political doctrine, both carries within itself the image in reverse of a certain universality, and stands as its correction. This thorn in the flesh is not a demand to be pitied. It is the scale and the strange firmness of an interiority, a lack of any support in the world, that is, an absence of any 'pre-prepared place of retreat', or means of escape, or last-ditch stand. Such is the land that Israel possesses as its State. The effort to build and defend it is made with the opposition and under the permanent and growing threat of all its neighbours. It is a State whose existence remains in question in everything that constitutes its essence; whereas for the political nations the land is always the famous 'never depleted stock' that remains when all else is lost. For Israel, the land is either what is at stake, or the point of impasse. This impasse is what is referred to in their expression: *en brera*, meaning 'there is no choice'! It is the position of an armed and dominant State, one of the great military powers of the Mediterranean basin facing the unarmed Palestinian people whose very existence Israel refuses to recognize! But is that the true state of affairs? Is not Israel, in its very real strength, also one of the most fragile and vulnerable things in the world, poised in the midst of unopposed nations, who are rich in natural allies, and surrounded by their lands? Land, land, land, as far as the eye can see.

This is the reason for the greatness and the importance of Sadat. His visit[2] was probably that exceptional, trans-historical, event that can be witnessed only once in a lifetime. For a brief moment everyone managed to forget all the political standards and clichés and all the false motives that a certain wisdom attributes even to the act of a man who transcends himself and rises above his own prudence and precautions. So prudence and precautions can be forgotten, but for how long? For a few days, a few hours? For an instant? Perhaps. But who can speak of the duration of a true event or of the advent of the true? Who has been able to measure the ephemeral dimension that works away in secret within the progress of History? Has Sadat himself perceived the entirely human humanity that unfolds within historical events in the form of Judaism, a patience and a Passion perpetually renewed, to the point of becoming an act that saves that same humanity? This is a politics and a precarious state of being that contain a despair to be transcended and yet despair of ever transcending themselves (*dont ne s'absente jamais le désespoir à dépasser*). Has Sadat sensed this in Zionism, which has been portrayed as imperialist in nature even though it still bears suffering and dereliction deep within itself and, outside of its own sense of truth, possesses no allotted and inalienable patrimony of the kind that supports those who elsewhere govern States? This struggle has always been, in one sense, like the uprising in the Warsaw ghetto where there is no hiding place and where each step back has implications for the whole struggle. Ah, what bad negotiators the Israelis are, even as they conduct a struggle from which the memory of Massada is never absent and which some dare to denounce as a derivative of western ideologies! In attacking Israeli suspicions, will they go as far as to strip the arms from the defenders on the last ramparts? Besides this, has not Sadat understood what opportunities are opened up by being friendly with Israel, or even simply by acknowledging its existence and entering into talks, and what prophetic promise is concealed beneath Zionism's claim to historical rights and its contortions under the yoke of politics? So many injustices are here no longer irreparable. So many impossibilities are here made possible. This is something that less elevated minds, among his enemies in the Near East or his friends in our proud West, have never sensed, immersed as they are in political book-keeping. Is it just 'a State like any other', plus a lot of eloquence? Really! Is there no alternative between having recourse to those unscrupulous methods typified by *Realpolitik*, and the irritating rhetoric of an incautious idealism that is lost in utopian dreams but turns to dust on contact with reality or becomes a dangerous, impudent and facile delirium that claims to speak again the language of the prophets? Beyond the concern to provide a shelter for those without a country, and beyond the sometimes astonishing, sometimes doubtful, accomplishments of the State of Israel, has it not been a matter above all of creating on its own land the concrete conditions for political innovation? That is Zionism's ultimate end, and probably one of the great events of human history. For two thousand years, the Jewish people was only the object of history, politically innocent because of its role as victim. That role does not answer its vocation. Since 1948, there it is, surrounded by enemies and still being called into question, but now it is also engaged in events, in order to think through – to build and rebuild – a State that should embody a prophetic morality and the idea of its peace. That this idea has been transmitted and grasped, in mid-flight, as it were, is a wonder of wonders. As we have said, Sadat's journey has opened up the only way to peace in the Near East, if that peace is to be possible: what is 'politically' weak about it is probably the expression of its daring and, in the end, of its strength. And perhaps of what, everywhere and for everyone, it brings to the very idea of peace: the suggestion that peace is a concept that goes beyond purely political thinking.

NOTES

1 Editor's note: Theodor Herzl (1860–1904), the founder of political Zionism, published *Der Judenstadt* (*The Jewish State*) in 1896.
2 On Saturday, 19 November 1977, President Sadat of Egypt made a historic visit to Israel to discuss the possibility of peace between the two nations.

Translated by Roland Lack

Assimilation and New Culture

In good sociology assimilation appears as an objective process, controlled by strict laws, even to the extent of being the social process par excellence. Among its factors figure the attraction exerted by a homogeneous majority over the minority, the difficulties of every kind that await those who obstinately make themselves the exception to this rule – and even to mere customs – and the economic necessities that, in modern society at least, break down these differences. The individual needs courage and strength to resist the natural current that would bear him away.

But, despite the evident constraints that determine such movement, assimilation is condemned as betrayal or decadence. The subject's intentions are put on trial. The defendants are suspected of egoism and opportunism, of aspiring to nothing more than a trouble-free life, and of being afraid to live dangerously.

I should not think of contesting this judgement when assimilation means de-judaification. But I should like to recall, or at least to underline the fact that, insofar as assimilation to Western culture is concerned, it cannot be thought to result only from its causes: it also involves spiritual reasons and necessities that impose themselves on active consciousness. This creates a serious problem for those who, whether they are educators or men of action, are concerned for the future of Judaism. The solution supposes more than simply a 'reorganizaton of communal services', more than a reform of the school curriculum, more than a new pedagogical politics: it requires an effort to create a culture, in other words a new Jewish life.

Insofar as they reflect the spiritual excellence of universality, the different forms of European life have conquered the Israelis. They have become the norm in thinking and feeling, and the source of science, art and modern technology. They are equally the origin of any reflection concerning democracy and the foundation of those institutions devoted to the ideal of liberty and the rights of man. Of course no one could forget the events of the twentieth century: two world wars, Fascism and the holocaust. The doctrines and institutions of Europe come out of it all highly compromised. But this does not stop us referring to them in order to distinguish between ourselves and their monstrous offspring or between a perversion and the good seed from which it sprang. We continue to admire universal principles and whatever can be deduced by sound logic from them.

Consequently, the problem of assimilation is still with us, and is so to the exact extent that we all – in Israel and among the Diaspora, Zionists and non-Zionists – acknowledge western civilizaton and lay claim to all that it has contributed and contributes still to our public and intellectual life, open as it is to the world's vast compass. But our belonging to a religious or national or linguistic Judaism is not something purely and simply to be added to our Western inheritance. One or other of the two factors becomes discredited. We must ask ourselves if there is not a permanent risk of the traditional aspect of our existence sinking, despite what affection and goodwill may attach to it, to the level of folklore.

The value-judgment that bears upon the public order to which we belong is not of the same force as that which is summoned up from our depths. It is the public order that counts. The maxim of the nineteenth-century Jewish *Haskalah*, the Jewish Enlightenment, 'Be a Jew at home and a man outside', no doubt was able to slow down the process of assimilation and guarantee the Jews of eastern Europe a double culture, and, in their consciousness, the happy co-existence of two worlds. But that had been possible only for as long as the Slavic civilizations remained closed, socially and politically, to the Jews and did not, intrinsically, elevate themselves from the outset to the heights of Western universalism. There, assimilation could be confined to a superficial adherence or adaptation to the surrounding world without requiring the soul's complete submission to it. The place of folklore was perhaps not on the Jewish side. It was sometimes the assimilating world that took on such an aspect in the popular imagination: the belonging to such a world of a collectivity that continued in practical terms to be excluded from it could sometimes seem like the unfolding of a masquerade.

Now, whatever may be, at the present time, our residual or acquired awareness or knowledge of the spiritual originality and richness of our Judaism, we cannot forget the eminence of the universal, to which we have been recalled in our passing through the West, where universality has been admirably explicated. This is a civilization, we might say, that is doubly universal. It displays itself as the common inheritance of humanity: every man and all peoples can enter on the same terms to occupy a place at the level suited to their innate powers and to their calling. And, at the same time, it bears the universal within itself as content: sciences, literature, plastic arts. The universal is elevated to the point of formalism and in it this civilization discovers its values and the principle of its will, in other words its ethics. Above all it discovers philosophy, which is principally a certain language whose semantics encounter no incommunicable mystery, or object without resemblance, but equally a language that has been able to sublimate metaphors into concepts and to express all lived experience, whatever the original language veiled by the experience and whether or not such a language were unutterable.

The nations that make up the West have as their particular features only those elements that, logically, appertain to any individual member of a species. Their belonging to humanity signifies precisely the possibility, to which each one of them aspires and accedes, of being translated into and spoken in this language of philosophy, a kind of Greek generously distributed around Europe within cultivated discourse. The rest is no more than local colour. On the other hand, the congenital universality of the Jewish mind, recorded in the riches of Scripture and by rabbinical literature, involves an ineradicable moment of isolation and distancing, a peculiarity that is not simply the fruit of exile and the ghetto, but probably a withdrawal into the self essential to one's awareness of a surfeit of responsibility towards humanity. It is a strange and uncomfortable privilege, a peculiar inequality that imposes obligations towards the Other which are not demanded of the Other in return. To be conscious of having been chosen no doubt comes down to this. Nevertheless, in the eyes of the nations and to ourselves as assimilated individuals, this inequality happens to take on the air of an irremediable characteristic, that of a petitioning nationalism. This misunderstanding is held both in general and among ourselves.

Despite the many criticisms made of assimilation, we benefit from the enlightenment it has brought, and we are fascinated by the vast horizons it has revealed to us, breathing in deeply the air of the open sea. As a result, Jewishness, that difficult destiny, is constantly in danger of appearing archaic and of having the effect, in the growing ignorance of Hebrew characters and the inability to make them speak, of diminishing our vision. It seems something which can no longer be justified in the modern world we have entered, a world belonging to all in which, up until the holocaust, our presence was never seriously called into question.

This is the opposite of a religious particularism. Instead, it presents the excellence of an exceptional message, albeit addressed to all. This is the paradox of Israel and one of the mysteries of the Spirit. Of this we are persuaded and this is at the heart of the present argument. But who, within assimilated Judaism and among the nations, still believes that a singularity is conceivable beyond universality, that it could incorporate the irrefutable values of the West but also lead beyond them? A thinking and a singularity of which Judaism, as fact, as history and as Passion, is actually the mode of entry and the figure, made manifest long before the distinction between the particular and the universal makes its appearance in the speculations of logicians. But – and this too is a point that matters – never, since our emancipation, have we formulated in Western language the sense (*sens*) of this beyond, whether despite or because of our assimilation. Until now all we have attempted is an apologetics limited, without great difficulty, to bringing the truths of the Torah into line with the West's noble models. The Torah demands something more.

What have we made of certain other themes? And, to give as examples only the best known of them, what have we made of: 'a people dwelling alone, and not reckoning itself among the nations' (Numbers 23: 9)? Of Abraham, who shall be called *hebrew* 'because he is able to remain alone to one side (*me-eber ahad*) when others remain on the other side (*Bereshit Rabah* 42: 8)?

Of the 613 commandments constraining the children of Israel, whereas seven only sufficed for the children of Noah? To owe the Other more than is asked! A cursory glance, blinded by the too bright sun of the West, sees in this only separation and pride. This is fatal. For it would be our right to ask if this apparent limiting of universalism is not what preserves it from totalitarianism, if it does not awaken our attention to the murmur of inner voices, if it does not turn eyes towards those faces that illuminate and allow the control of social anonymity, towards the defeated in the reasonable history of humanity, where the proud are not all that fall.

For as long as this fatal confusion persists, none of us, not even the strongest advocate of hebraism, will overcome the temptation of assimilation. And this is true however tenderly we look upon the traditional memories and the moving accents of familiar but disappearing dialects, upon all that folklore which our assimilation has taught us – for good reason! – not to mistake for the essential.

We Jews who wish to remain Jews know that our heritage is no less human than that of the West, and is capable of integrating all that our Western past has awakened within our own potential. Let us be grateful to assimilation. If, at the same time, we oppose it, it is because this 'withdrawal into the self' which is essential to us and which is so often disparaged is not the symptom of an outmoded phase of existence, but reveals a 'beyond' to universalism, which is what completes or perfects human fraternity. In the singularity of Israel a peak is attained that justifies the very perenniality of Judaism. It is not a permanent relapse into an antiquated provincialism.

But this is a singularity that the long history from which we are emerging has left at the level of sentiment or faith. It needs to be made explicit to thought. It cannot here and now furnish rules for education. It still needs to be translated into that Greek language which, thanks to assimilation, we have learnt in the West. We are faced with the great task of articulating in Greek those principles of which Greece had no knowledge. The singularity of the Jews awaits its philosophy. The servile imitation of European models is no longer enough. The search for references to universality in the Scriptures and in the texts of the spoken Law still derives from the process of assimilation. These texts, across two thousand years of commentary, still have something other to say.

In offering these remarks in this exalted place, the palace of the President of the State, in Jerusalem, I am certainly addressing the right audience. Only a Jewish culture called upon to develop itself on the basis of a new life in Israel could put an end – for the Jews above all but also for the nations – to a persistent misunderstanding. It will open our closed books and our eyes. That is our hope. To this effect also, the State of Israel will be the end of assimilation. It will make possible, in all its plenitude, the conception of concepts whose roots reach down to the depths of the Jewish soul. The explication and elaboration of these concepts are decisive for the struggle against assimilation, and are preliminaries necessary to any kind of effort on the part of generous organizations, or abnegation on the part of the masters of an elite. This is a task that is not only speculative but rich in practical, concrete and immediate consequences.

Translated by Roland Lack

18

Ethics and Politics

On 14 September 1982, a bomb demolished a party headquarters building in East Beirut, in which Bashir Gemayel, the President of Lebanon, was speaking. He and twenty-six others were killed. The following day, the Israelis responded by occupying West Beirut, in order 'to prevent any possible incident and to secure quiet'. The phrase forced the Begin Government to accept responsibility for what then occurred. While the move into West Beirut was supposedly made in order to protect the Muslims from the revenge of the Phalangists, the Israel Defence Forces (IDF) actually introduced Phalangists into the Palestinian camps with the mission of clearing out suspected *fedayeen*, or Arab infiltrators, who carried out hit-and-run raids inside Israel. The Christian soldiers massacred several hundred people in Sabra and Chatila camps over a period of nearly two days with no intervention on the part of the IDF. At first Begin refused to set up a judicial enquiry, commenting in the *New York Times* on 26 September that '*Goyim* kill *goyim*, and they immediately come to hang the Jews.'

In the aftermath of the massacre, Levinas and Alain Finkielkraut were invited by Shlomo Malka to discuss the theme of Israel and Jewish ethics on Radio Communauté, 28 September 1982. This is the transcript of that interview, published in *Les Nouveaux Cahiers*, 18 (1982–3), 71, 1–8. In its rigour and clarity, it is a model of its kind.

S.H.

SHLOMO MALKA: The events at Sabra and Chatila have shaken Jewish communities throughout the world, beginning with Israeli society itself. It is as if the very essence of Judaism were wavering, as if a sort of moral virginity of Judaism were at stake. Beyond the obscure motives of various parties, and however the situation may be exploited here and there, the extremeness of the reactions is perhaps also indicative of a certain ambition for Judaism. Emmanuel Levinas is without doubt the philosopher who has given Judaism its most exacting expression. Rarely, I believe, has Judaism's encounter with its times been taken so far, and without sacrificing anything of the essence of the question. That is why we at Radio Communauté hoped that he would break the silence on these events which confront us, and him in particular, with a series of vital questions.

I thought Alain Finkielkraut would be the person best suited to talk to Emmanuel Levinas on this subject. We have chosen him to take part in this discussion because of a very powerful talk he recently gave at the Memorial, in which he defined the terms of tonight's debate by evoking what he called 'the temptation of innocence'. I should like to quote the last main point of that talk: 'We are split between a feeling of innocence and a feeling of responsibility, both of which are anchored in our traditions and our ordeals. I do not yet know which of the two, innocence or responsibility, we will choose as Jews. But I believe that our decision will determine the meaning that we give to the ordeal of genocide.

Emmanuel Levinas, first of all I'd like to ask you whether Israel is innocent or responsible for what happened at Sabra and Chatila.

EMMANUEL LEVINAS: Let me begin with our immediate reactions on learning of this catastrophe. Despite the lack of guilt here – and probably there, too – what gripped us right away was the honour of responsibility. It is, I think, a responsibility which the Bible of course teaches us, but it is one which constitutes every man's responsibility towards all others, a responsibility which has nothing to do with any acts one may really have committed. Prior to any act, I am concerned with the Other, and I can never be absolved from this responsibility. To use an expression close to my heart, 'Even when he does not regard me, he regards me'. Consequently, I shall speak of the responsibility of those 'who have done nothing', of an original responsibility of man for the other person. It is all the more overwhelming and direct for existing in the space between two people who are regarding one another. This is the responsibility of those we call innocent! But it is no more light or more comfortable for all that; it doesn't let you sleep any the easier. I would insist on this responsibility, even if I am not speaking of direct guilt.

I have always thought of Jewish consciousness as an attentiveness which is kept alert by centuries of inhumanity and pays particular attention to what occasionally is human in man: the feeling that you personally are implicated each time that somewhere – especially when it's somewhere close to you – humanity is guilty. Close to you – as if one could anticipate that!

ALAIN FINKIELKRAUT: I'd like to mention two points here: after the massacres at Sabra and Chatila, the Israeli government at first refused to set up a board of inquiry, saying. 'Nobody can teach us anything about morals.' To which Meron Benvenisti, the former deputy mayor of Jerusalem, replied: 'That was perhaps the ultimate moral wound the Germans inflicted on us: "no-one can teach us anything, no-one can say anything more to us".' That is what I would call the temptation of innocence. From the moment that Israel's slightest act is greeted with rage by detractors guilty of bad faith, we see an exchange, a subtle, dangerous dialectic, start to take place between that bad faith and our good conscience. Criticisms of Israel are so intolerable that we devote all our time to those criticisms without always thinking about the acts that have been committed.

Graver still is our propensity to think: since antisemitism has marked us out as the 'other', what then, in concrete terms, can be our responsibility towards the Other, towards those who are not us? If we are the absolute victims, the insulted and injured of history, trapped between an ordeal that has led us to catastrophe and the various threats which weigh upon us, caught between Hitler and Ben Bella, then perhaps we have no responsibility towards the non-Jew. We have no room for any imperative other than self-defence. Certain Jews call upon the complex of persecution, the particular status which human history has given to the Jewish being, in order to escape here from the demands of responsibility. How would you, Emmanuel Levinas, react to that temptation?

E.L.: First of all, to return to the facts, I'd also like to remind you of the reaction of a great many Israeli Jews, the majority. I'd say. We here are not the only ones to have had this feeling of responsibility, there too they've felt it to the highest degree. Real innocence clearly arises in this feeling of responsibility. And consequently, we ought absolutely to glorify this reaction, which is not morbid, but a moral one. It's an ethical reaction on the part of what I think is the majority of the Jewish people, the Israeli people, beginning with President Navon, who felt it immediately, and who was the first to demand a board of enquiry. But you're quite right to denounce the 'temptation of innocence'. Innocence is not the zero degree of conscience, but merely an exalted state of responsibility, which is perhaps the final nodal point of the Jewish conscience, among all those symbolized by the knots of our *tzitzit*: the more innocent we are, the more we are responsible.

But this is not to forget the Holocaust. No-one has forgotten the Holocaust, it's impossible to forget things which belong to the most immediate and the most personal memory of every one of us, and pertaining to those closest to us, who sometimes make us feel guilty for surviving. That in no way justifies closing our ears to the voice of men, in which sometimes the voice of God can also resound. Evoking the Holocaust to say that God is with us in all circumstances is as odious as the words 'Gott mit uns' written on the belts of the executioners. I don't at all believe that there are limits to responsibility, that there are limits to responsibility in 'myself'. My *self*, I repeat, is never absolved from responsibility towards the Other. But I think we should also say that all those who attack us with such venom have no right to do so, and that consequently, along with this feeling of unbounded responsibility, there is certainly a place for a defence, for it is not always a question of 'me', but of those close to me, who are also my neighbours. I'd call such a defence a politics, but a politics that's ethically necessary. Alongside *ethics*, there is a place for *politics* – I may come back to this question later.

A.F.: Beyond this plea of innocence that we've just talked about, by which some try to justify Israel's attitude during the Sabra and Chatila massacres or the refusal of a board of enquiry, there is also the 'reason of State'. In other words, political necessities are held up as justification. These are necessities of which everyone in Israel is aware. But at the same time, it seems to me that the demonstrators who gathered in Tel Aviv, three hundred thousand of them, precisely wanted to rethink the relations between ethics and politics. It was as if a slippage had taken place, as if certain moral demands, certain ethical imperatives had been forgotten in the name of political necessity. And these people who are obsessed by the concern for security at the same time also manifested another obsession, an ethical concern, and what this demonstration seemed to be saying was that the two are incompatible, or that in any case they shouldn't come into open contradiction. What do you think of that?

E.L.: I think that there's a direct contradiction between ethics and politics, if both these demands are taken to the extreme. It's a contradiction which is usually an abstract problem. Unfortunately for ethics, politics has its own justification. In mankind, there is a justification for politics. The Zionist idea, as I now see it, all mysticism or false immediate messianism aside, is nevertheless a political idea which has an ethical justification. It has an ethical justification insofar as a political solution imposes itself as a way of putting an end to the arbitrariness which marked the Jewish condition, and to all the spilt blood which for centuries has flowed with impunity across the world. This solution can be summed up as the existence, in conditions which are not purely abstract, that is, not just anywhere, of a political unity with a Jewish majority. For me, this is the essence of Zionism. It signifies a State in the fullest sense of the term, a State with an army and arms, an army which can have a deterrent and if necessary a defensive significance. Its necessity is ethical – indeed, it's an old ethical idea which commands us precisely to defend our neighbours. My people and my kin are still my neighbours. When you defend the Jewish people, you defend your neighbour; and every Jew in particular defends his neighbour when he defends

However, there is also an ethical limit to this ethically necessary political existence. But what is this limit? Perhaps what is happening today in Israel marks the place where ethics and politics will come into confrontation and where their limits will be sought. Unfortunately, contradictions like those at play between morals and politics are not only resolved in the reflections of philosophers. It takes events, that is, human lived experience. And perhaps this is where we might find the solution to the universal human problem of the relationship between ethics and politics; the people 'engaged' (*engagé*) in this 'contradiction' and for whom, despite the war, it is an everyday thought, is a people with a long ethical tradition. The events over there, which we would rather hadn't happened, will therefore take on a significance for the general history of the mind. Perhaps that's where some light will be shed on the matter, in the concrete consciousness of those who suffer and struggle.

I'm not saying that Israel is a State like any other, nor a people unlike any other. I'm saying that in the political and moral ordeal, in the Passion of this war – and every time the Jewish people is implicated in an event, something universal is also at stake – it's there that the relationship between ethics and politics is being decided, it's there that 'in and for itself', as philosophical jargon puts it, it is being defined; alas, it's a dangerous game that's afoot.

A.F.: It was Begin who said: 'Jewish blood must not flow with impunity.' It was in reference to that precept, on which, as you've shown, Zionism was practically founded, that Operation Peace for Galilee was run. Some would say, all right, from then on, an aberration has set in, the copybook has been blotted, something serious happened at Sabra and Chatila, but that doesn't mean everything is cast in doubt, and to revolt against this phenomenon is nothing but the reflex of a noble soul, the luxury of a pure conscience exempted from the mudpit of history.

E.L.: I haven't said within what limits the State seems to me to be justified by Begin's phrase; but we mustn't forget that it's a phrase of his that is quite invaluable. It doesn't set the limits within which a political action, or even warlike measures, would be justified. We mustn't forget that. That's what is being debated in the first two phases of the conflict: Peace for Galilee and the Beirut siege. But the place where everything is interrupted, where everything is disrupted, where everyone's moral responsibility comes into play, a responsibility that concerns and engages even innocence, unbearably so, that place lies in the events at Sabra and Chatila. Everyone's responsibility. Over there, no-one can say to us: 'you're in Europe and at peace, you're not in Israel, and yet you take it upon yourself to judge.' I think that in this case, this distinction between the ones and the others, for once at least, disappears. People will also say to us, as you have just done, 'You're noble souls.' Hegel teaches us that we must be anything rather than noble souls. But because we are afraid to become noble souls, we become base souls instead.

S.M.: Emmanuel Levinas, you are the philosopher of the 'other'. Isn't history, isn't politics the very site of the encounter with the 'other', and for the Israeli, isn't the 'other' above all the Palestinian?

E.L.: My definition of the other is completely different. The other is the neighbour, who is not necessarily kin, but who can be. And in that sense, if you're for the other, you're for the neighbour. But if your neighbour attacks another neighbour or treats him unjustly, what can you do? Then alterity takes on another character, in alterity we can find an enemy, or at least then we are faced with the problem of knowing who is right and who is wrong, who is just and who is unjust. There are people who are wrong.

S.M.: At this stage in the debate I'd like to ask you both a question. In an issue of *Débat*, Monsignor Lustiger wrote a very fine article on the vocation of Judaism. After expounding the vocation of Judaism as he sees it, he says, 'but we must pay attention to a mysticism which can degenerate into politics'. Do you think this risk exists in Israel?

A.F.: I think the opposite is true: the risk that Israel runs is one of a too hasty and summary transformation of politics into mysticism. As Emmanuel Levinas has just shown, we're now witnessing a passionate examination of the contradictions between ethics and politics, and of the necessity, that is both vital and almost impossible, of conforming the demands of collective action to fundamental ethical principles. So the danger is one of the autonomy of politics, of submission to the reason of State. But the other peril facing Israel lies is not taking account of the everyday practicalities of politics, in forgetting that it's a specific domain in the life of men, and in preferring to read into it, in mystical fashion, the presence of God and the signs of Providence.

We can't think enough about the effects of the 1967 victory on the Israeli psyche. The victory, in its scope and its speed, was so unexpected, so miraculous, that some couldn't resist seeing it as a messianic moment. So the Israeli government hadn't included the conquest of the West Bank on its agenda? Then that proves that we're living through the 'first pains of redemption', and that God is giving the Jews back the Promised Land.

So if there is a danger, it's not one of mysticism degenerating into politics, but rather of an ill-considered elevation of politics onto the level of mysticism, a confusion of the two spheres.

E.L.: I would say that this risk is run less there than anywhere else. When you compare world history, where there are so many mystical thoughts and movements, so many movements and doctrines of peace and love, with the true political course of this history made up of wars, violence, conquests and the oppression of men by their fellows, then you have less cause to worry about Israel's soul and political history. Ethics will never, in any lasting way, be the good conscience of corrupt politics – the immediate reactions we've witnessed these last few days prove it; and transgression of ethics made 'in the name of ethics' is immediately perceived as a hypocrisy and as a personal offence.

Just now when I was denouncing the confusion between Zionism and messianism, or rather when I wanted to distinguish Zionism from the mysticism which sees in it the first labour pains of the Messiah's birth, I didn't in any way mean to belittle the Zionist struggle. It was simply to separate it from the simplistic image of messianism, which is dangerous as a political principle. On the contrary, I believe that Zionism comprises a genuine messianic element, which is the day-to-day life in Israel of Israel itself. It lies in hard work, the daily sacrifice made by people who've left secure positions and often abundance in order to lead a difficult life, to lead an ethical life, to lead a life which isn't disturbed by the values of our Western comfort, people who like Rabbi Akiva, on the last page of the Talmudic treatise *Makkoth*, are not troubled by the 'noise of Rome', which can be heard even at great distances. I would say that in this sense one is closer to the Messiah in Israel than here.

A.F.: I'd like to clarify one point. What is happening around this demonstration is of the utmost importance. I think we're seeing a reconciliation of the Israeli elite with its own country. Let me explain what I mean by the word 'elite'. I don't simply mean, as in other Western countries, the intelligentsia or the technostructure. The Israeli elite is made up of kibbutz workers, of the intellectual world, and of the military aristocracy. From 1977 up until the demonstration of the 25 September, this elite suffered from a feeling deeper and more painful than simple political disappointment: it was almost an internal exile. People who felt they had built Israel no longer recognized Israel. Hearing them today, the three hundred thousand people of Tel Aviv have proved that the Zionism of Ben Gurion and Levi Eshkol is still alive. It's not euphoria, but it's no longer *estrangement*. This idea can only soothe our hearts: within the measure of our means, and with the humility that our distance from Israel requires, we

Jews of the Diaspora must uphold these values, this image of Zionism, this truth of Israel.

E.L.: The truth of Israel! It's because a profound attachment to Israel – and to the new mode of life we find there – can only be found precisely in conformity with the heritage of our scriptures. Not enough has been said about this, not enough has been said about the shock that the human possibility of the events at Sabra and Chatila – whoever is behind them – signifies for our entire history as Jews and as human beings. It's not only our thought that we must defend and protect, it's our souls, and that which upholds our souls: our books! Yes, for Jews, this is an enormous question, and the supreme threat: that our books should be in jeopardy! The books which carry us through history, and which, even more deeply than the earth, are our support.

A.F.: Could you elaborate on that idea? Why is it our books that are in question? Why is it a wound of all history?

E.L.: I'm not going to give a summing-up of our books . . . but here's a text that occurs three times in the Talmud. Let me recite it purely and simply: 'Our masters have said: those that are offended without giving offence, those who are defamed without defaming, those who obey in love and rejoice in suffering, are like the sun that rises in its glory.' And this metaphor of the sun rising in its glory is borrowed by the Talmudic scholars from Judges, chapter 5, the verse which ends the glorious song of the military victory of Deborah, as if the true light of the sun of victory shone only on those who can 'bear defamation without defaming'. Or as if all Deborah's military combat simply stood for a moral combat.

I'd also like to mention another talmudic text, for the benefit of those who confuse Zionism – or the relationship to the world and to human beings that its message entails – with some sort of commonplace mystique of the earth as native soil. It is a text that deals with the condemnation of calumny. But the Talmud always says one thing in order to say another as well. Calumny is to be condemned. How do we know? We know it of course, from the Book, from a passage in Numbers, where Moses sends explorers to spy out the land the people of Israel must enter. But the explorers vilify that land. According to the text, they are punished with death. And here the Talmud asks: 'What do we learn from this condemnation and this punishment of the explorers who have maligned the land?'. Above all, it should teach us the gravity of calumny concerning persons. For if calumny of that which is 'but stones and trees' already merits death, then how serious, *a fortiori*, must be calumny relating to human beings. The argument – the *a fortiori* of it – is remarkable. A person is more holy than a land, even a holy land, since, faced with an affront made to a person, this holy land appears in its nakedness to be but stone and wood.

Translated by Jonathan Romney

Glossary

For full references to the Judaic terms used here, readers should consult the *Encyclopaedia Judaica*, edited by Cecil Roth (Jerusalem, Israel: Keter, 1971–2), 16 vols.

Aggadah	Those sections of the *Talmud* and *Midrash* devoted to ethical and moral teaching, legends, folklore, and so on, as opposed to the legal sections, the *Halakhah*. Aggadah is therefore essentially the refinement of *halakhah*.
Amora	Speaker, interpreter. Originally the interpreter who attended upon the public preacher or lecturer for the purpose of expounding at length. This led to the plural, *Amoraim*, a name given to Rabbinic authorities responsible for the *Gemara* as opposed to *Mishnah* or *Baraitha*.
Baraitha	A teaching or a tradition of the *Tennaim* that has been excluded from the Mishnah and incorporated in a later collection compiled by R. Hiyya and R. Oshaiah, generally introduced by 'Our Rabbis taught', or 'It has been taught'.
BCE	Before Common Era (or Before Christ).
CE	Common Era (or AD).
Diaspora	From the Greek, meaning 'dispersion'. Refers normally to the voluntary dispersion of the Jewish people as distinct from their forced dispersion. It therefore applies originally to the period of the First Temple and the Second Temple. But after the establishment of the State of Israel, the Jewish community outside Israel constitutes a Diaspora.
Gemara	The traditions, discussions and rulings of the *Amoraim*, based mainly on the Mishnah and forming (a) the Babylonian Talmud and (b) the Palestinian Talmud.
Halakhah	The legal side of Judaism, as contrasted with *Aggadah*. Originally *Halakhah* was a legal formula laid down in the oral Law. In the rabbinic period and beyond the study of the *Halakhah* became the supreme religious duty.
Hasidism	Religious movement founded in the eighteenth century by Israel Baal Shem Tov, whose teachings placed zeal and emo-

tion over study, and have always had a mystical basis. In the twentieth century neo-Hasidism has been popularized by such writers as Martin Buber and Elie Wiesel.

Haskalah	The word means 'Enlightenment' and designates a movement which in the mid-eighteenth century aimed to break with the exclusiveness of Jewish life by spreading modern European culture among Jews. It developed Hebrew as a literary language to the neglect of Yiddish. Towards the end of the century it disappeared under the combined impact of assimilation on the one hand and nationalism on the other.
Hiddushim	or *novellae*. Commentaries on the *Talmud* or rabbinic literature that extract new facts or theories from the text. From the sixteenth century, these have placed less of an emphasis on sober analysis than on novelty.
Hittel	First century BCE rabbinic authority and Pharisaic leader.
Kabbalah	('Tradition'). Taken generally to mean the mystical tradition in Judaism.
Kibbutz	Voluntary collective, mainly agricultural, community where there is no private wealth.
Massektoth	The sixty-three subsections of *Sederim*, or tractates.
Mezuzah	Literally a 'door-post' (see Deuteronomy 6: 9). A piece of parchment inscribed with the two passages Deuteronomy 6: 4–8 and 11: 13–21, placed in a small wooden or metal container and fixed to the upper right-hand door-post as one enters.
Midrash	The discovery of meanings other than the literal one in the Bible. The word comes from 'darash', to inquire (see Leviticus 10: 16 or Deuteronomy 13: 15). In general, it therefore designates a particular genre of rabbinic literature which continued until about the thirteenth century and was composed of homilies dealing with both biblical exegesis and public sermons.
Mishnah	Codification of Jewish law compiled by Judah ha-Nasi *c.*200 CE, which contains the basis of the oral Law traditionally given to Moses at Sinai and handed down by word of mouth alongside the written Law or Pentateuch. The teachers quoted in the *Mishnah* are called *Tannaim*.
Mishneh Torah	Otherwise known as *Yad ha-Hazakah*. Maimonides' great work on Jewish law and the first complete compendium of its kind. It is known as the *Yad ha-Hazakah* (the strong hand) because it consists of fourteen books, and the Hebrew numeral fourteen, *Yod Daleth*, can be read as *yad*, hand.
Mitzvah	A commandment or religious duty contained in the Pentateuch. Traditionally there are a total of 613 positive and negative commandments. A boy becomes liable to perform these at the age of thirteen (hence the ceremony of Bar Mitz-

	vah) and a girl at twelve (Bat Mitzvah). In general, the term *mitzvah* can refer to any good deed.
Sederim	The six main sections of the oral Law.
Soferim	Scribes.
Talmud	('Learning'.) Comprehensive term for *Mishnah* and *Gemara*, traditionally based on the oral Law transmitted at Mt Sinai, and composed of laws from the Mishnah, discussions on each one, plus elements from *Halakhah* or *Aggadah*.
Tannaim	Teachers of the oral Law. A *Tanna* is therefore: (a) a Rabbi quoted in the *Mishnah* or *Baraitha*; (b) in the Amoraic period, a scholar whose special task was to memorize and recite *Baraithas* in the presence of expounding teachers.
Torah	*The Law.*
Tzitzit	The word refers to the *fringes* attached to each of the four corners of a garment (see Deuteronomy, 22: 12). Originally such a garment was worn by male Jews at all times. A blessing is recited as it is donned.
Yad ha-Hazakah	See *Mishneh Torah.*
Yeshivah	A house of study. The oldest institution for higher talmudic learning in Judaism, dating back to second-century Babylonia. Its modern existence stems from the foundation of the *Yeshivah* at Volozhin in 1803.
Zionism	In very general terms, Zionism was a movement aiming at the return of the Jewish people to the land of Israel (Palestine). From 1896 on it referred to the political movement founded by Theodor Herzl. After the establishment of the Jewish State the concept was widened to include material and moral support of Israel. For a full explanation of the term's ideological evolution, see the *Encyclopaedia Judaica*.

Bibliography

The standard bibliography of studies both by and on Levinas is Roger Burggraeve, *Emmanuel Levinas. Une bibliographie primaire et secondaire (1929–1985)*, Leuven, the Centre for Metaphysics and Philosophy of God, 1986. Also useful is the bibliography compiled by Robert Bernasconi for *The Provocation of Levinas: Rethinking the Other*, edited by Robert Bernasconi and David Wood (London and New York: Routledge, 1988) pp. 181–8, and the bibliography to François Poirié, *Emmanuel Levinas, Qui êtes-vous?* (Lyon: La Manufacture, 1987) pp. 175–82. My selected bibliography is greatly indebted to all these sources.

Works by Levinas

Articles are not listed separately if subsequently collected by Levinas in book form. I have not included reviews, translations, correspondence or allocutions.

1929
'Sur les "Ideen" de M. E. Husserl', *Revue Philosophique de la France et de l'Etranger*, CVII, 3–4, 230–65.

1930
La théorie de l'intuition dans la phénoménologie de Husserl, Paris: Alcan (Vrin, 1963). Translated as *The Theory of Intuition in Husserl's Phenomenology* by A. Orianne (Evanston: Northwestern University Press, 1973).

1931
'Fribourg, Husserl et la phénoménologie', *Revue d'Allemagne et des pays de langue allemande*, v, 43, 402–14.

1934
'Quelques reflexions sur la philosophie de l'hitlérisme', *Esprit*, II, 26, 199–208.

1935
'L'actualité de Maïmonide', *Paix et Droit*, XV, 4, 6–7.
'L'inspiration religieuse de l'Alliance', *Paix et Droit*, XV, 8, 4.

1938
'L'essence spirituelle de l'antisémitisme d'après Jacques Maritain', *Paix et Droit*, XVIII, 5, 3–4.

1939
'A propos de la mort du Pope Pie XI', *Paix et Droit*, XIX, 3, 3.

1946
'Tout est-il vanité?', *Les Cahiers de l'Alliance Israélite Universelle*, IX, 1–2.
'Le récouverture de l'Ecole Normale Israélite Orientale', *Les Cahiers de l'Alliance Israélite Universelle*, XI, 2–3.

1947
De l'existence à l'existant, Paris: Fontaine (Vrin, 1973). Translated as *Existence and Existents* by A. Lingis (The Hague: Martinus Nijhoff, 1978).
'Etre juif', *Confluences*, VIII, 15–17, 253–64.
'Existentialisme et antisémitisme', *Les Cahiers de l'Alliance Israélite Universelle*, 14–15, 2–3.

1949
En découvrant l'existence avec Husserl et Heidegger, Paris: Vrin (1967). Translated by R. A. Cohen (Bloomington, Ill.: Indiana University Press, forthcoming).
'Quand les mots reviennent de l'exil', *Les Cahiers de l'Alliance Israélite Universelle*, XXXII, 4.
'En marge d'une enquête: L'érotisme ne ravale pas l'esprit', *Combat*, 30 June 1949.

1951
'L'ontologie est-elle fondamentale?', *Revue de Métaphysique et de Morale*, LVI, 1, 88–98.
'Deux promotions', *Les Cahiers de l'Alliance Israélite Universelle*, LIV–LV, 1–2.
'Préface (sur Jacob Gordin)', *Evidences*, XXI, 22.

1952
'Eternité et domicile', *Evidences*, XXVIII, 35–6.

1953
'L'unique apaisement', *Combat*, 2 April.
'Liberté et commandement', *Revue de Métaphysique et de Morale*, LVIII, 3, 264–72.

1954
'Noé Gottlieb', *Les Cahiers de l'Alliance Israélite Universelle*, LXXXII, 1–3.
'Le moi et la totalité', *Revue de Métaphysique et de Morale*, LIX, 4, 353–73.
'L'hébreu dans les écoles de l'Alliance', *Revue du Fonds Social Juif Unifié*, X, 17–18.

1955
'Le rôle de l'Ecole Normale Israélite Orientale', *Les Cahiers de l'Alliance Israélite Universelle*, XCI, 32–8.

1956
'L'Ecole Normale Israélite Orientale', *Les Cahiers de l'Alliance Israélite Universelle*, C, 16–17.

1957
'L'Ecole Normale Israélite Orientale', *Les Cahiers de l'Alliance Israélite Universelle*,

CX, 15–17.

'Lévy-Bruhl et la philosophie contemporaine', *Revue Philosophique de la France et de l'Etranger*, CXLVII, 4, 551–69.

'Rencontres', *Les Cahiers de l'Alliance Israélite Universelle*, CXII, 13–14.

1958

'La civilisation juive (débat entre E. Berl, E. Levinas, G. Lévitte, J. Lindon, J. Neher, P. Sipriot et C. Tresmontant)', *Les Cahiers de l'Alliance Israélite Universelle*, CXV, 3–12.

'Une mission à Tioumliline', *Les Cahiers de l'Alliance Israélite Universelle*, CXIX, 25–7.

1960

'La laïcité et la pensée d'Israël', in A. Audibert et al., *La laïcité* (Paris: Presses Universitaires de France), pp. 45–58.

'La laïcité dans l'état d'Israël', in A. Audibert et al., *La laïcité* (Paris: Presses Universitaires de France), pp. 549–62.

'Le problème scolaire et nous', *L'Arche*, XXXVIII, 11–15.

'Que nous apporte l'accord culturel franco-israélien? (table rond avec P.–E. Gilbert, A. Neher, E. Levinas, D. Catarivas, Ph. Rebeyrol, A. Chouraqui, M. Salomon)', *L'Arche*, XXXVIII, 28–32, 61–3.

'L'accord culturel franco-israélien et les Juifs de la dispersion', *Les Cahiers de l'Alliance Israélite Universelle*, CXXVIII, 1–4.

'Le permanent et l'humain chez Husserl', *L'Age Nouveau*, CX, 51–6.

'L'heure de la rédemption', *Le Journal des communautés*, CCLI, 4.

1961

'L'Ecole Normale Israélite Orientale: perspectives d'avenir', in *Les droits de l'homme et de l'éducation* (Paris: Presses Universitaires de France), pp. 73–9.

Totalité et Infini. Essai sur l'extériorité (The Hague: Martinus Nijhoff).

'L'Ecole Normale Israélite Orientale', *Les Cahiers de l'Alliance Israélite Universelle*, CXXXIV, 9–10.

1962

'Transcendance et hauteur', *Bulletin de la Société Française de Philosophie*, LVI, 3, 89–101.

'Enseignement juif et culture contemporaine (interview)', *L'Arche*, LXV, 22–5.

'L'Ecole Normale Israélite Orientale', *Les Cahiers de l'Alliance Israélite Universelle*, CXXXVIII, 19–20.

1963

'Judaïsme et altruïsme', in *De l'identité juive à la communauté* (Paris: s.d.), pp. 11–15.

'L'Ecole Normale Israélite Orientale', *Les Cahiers de l'Alliance Israélite Universelle*, CXLV, 16–20.

Difficile Liberté (Paris: Albin Michel (2nd edn, 1976)), translated as *Difficult Freedom* by S. Hand (London: Athlone, forthcoming).

1964

Intervention, translated by R. Rosthal, 'Interrogation of Martin Buber conducted by

Maurice S. Friedman', in *Philosophical Interrogations*, edited by S. C. Rome and B. K. Rome (New York, Chicago and San Francisco: Holt, Rinehart and Winston), pp. 23–6.

1965
'Martin Buber', *L'Arche*, CII, 10–11.
'Martin Buber prophète et philosophe', *Informations catholiques internationales*, CCXVIII, 31–2.

1966
'De Sheylock à Swann', *Les Nouveaux Cahiers*, VI, 47–8.

1967
'Par delà le dialogue', *Journal des communautés*, CCCXCVIII, 1–3.

1968
'La renaissance culturelle juive en Europe continentale', in M. Davis et al., *Le renouveau de la culture juive* (Bruxelles: Editions de l'Institut de Sociologie de l'Université Libre de Bruxelles), pp. 21–34.
Quatre lectures talmudiques (Paris: Editions de Minuit). Translated by A. Aronowicz (Bloomington, Ill.: Indiana University Press, forthcoming).
'Un Dieu homme?', *Qui est Jésus-Christ*, LXII, 186–92.

1970
'Infini', *Encyclopaedia Universalis*, Paris, vol. 8, p. 991.
'Le surlendemain des dialectiques', *Hamoré*, XIII, 50, 38–40.
'Séparation des biens', *L'Arche*, CLXII-CLXIII, 101–2.

1971
'Préface' to T. G. Geraets, *Vers une nouvelle philosophie transcendentale. La genèse de la philosophie de Maurice Merleau-Ponty jusqu'à la Phénoménologie de la Perception* (The Hague, Martinus Nijhoff), pp. IX–XV.

1972
'Leçon talmudique', *Jeunesse et révolution dans la conscience juive. Données et débats*, edited by J. Halpérin and G. Lévitte (Paris: Presses Universitaires de France), pp. 59–80.
'Leçon talmudique', *Jeunesse et révolution dans la conscience juive. Données et débats*, edited by J. Halpérin and G. Lévitte (Paris: Presses Universitaires de France), pp. 279–92.
Humanisme de l'autre homme (Montpellier: Fata Morgana).
'Centenaire de la création de l'Ecole Normale Israélite Orientale', *Bulletin intérieur du Consistoire Central Israélite de France et d'Algérie*, V, 22, 16–18.
'Evolution et fidélité', *Les Cahiers de l'Alliance Israélite Universelle*, CLXXXII, 26–30.

1973
'Leçon talmudique', in *L'autre dans la conscience juive. Le sacré et le couple. Données et débats*, edited by J. Halpérin and G. Lévitte (Paris: Presses Universitaires de France), pp. 55–74.

'Leçon talmudique', in *L'autre dans la conscience juive. Le sacré et le couple. Données et débats*, edited by J. Halpérin and G. Lévitte (Paris: Presses Universitaires de France), pp. 173–86.

'Totalité et totalisation', *Encyclopaedia Universalis*, Paris, vol. 16, p. 192.

1974

Autrement qu'être ou au-delà de l'essence (The Hague: Martinus Nijhoff), translated as *Otherwise than Being or Beyond Essence* by A. Lingis (The Hague, Martinus Nijhoff, 1981).

'Karl Kerényi', *Les Etudes Philosophiques*, XXIX, 2, 185.

'La mort du P. Van Breda', *Les Etudes Philosophiques*, XXIX, 2, 285–7.

'Leçon talmudique', *Consistoire Central Israélite*, pp. 57–67.

1975

Sur Maurice Blanchot (Montpellier: Fata Morgana).

'Trois notes sur la positivité et la transcendance', in *Mélanges André Néher* (Paris: Adrien-Maisonneuve), pp. 21–7.

1976

Noms propres (Montpellier: Fata Morgana).

'Philosophie et positivité', in *Savoir, faire, espérer: les limites de la raison* (Bruxelles: Editions Facultés Universitaires Saint-Louis), vol. 1, pp. 194–206.

'Les dommages causés par le feu: Leçon talmudique', in *La conscience juive face à la guerre*, edited by J. Halpérin and G. Lévitte (Paris: Presses Universitaires de France), pp. 13–26.

'Sécularisation et faim', in *Herméneutique de la sécularisation*, edited by E. Castelli (Paris: Aubier-Montaigne), pp. 101–9.

1977

Du sacré au saint (Paris: Editions de Minuit). Translated by A. Aronowicz (Bloomington, Ill.: Indiana University Press, forthcoming).

'Modèles de la permanence' in *Le modèle de l'Occident. Données et débats*, edited by J. Halpérin and G. Lévitte (Paris: Presses Universitaires de France), pp. 199–215.

'Pensée et prédication' in *The Self and the Other. The irreducible element in man*, edited by Anna-Teresa Tymieniecka (Dordrecht and Boston: D. Reidel), pp. 3–6.

'Préface' to M. Buber, *Utopie et socialisme* (Paris: Aubier-Montagne), pp. 9–11.

'La lettre ouverte', *Rencontres. Chrétiens et Juifs*, LI, 118–20.

'La philosophie de l'éveil', *Les études philosophiques*, III, 307–17.

1978

'Un nouvel esprit de coexistence', *Les nouveaux cahiers*, LIV, pp. 40–2.

1979

Le temps et l'autre [1947], Montpellier: Fata Morgana (Paris: Presses Universitaires de France, 1983), translated as *Time and the Other* by R. Cohen (Pittsburgh: Duquesne University Press, 1987).

'Les villes refuges', in *Jérusalem, l'Unique et l'Universelle*, edited by J. Halpérin and G. Lévitte, (Paris: Presses Universitaires de France), pp. 35–48.

'Un éveil qui signifie une responsabilité, in *Gabriel Marcel et la pénsée allemande. Nietzsche, Heidegger, Ernst Bloch*, (Paris: Présence de Gabriel Marcel), pp. 92–5.

'Lettre à *Terriers* (à propos de Paul Celan)', *Terriers*, VI, 11–12.

'De la lecture juive des Ecritures', *Lumière et Vie*, XXVIII, 144, 5–23.

1980

'Exégèse et transcendance. A propos d'un texte du Makoth 23b', in *Hommage à Georges Vajda. Etudes d'histoire et de pensée juives*, edited G. Nahon and Ch. Touati, (Louvain: Peeters), pp. 99–104.

'Le dialogue. Conscience de soi et proximité du prochain', in *Esistenza, unito, ermeneutica. Scritti per Enrico Castelli* (Padova: Cedam), pp. 345–57.

'Un langage pour nous familier (à propos de Sartre)', *Le Matin*, March.

'Exigeant Judaïsme', *Le débat*, V, 11–19.

'Du langage religieux et de la "Crainte de Dieu" (sur un texte talmudique)', *Man and World*, XIII, 3–4, 265–79.

1982

L'Au-Delà du Verset (Paris: Editions de Minuit).

De Dieu qui vient à l'idée, (Paris: Vrin).

De l'évasion [1935], (Paris: Fata Morgana).

Ethique et Infini (Paris: Fayard), translated as *Ethics and Infinity* by R. A. Cohen, (Pittsburgh: Duquesne University Press, 1985).

1984

Transcendance et intelligibilité (Genève: Labor et Fides).

1987

Collected Philosophical Papers, translated by A. Lingis (Dordrecht: Martinus Nijhoff).

Hors sujet (Montpellier: Fata Morgana).

'De l'écrit à l'oral', preface to D. Banon, *La lecture infinie* (Paris: Editions du Seuil), pp. 7–11.

1988

A l'heure des nations (Paris: Editions de Minuit).

Selected Works on Levinas

Bernasconi, Robert, 'Levinas Face to Face – with Hegel', *Journal of the British Society for Phenomenology*, 13 (1982), no. 3, 267–76.

Burggraeve, Roger, 'The Ethical Basis for a Humane Society according to Emmanuel Levinas', translated by C. Vanhove-Romanik, in *Emmanuel Levinas*, (Leuven: The Centre for Metaphysics and Philosophy of God, 1981), pp. 5–57.

——, *From Self-Development to Solidarity: an Ethical Reading of Human Desire in its Socio-Political Relevance according to Emmanuel Levinas*, translated by C. Vanhove-Romanik, (Leuven, The Centre for Metaphysics and Philosophy of God, 1985).

Chalier, Catherine, *Figures du Féminin. Lecture d'Emmanuel Lévinas*, (Paris, La nuit surveillée, 1982).

Cohen, Richard A., 'The Privilege of Reason and Play: Derrida and Levinas', *Tijdschrift voor Filosofie*, 45 (1983), no. 2, 242–55.

Derrida, Jacques, 'Violence and Metaphysics', in *Writing and Difference*, translated by Alan Bass (London: Routledge and Kegan Paul and Chicago: Chicago University Press, 1978), pp. 79–153.

Forthomme, Bernard, *Une philosophie de la transcendance: la métaphysique d'Emmanuel Levinas*, (Paris: Vrin, 1984).

Gans, Steven, 'Ethics or Ontology', *Philosophy Today*, 16 (1972), no. 2, 117–21.

Libertson, Joseph, *Proximity, Levinas, Blanchot, Bataille and Communication* Phaenomenologica, 87, (The Hague: Martinus Nijhoff, 1982).

Lingis, Alphonso, *Libido: the French Existential Theories* (Bloomington, Ill.: Indiana University Press, 1985), pp. 58–73 and 103–20.

Lyotard, Jean-François, 'Jewish Oedipus' in *Driftworks*, (New York, Semiotext(e), 1984), pp. 35–55.

Malka, Salomon, *Lire Levinas*, (Paris: Le Cerf, 1984).

Peperzak, Adriaan, 'Beyond Being', *Research in Phenomenology*, 8 (1978), 239–61.

——, 'Emmanuel Levinas: Jewish Experience and Philosophy', *Philosophy Today*, 27 (1983), no. 4, 297–306.

——, 'Phenomenology – Ontology – Metaphysics: Levinas' Perspective on Husserl and Heidegger', *Man and World*, 16 (1983), 113–27.

Petrosino, Silvano and Rolland, Jacques, *La Vérité nomade. Introduction à Emmanuel Levinas*, (Paris: La Découverte, 1984).

Poirié, François, *Emmanuel Levinas, Qui etes-vous?* (Lyon: La Manufacture, 1987).

Volumes devoted to Levinas

Exercises de la patience, no. 1, (Paris: Obsidiane, 1980).

Textes pour Emmanuel Lévinas, edited by F. Laruelle (Paris: J.-M. Place, 1980). (Includes essays by M. Blanchot, J. Derrida, M. Dufrenne, E. Jabès, J.-F. Lyotard, P. Ricoeur.)

Les Cahiers de la nuit surveillée, no. 3, edited by J. Rolland (Lagrasse: Verdier, 1984). (Includes essays by F. Wybrands, C. Chalier, D. Banon, J. Rolland, S. Petrosino, A. Fernandez-Zoila.)

Face to Face with Levinas, edited by R. Cohen, (Albany: State University of New York Press, 1986). (Includes essays by Th. de Boer, J.-F. Lyotard, R. Bernasconi, A. Peperzak, A. Lingis, L. Irigaray.)

The Provocation of Levinas: Rethinking the Other, edited by R. Bernasconi and D. Wood (London and New York: Routledge, 1988). (Includes essays by T. Chanter, S. Gans, C. Howells, R. Bernasconi, J. Llewelyn.)

Index

MAY 0 6 1993

ECHEANCE   *DATE DUE*

15 1.0 92

UNIV. OF/DE SUDBURY

3 0007 00469722 2